# Afro

13

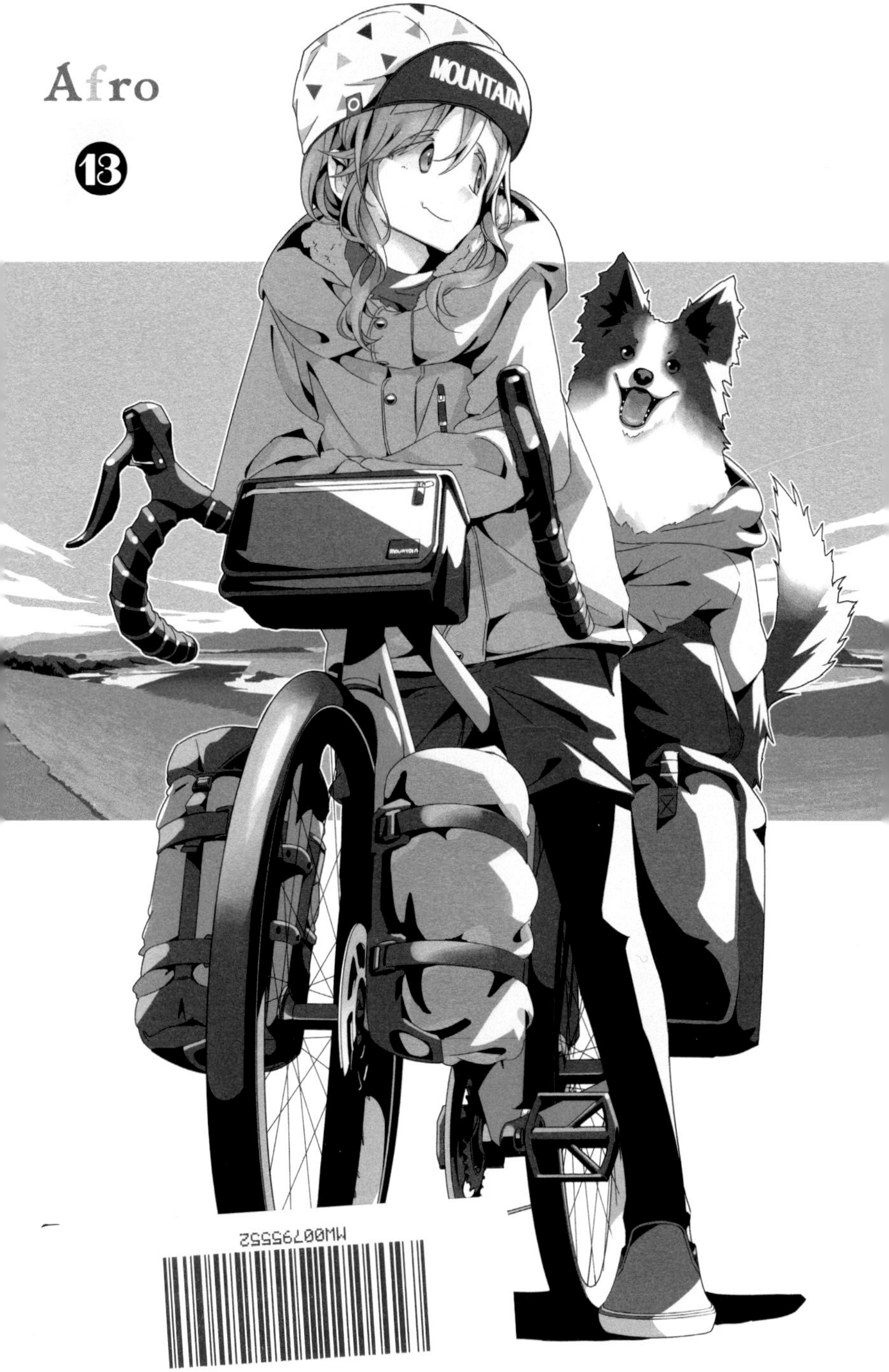
MOUNTAIN

13

LAID-BACK CAMP

contents



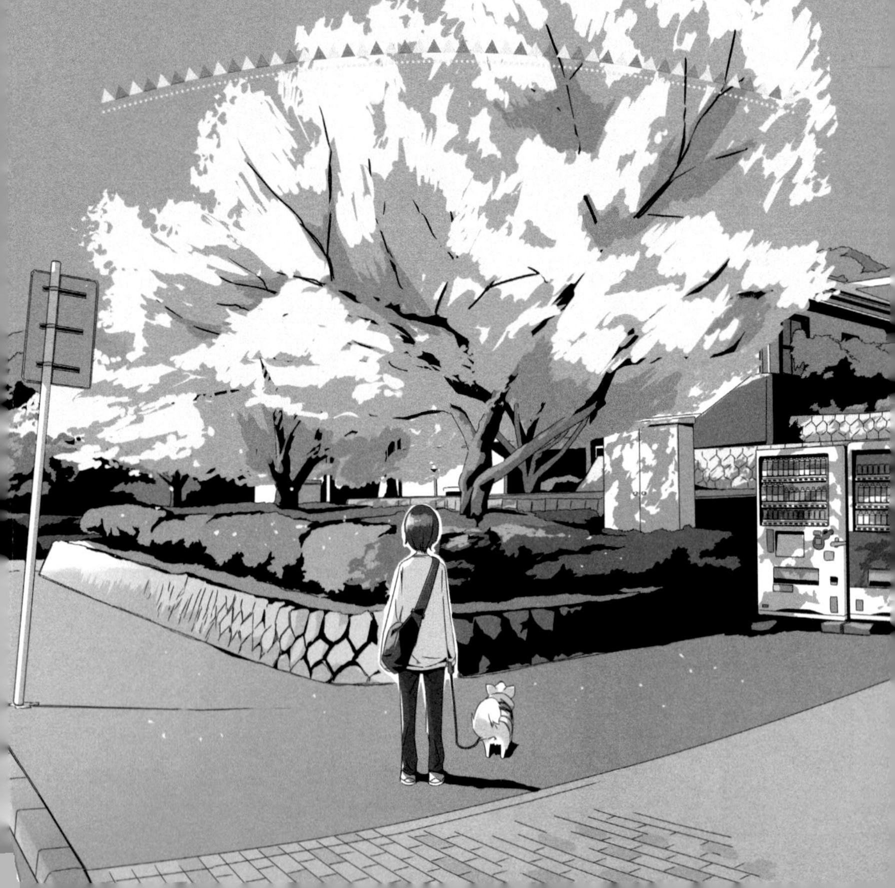

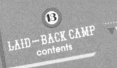

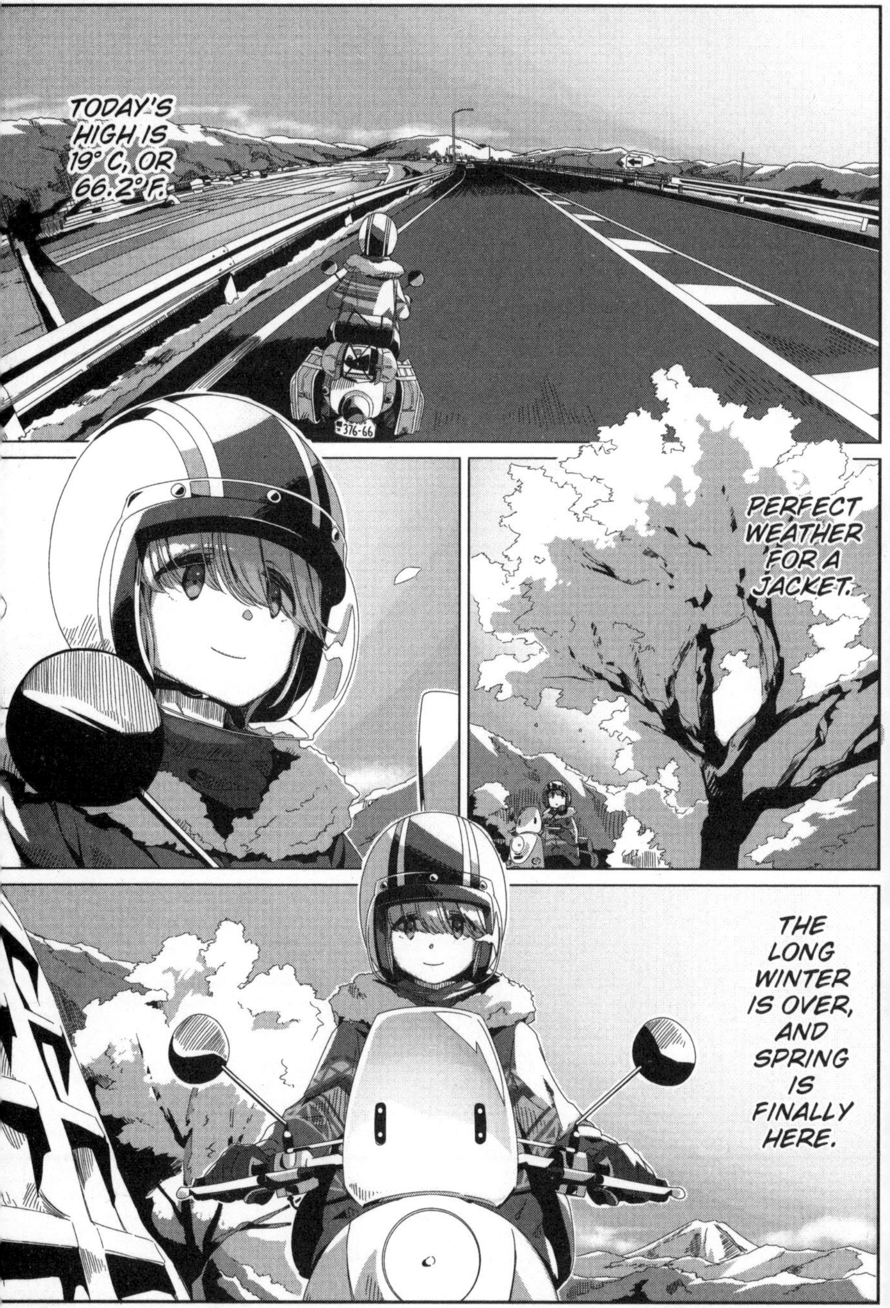
TODAY'S HIGH IS 19° C, OR 66.2° F.
PERFECT WEATHER FOR A JACKET.
THE LONG WINTER IS OVER, AND SPRING IS FINALLY HERE.

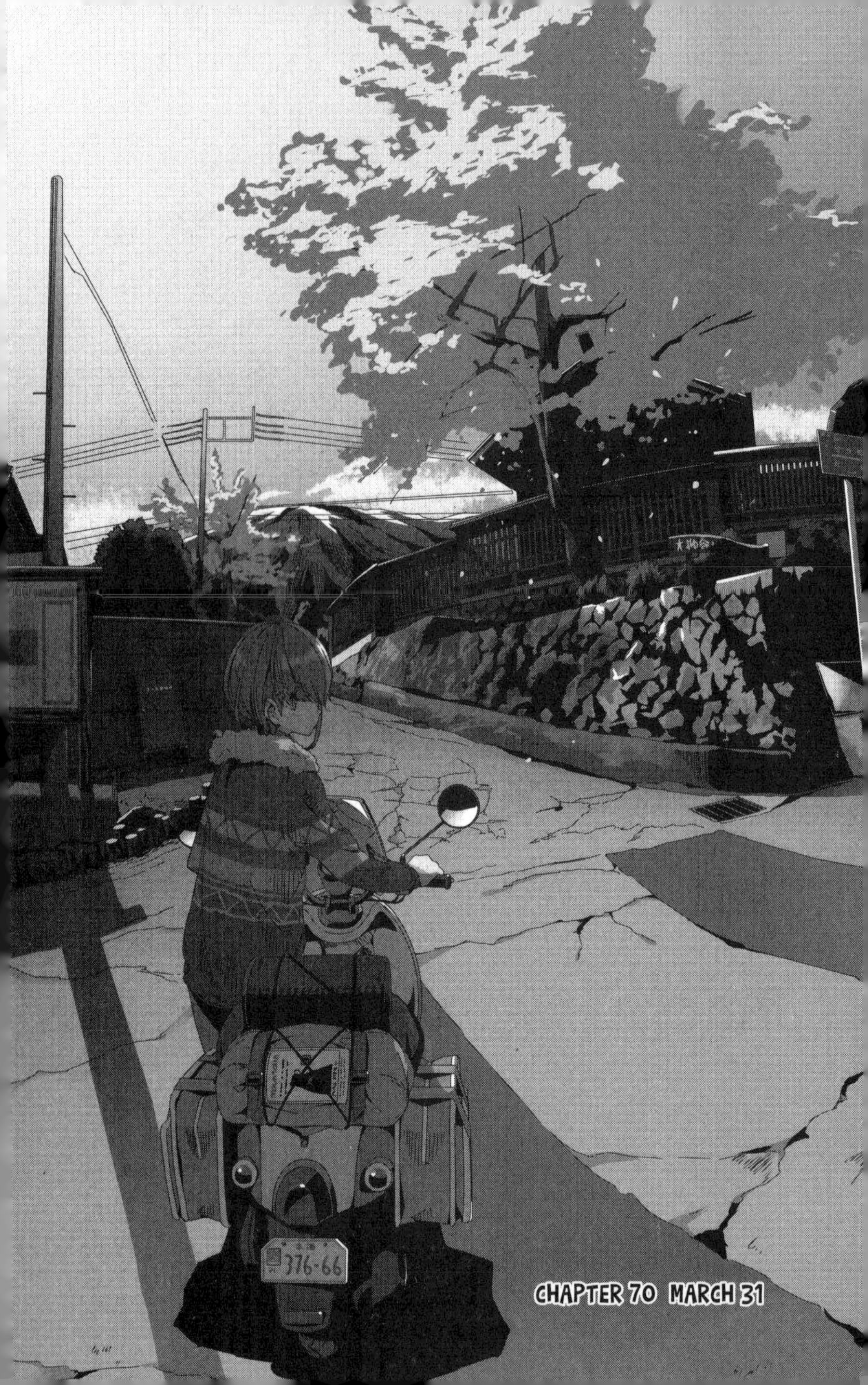
376-66
CHAPTER 70 MARCH 31

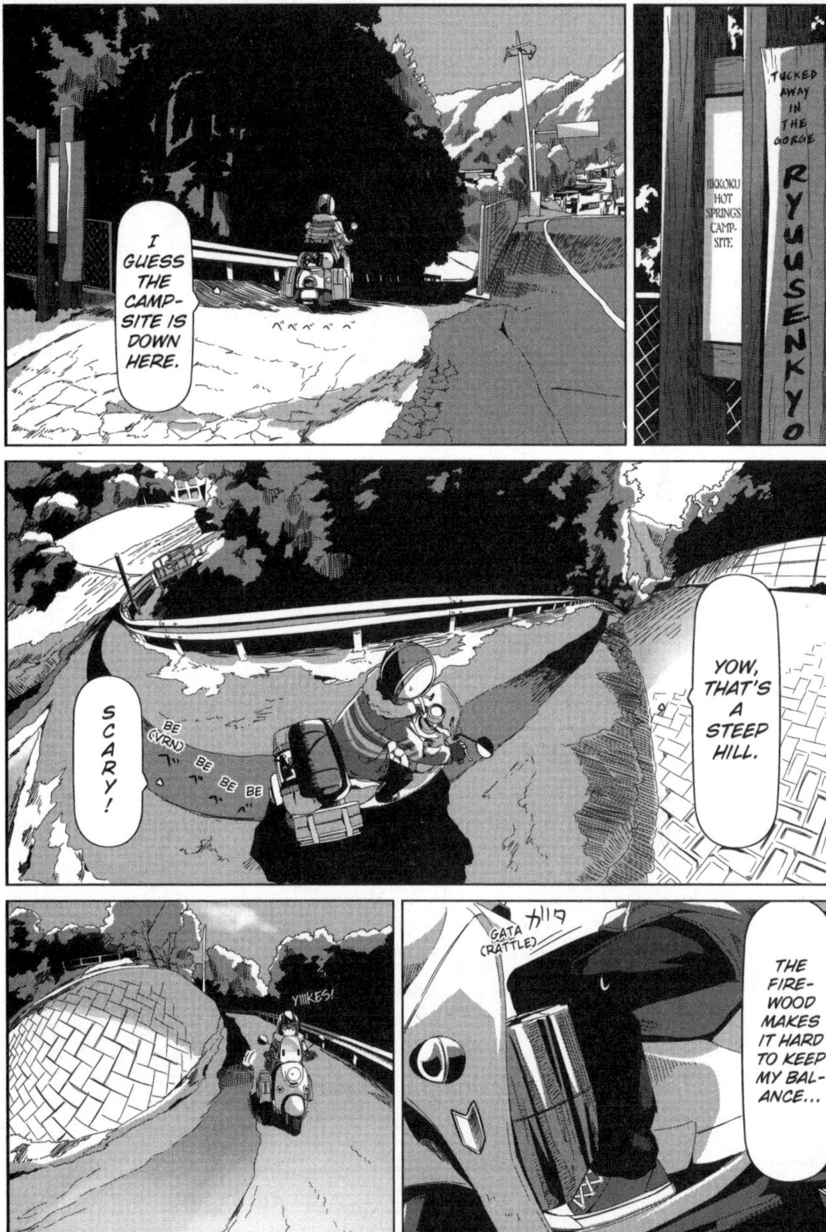
TUCKED AWAY IN THE GORGE
RYUUSENKYO
JIKKOKU HOT SPRINGS CAMP-SITE
I GUESS THE CAMP-SITE IS DOWN HERE.
べべべべべ
YOW, THAT'S A STEEP HILL.
SCARY!
BE (VRN) ブ BE ブ BE ベ BE ベ
THE FIRE-WOOD MAKES IT HARD TO KEEP MY BAL-ANCE...
GATA (RATTLE) ガタ
GATA ガタ
YIIIKES!

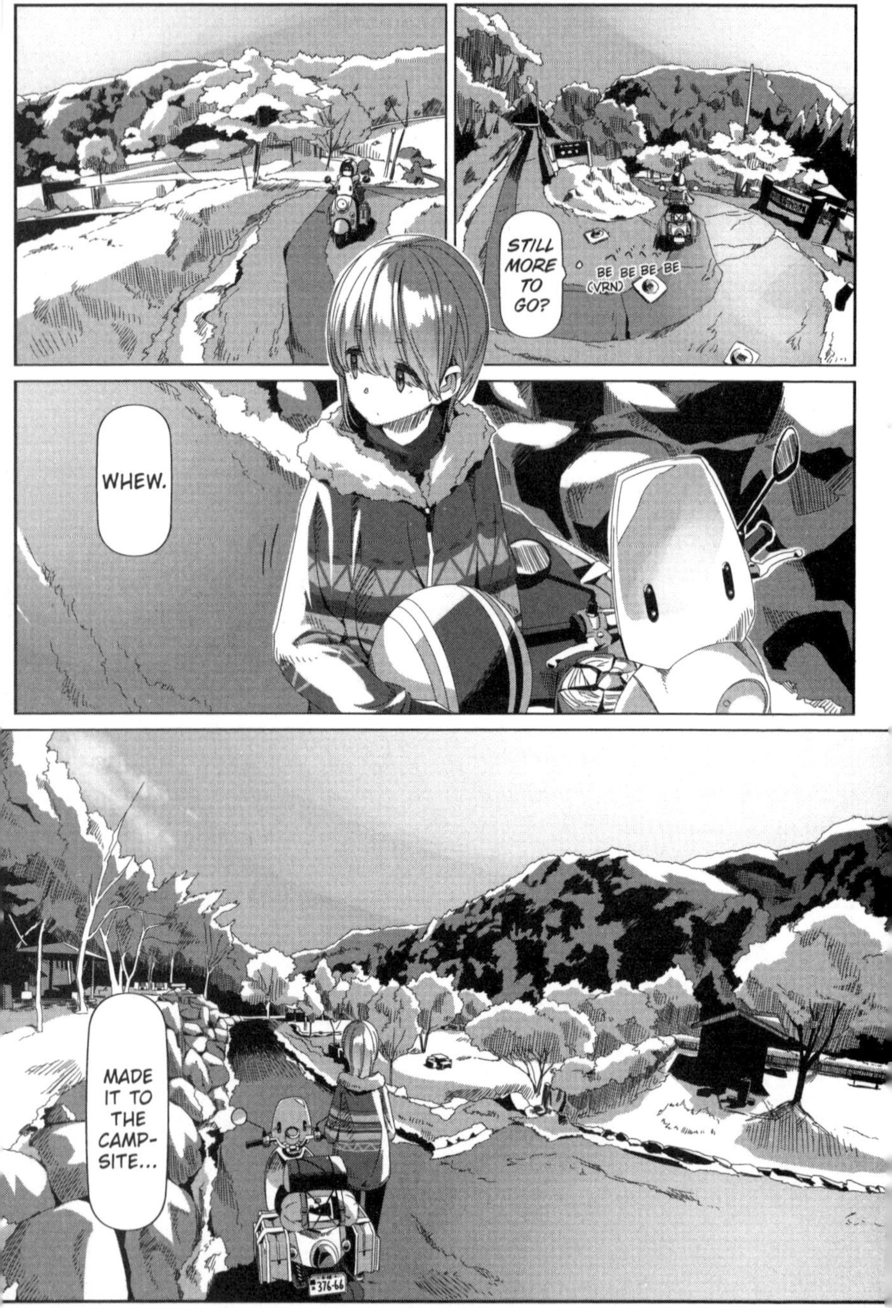
STILL MORE TO GO?
BE BE BE BE
(VRN)
WHEW.
MADE IT TO THE CAMP-SITE...

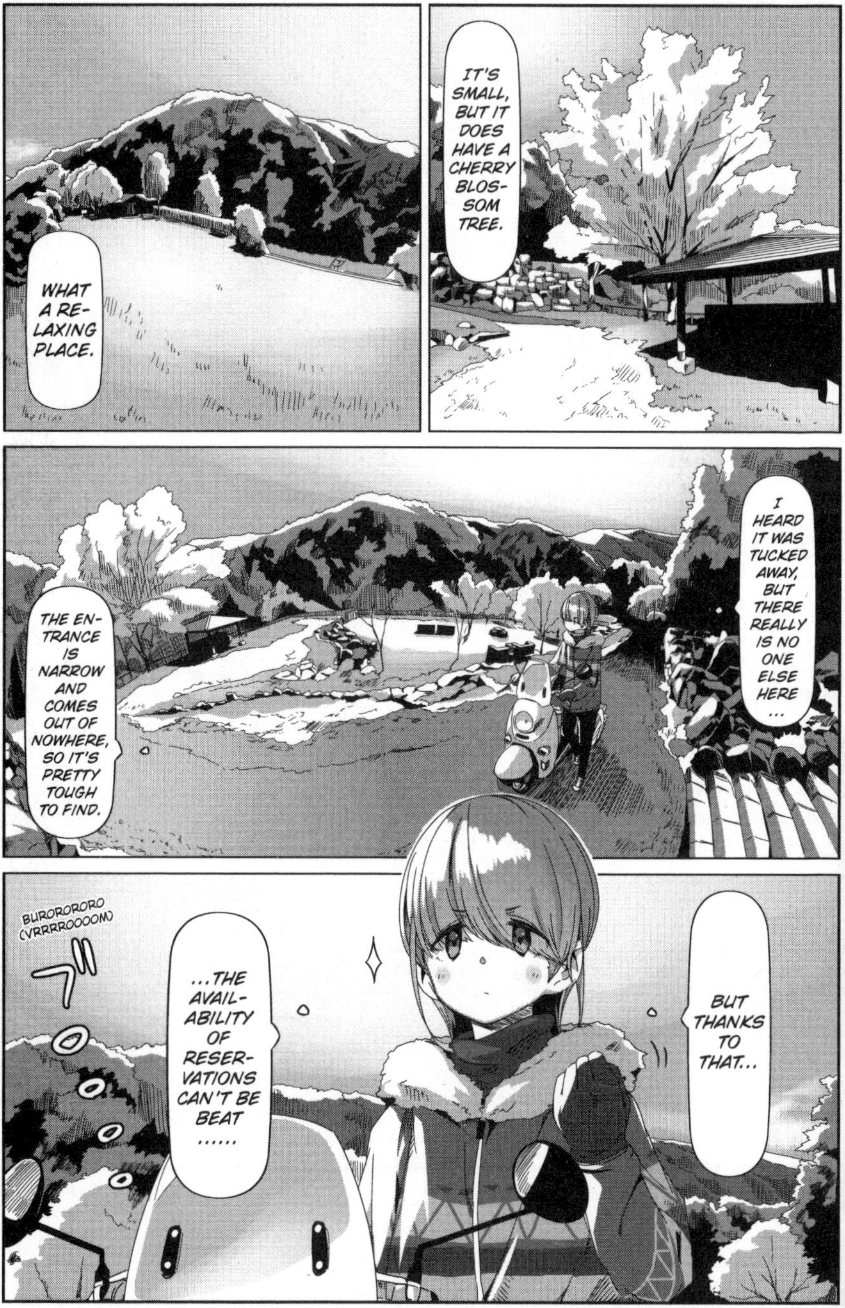
IT'S SMALL, BUT IT DOES HAVE A CHERRY BLOSSOM TREE.
WHAT A RELAXING PLACE.
I HEARD IT WAS TUCKED AWAY, BUT THERE REALLY IS NO ONE ELSE HERE...
THE ENTRANCE IS NARROW AND COMES OUT OF NOWHERE, SO IT'S PRETTY TOUGH TO FIND.
BUT THANKS TO THAT...
...THE AVAILABILITY OF RESERVATIONS CAN'T BE BEAT......
BURORORORO (VRRRROOOOM)

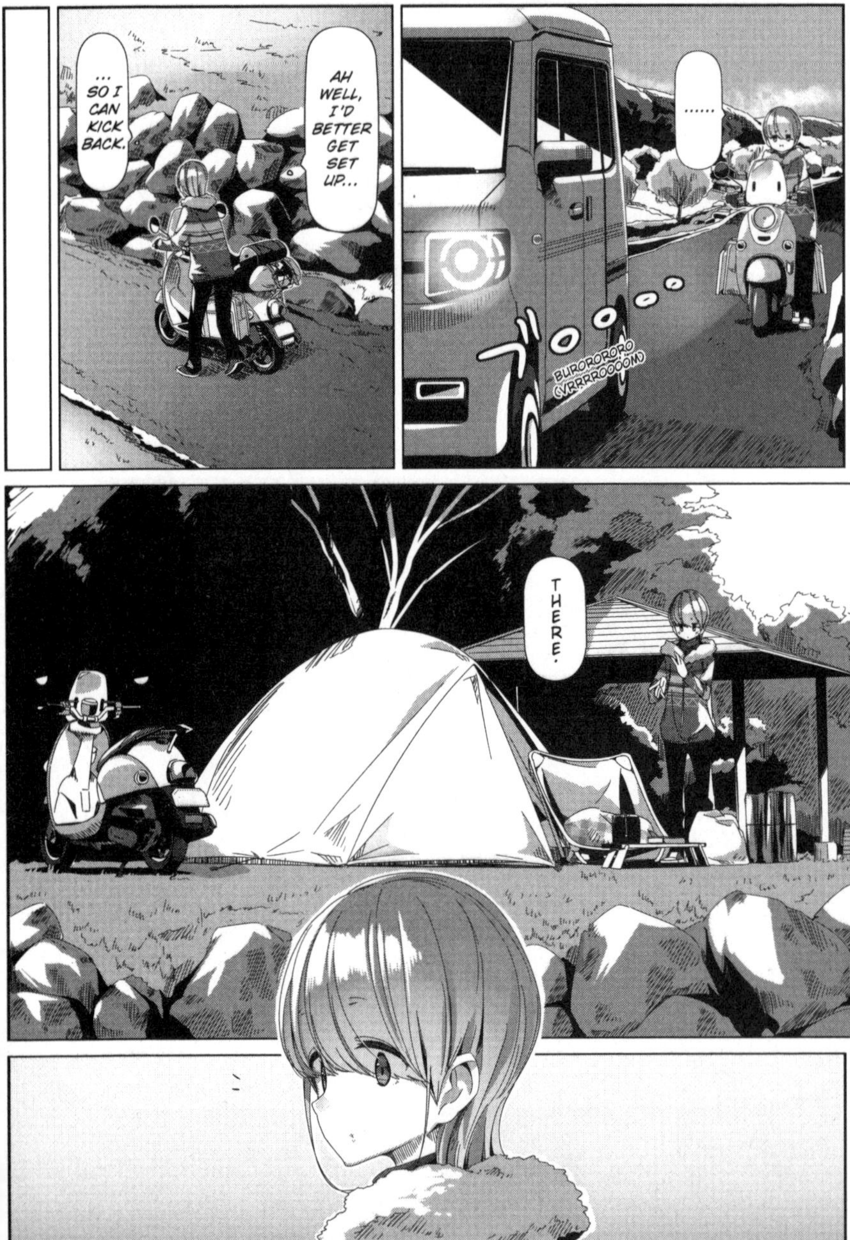
......
BUROROROROO (VRRRROOOOM)
AH WELL, I'D BETTER GET SET UP...
... SO I CAN KICK BACK.
THERE.

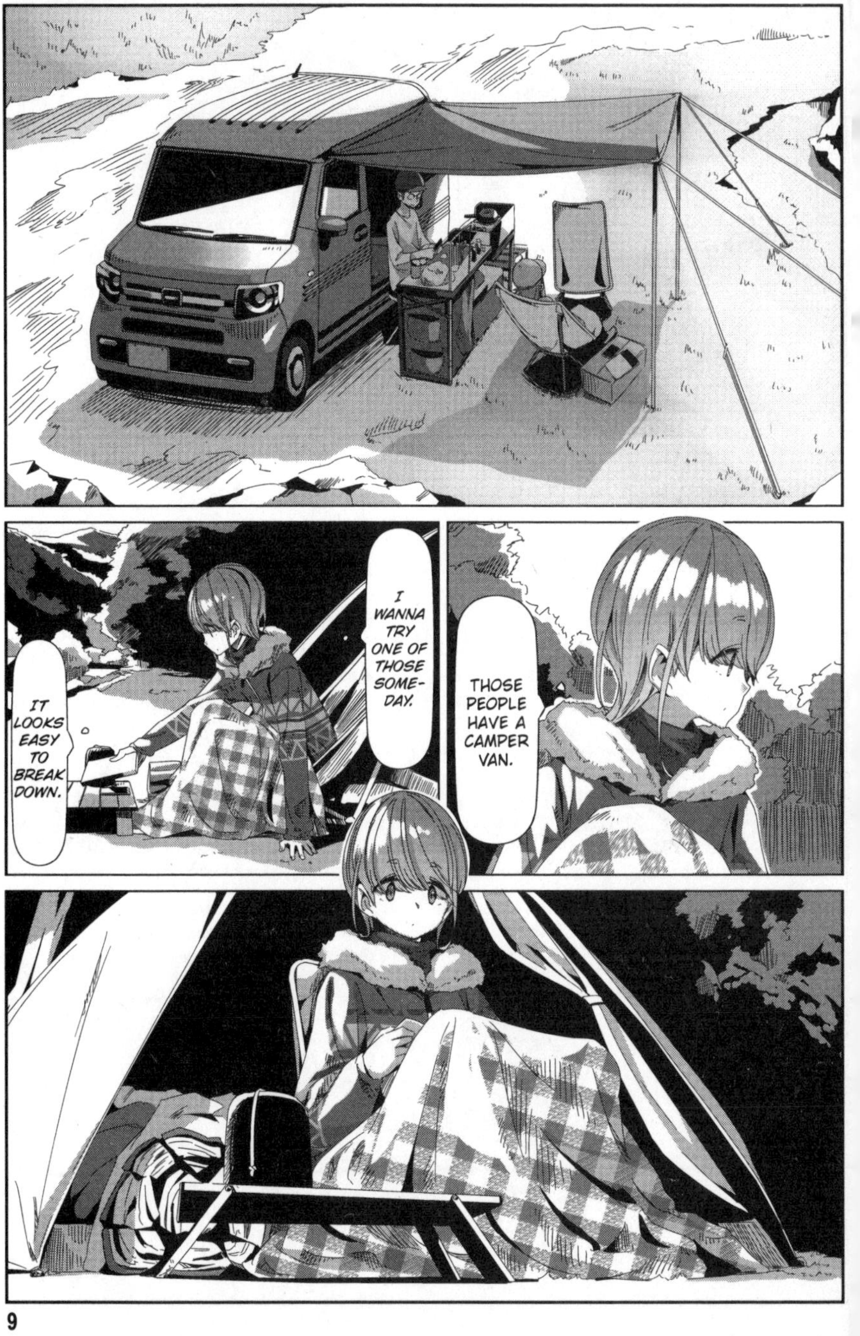
THOSE PEOPLE HAVE A CAMPER VAN.
I WANNA TRY ONE OF THOSE SOME-DAY.
IT LOOKS EASY TO BREAK DOWN.

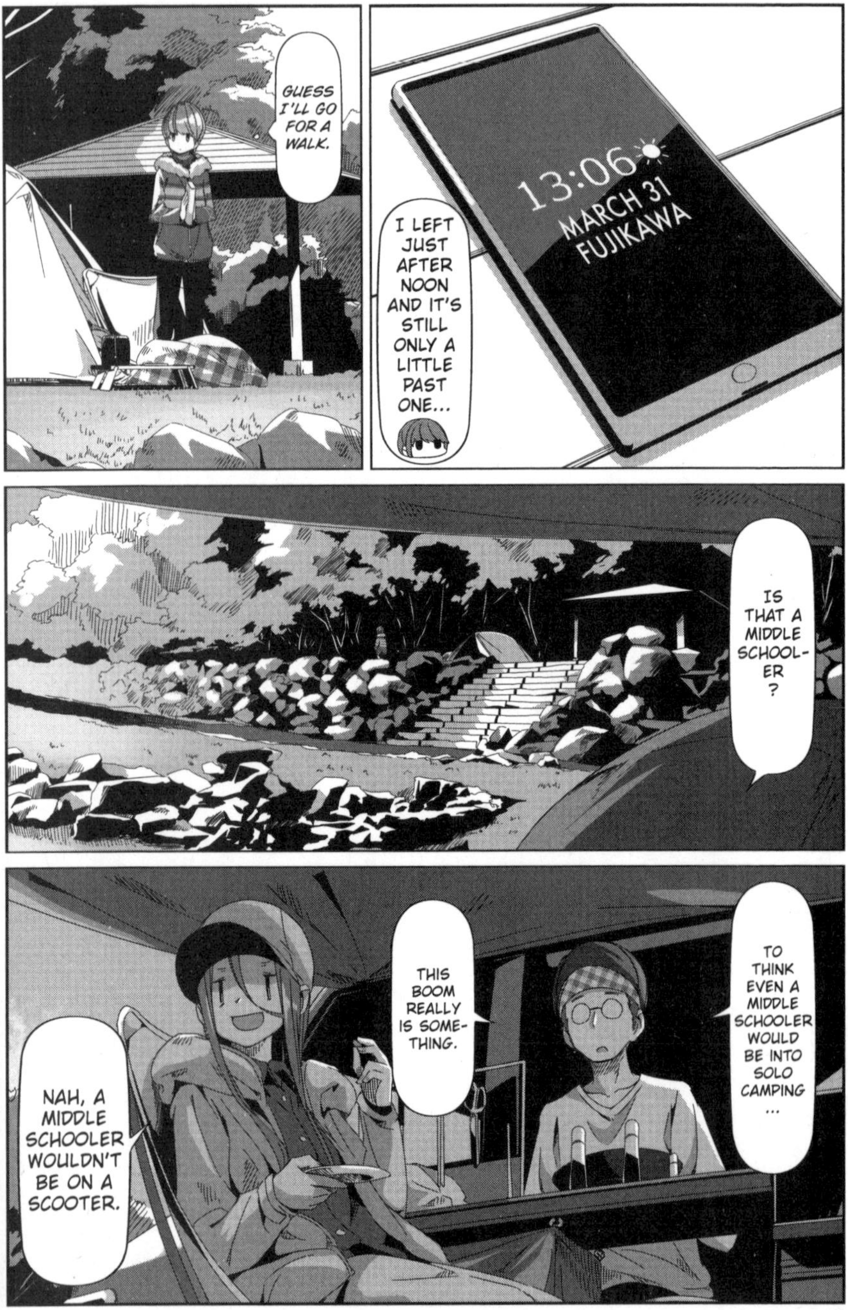
13:06
MARCH 31
FUJIKAWA
I LEFT JUST AFTER NOON AND IT'S STILL ONLY A LITTLE PAST ONE...
GUESS I'LL GO FOR A WALK.
IS THAT A MIDDLE SCHOOL-ER?
TO THINK EVEN A MIDDLE SCHOOLER WOULD BE INTO SOLO CAMPING...
THIS BOOM REALLY IS SOME-THING.
NAH, A MIDDLE SCHOOLER WOULDN'T BE ON A SCOOTER.

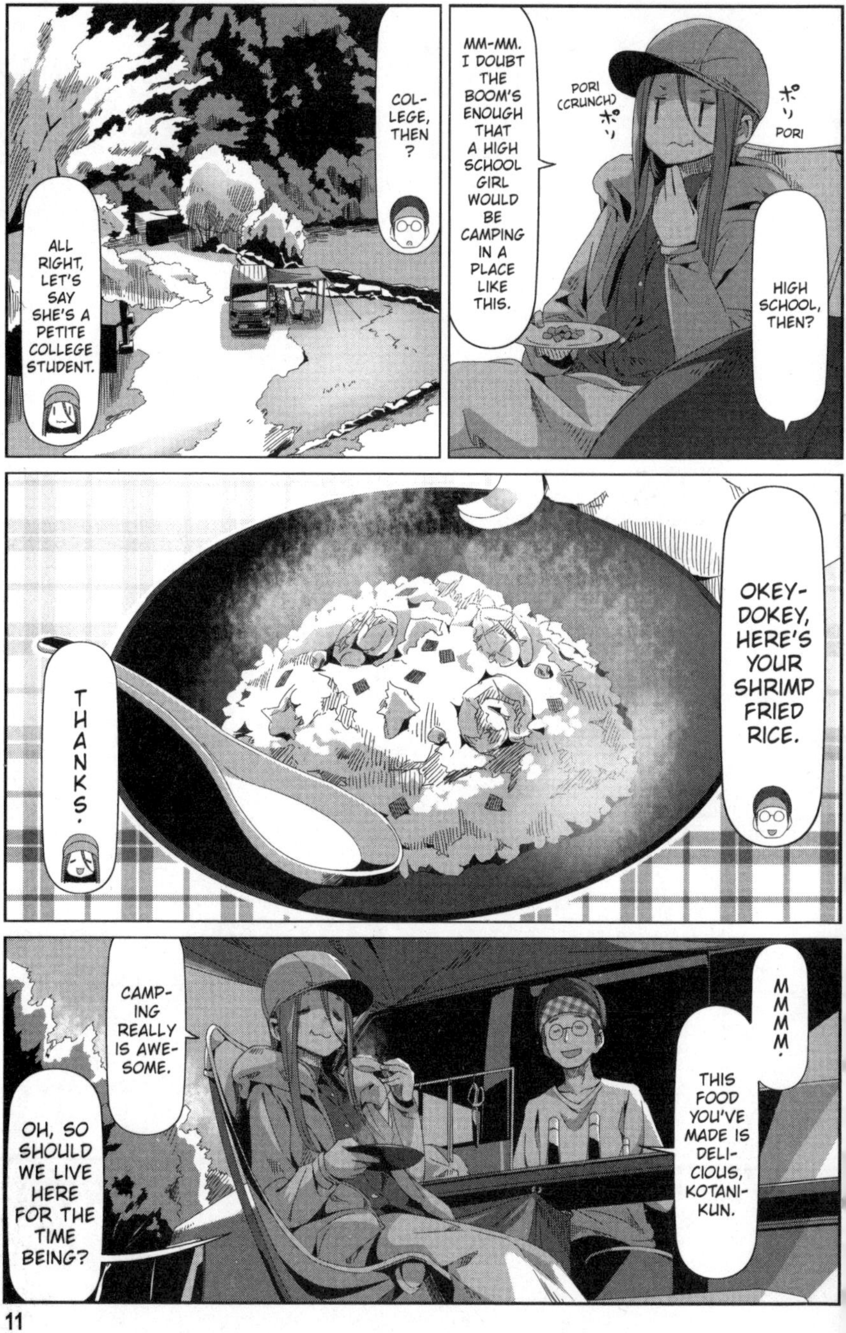
ポリ
PORI
PORI (CRUNCH)
ポリ
MM-MM. I DOUBT THE BOOM'S ENOUGH THAT A HIGH SCHOOL GIRL WOULD BE CAMPING IN A PLACE LIKE THIS.
HIGH SCHOOL, THEN?
COL-LEGE, THEN?
ALL RIGHT, LET'S SAY SHE'S A PETITE COLLEGE STUDENT.
OKEY-DOKEY, HERE'S YOUR SHRIMP FRIED RICE.
THANKS.
MMMM.
THIS FOOD YOU'VE MADE IS DELI-CIOUS, KOTANI-KUN.
CAMP-ING REALLY IS AWE-SOME.
OH, SO SHOULD WE LIVE HERE FOR THE TIME BEING?

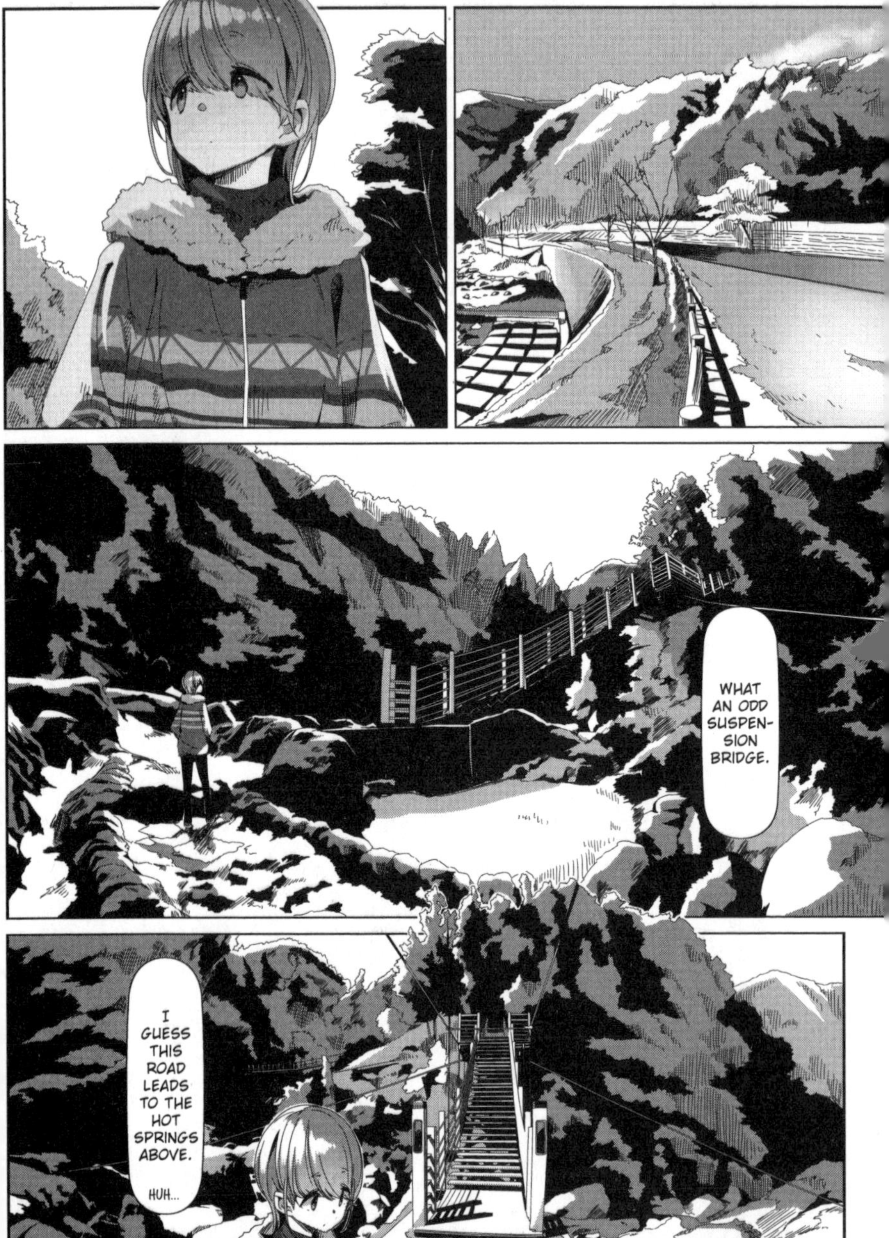
WHAT AN ODD SUSPENSION BRIDGE.
I GUESS THIS ROAD LEADS TO THE HOT SPRINGS ABOVE.
HUH...

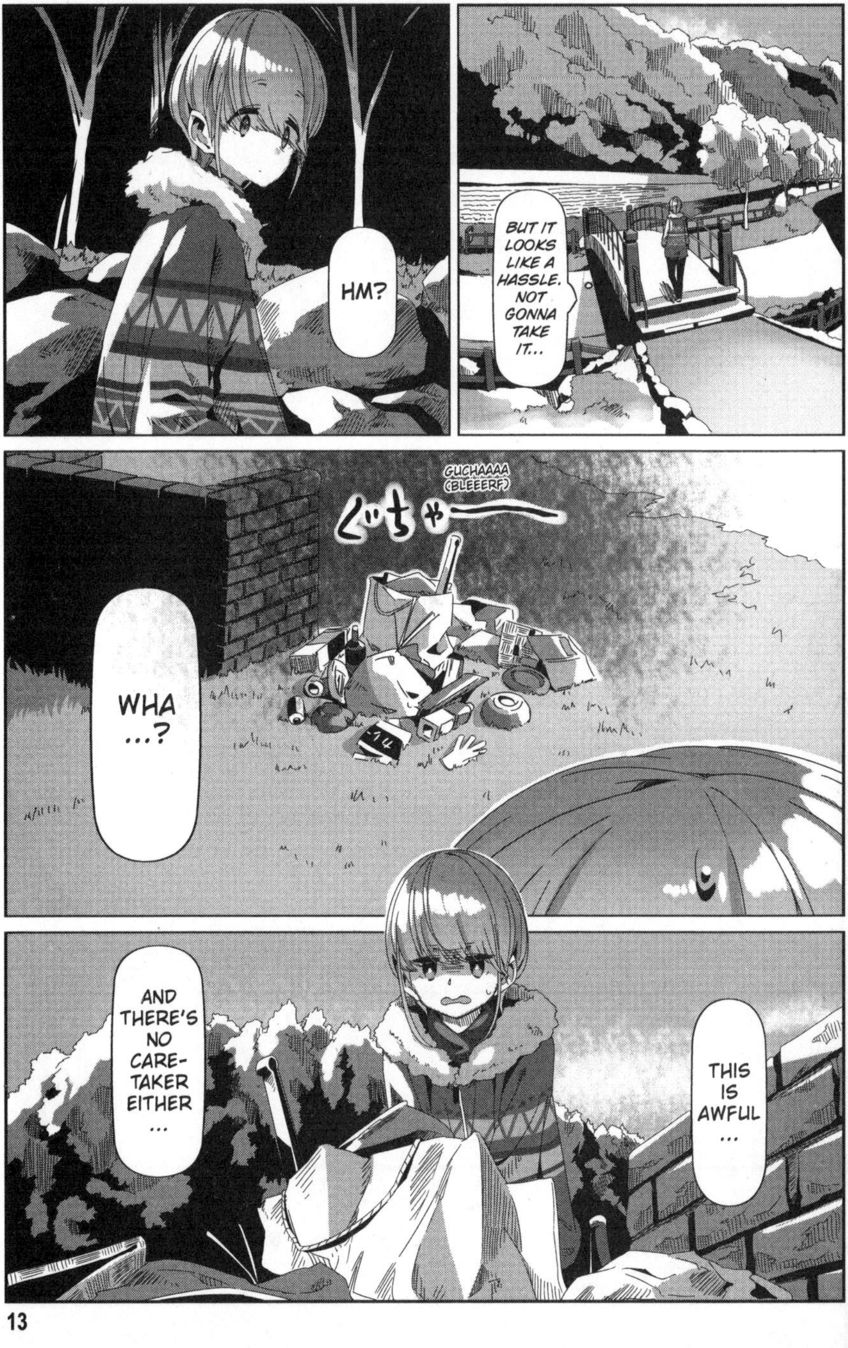
BUT IT LOOKS LIKE A HASSLE. NOT GONNA TAKE IT...
HM?
GUCHAAAA (BLEEERF)
ぐちゃーー
WHA ...?
THIS IS AWFUL ...
AND THERE'S NO CARE-TAKER EITHER ...

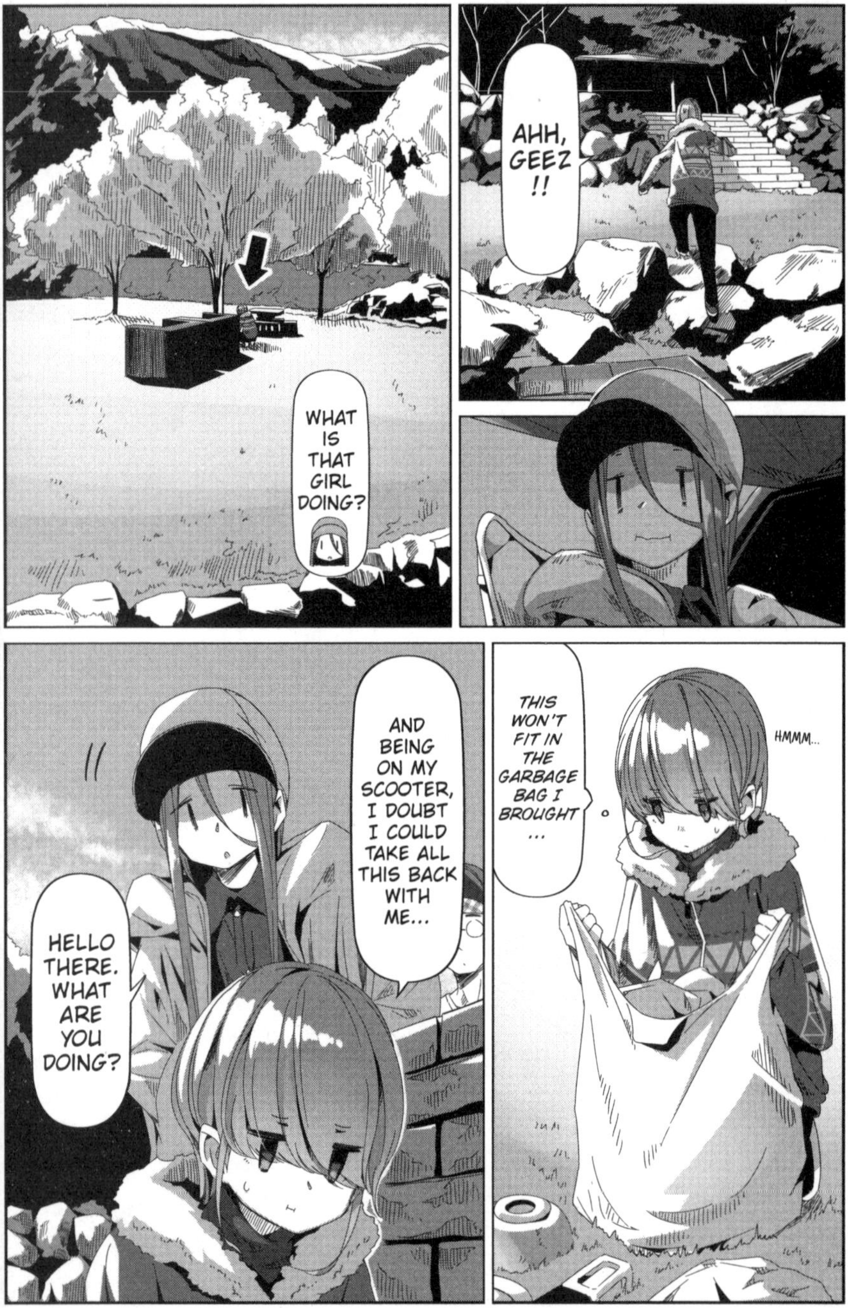
AHH, GEEZ!!
WHAT IS THAT GIRL DOING?
HMMM...
THIS WON'T FIT IN THE GARBAGE BAG I BROUGHT...
AND BEING ON MY SCOOTER, I DOUBT I COULD TAKE ALL THIS BACK WITH ME...
HELLO THERE. WHAT ARE YOU DOING?

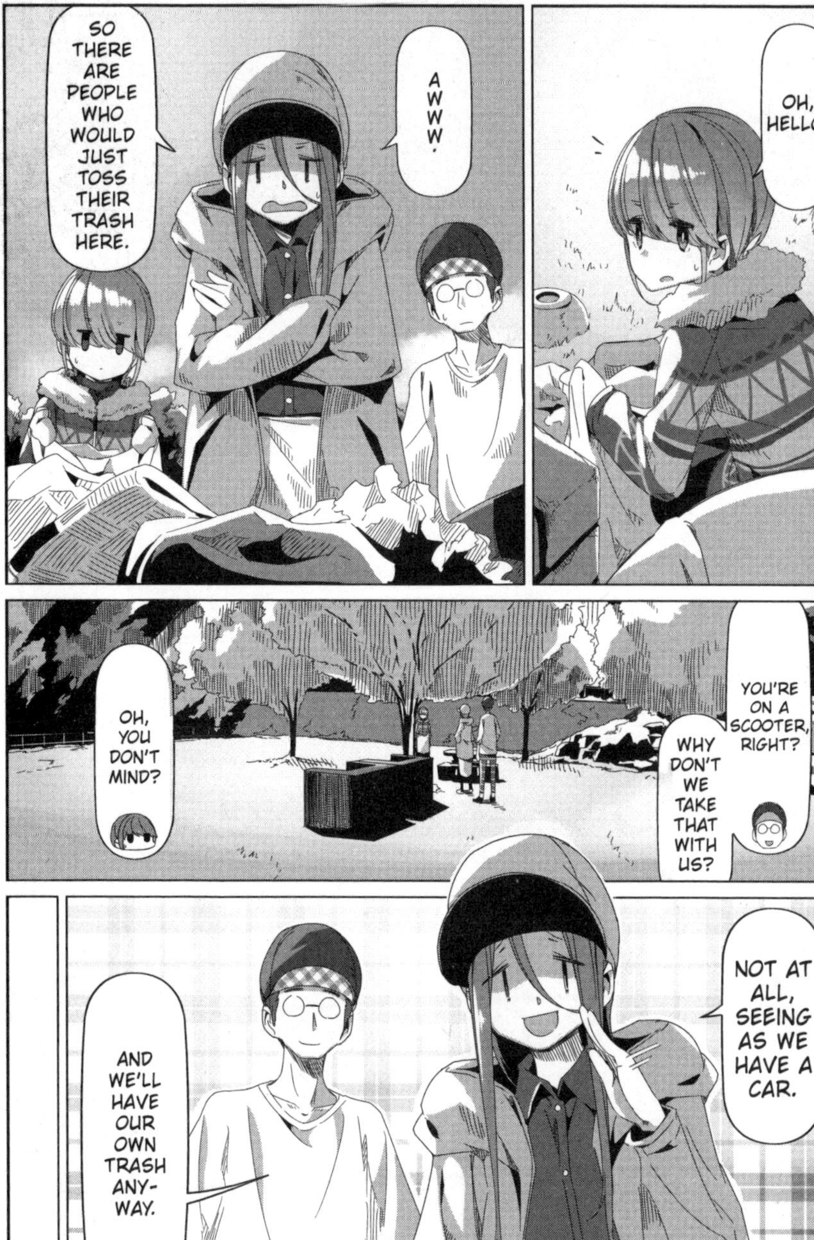
OH, HELLO.
AWWW.
SO THERE ARE PEOPLE WHO WOULD JUST TOSS THEIR TRASH HERE.
YOU'RE ON A SCOOTER, RIGHT?
WHY DON'T WE TAKE THAT WITH US?
OH, YOU DON'T MIND?
NOT AT ALL, SEEING AS WE HAVE A CAR.
AND WE'LL HAVE OUR OWN TRASH ANY-WAY.

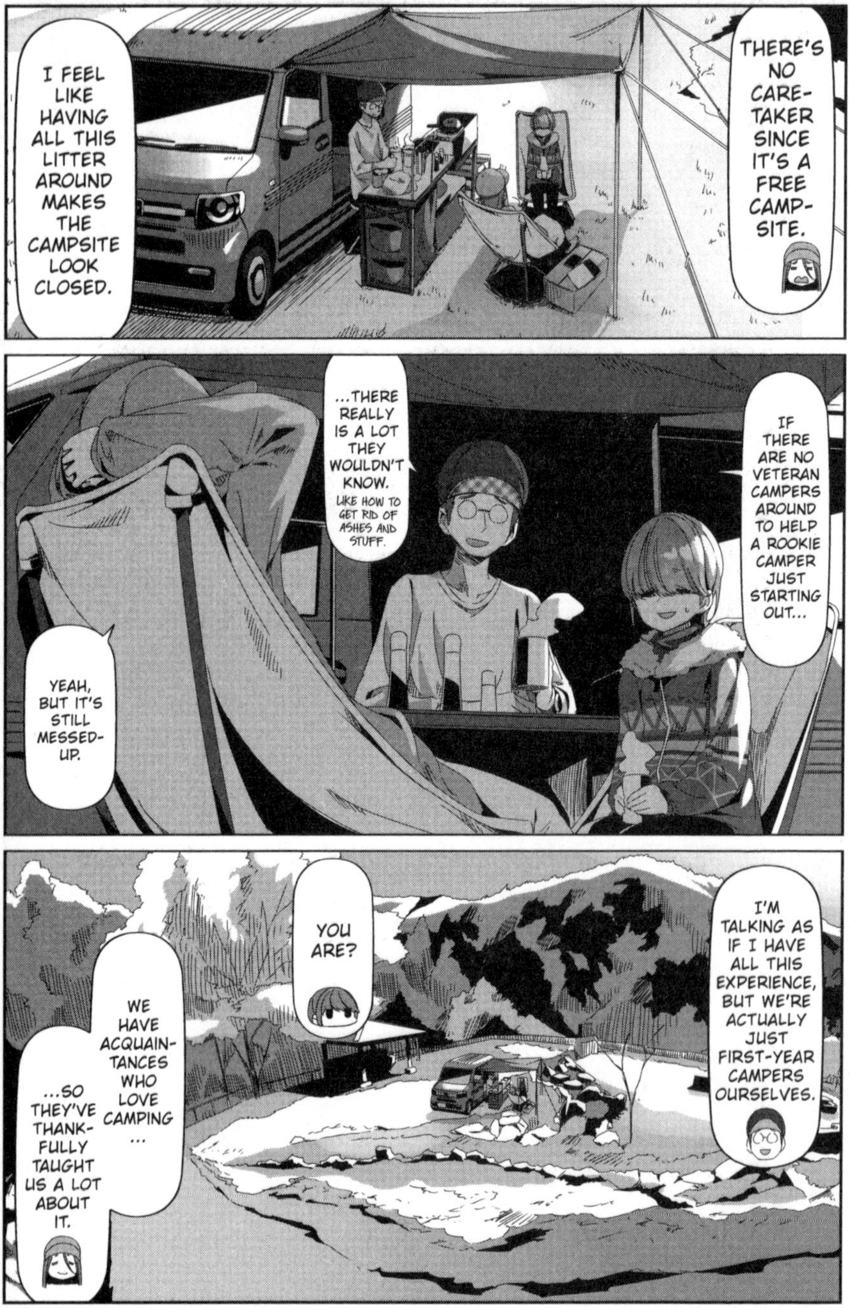
THERE'S NO CARE-TAKER SINCE IT'S A FREE CAMP-SITE.
I FEEL LIKE HAVING ALL THIS LITTER AROUND MAKES THE CAMPSITE LOOK CLOSED.
IF THERE ARE NO VETERAN CAMPERS AROUND TO HELP A ROOKIE CAMPER JUST STARTING OUT...
...THERE REALLY IS A LOT THEY WOULDN'T KNOW.
LIKE HOW TO GET RID OF ASHES AND STUFF.
YEAH, BUT IT'S STILL MESSED-UP.
I'M TALKING AS IF I HAVE ALL THIS EXPERIENCE, BUT WE'RE ACTUALLY JUST FIRST-YEAR CAMPERS OURSELVES.
YOU ARE?
WE HAVE ACQUAIN-TANCES WHO LOVE CAMPING...
...SO THEY'VE THANK-FULLY TAUGHT US A LOT ABOUT IT.

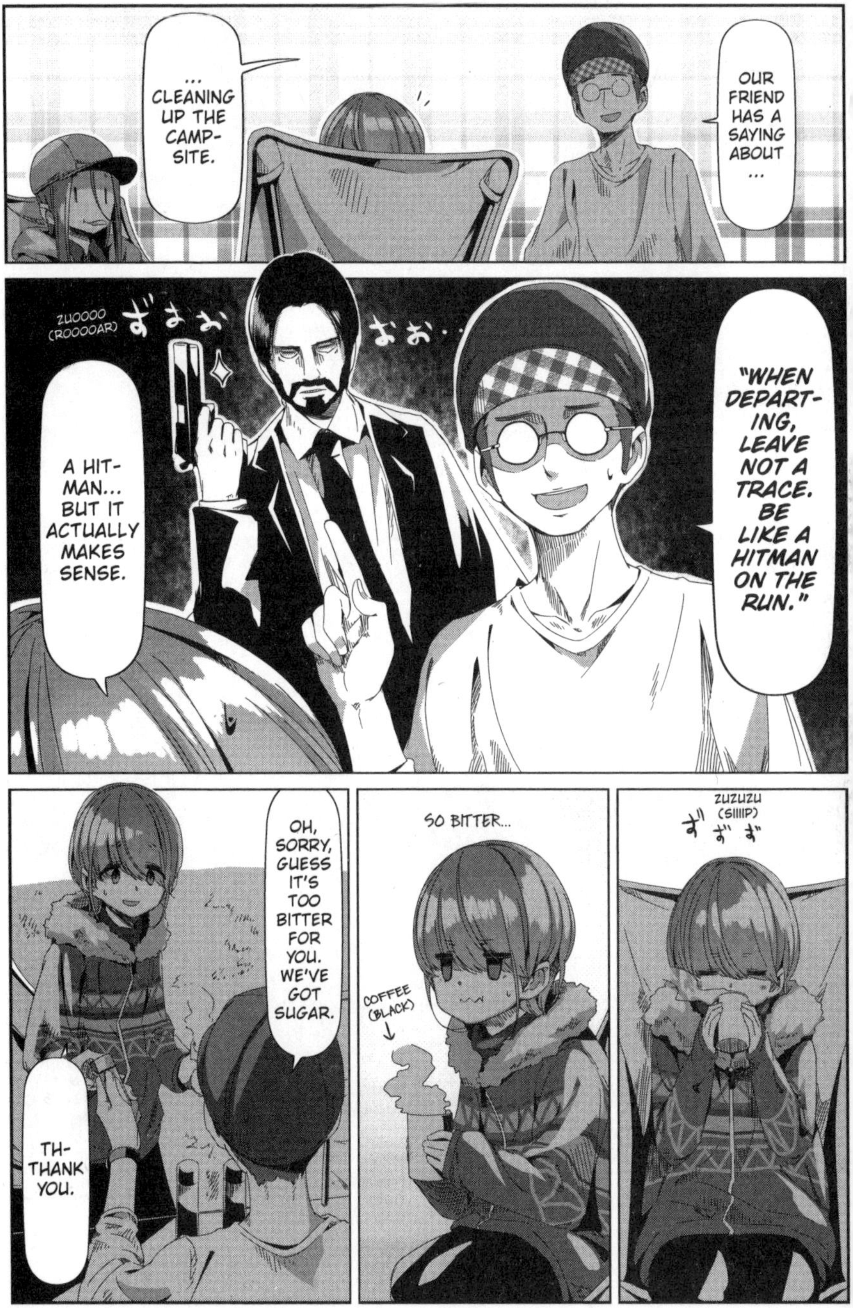
OUR FRIEND HAS A SAYING ABOUT ...
... CLEANING UP THE CAMP-SITE.
"WHEN DEPART-ING, LEAVE NOT A TRACE. BE LIKE A HITMAN ON THE RUN."
ZUOOOO (ROOOOAR)
ずぉぉ ぉぉ...
A HIT-MAN... BUT IT ACTUALLY MAKES SENSE.
ZUZUZU (SIIIIP)
ずずず
SO BITTER...
COFFEE (BLACK)
OH, SORRY, GUESS IT'S TOO BITTER FOR YOU. WE'VE GOT SUGAR.
TH-THANK YOU.

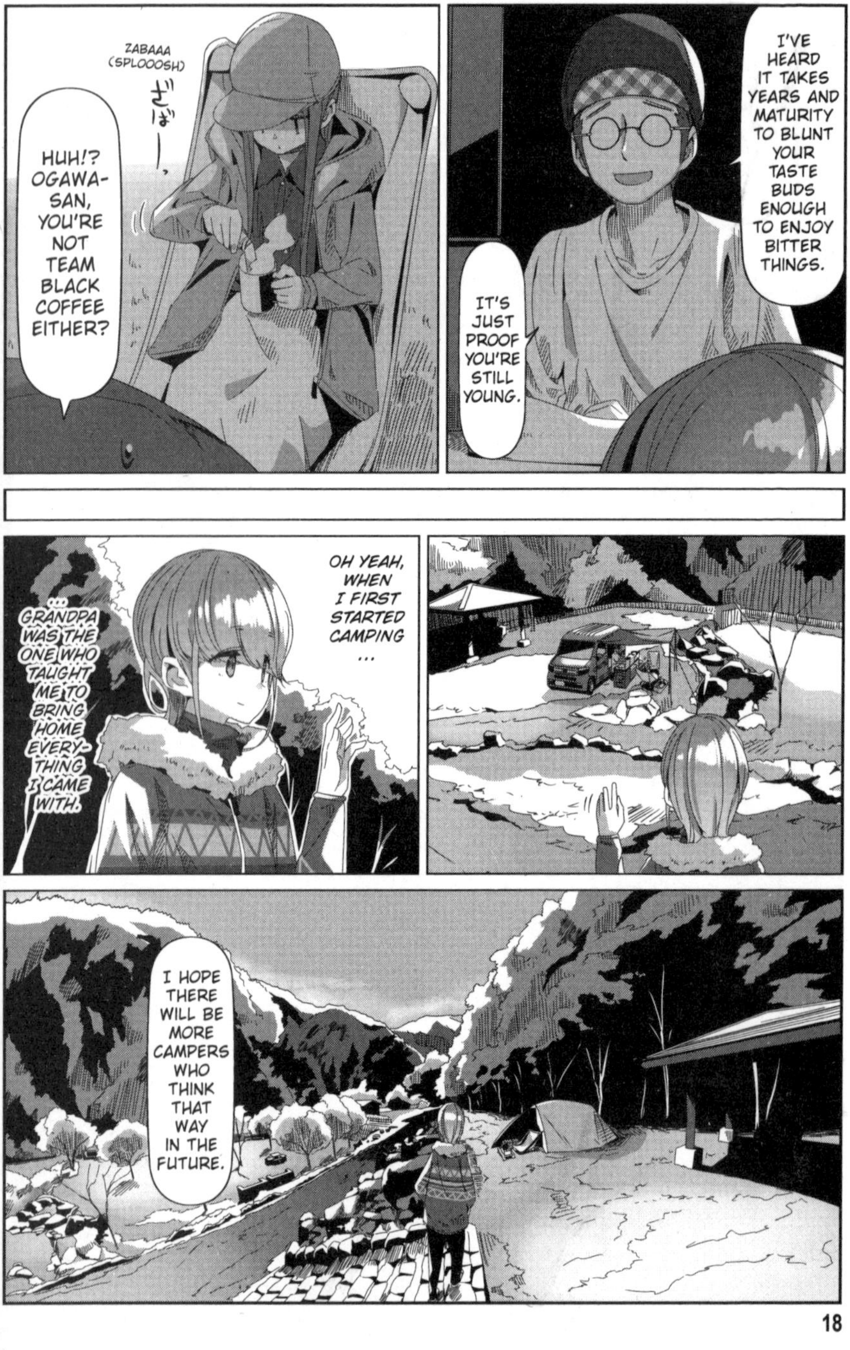

I'VE HEARD IT TAKES YEARS AND MATURITY TO BLUNT YOUR TASTE BUDS ENOUGH TO ENJOY BITTER THINGS.
IT'S JUST PROOF YOU'RE STILL YOUNG.
ZABAAA (SPLOOOSH)
ざばー
HUH!? OGAWA-SAN, YOU'RE NOT TEAM BLACK COFFEE EITHER?
OH YEAH, WHEN I FIRST STARTED CAMPING...
...GRANDPA WAS THE ONE WHO TAUGHT ME TO BRING HOME EVERYTHING I CAME WITH.
I HOPE THERE WILL BE MORE CAMPERS WHO THINK THAT WAY IN THE FUTURE.

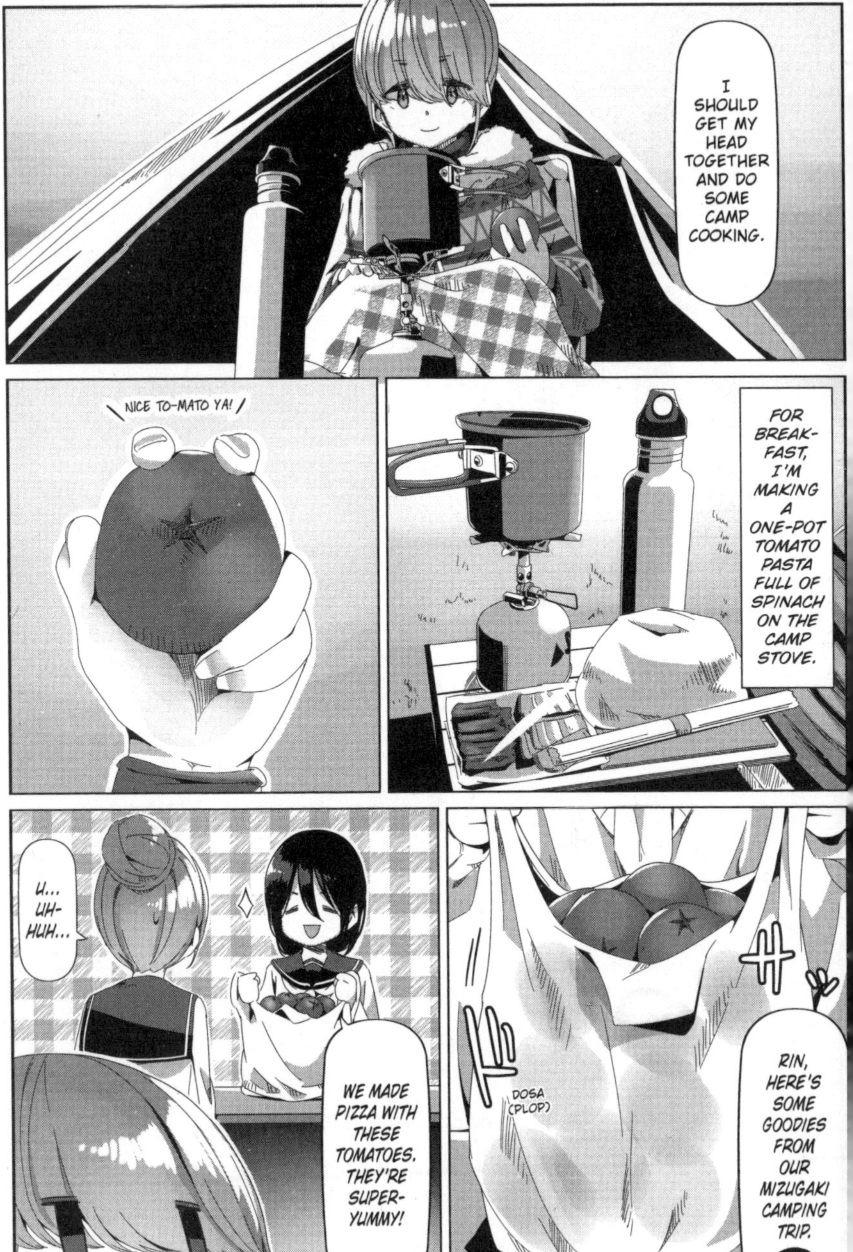
I SHOULD GET MY HEAD TOGETHER AND DO SOME CAMP COOKING.
FOR BREAK-FAST, I'M MAKING A ONE-POT TOMATO PASTA FULL OF SPINACH ON THE CAMP STOVE.
NICE TO-MATO YA!
RIN, HERE'S SOME GOODIES FROM OUR MIZUGAKI CAMPING TRIP.
DOSA (PLOP)
WE MADE PIZZA WITH THESE TOMATOES. THEY'RE SUPER-YUMMY!
U... UH-HUH...

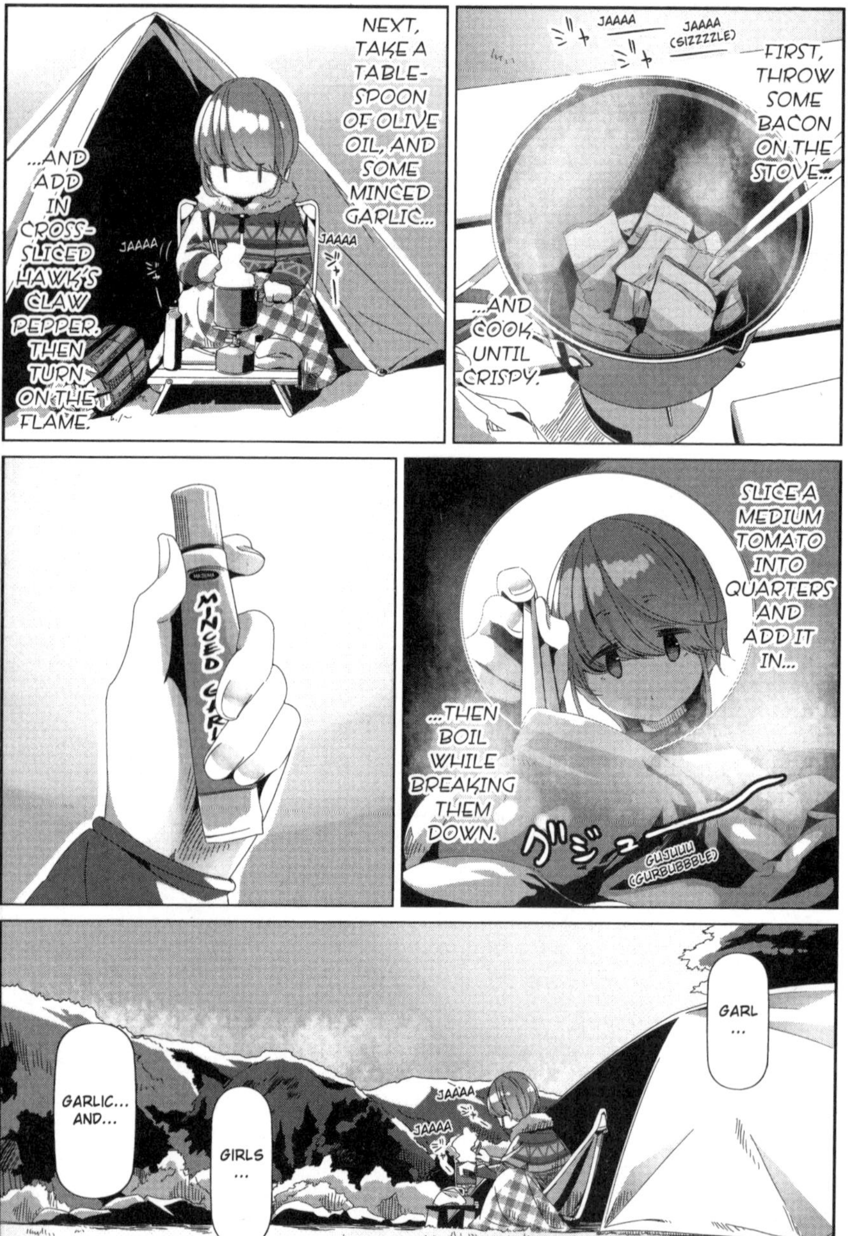
JAAAA
JAAAA (SIZZZZLE)
FIRST, THROW SOME BACON ON THE STOVE...
...AND COOK UNTIL CRISPY.
NEXT, TAKE A TABLE-SPOON OF OLIVE OIL, AND SOME MINCED GARLIC...
JAAAA
JAAAA
...AND ADD IN CROSS-SLICED HAWK'S CLAW PEPPER. THEN TURN ON THE FLAME.
SLICE A MEDIUM TOMATO INTO QUARTERS AND ADD IT IN...
...THEN BOIL WHILE BREAKING THEM DOWN.
GUJUUU (GURBUBBBLE)
MINCED GIRL
GARL...
JAAAA
JAAAA
GIRLS...
GARLIC... AND...

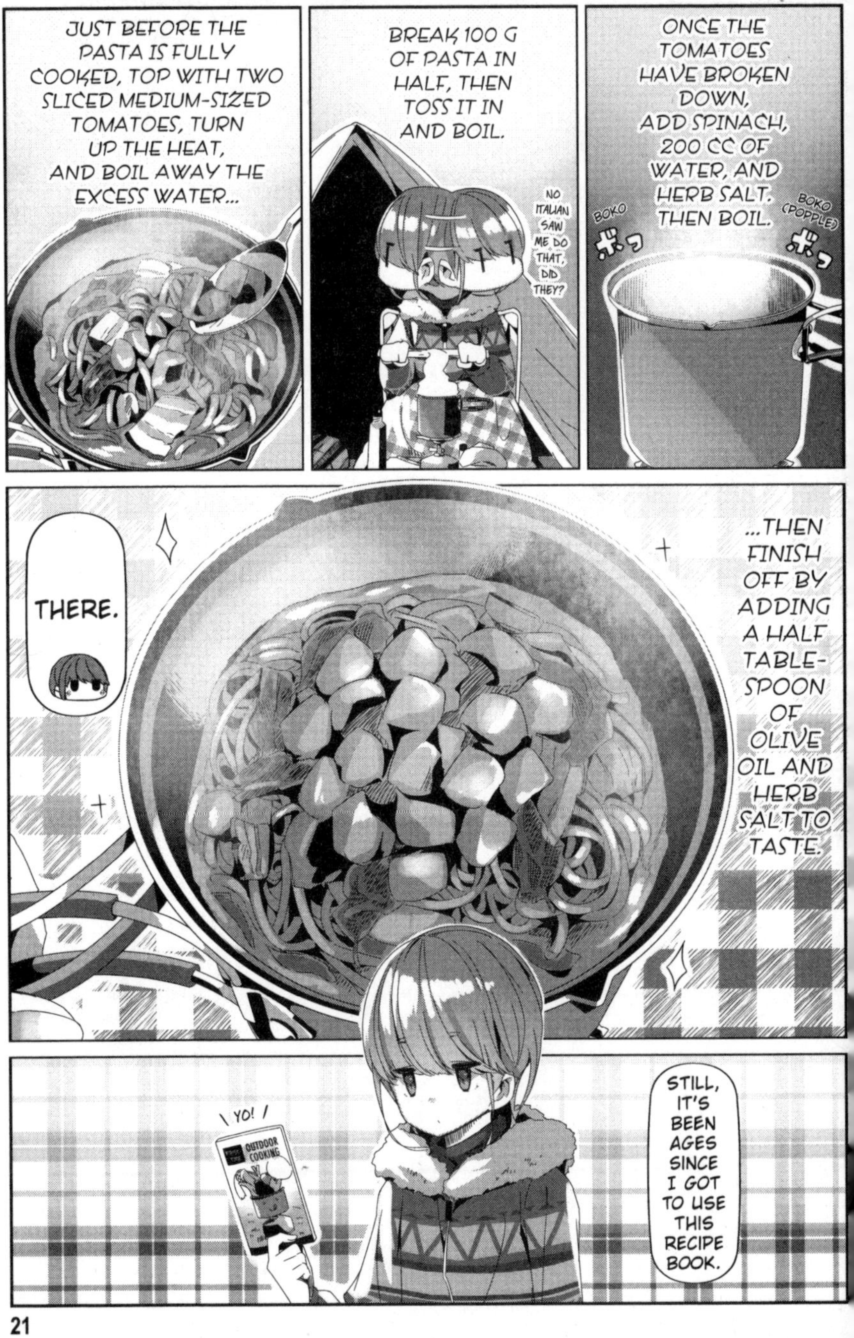
ONCE THE TOMATOES HAVE BROKEN DOWN, ADD SPINACH, 200 CC OF WATER, AND HERB SALT. THEN BOIL.
BOKO (POPPLE)
ボッ
BOKO
ボッ
BREAK 100 G OF PASTA IN HALF, THEN TOSS IT IN AND BOIL.
NO ITALIAN SAW ME DO THAT, DID THEY?
JUST BEFORE THE PASTA IS FULLY COOKED, TOP WITH TWO SLICED MEDIUM-SIZED TOMATOES, TURN UP THE HEAT, AND BOIL AWAY THE EXCESS WATER...
...THEN FINISH OFF BY ADDING A HALF TABLE-SPOON OF OLIVE OIL AND HERB SALT TO TASTE.
THERE.
STILL, IT'S BEEN AGES SINCE I GOT TO USE THIS RECIPE BOOK.
\ YO! /
OUTDOOR COOKING

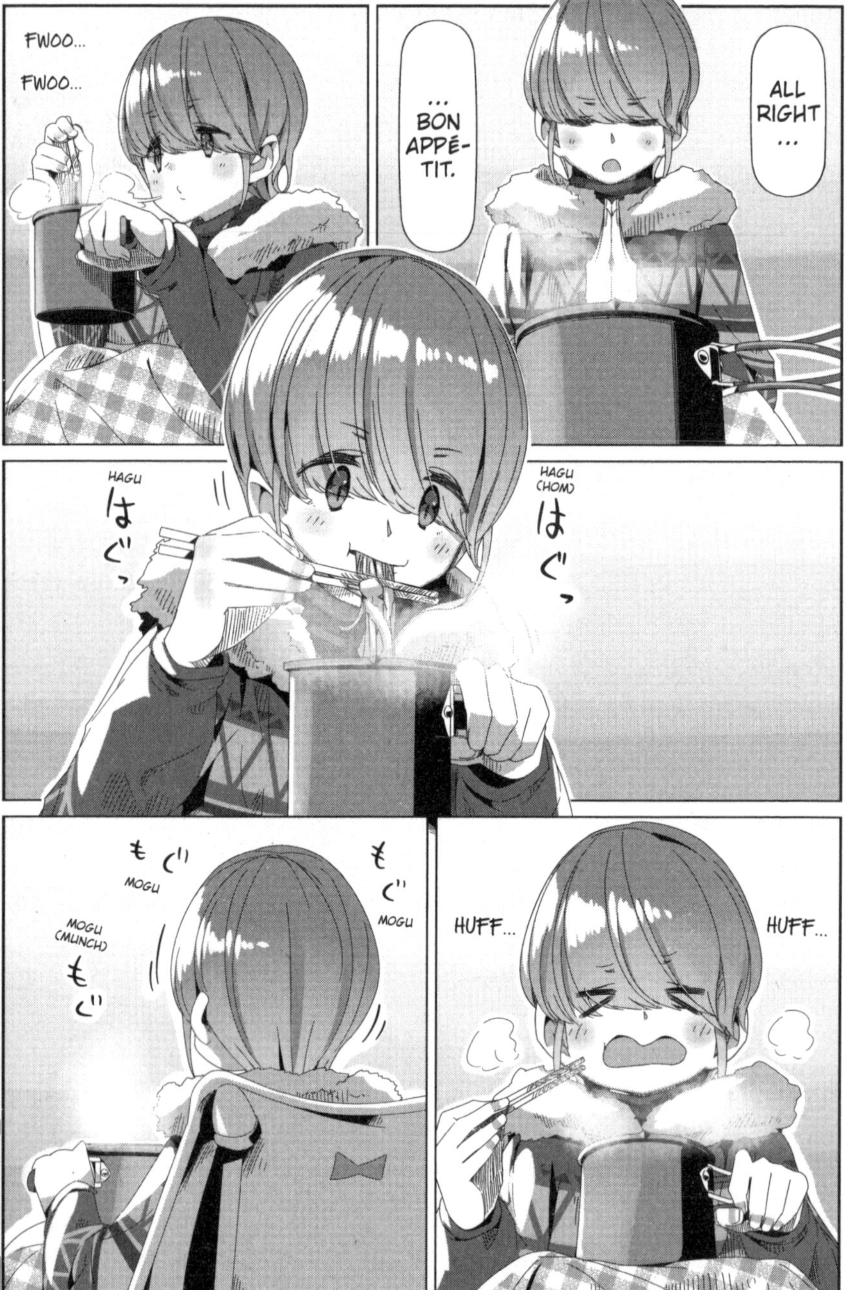
ALL RIGHT ...
... BON APPÉ-TIT.
FWOO...
FWOO...
HAGU (HOM)
はぐっ
HAGU
はぐっ
HUFF...
HUFF...
もぐ
MOGU
もぐ
MOGU
MOGU (MUNCH)
もぐ

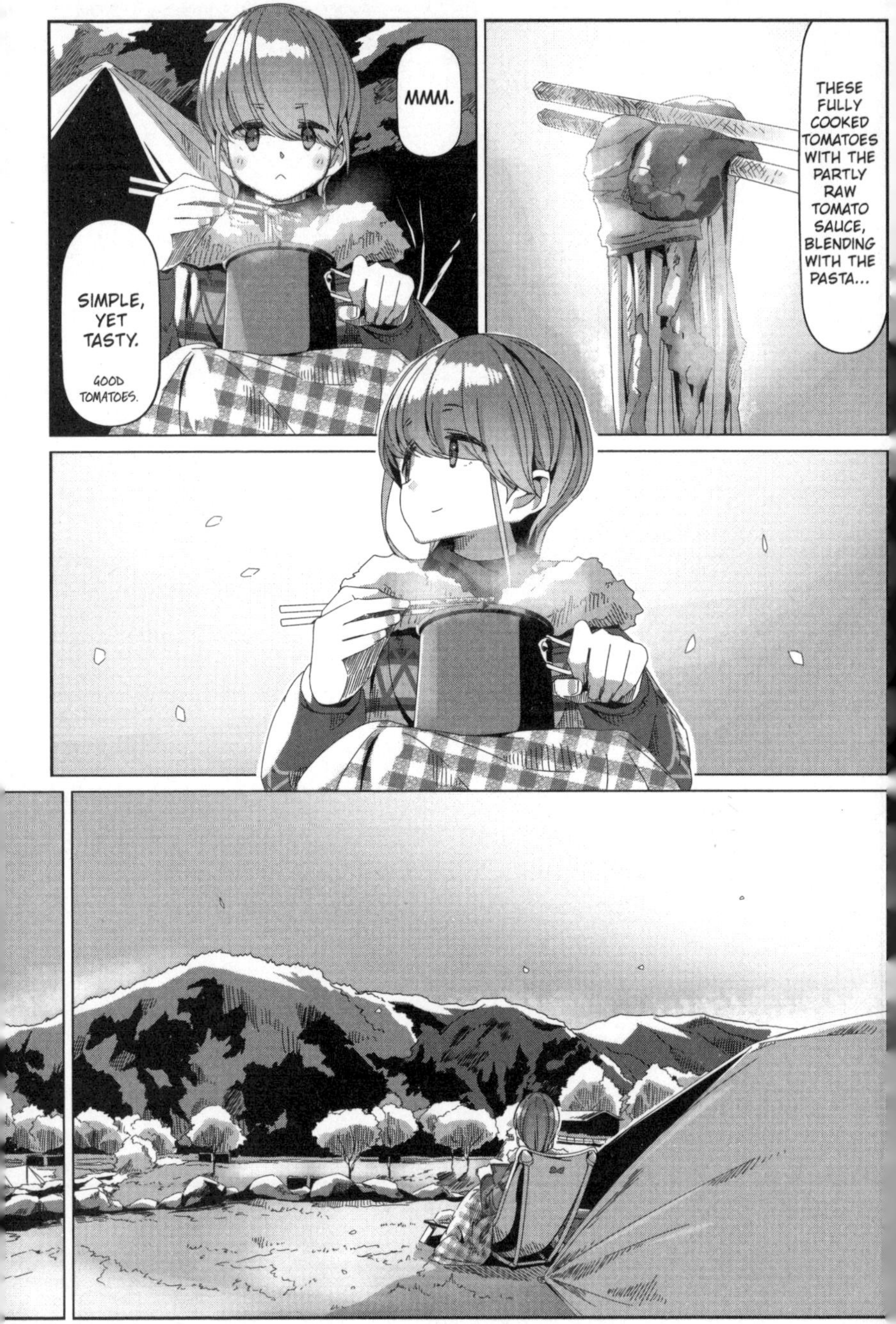
THESE FULLY COOKED TOMATOES WITH THE PARTLY RAW TOMATO SAUCE, BLENDING WITH THE PASTA...
MMM.
SIMPLE, YET TASTY.
GOOD TOMATOES.

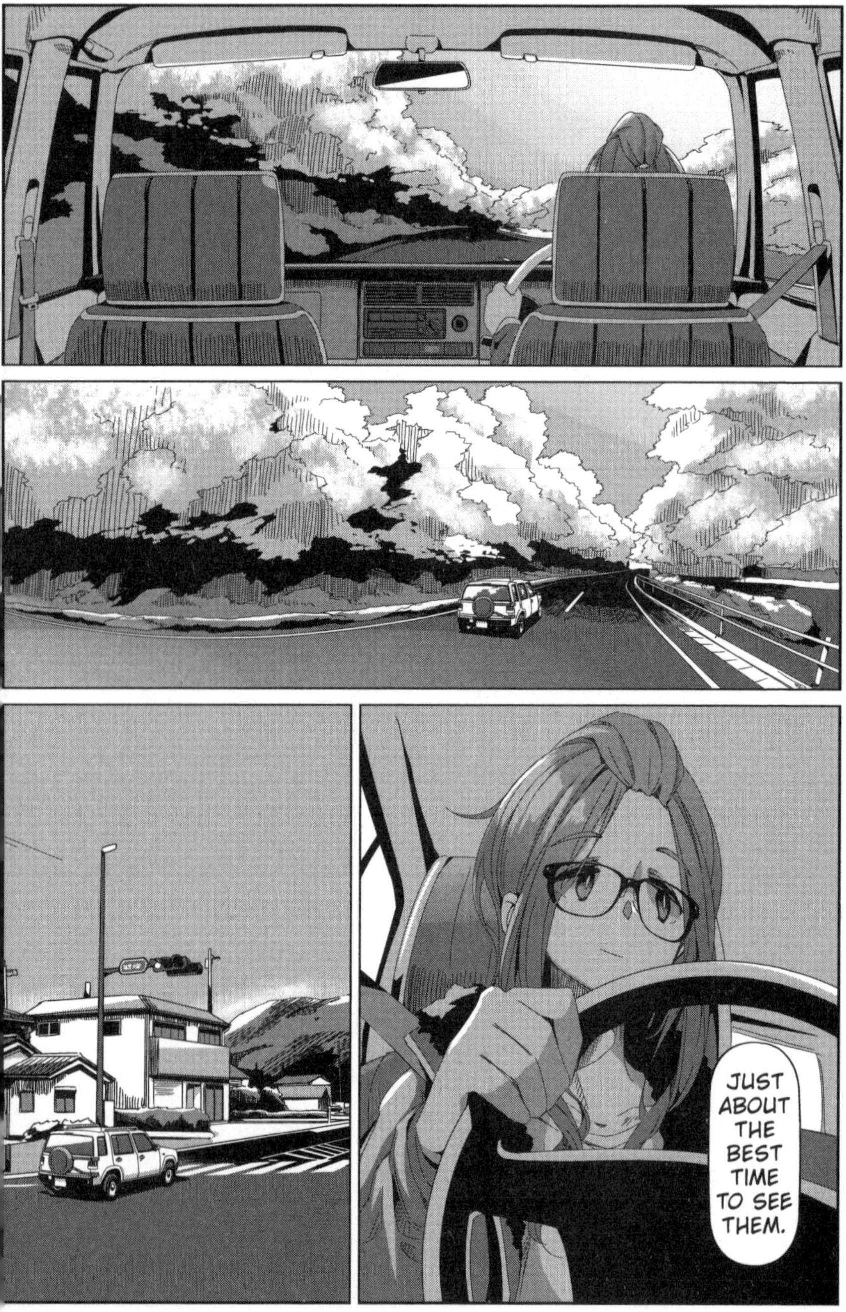
JUST ABOUT THE BEST TIME TO SEE THEM.

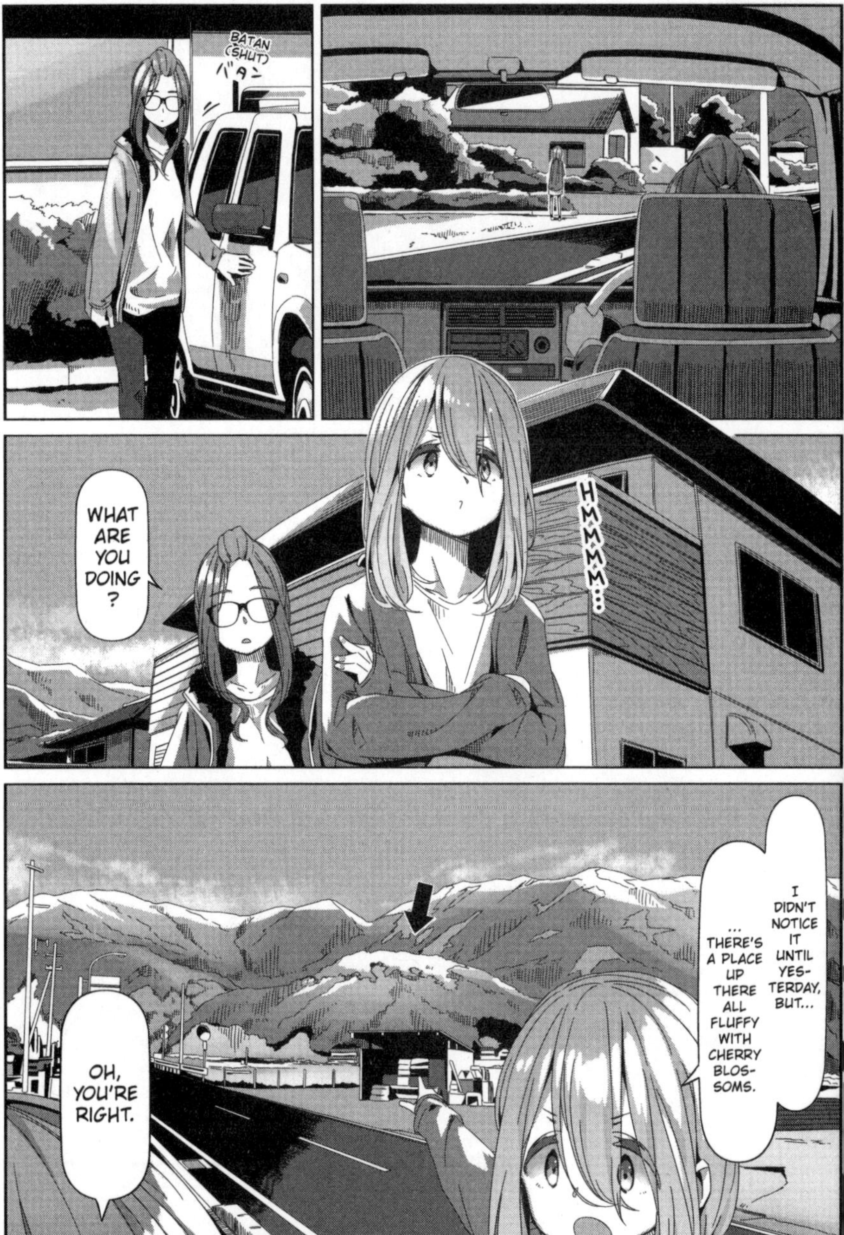
BATAN (SHUT)
バタン
HMMMM...
WHAT ARE YOU DOING?
I DIDN'T NOTICE IT UNTIL YES-TERDAY, BUT...
... THERE'S A PLACE UP THERE ALL FLUFFY WITH CHERRY BLOS-SOMS.
OH, YOU'RE RIGHT.

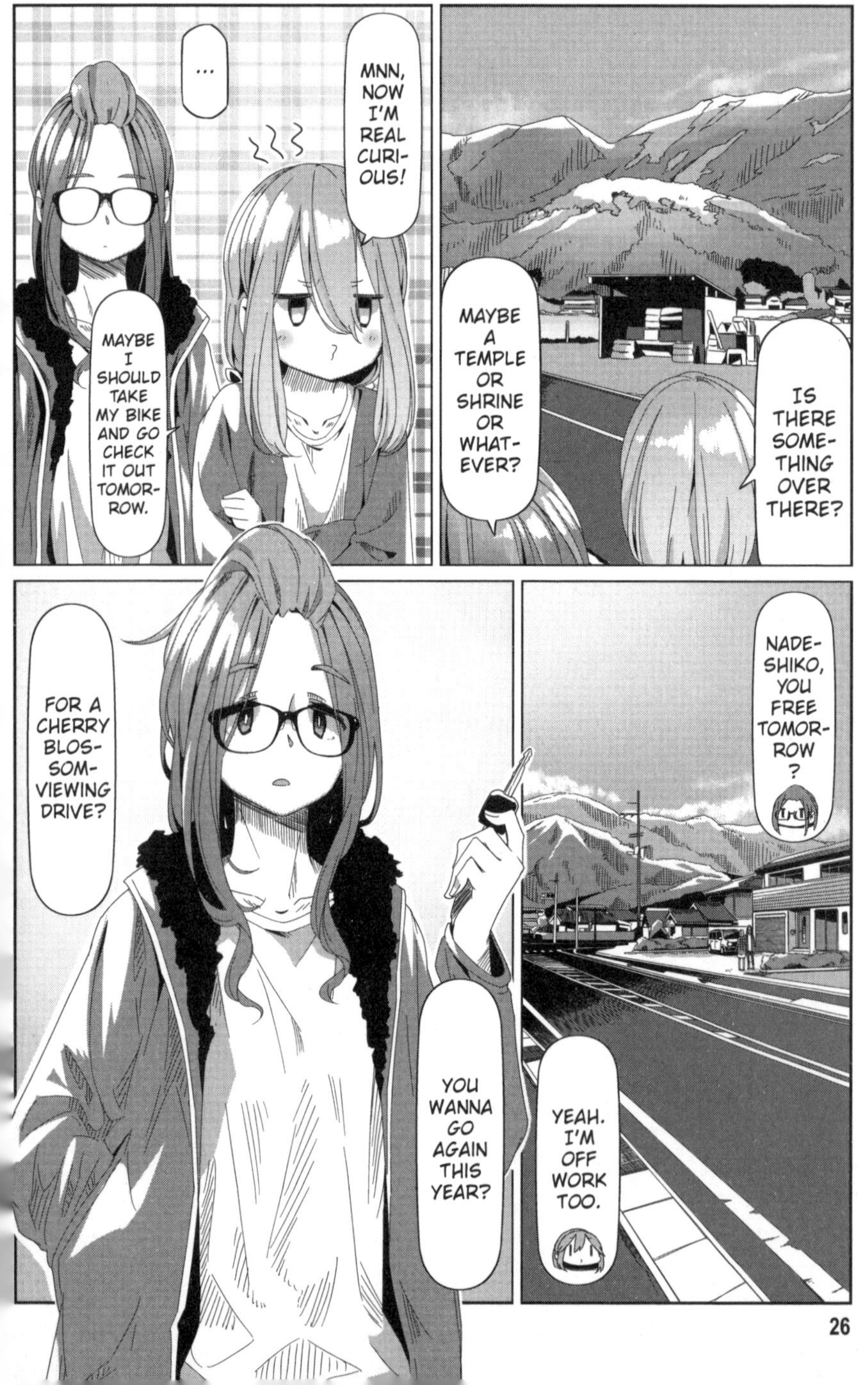

IS THERE SOMETHING OVER THERE?
MAYBE A TEMPLE OR SHRINE OR WHATEVER?
MNN, NOW I'M REAL CURIOUS!
...
MAYBE I SHOULD TAKE MY BIKE AND GO CHECK IT OUT TOMORROW.
NADESHIKO, YOU FREE TOMORROW?
YEAH. I'M OFF WORK TOO.
YOU WANNA GO AGAIN THIS YEAR?
FOR A CHERRY BLOSSOM-VIEWING DRIVE?

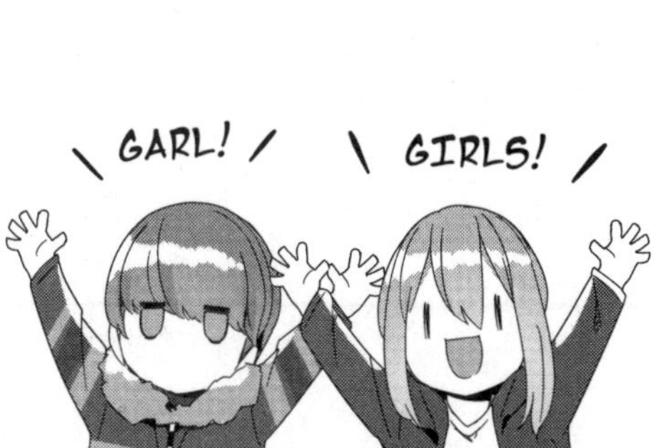
GARL!
GIRLS!

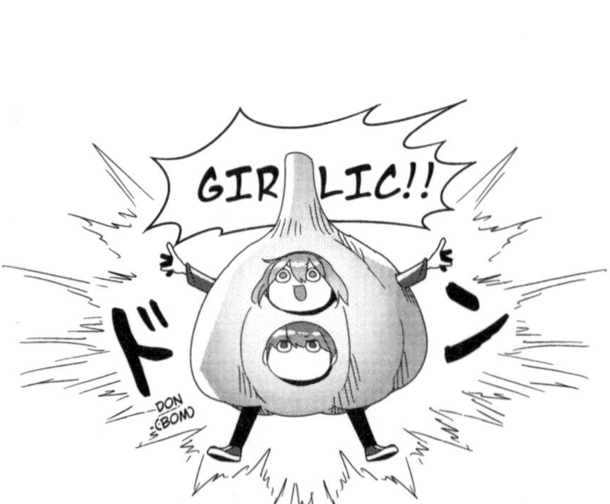
GIRLIC!!
ド
ン
DON (BOM)

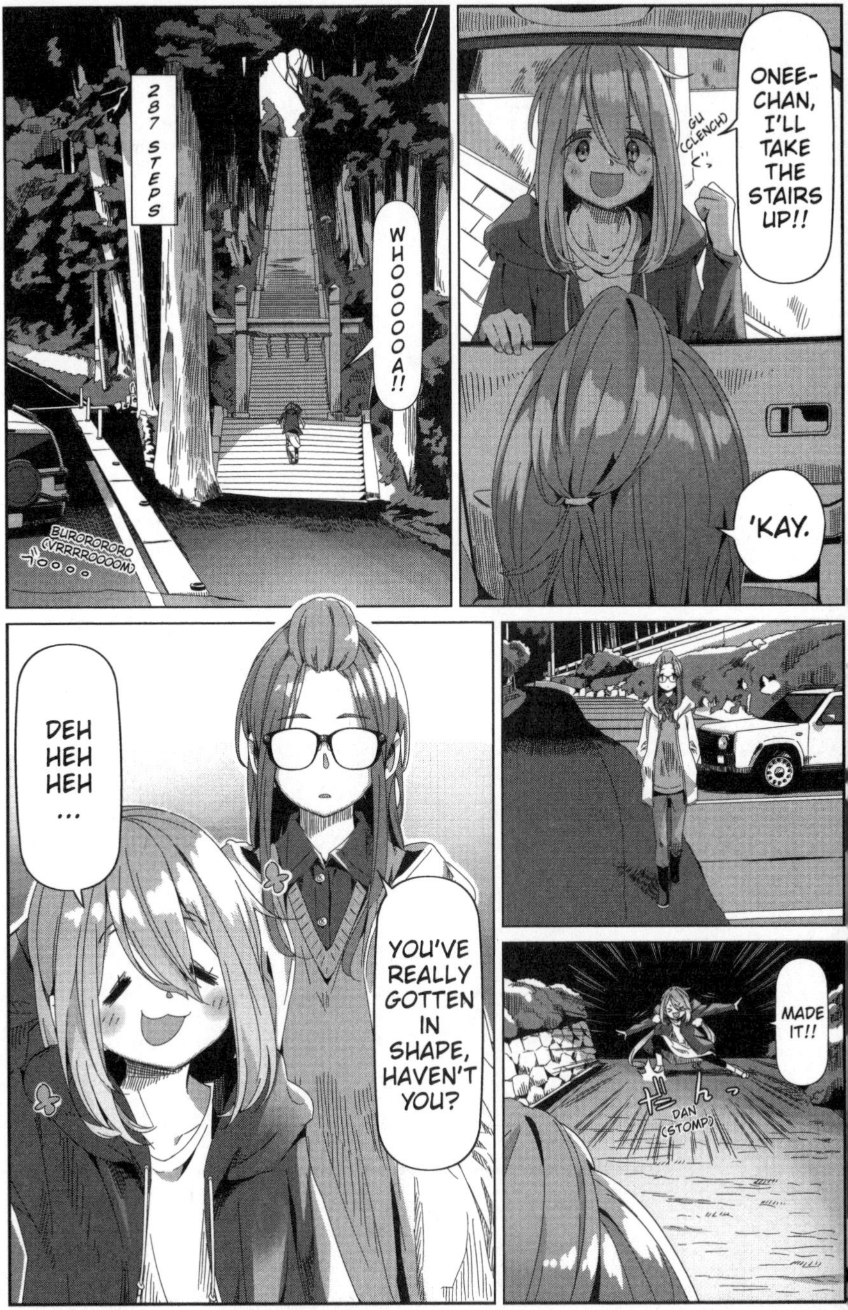
ONEE-CHAN, I'LL TAKE THE STAIRS UP!!
GU (CLENCH)
'KAY.
287 STEPS
WHOOOOOOA!!
BURORORORO (VRRRROOOOM)
MADE IT!!
DAN (STOMP)
YOU'VE REALLY GOTTEN IN SHAPE, HAVEN'T YOU?
DEH HEH HEH ...

# Chapter 71 The Kagamihara Sisters' Cherry-Blossom Excursion

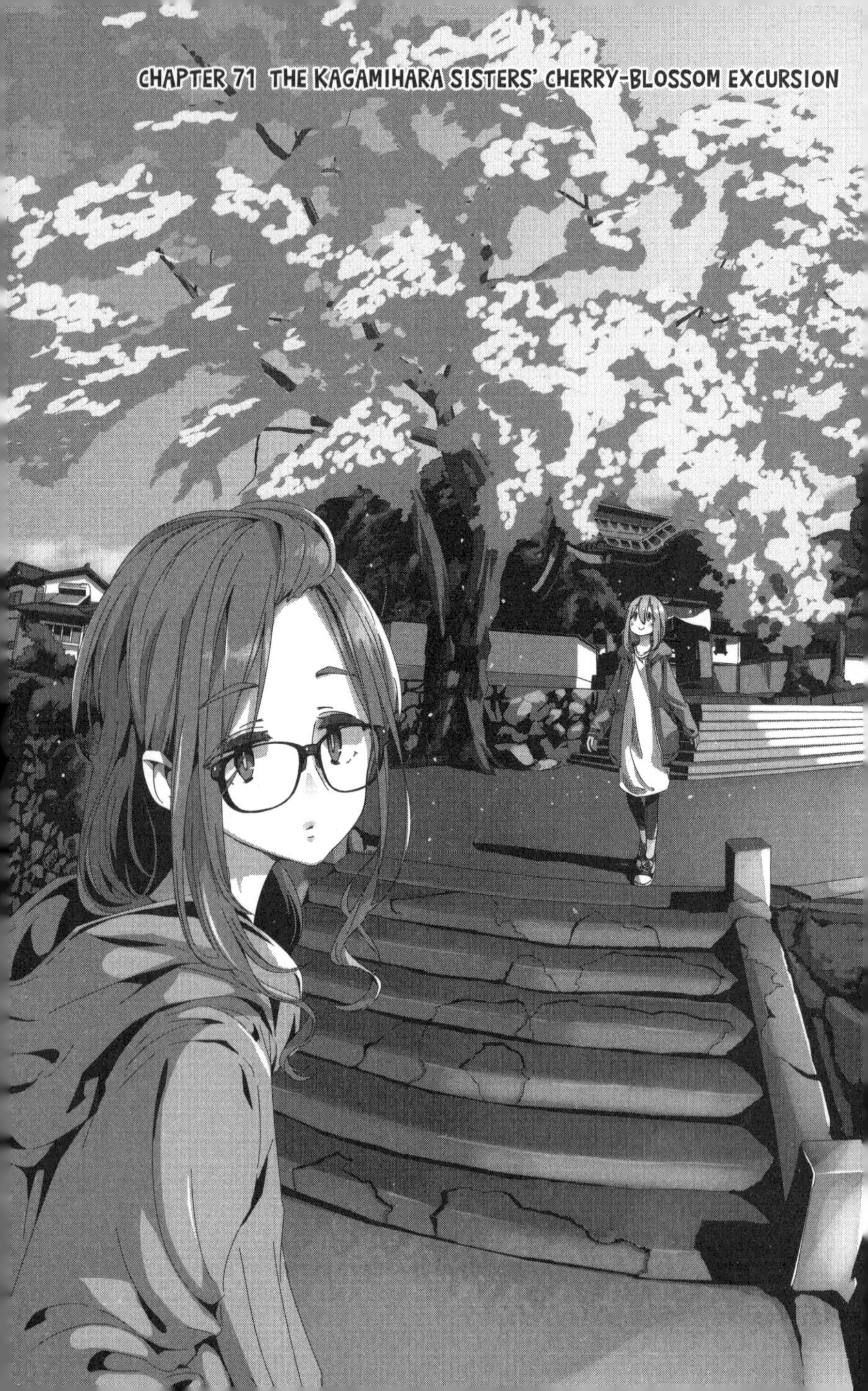

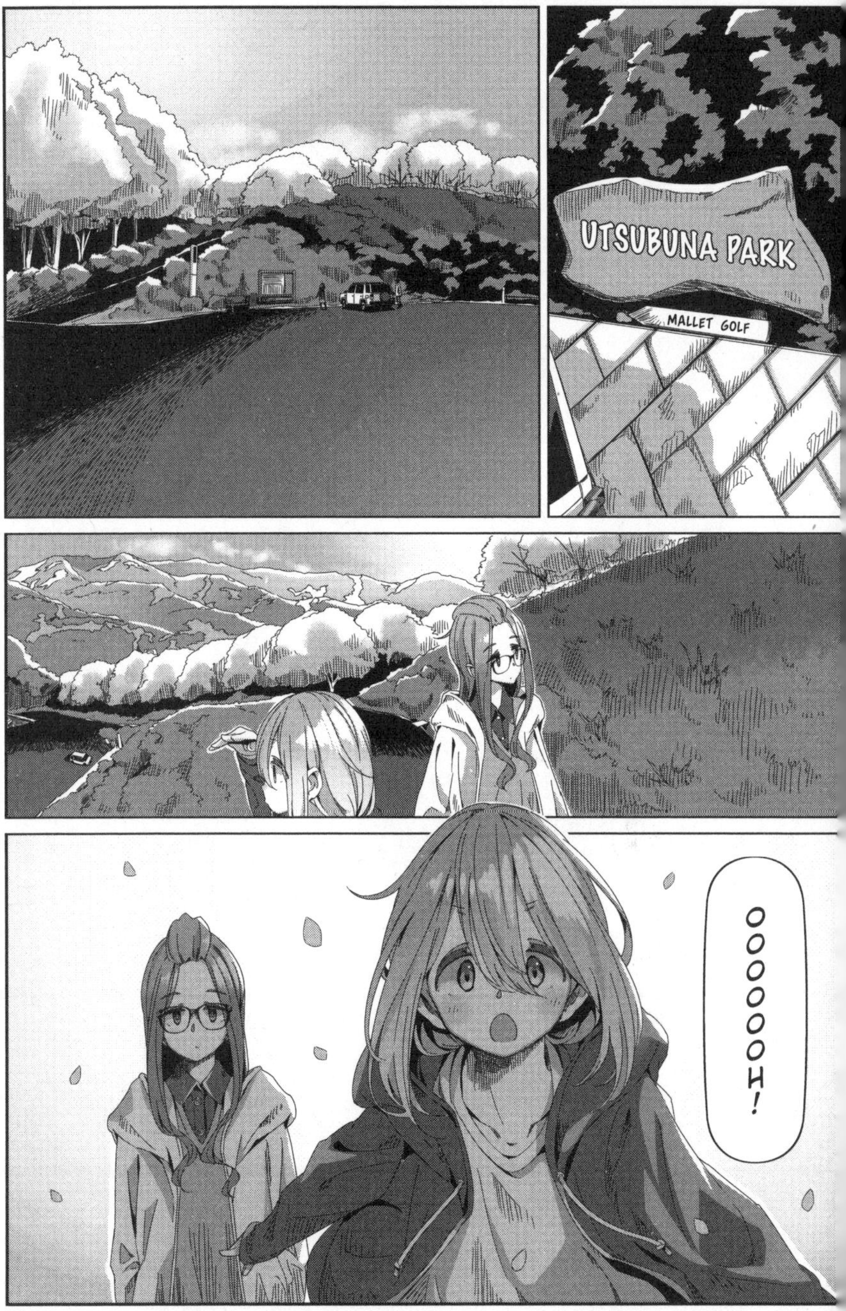
UTSUBUNA PARK
MALLET GOLF
OOOOOOOH!

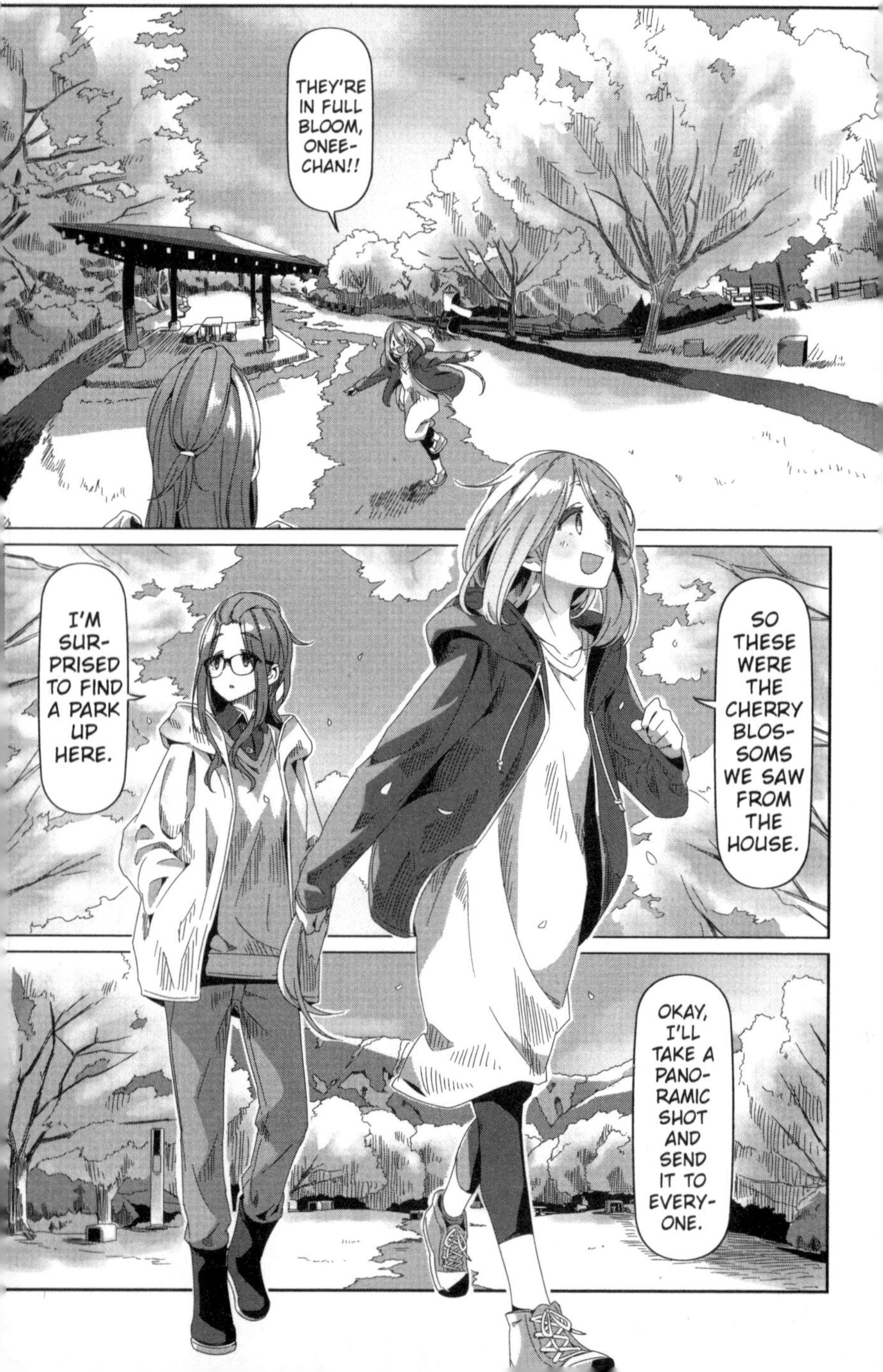
THEY'RE IN FULL BLOOM, ONEE-CHAN!!
SO THESE WERE THE CHERRY BLOS-SOMS WE SAW FROM THE HOUSE.
I'M SUR-PRISED TO FIND A PARK UP HERE.
OKAY, I'LL TAKE A PANO-RAMIC SHOT AND SEND IT TO EVERY-ONE.

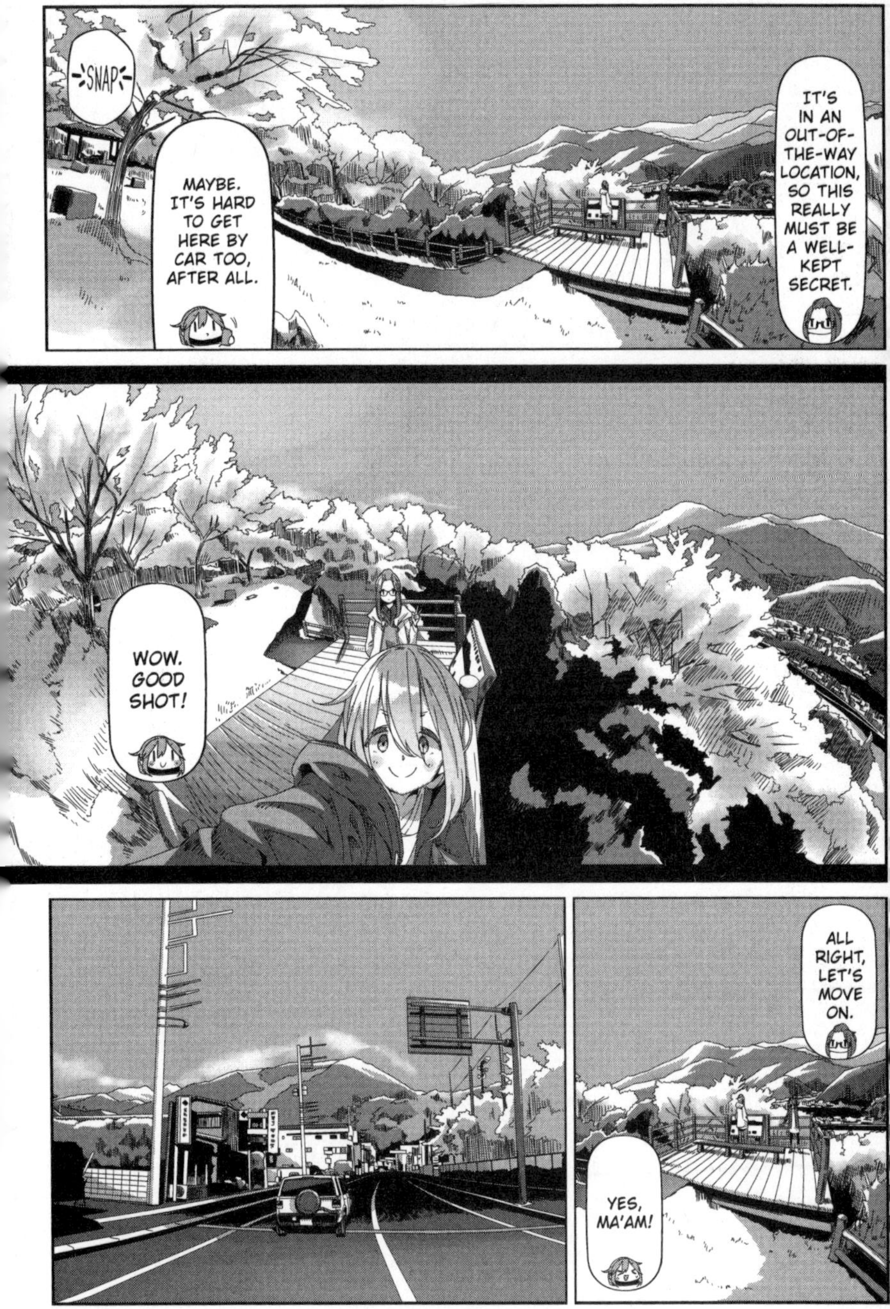
IT'S IN AN OUT-OF-THE-WAY LOCATION, SO THIS REALLY MUST BE A WELL-KEPT SECRET.
MAYBE. IT'S HARD TO GET HERE BY CAR TOO, AFTER ALL.
SNAP
WOW. GOOD SHOT!
ALL RIGHT, LET'S MOVE ON.
YES, MA'AM!

SIGNS: MT. MINOBU KUON-JI TEMPLE / SALVATION TO ALL

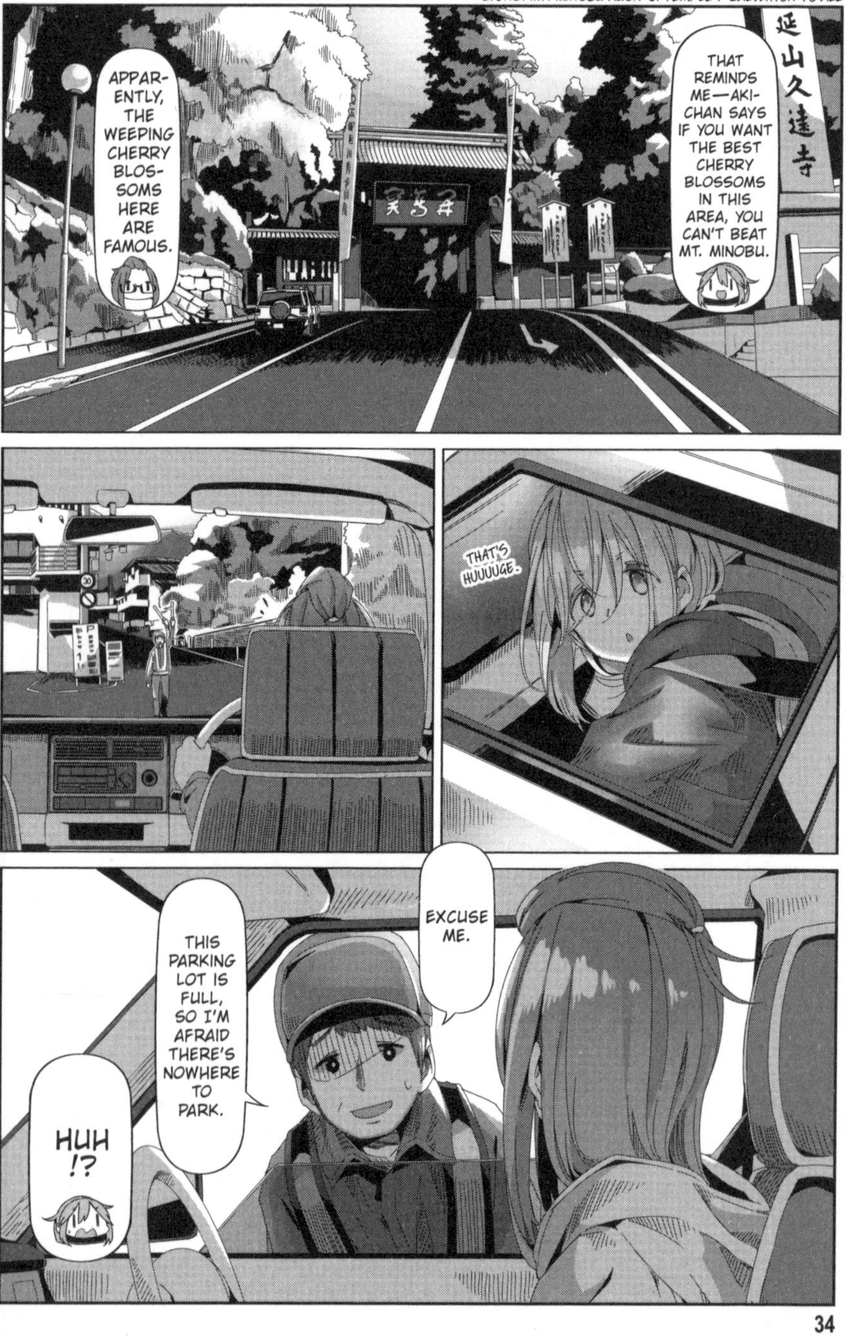
延山久遠寺
THAT REMINDS ME—AKI-CHAN SAYS IF YOU WANT THE BEST CHERRY BLOSSOMS IN THIS AREA, YOU CAN'T BEAT MT. MINOBU.
APPARENTLY, THE WEEPING CHERRY BLOSSOMS HERE ARE FAMOUS.
THAT'S HUUUUGE.
EXCUSE ME.
THIS PARKING LOT IS FULL, SO I'M AFRAID THERE'S NOWHERE TO PARK.
HUH!?

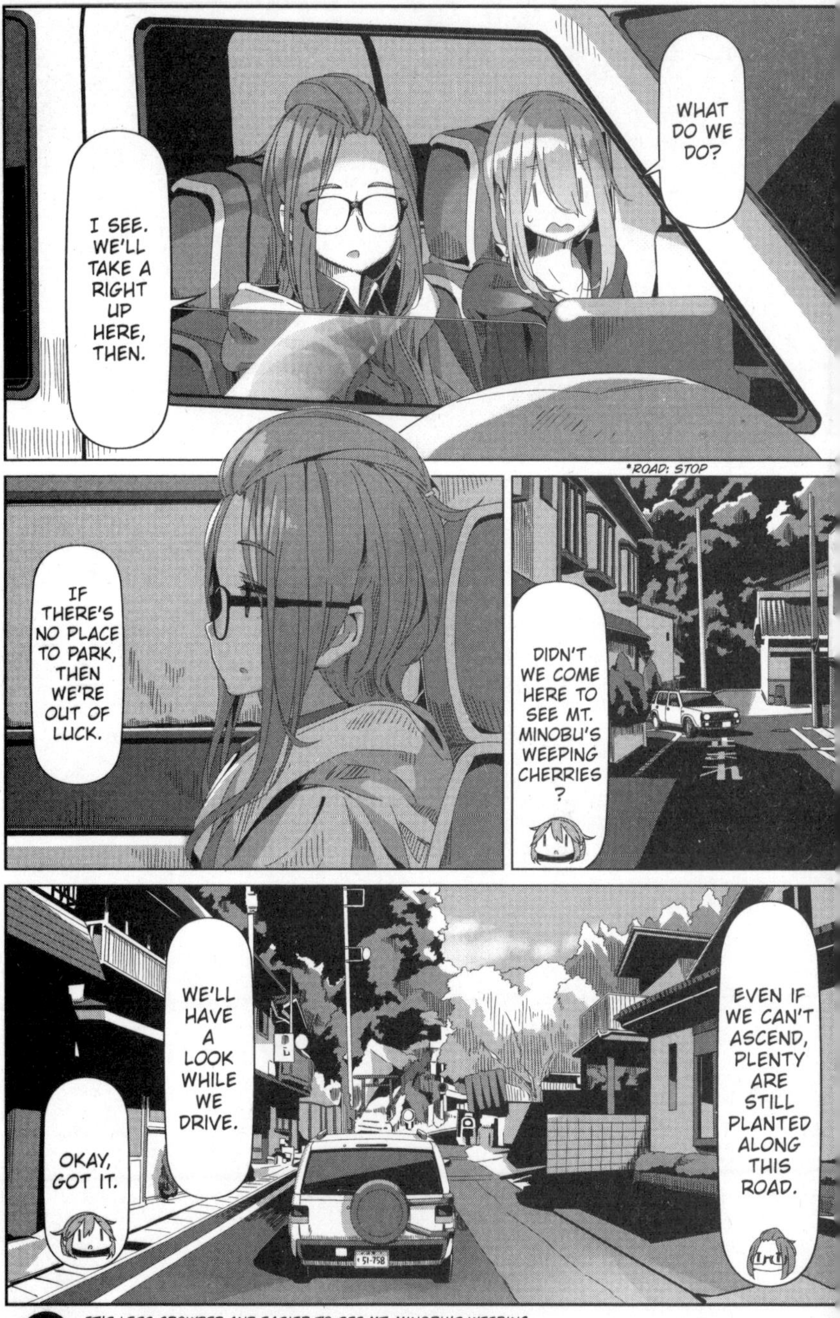
WHAT DO WE DO?
I SEE. WE'LL TAKE A RIGHT UP HERE, THEN.
*ROAD: STOP
DIDN'T WE COME HERE TO SEE MT. MINOBU'S WEEPING CHERRIES?
IF THERE'S NO PLACE TO PARK, THEN WE'RE OUT OF LUCK.
EVEN IF WE CAN'T ASCEND, PLENTY ARE STILL PLANTED ALONG THIS ROAD.
WE'LL HAVE A LOOK WHILE WE DRIVE.
OKAY, GOT IT.

*IT'S LESS CROWDED AND EASIER TO SEE MT. MINOBU'S WEEPING CHERRIES IF YOU GO IN THE EARLY MORNING OR IN THE EVENING.*

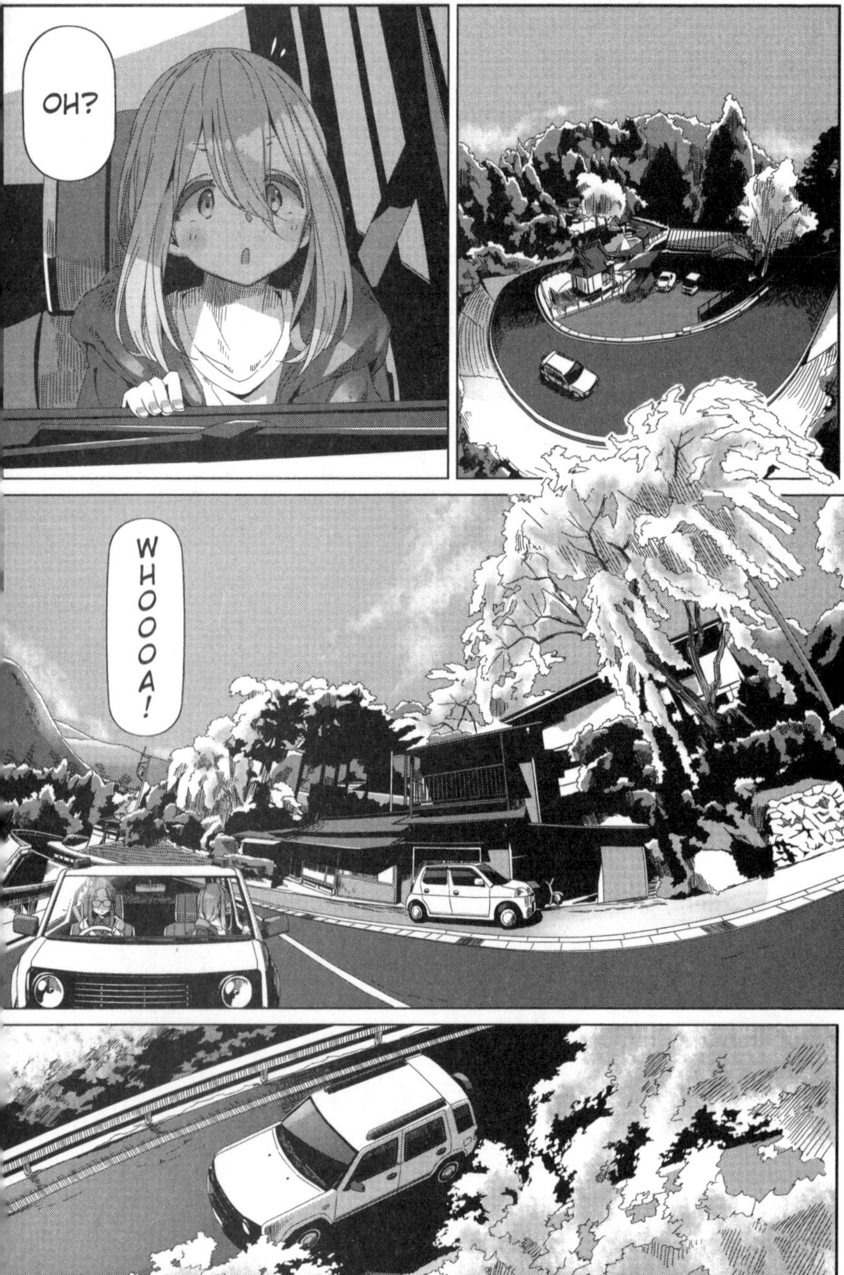
OH?
WHOOOA!

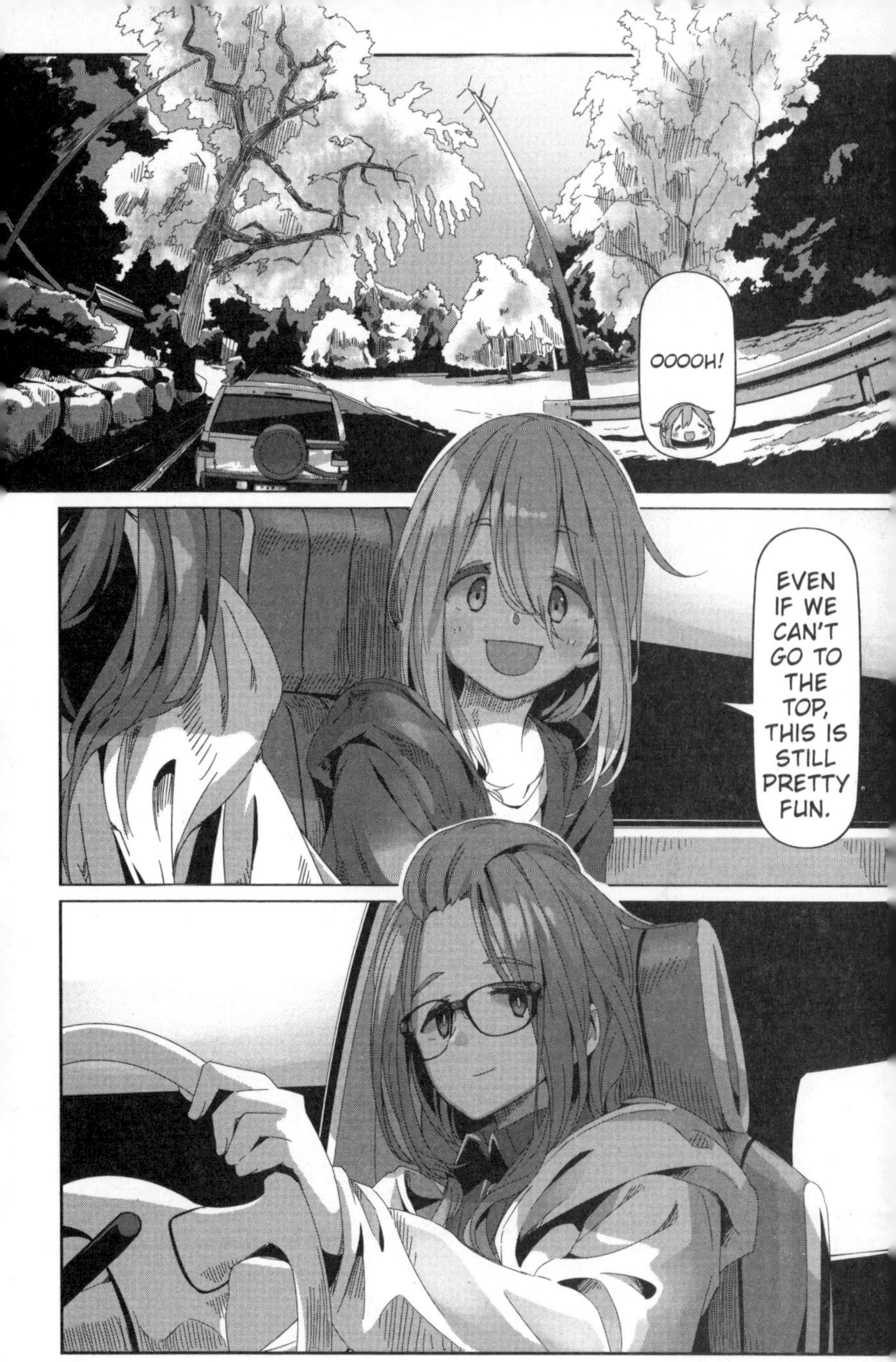
OOOOH!
EVEN IF WE CAN'T GO TO THE TOP, THIS IS STILL PRETTY FUN.

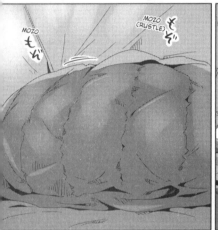

MOZO
もぞ

MOZO
(RUSTLE)
もぞ

-BZZT-
-BZZT-

A
FLOWER-
VIEWING
......

10:05

Heading out for a flower-viewing drive with my sister. (￣▽￣)

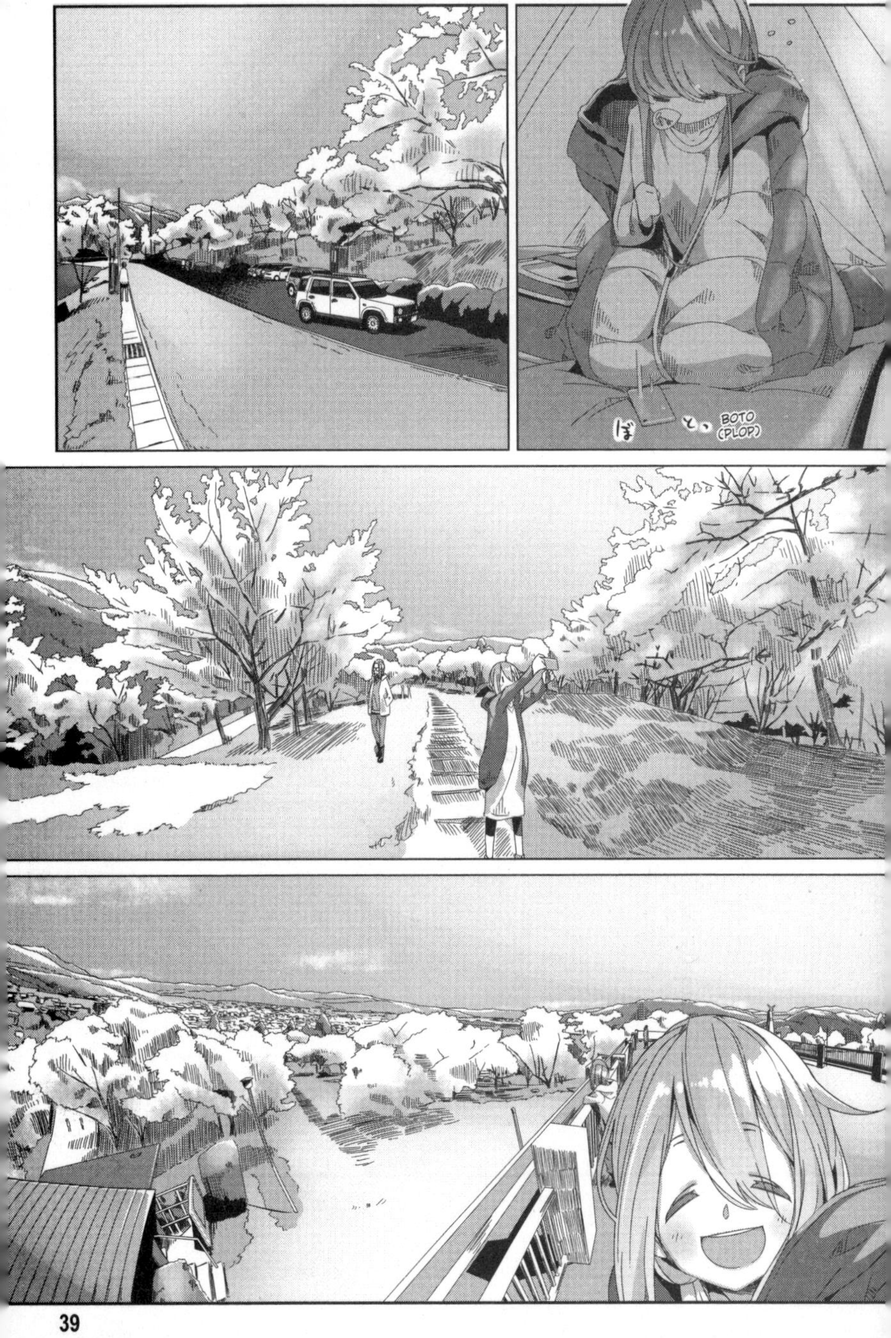
ぼと、
BOTO
(PLOP)

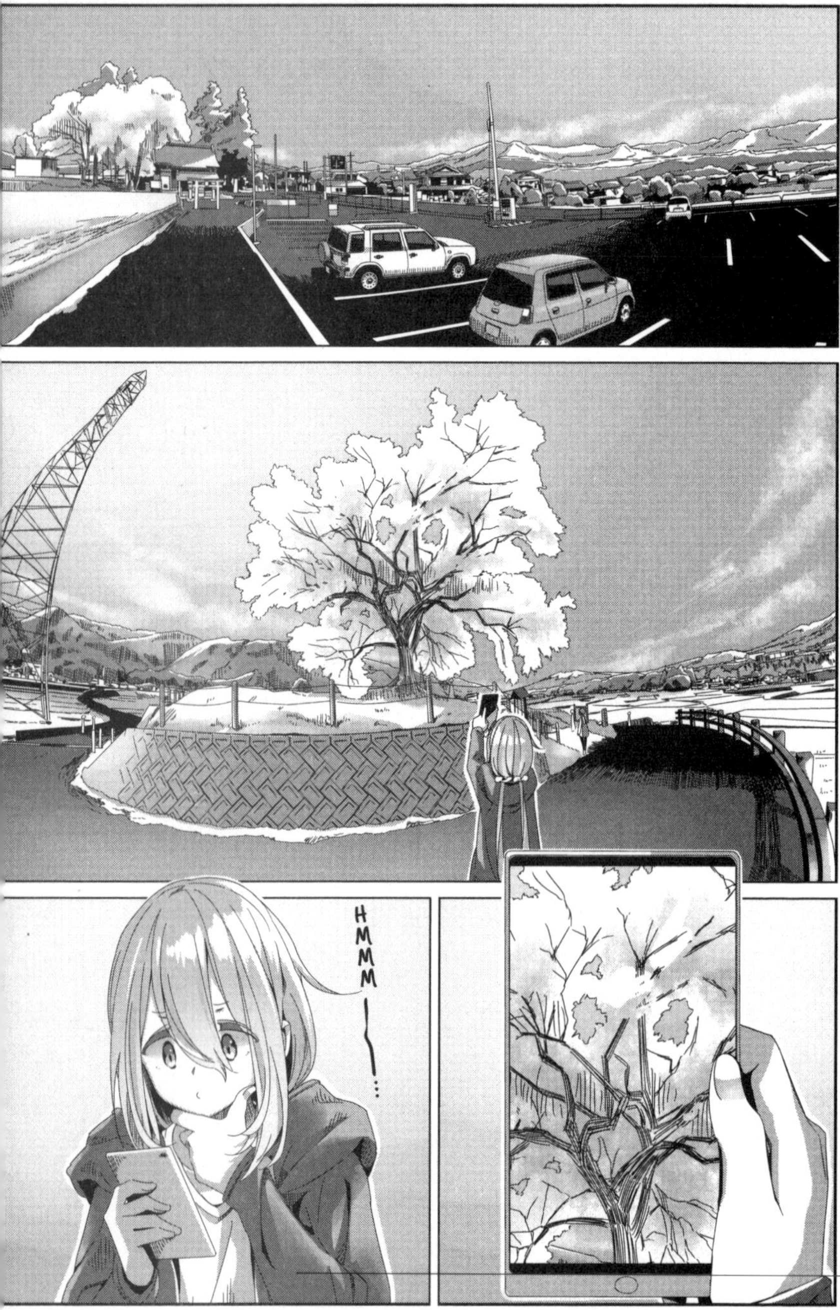
HMMM~~...

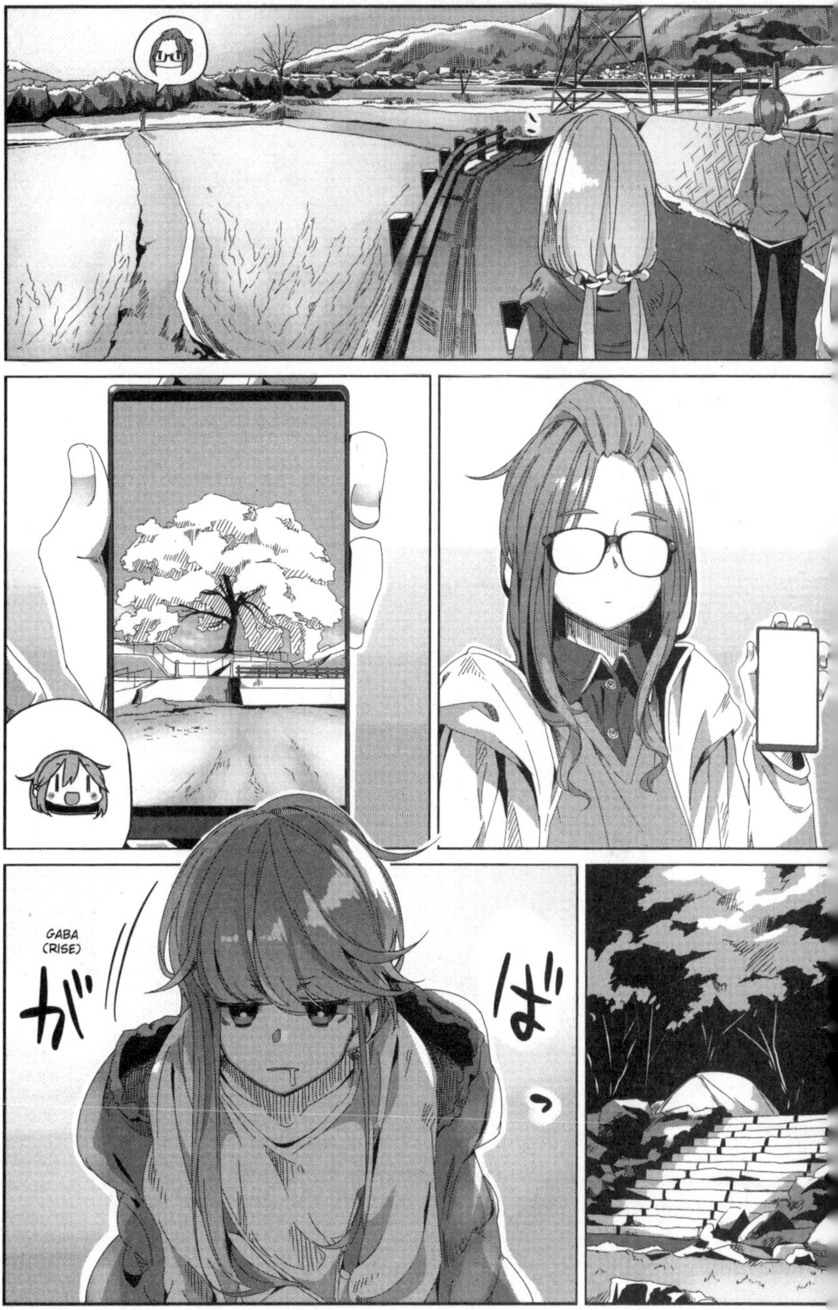
GABA
(RISE)
ガば

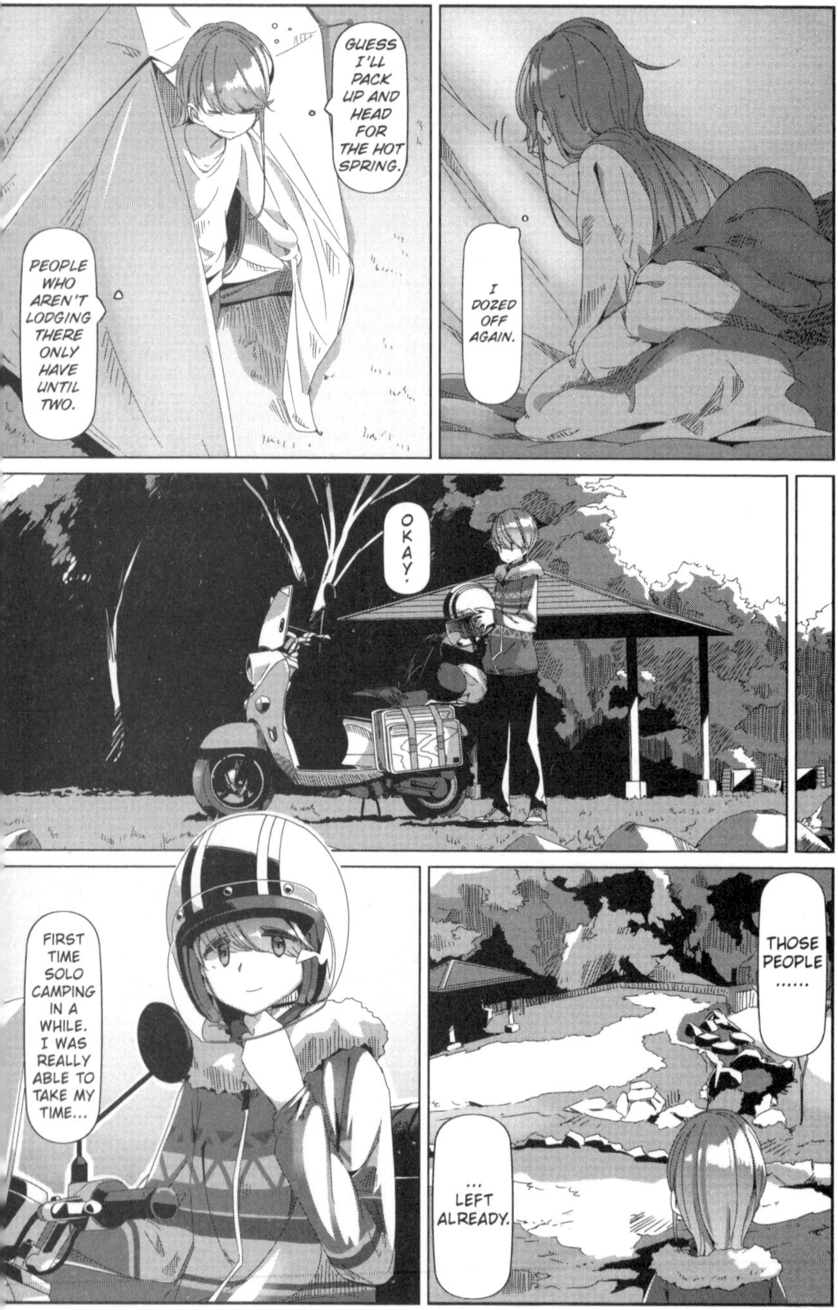

I DOZED OFF AGAIN.
GUESS I'LL PACK UP AND HEAD FOR THE HOT SPRING.
PEOPLE WHO AREN'T LODGING THERE ONLY HAVE UNTIL TWO.
OKAY.
THOSE PEOPLE ......
... LEFT ALREADY.
FIRST TIME SOLO CAMPING IN A WHILE. I WAS REALLY ABLE TO TAKE MY TIME...

I'LL HAVE TO ASK TO USE THIS AGAIN NEXT TIME I'M SOLO.
MOTOSU
み 376-66
BUBEBE (BRRBRNBRN)
ブベベ・・・
TH—
ZUUUUUUN (LOOOOM)
ずぅぅぅん
THIS HILL IS WAY TOO STEEP! I CAN'T CLIMB IIIT!!
376-66

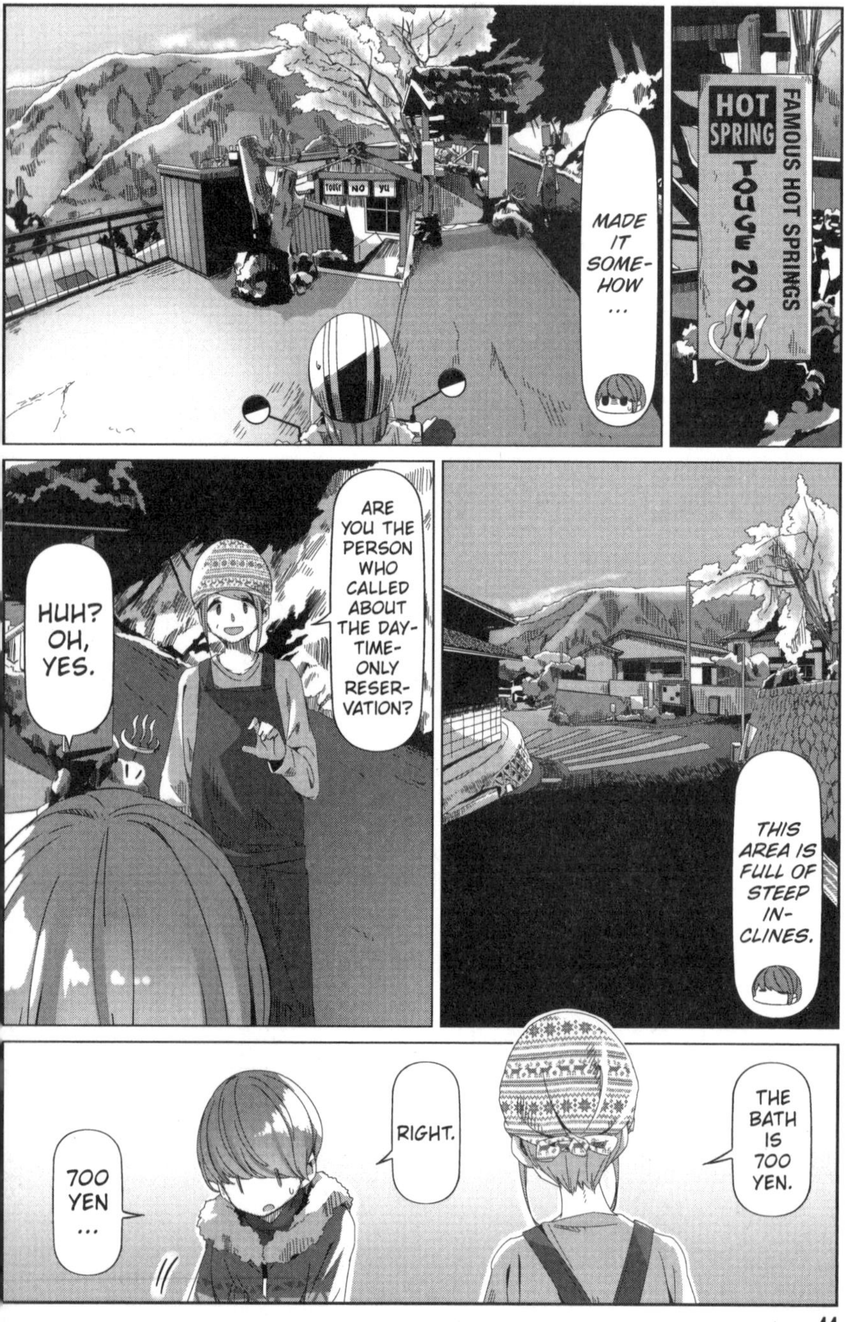
HOT SPRING
FAMOUS HOT SPRINGS
TOUGE NO YU
MADE IT SOMEHOW...
TOUGE NO YU
THIS AREA IS FULL OF STEEP INCLINES.
ARE YOU THE PERSON WHO CALLED ABOUT THE DAYTIME-ONLY RESERVATION?
HUH? OH, YES.
THE BATH IS 700 YEN.
RIGHT.
700 YEN...

THE BATH IS OVER THERE.
THANK YOU.
ENJOY.
GUESS SHE WORKS HERE...
I THOUGHT SHE WAS SOME RANDOM PERSON OUT FOR A WALK...
THIS PLACE JUST SCREAMS "MOUNTAIN HOT SPRING"...

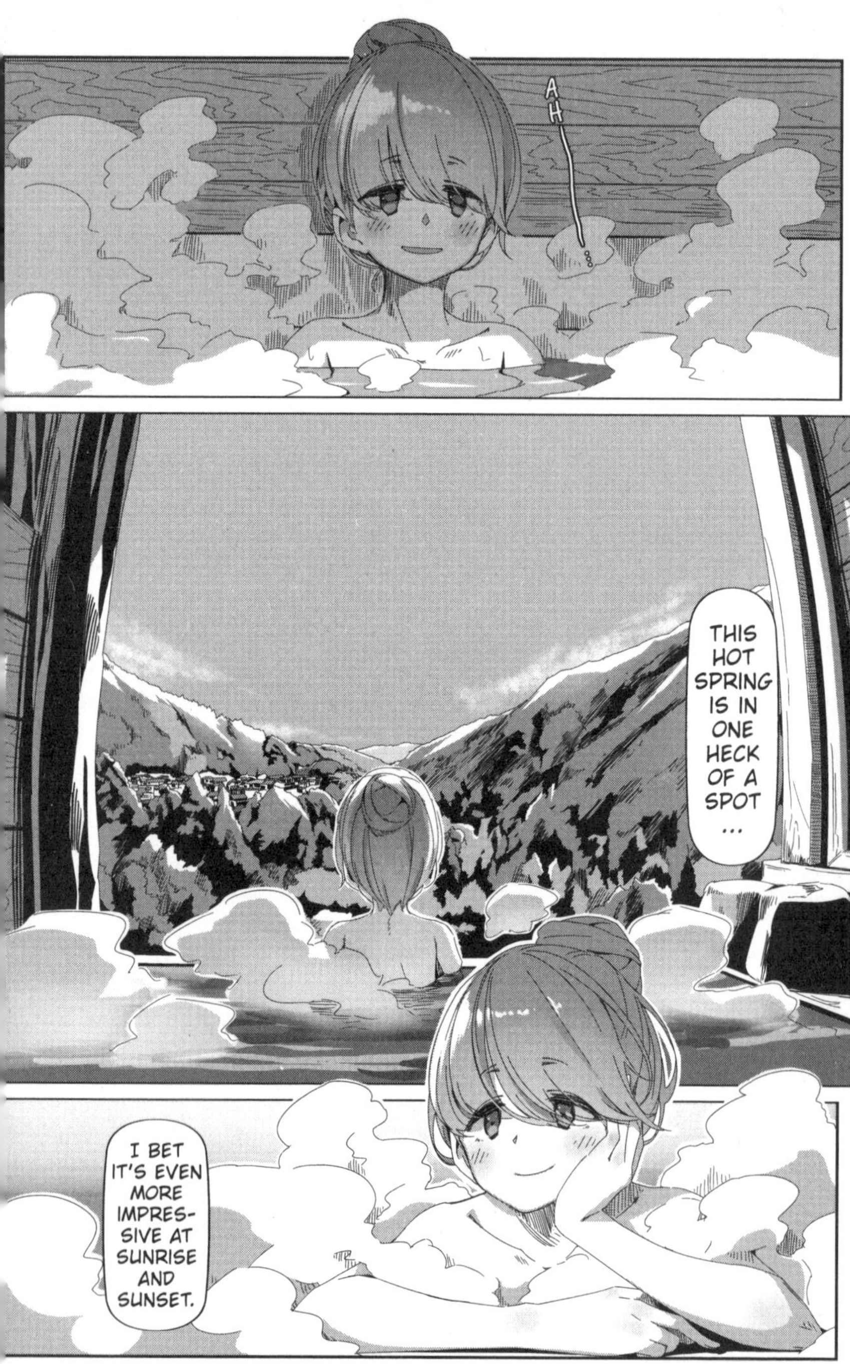
AH...
THIS HOT SPRING IS IN ONE HECK OF A SPOT...
I BET IT'S EVEN MORE IMPRESSIVE AT SUNRISE AND SUNSET.

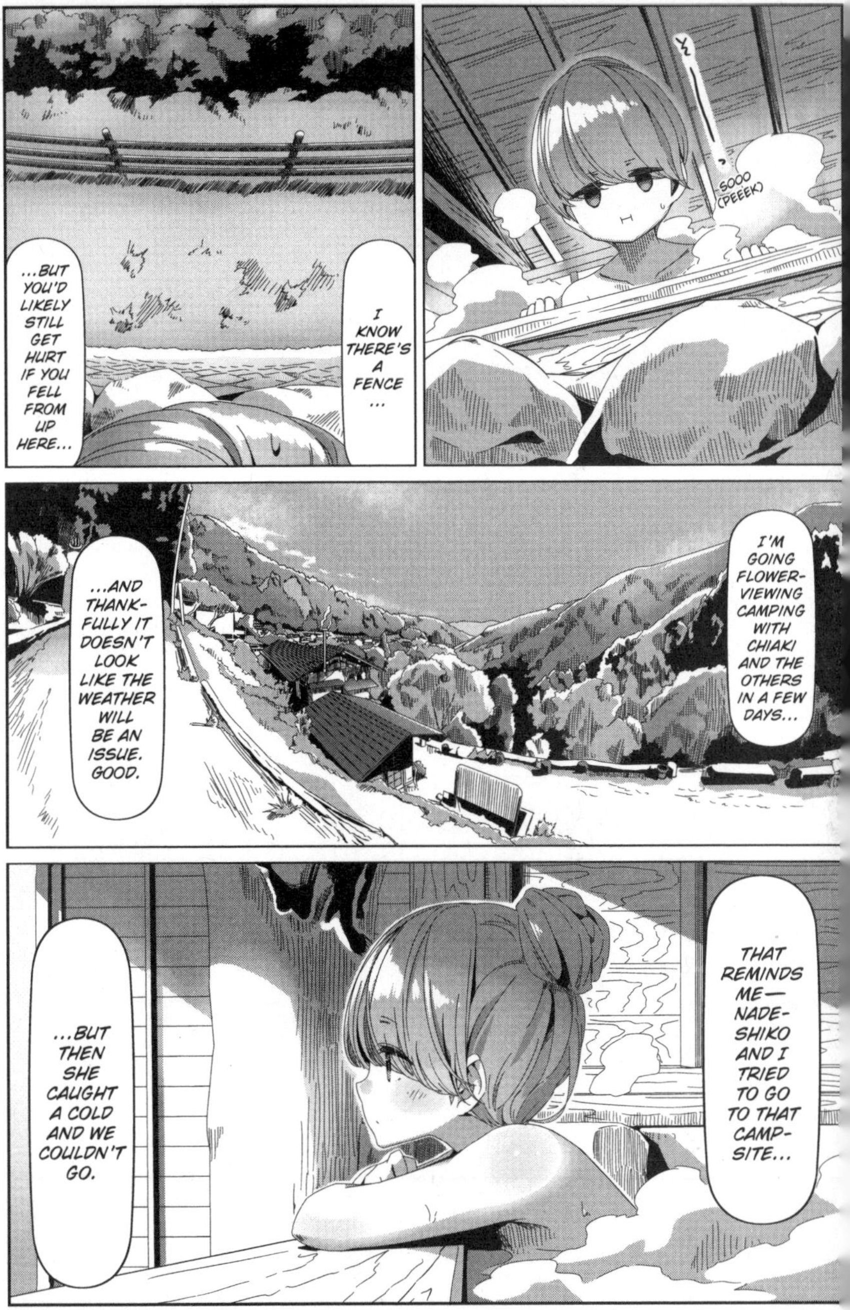
SOOO (PEEEK)
I KNOW THERE'S A FENCE...
...BUT YOU'D LIKELY STILL GET HURT IF YOU FELL FROM UP HERE...
I'M GOING FLOWER-VIEWING CAMPING WITH CHIAKI AND THE OTHERS IN A FEW DAYS...
...AND THANKFULLY IT DOESN'T LOOK LIKE THE WEATHER WILL BE AN ISSUE. GOOD.
THAT REMINDS ME—NADESHIKO AND I TRIED TO GO TO THAT CAMPSITE...
...BUT THEN SHE CAUGHT A COLD AND WE COULDN'T GO.

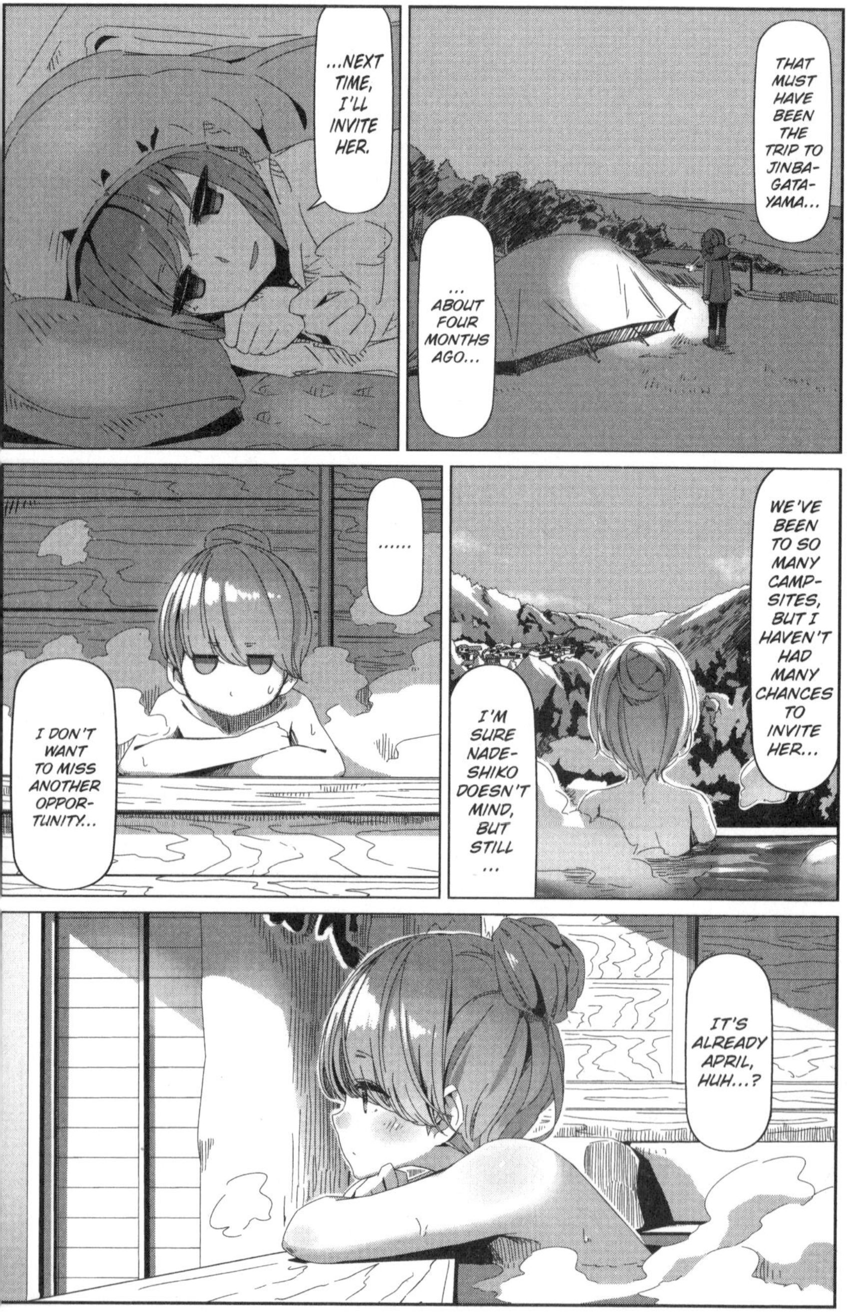
THAT MUST HAVE BEEN THE TRIP TO JINBA-GATA-YAMA...
...ABOUT FOUR MONTHS AGO...
...NEXT TIME, I'LL INVITE HER.
WE'VE BEEN TO SO MANY CAMP-SITES, BUT I HAVEN'T HAD MANY CHANCES TO INVITE HER...
I'M SURE NADE-SHIKO DOESN'T MIND, BUT STILL...
......
I DON'T WANT TO MISS ANOTHER OPPOR-TUNITY...
IT'S ALREADY APRIL, HUH...?

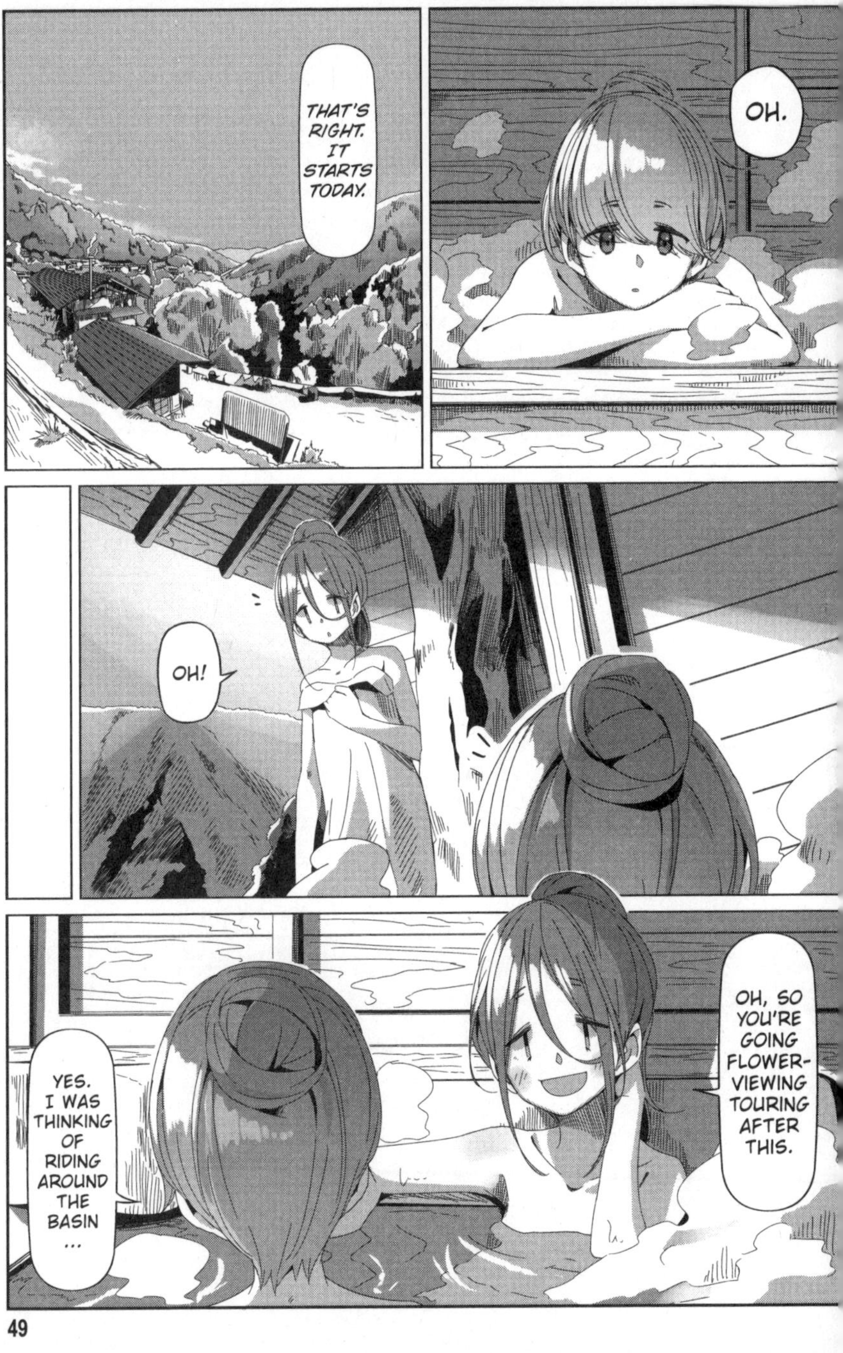
OH.
THAT'S RIGHT. IT STARTS TODAY.
OH!
OH, SO YOU'RE GOING FLOWER-VIEWING TOURING AFTER THIS.
YES. I WAS THINKING OF RIDING AROUND THE BASIN ...

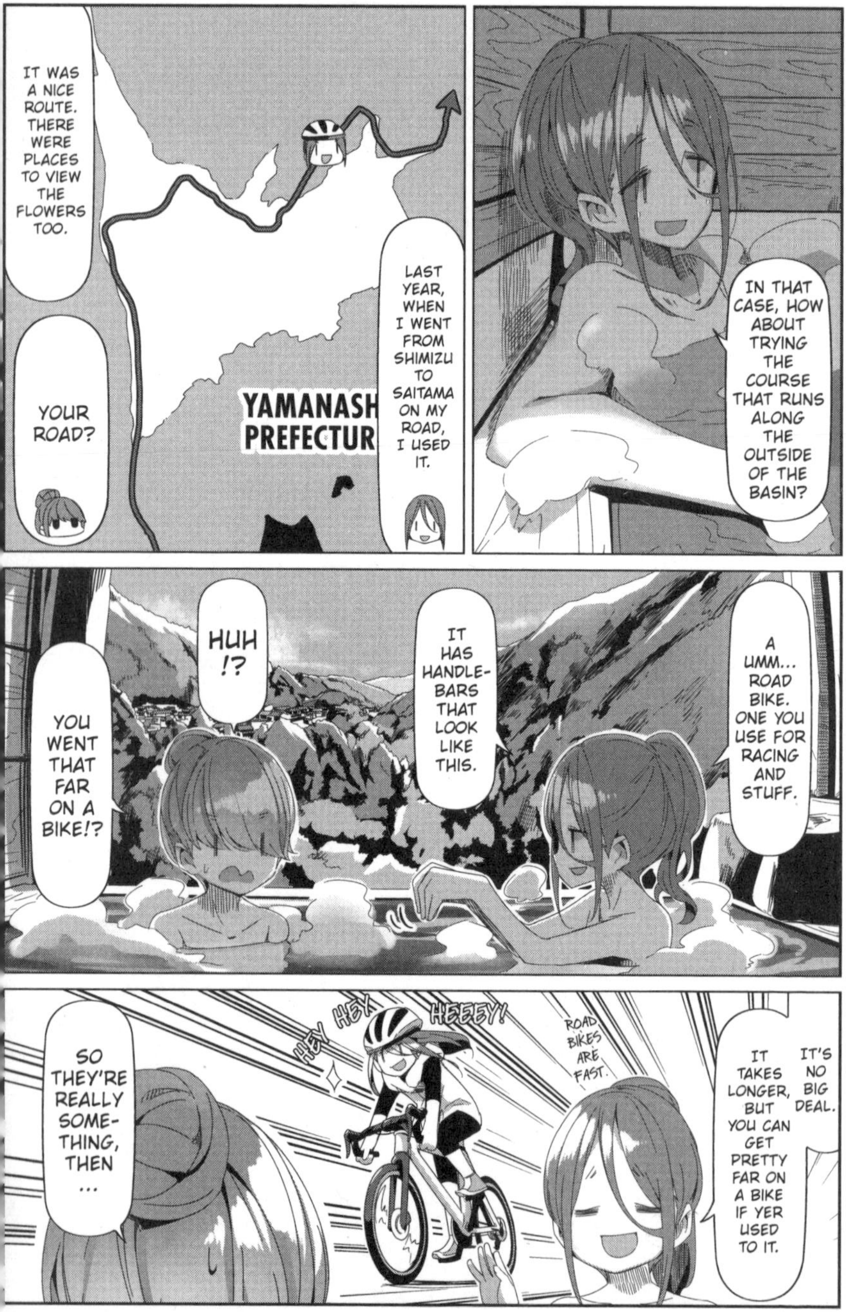
IN THAT CASE, HOW ABOUT TRYING THE COURSE THAT RUNS ALONG THE OUTSIDE OF THE BASIN?
LAST YEAR, WHEN I WENT FROM SHIMIZU TO SAITAMA ON MY ROAD, I USED IT.
IT WAS A NICE ROUTE. THERE WERE PLACES TO VIEW THE FLOWERS TOO.
YAMANASH PREFECTUR
YOUR ROAD?
A UMM... ROAD BIKE. ONE YOU USE FOR RACING AND STUFF.
IT HAS HANDLE-BARS THAT LOOK LIKE THIS.
HUH!?
YOU WENT THAT FAR ON A BIKE!?
IT'S NO BIG DEAL.
IT TAKES LONGER, BUT YOU CAN GET PRETTY FAR ON A BIKE IF YER USED TO IT.
ROAD BIKES ARE FAST.
HEY HEY HEEEY!
SO THEY'RE REALLY SOME-THING, THEN ...

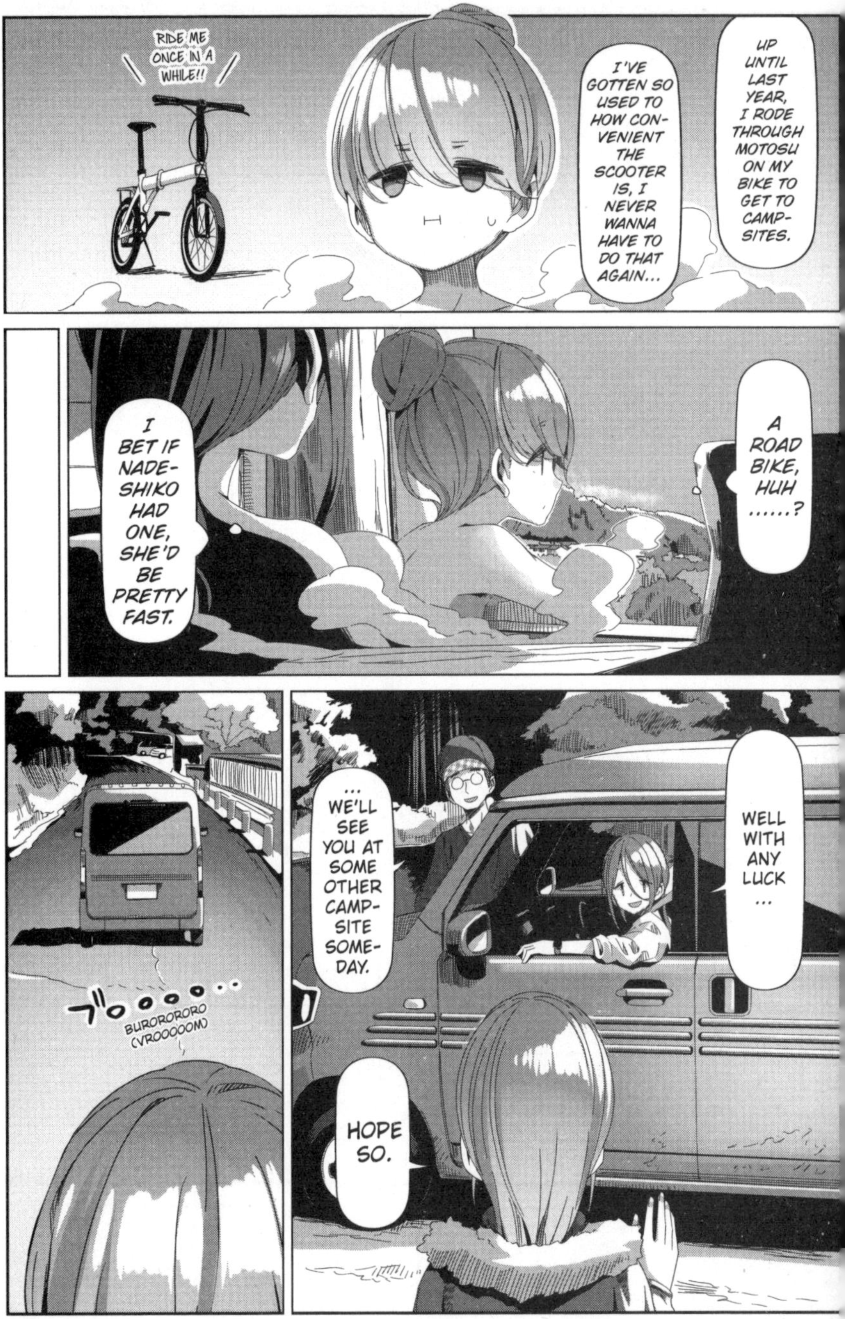
UP UNTIL LAST YEAR, I RODE THROUGH MOTOSU ON MY BIKE TO GET TO CAMP-SITES.
I'VE GOTTEN SO USED TO HOW CON-VENIENT THE SCOOTER IS, I NEVER WANNA HAVE TO DO THAT AGAIN...
RIDE ME ONCE IN A WHILE!!
A ROAD BIKE, HUH ......?
I BET IF NADE-SHIKO HAD ONE, SHE'D BE PRETTY FAST.
WELL WITH ANY LUCK ...
... WE'LL SEE YOU AT SOME OTHER CAMP-SITE SOME-DAY.
HOPE SO.
BURORORORO (VROOOOOM)

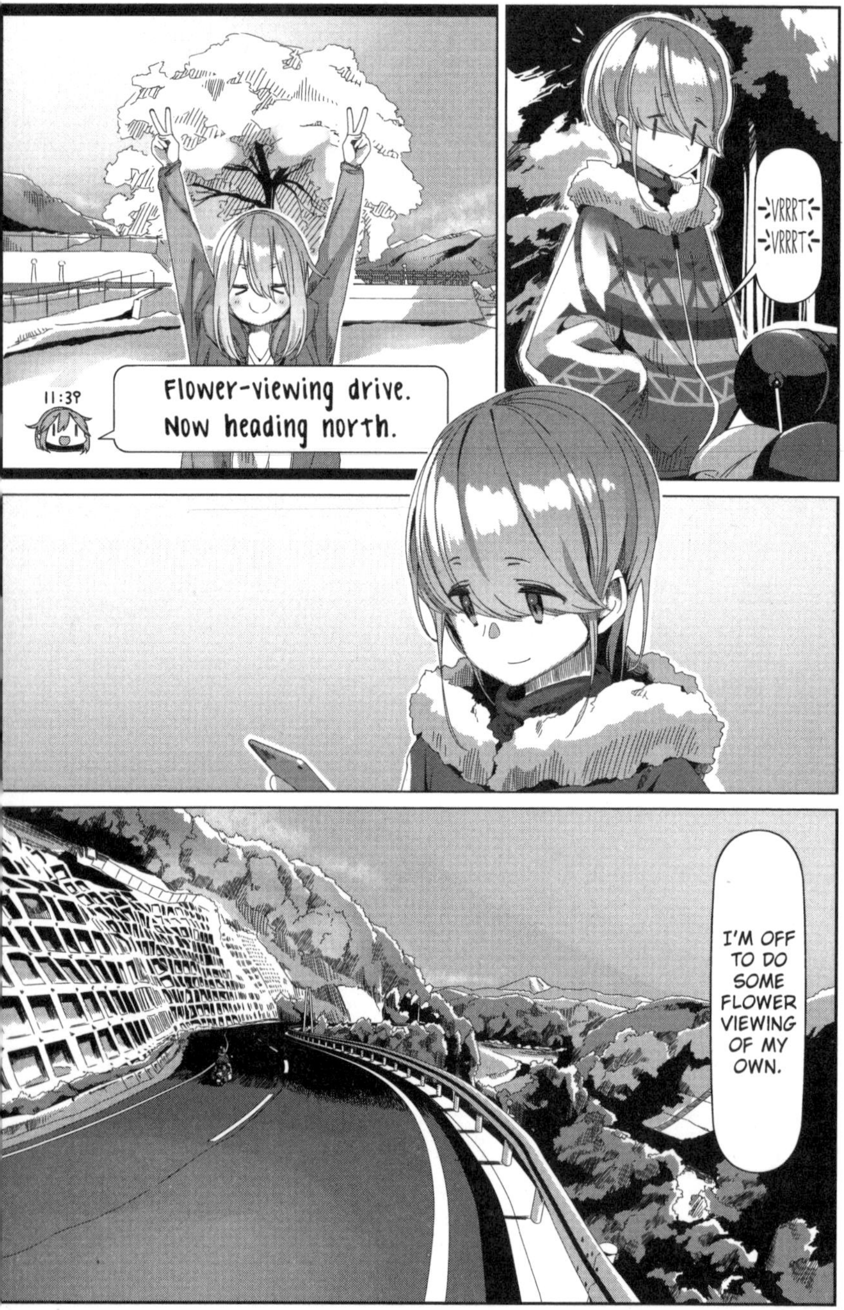

VRRRT VRRRT
11:39
Flower-viewing drive. Now heading north.
I'M OFF TO DO SOME FLOWER VIEWING OF MY OWN.

I BET IF NADESHIKO HAD ONE, SHE'D BE PRETTY FAST.

ENGINE
MODEL: KAGAMIHARA NADESHIKO
MAXIMUM OUTPUT:          43 PS
MAX TORQUE:          45.3N/M
FUEL TYPE:     MINOBU MANJUU
FUEL ECONOMY:   20 M/1 MANJUU

※ FUEL ECONOMY VALUES TAKEN WHILE IN
   SPORTS MODE.

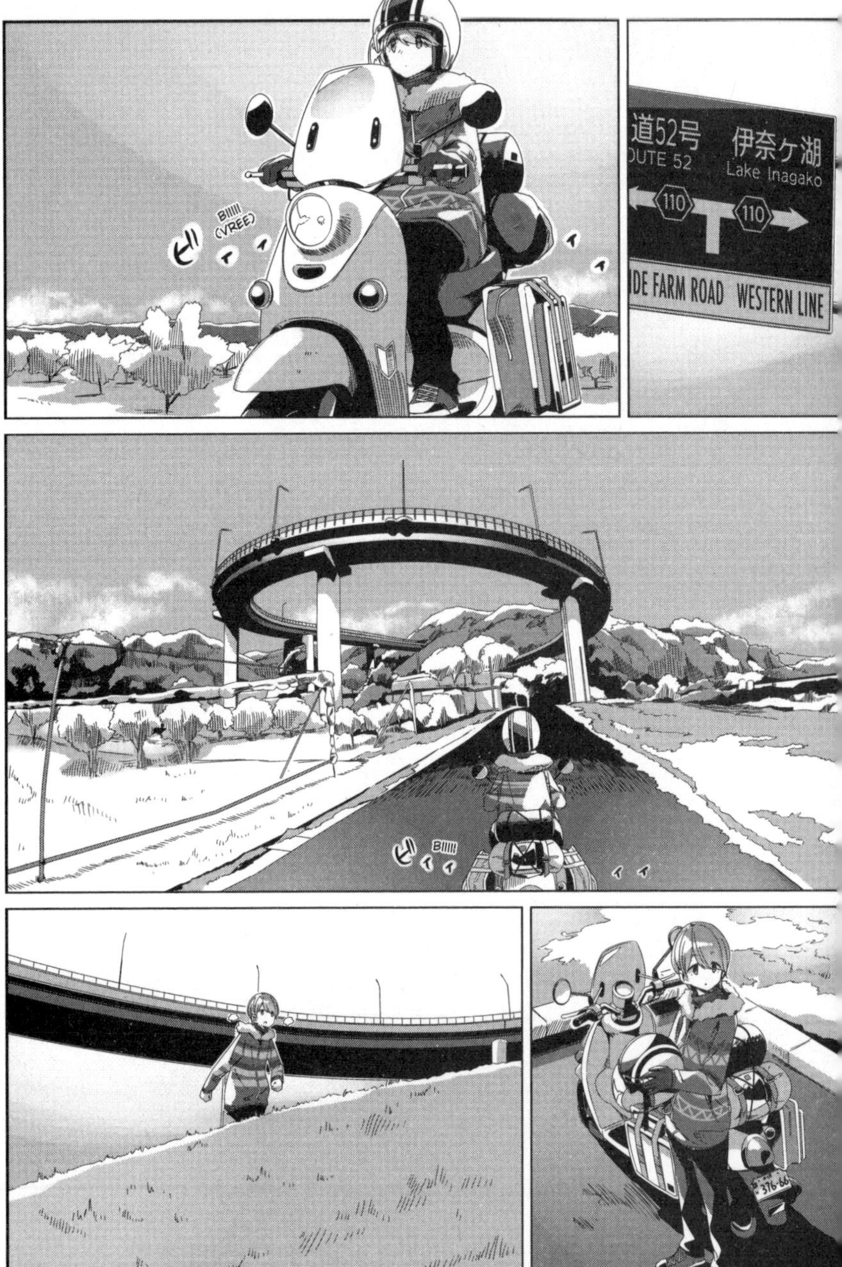
道52号
DUTE 52
伊奈ヶ湖
Lake Inagako
110
110
DE FARM ROAD
WESTERN LINE
ビィィィィ
BIIIII (VREE)
ビィィィィ
BIIIII

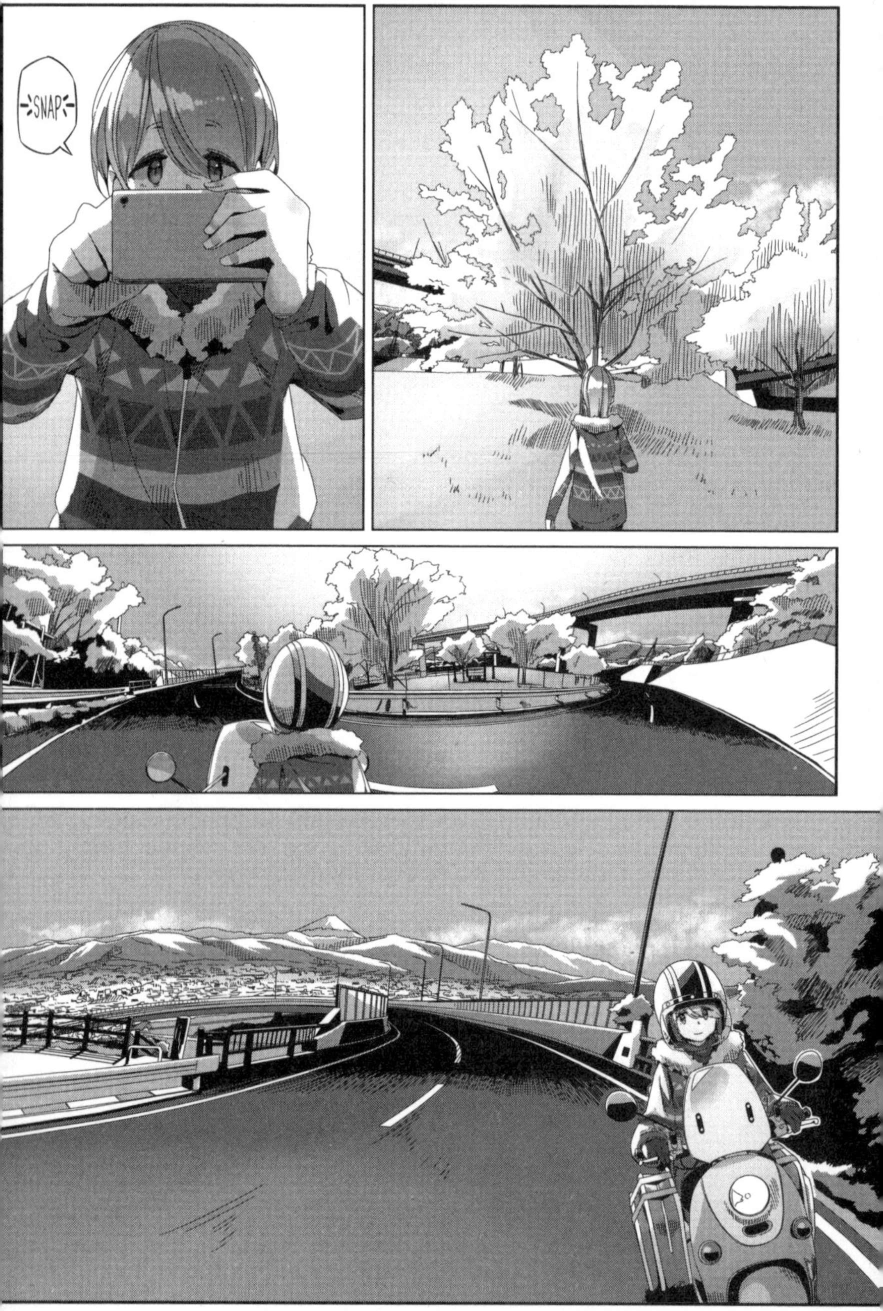
SNAP

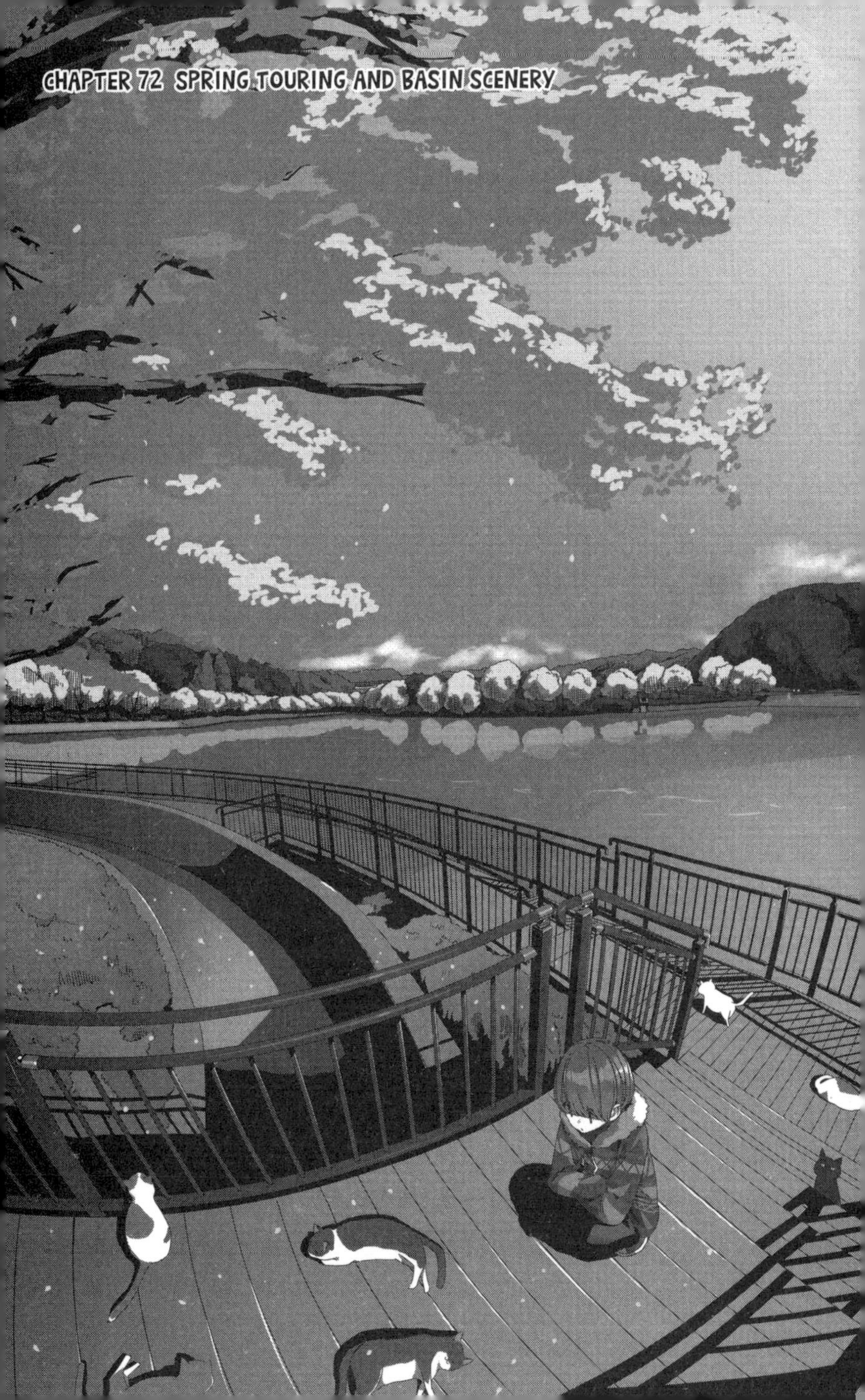
CHAPTER 72 SPRING TOURING AND BASIN SCENERY

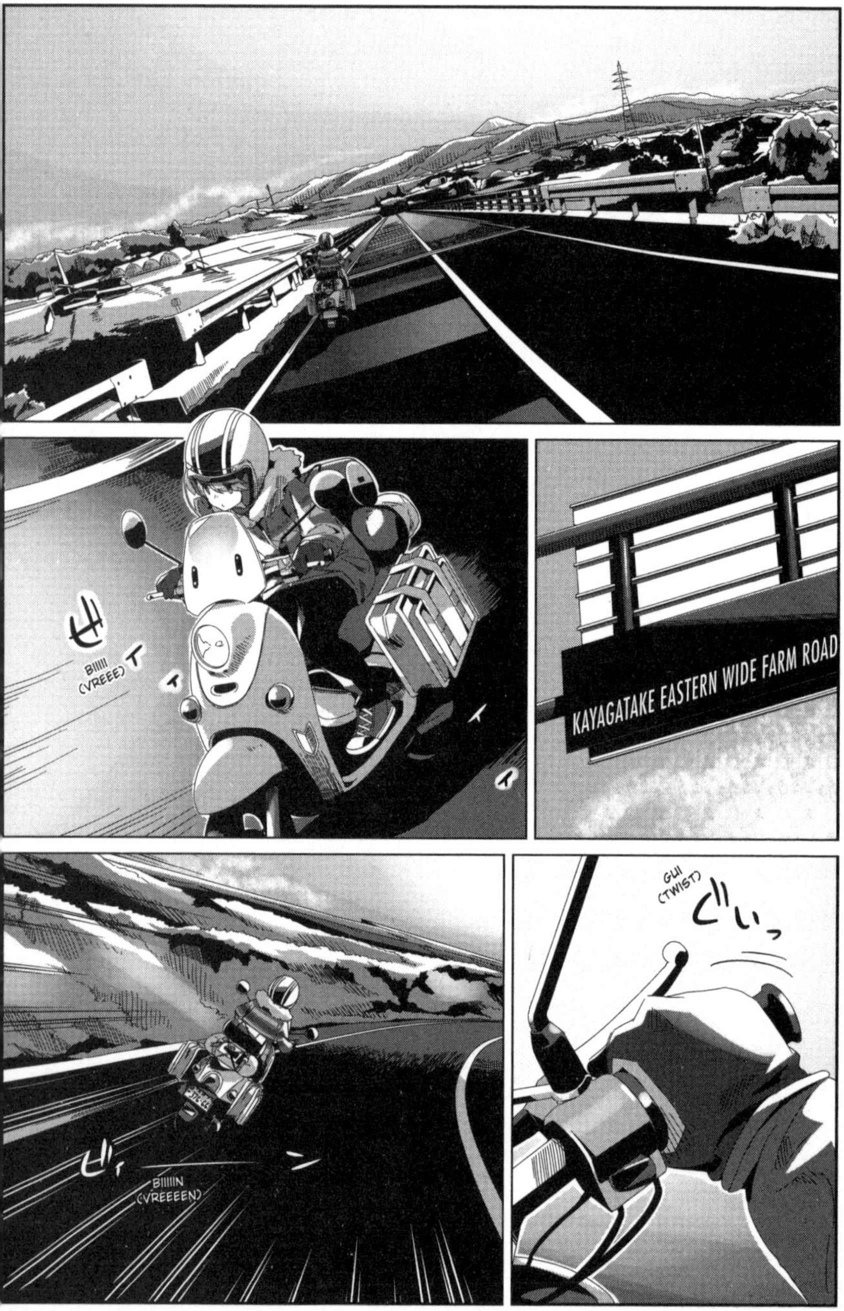
KAYAGATAKE EASTERN WIDE FARM ROAD
BIIIII (VREEE)
GUI (TWIST)
ぐいっ
BIIIIN (VREEEEN)

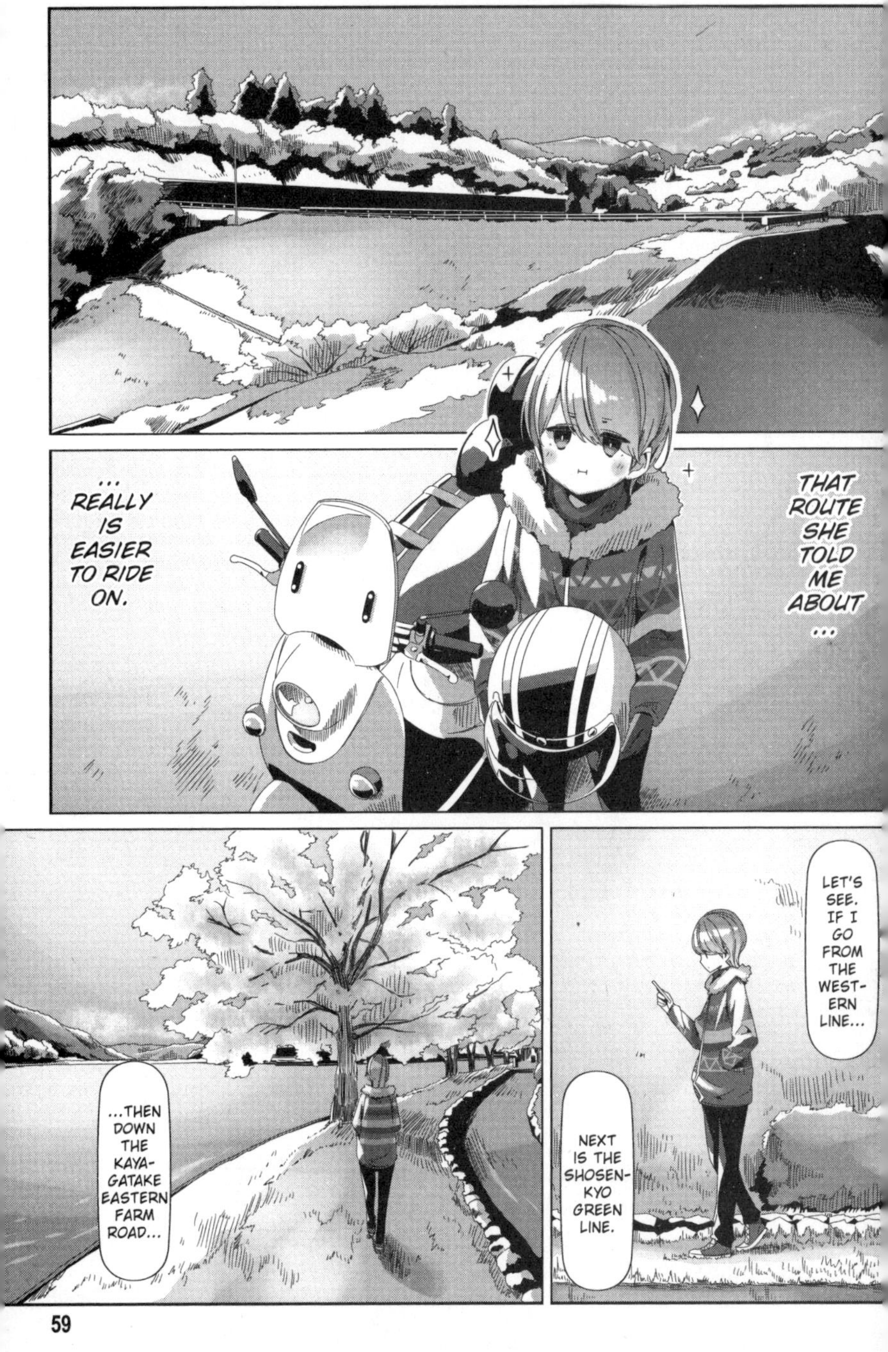
THAT ROUTE SHE TOLD ME ABOUT...
...REALLY IS EASIER TO RIDE ON.
LET'S SEE. IF I GO FROM THE WESTERN LINE...
NEXT IS THE SHOSENKYO GREEN LINE.
...THEN DOWN THE KAYAGATAKE EASTERN FARM ROAD...

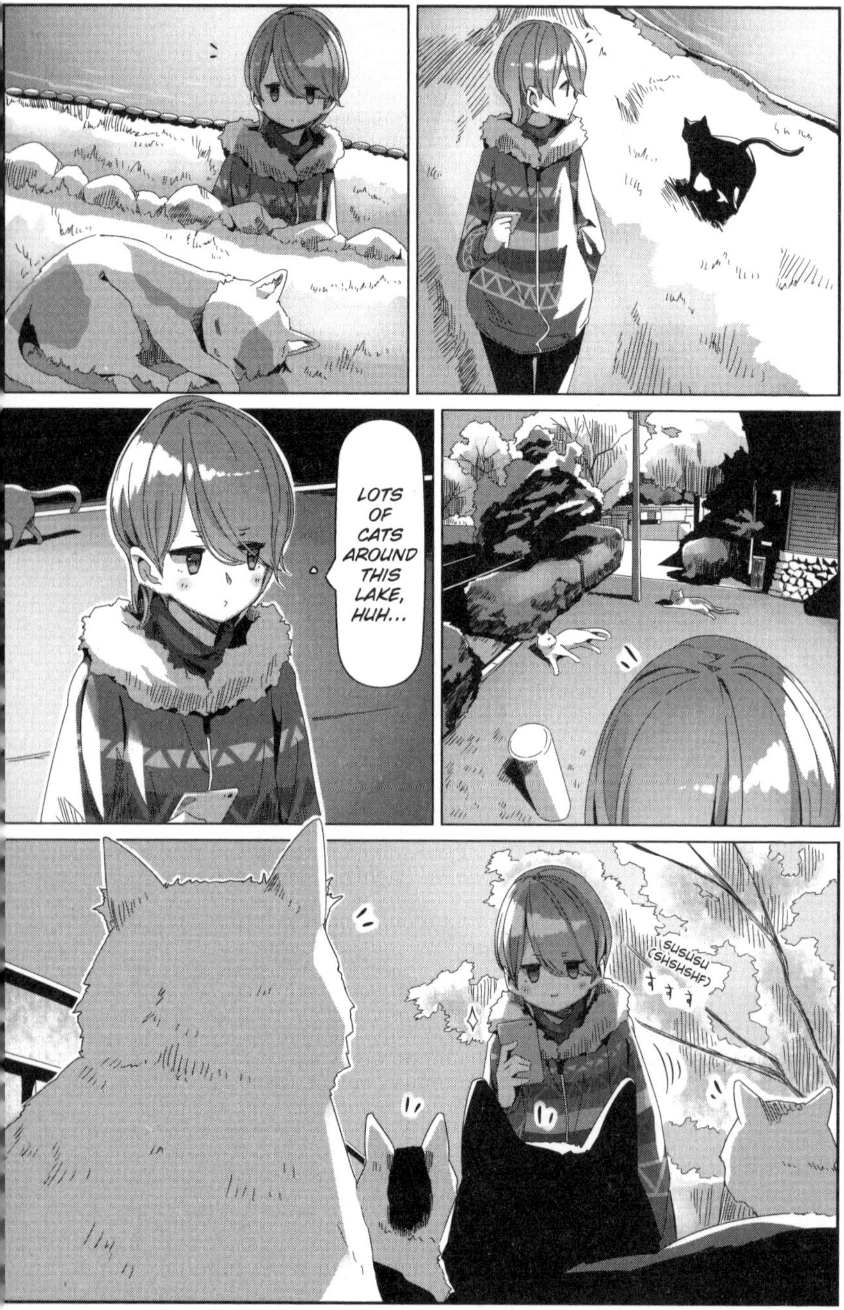
LOTS OF CATS AROUND THIS LAKE, HUH...
すすす
SUSUSU (SHSHSHF)

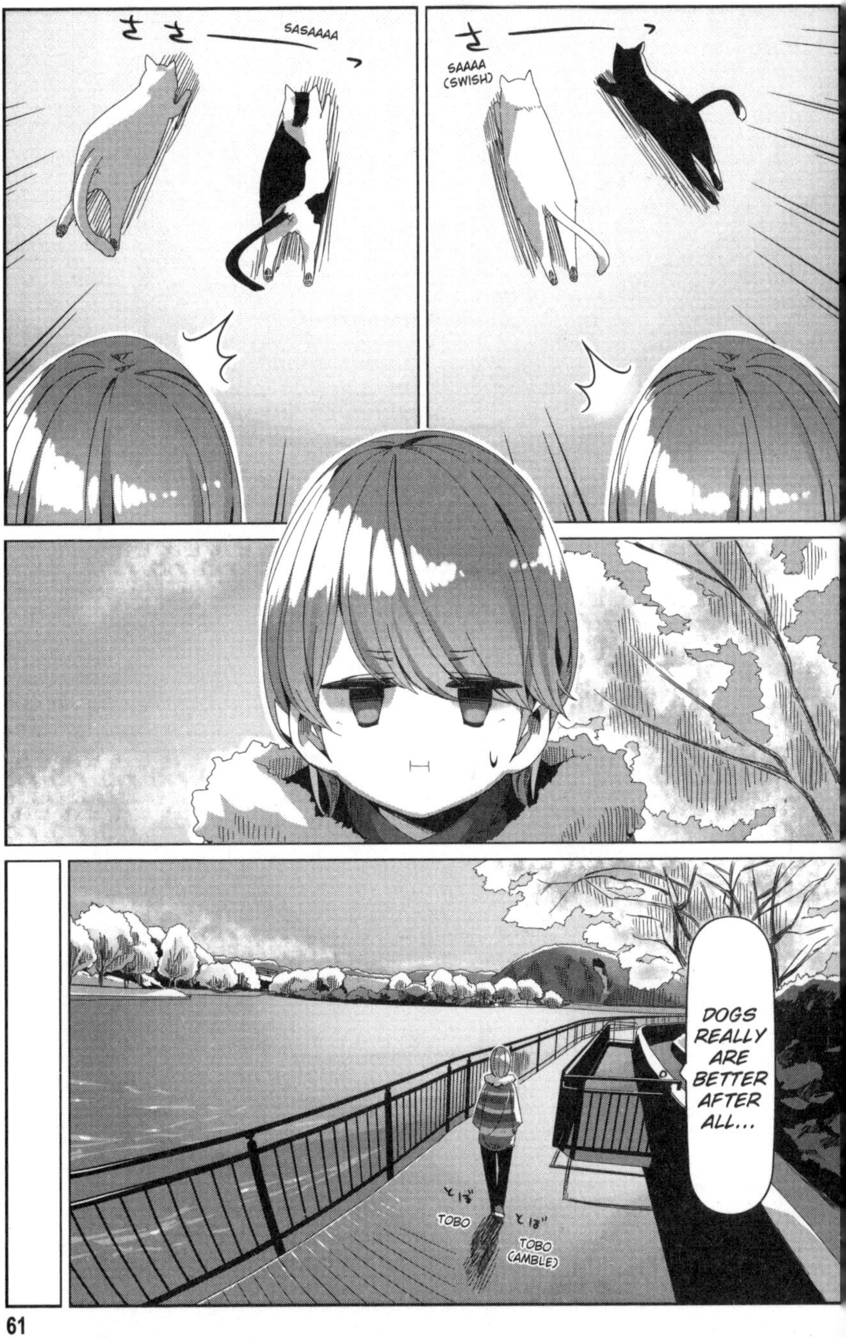

さーっ
SAAAA (SWISH)
ささーっ
SASAAAA
DOGS REALLY ARE BETTER AFTER ALL...
とぼ
TOBO
とぼ
TOBO (AMBLE)

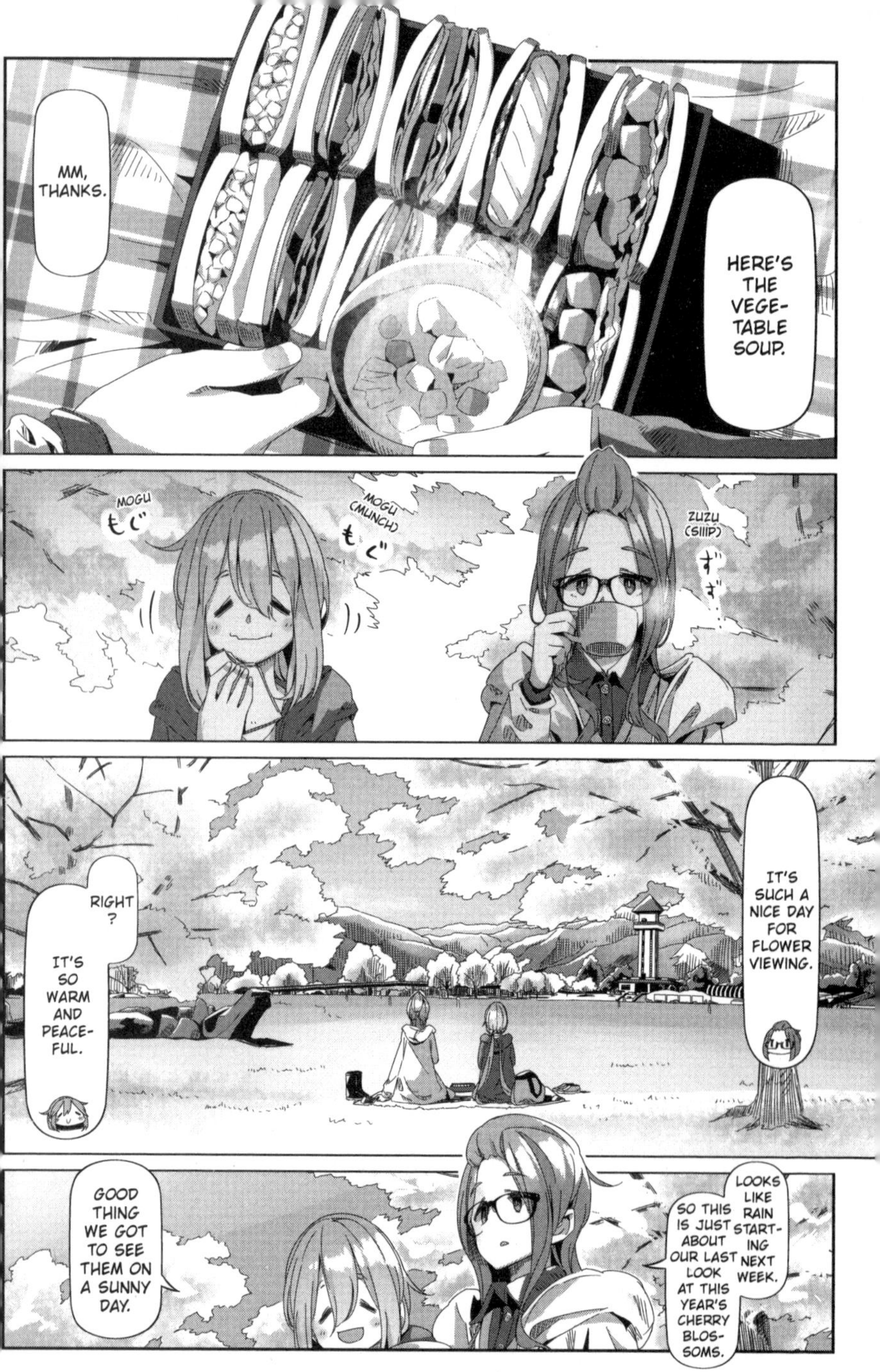

HERE'S THE VEGE-TABLE SOUP.
MM, THANKS.
ZUZU (SIIIP)
ずず
MOGU (MUNCH)
もぐ
MOGU
もぐ
IT'S SUCH A NICE DAY FOR FLOWER VIEWING.
RIGHT? IT'S SO WARM AND PEACE-FUL.
LOOKS LIKE RAIN START-ING NEXT WEEK.
SO THIS IS JUST ABOUT OUR LAST LOOK AT THIS YEAR'S CHERRY BLOS-SOMS.
GOOD THING WE GOT TO SEE THEM ON A SUNNY DAY.

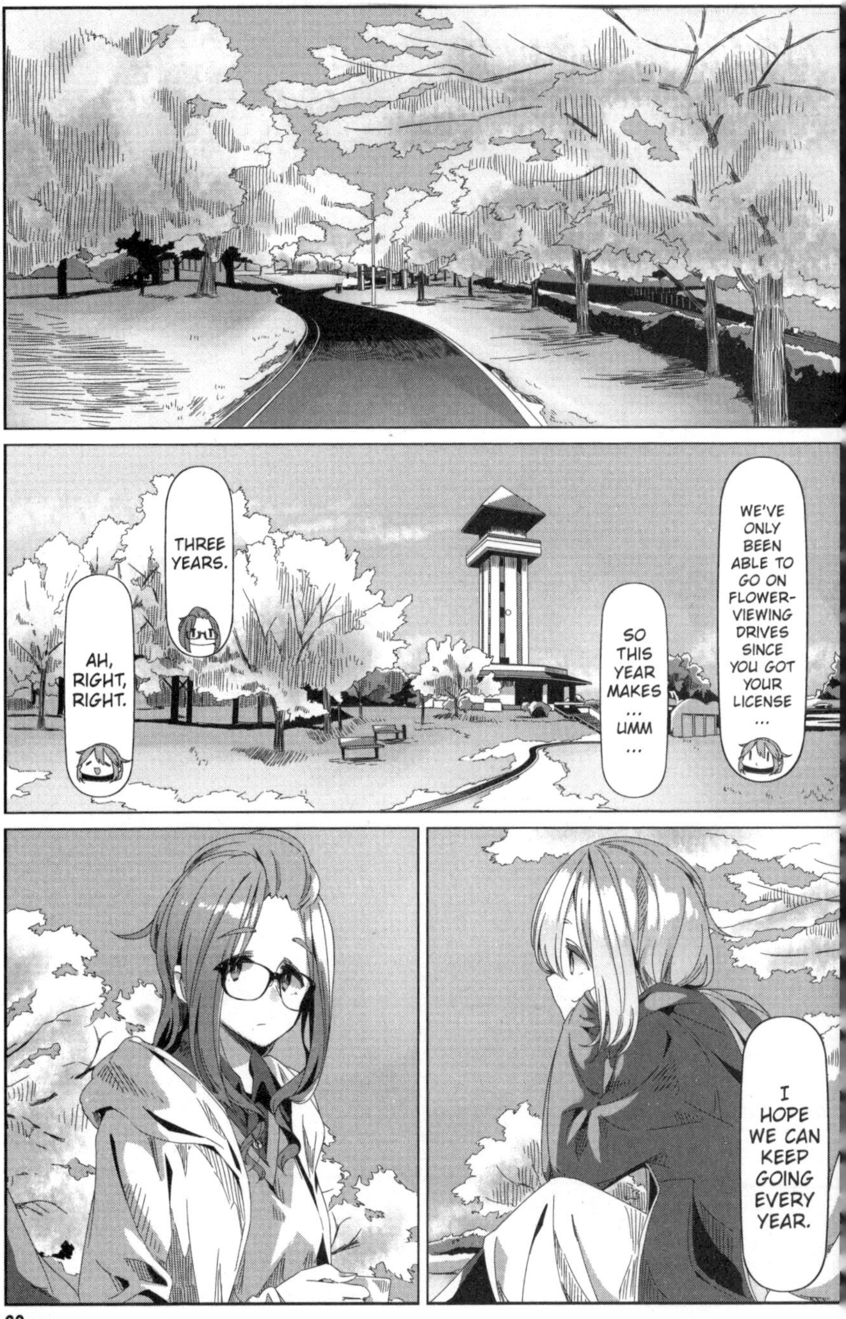
WE'VE ONLY BEEN ABLE TO GO ON FLOWER-VIEWING DRIVES SINCE YOU GOT YOUR LICENSE ...
SO THIS YEAR MAKES ... UMM ...
THREE YEARS.
AH, RIGHT, RIGHT.
I HOPE WE CAN KEEP GOING EVERY YEAR.

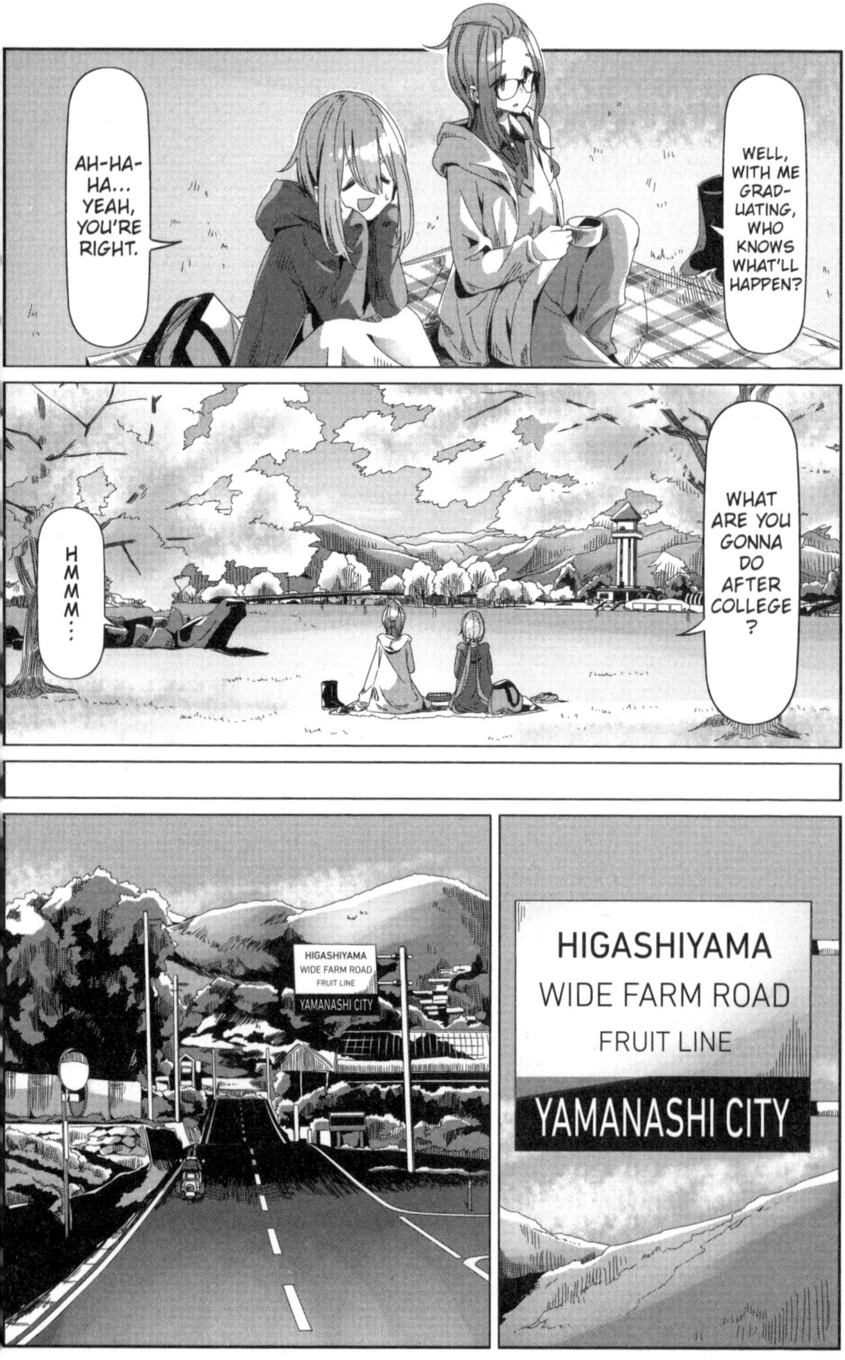
WELL, WITH ME GRAD-UATING, WHO KNOWS WHAT'LL HAPPEN?
AH-HA-HA... YEAH, YOU'RE RIGHT.
WHAT ARE YOU GONNA DO AFTER COLLEGE?
HMMM...
HIGASHIYAMA WIDE FARM ROAD FRUIT LINE
YAMANASHI CITY
HIGASHIYAMA WIDE FARM ROAD FRUIT LINE
YAMANASHI CITY

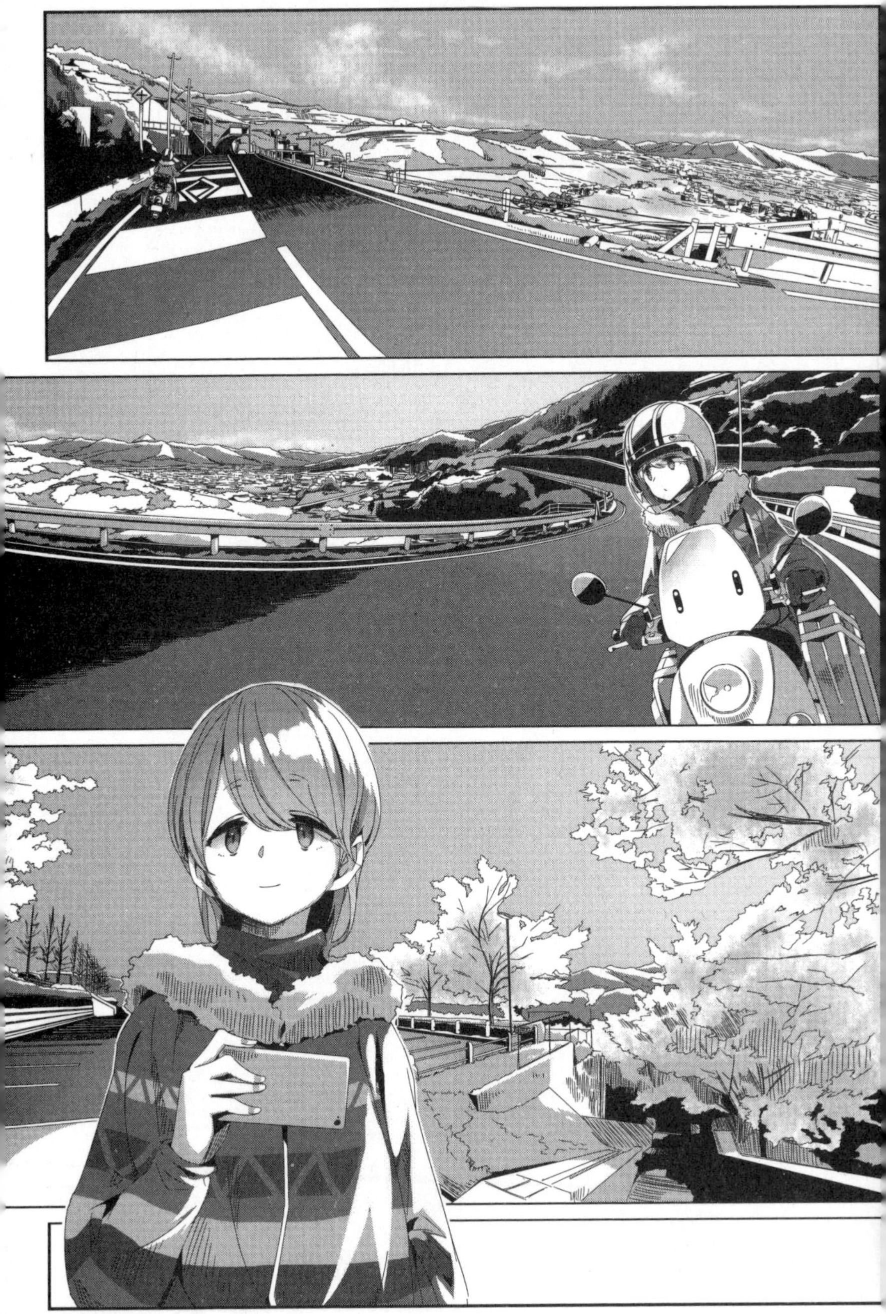

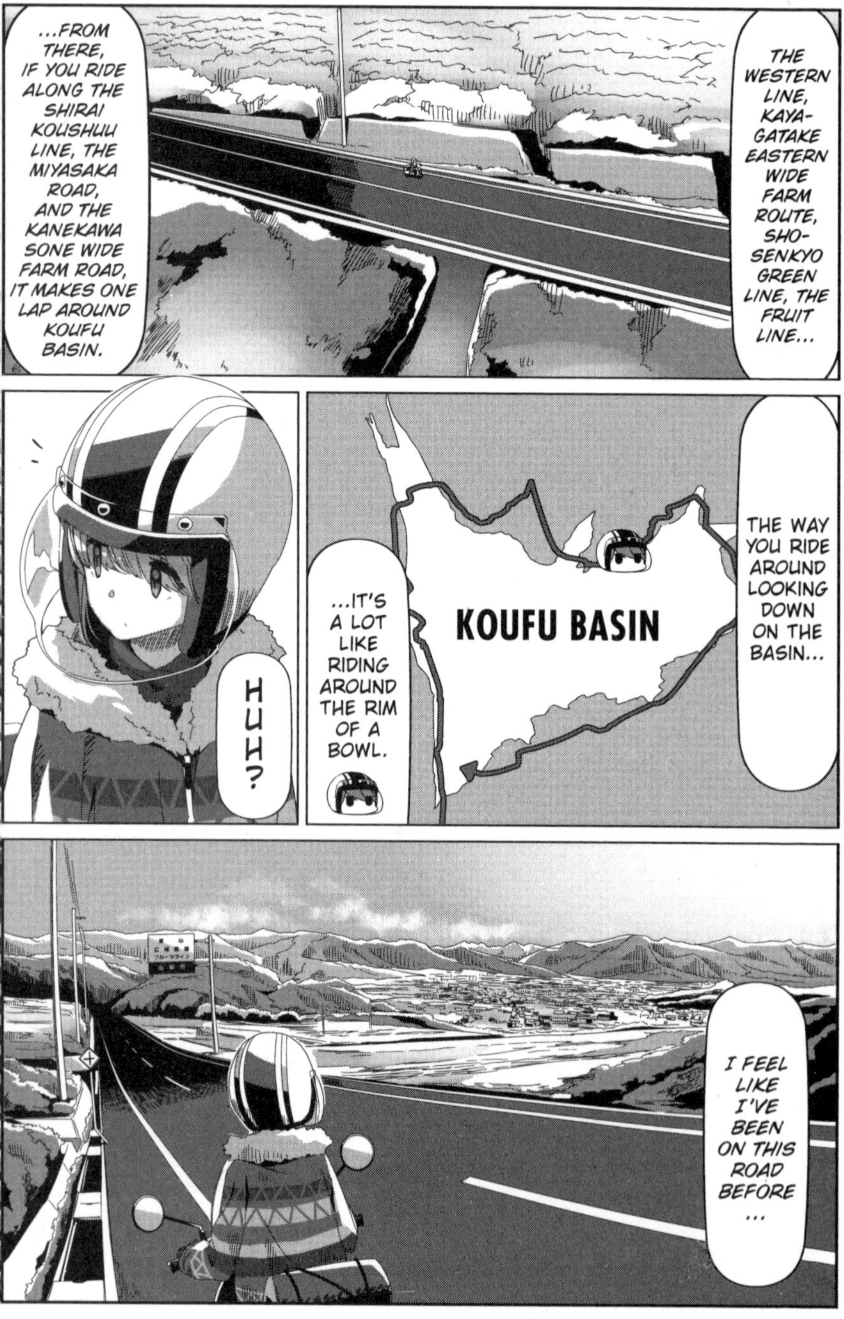
THE WESTERN LINE, KAYA-GATAKE EASTERN WIDE FARM ROUTE, SHO-SENKYO GREEN LINE, THE FRUIT LINE...
...FROM THERE, IF YOU RIDE ALONG THE SHIRAI KOUSHUU LINE, THE MIYASAKA ROAD, AND THE KANEKAWA SONE WIDE FARM ROAD, IT MAKES ONE LAP AROUND KOUFU BASIN.
THE WAY YOU RIDE AROUND LOOKING DOWN ON THE BASIN...
KOUFU BASIN
...IT'S A LOT LIKE RIDING AROUND THE RIM OF A BOWL.
HUH?
I FEEL LIKE I'VE BEEN ON THIS ROAD BEFORE...

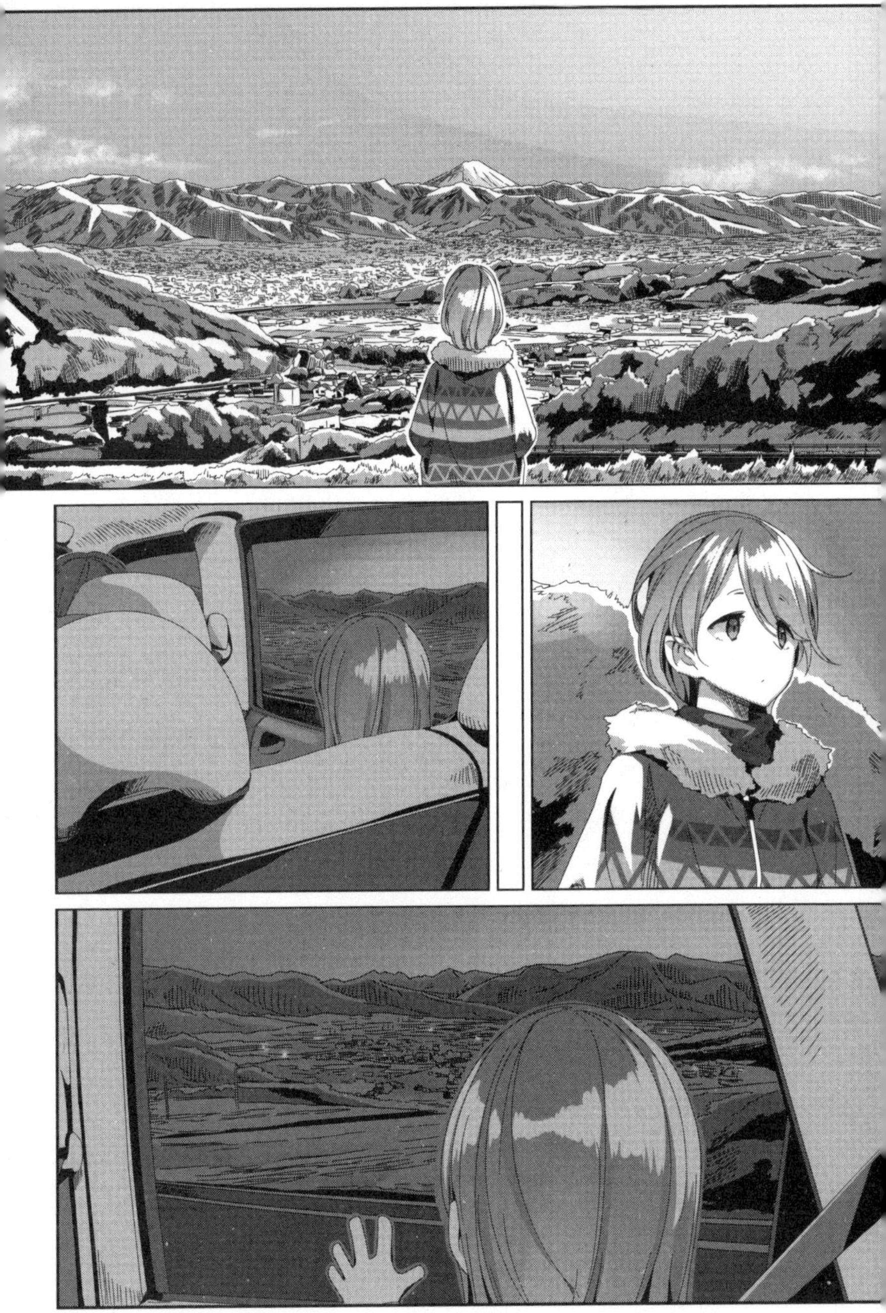

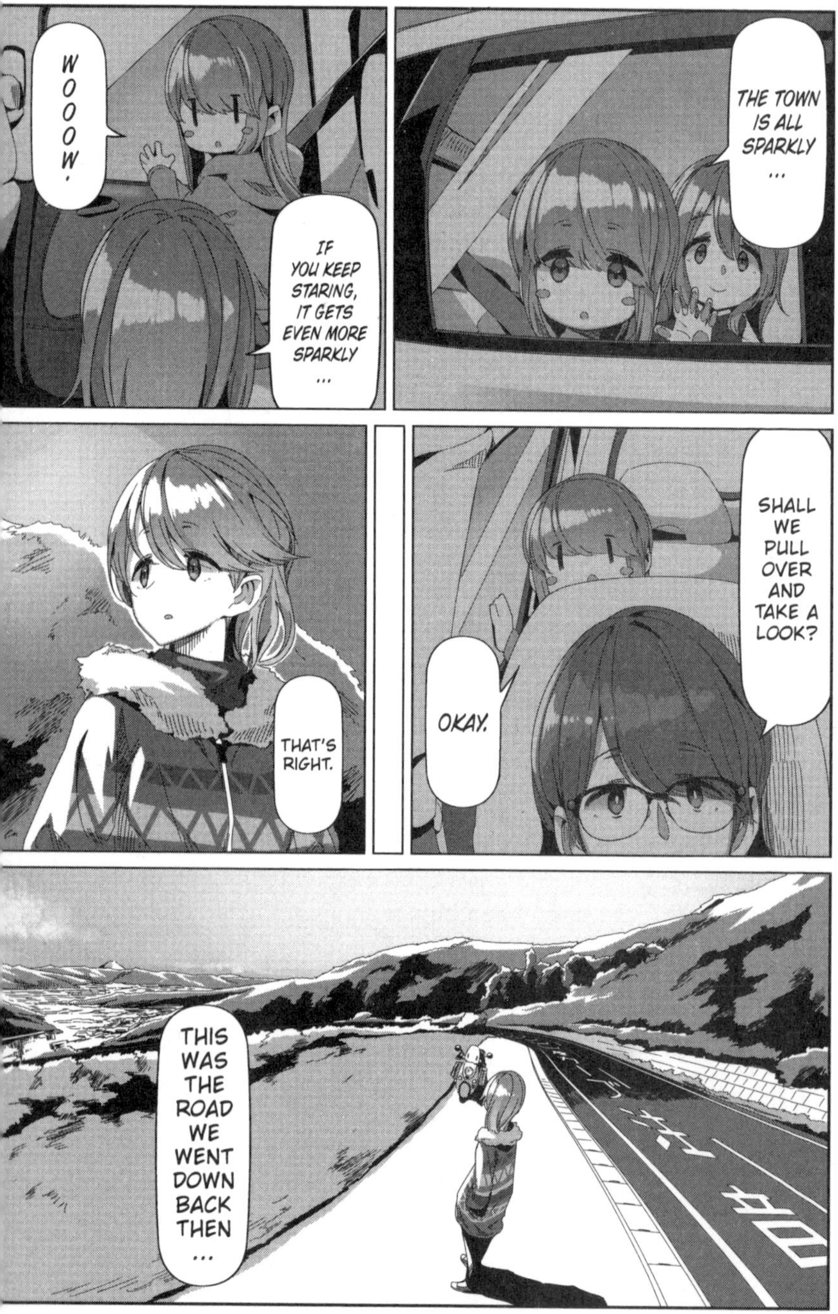
THE TOWN IS ALL SPARKLY ...
WOOOOW.
IF YOU KEEP STARING, IT GETS EVEN MORE SPARKLY ...
SHALL WE PULL OVER AND TAKE A LOOK?
OKAY.
THAT'S RIGHT.
THIS WAS THE ROAD WE WENT DOWN BACK THEN ...

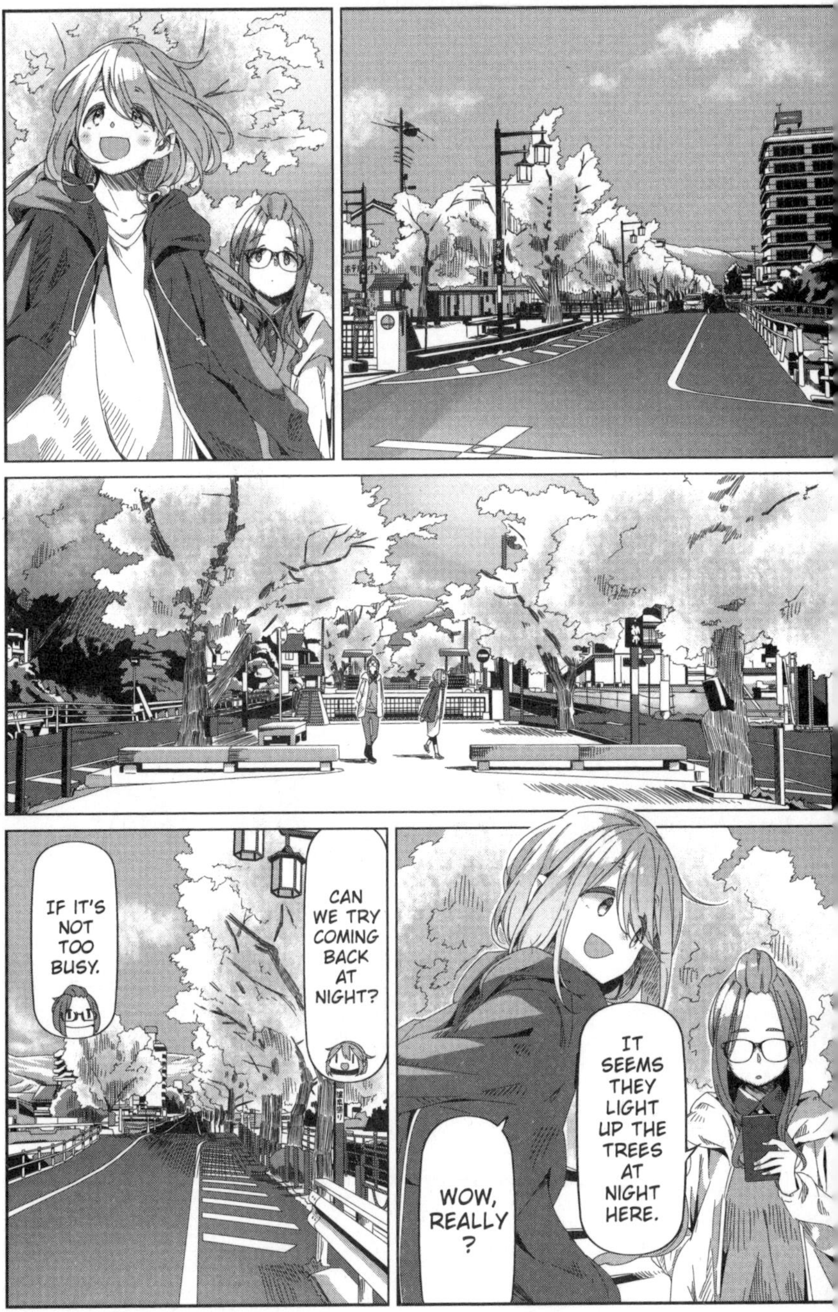
IT SEEMS THEY LIGHT UP THE TREES AT NIGHT HERE.
WOW, REALLY?
CAN WE TRY COMING BACK AT NIGHT?
IF IT'S NOT TOO BUSY.

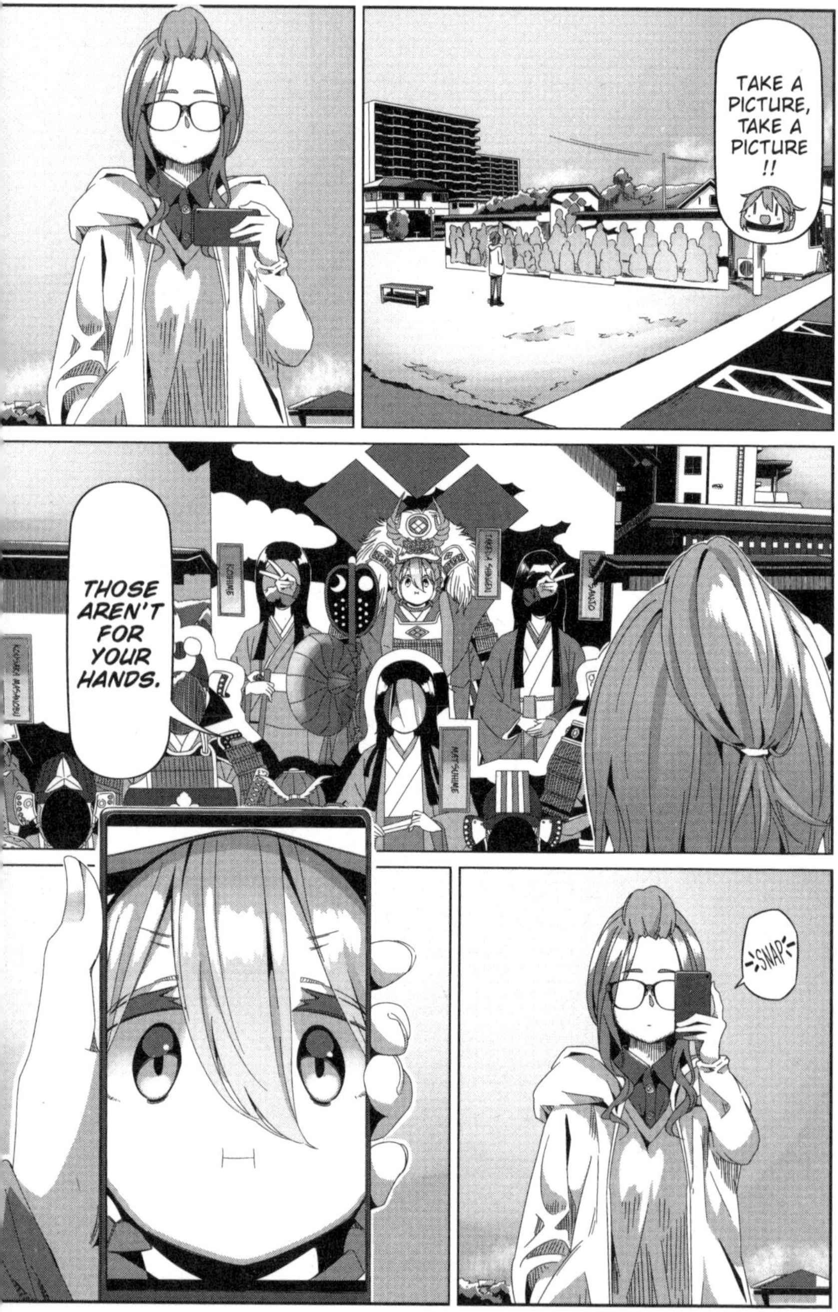
TAKE A PICTURE, TAKE A PICTURE !!
THOSE AREN'T FOR YOUR HANDS.
SNAP

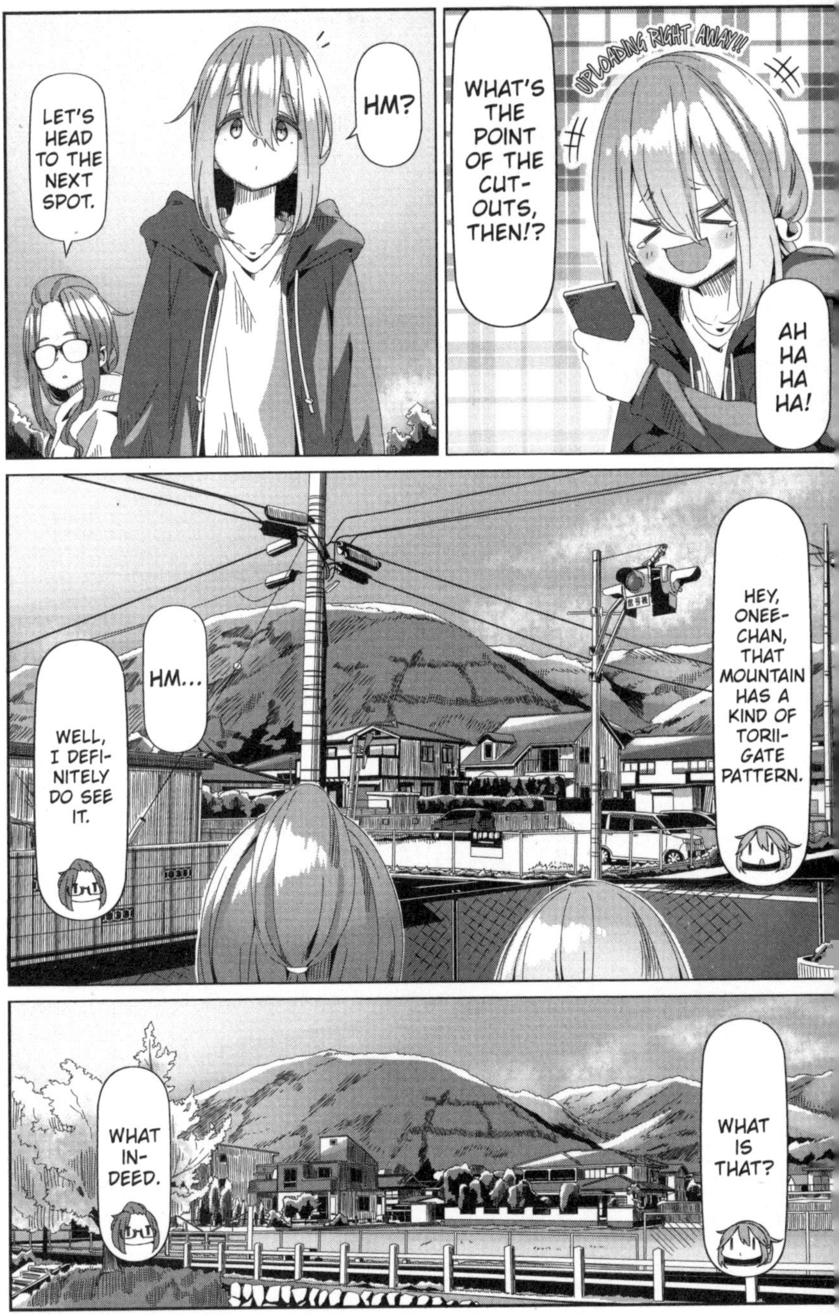
UPLOADING RIGHT AWAY!!
AH HA HA HA!
WHAT'S THE POINT OF THE CUT-OUTS, THEN!?
HM?
LET'S HEAD TO THE NEXT SPOT.
HEY, ONEE-CHAN, THAT MOUNTAIN HAS A KIND OF TORII-GATE PATTERN.
HM...
WELL, I DEFINITELY DO SEE IT.
WHAT IS THAT?
WHAT IN-DEED.

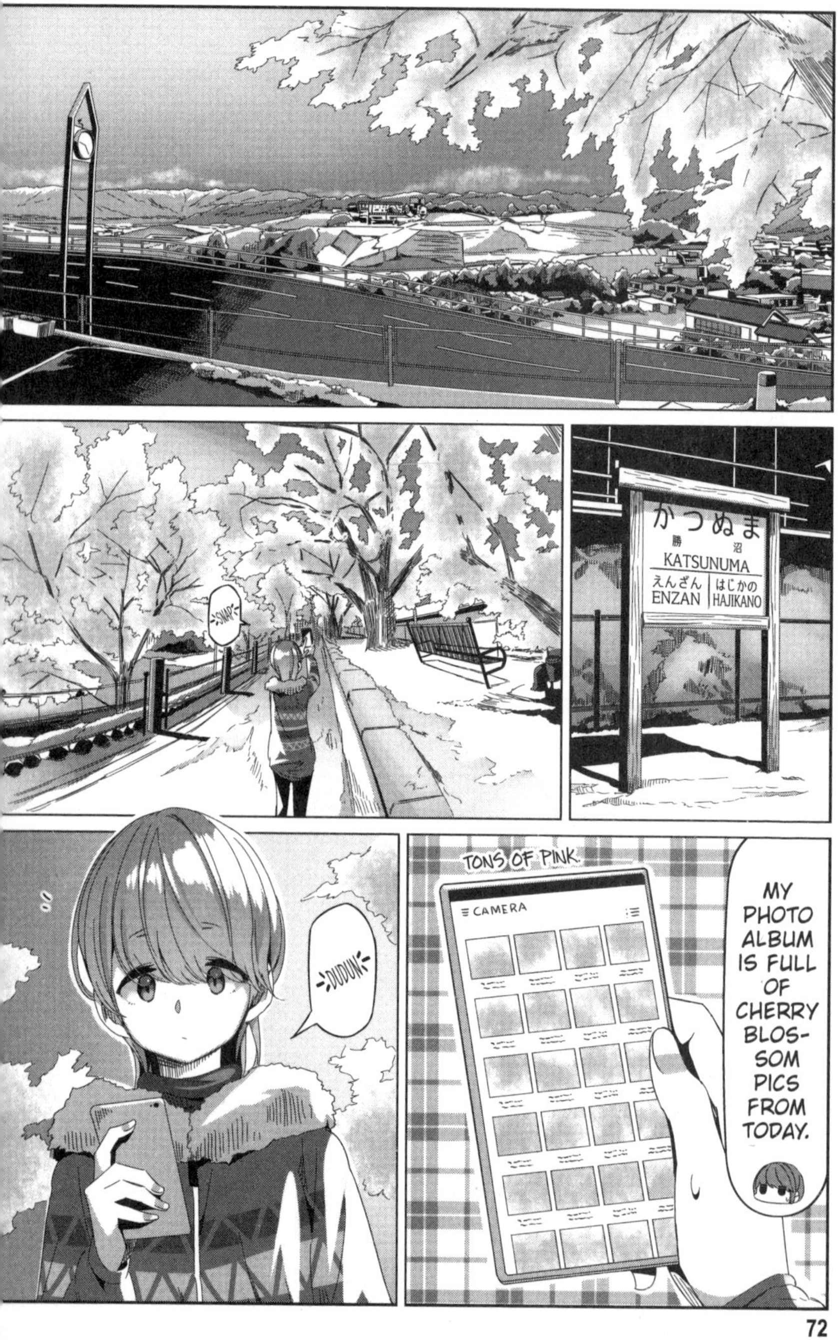
かつぬま
勝沼
KATSUNUMA
えんざん ENZAN
はじかの HAJIKANO
SNAP
TONS OF PINK.
MY PHOTO ALBUM IS FULL OF CHERRY BLOSSOM PICS FROM TODAY.
CAMERA
DUDUN

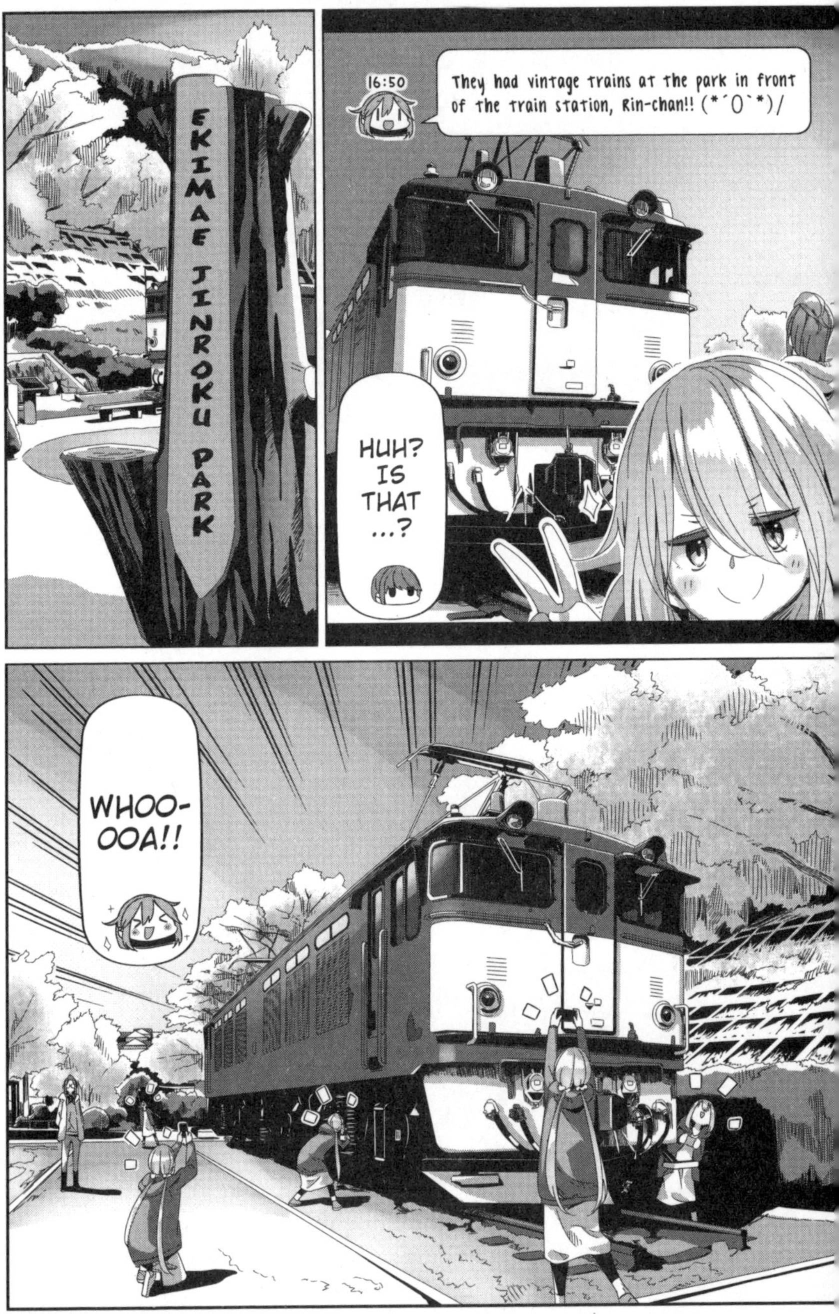
16:50
They had vintage trains at the park in front of the train station, Rin-chan!! (*´O`*)/
HUH? IS THAT ...?
EKIMAE JINROKU PARK
WHOO-OOA!!

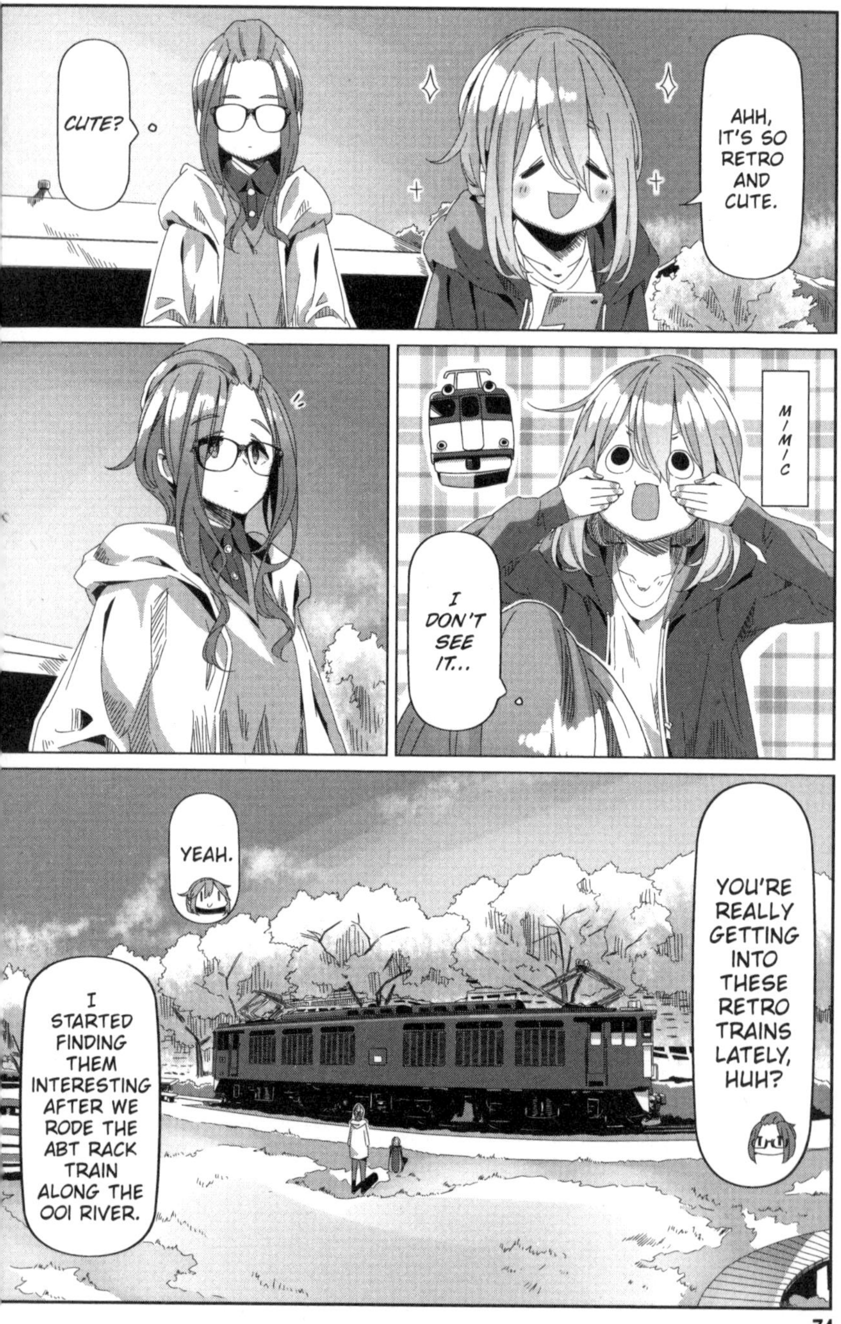
AHH, IT'S SO RETRO AND CUTE.
CUTE?
MIMIC
I DON'T SEE IT...
YOU'RE REALLY GETTING INTO THESE RETRO TRAINS LATELY, HUH?
YEAH.
I STARTED FINDING THEM INTERESTING AFTER WE RODE THE ABT RACK TRAIN ALONG THE OOI RIVER.

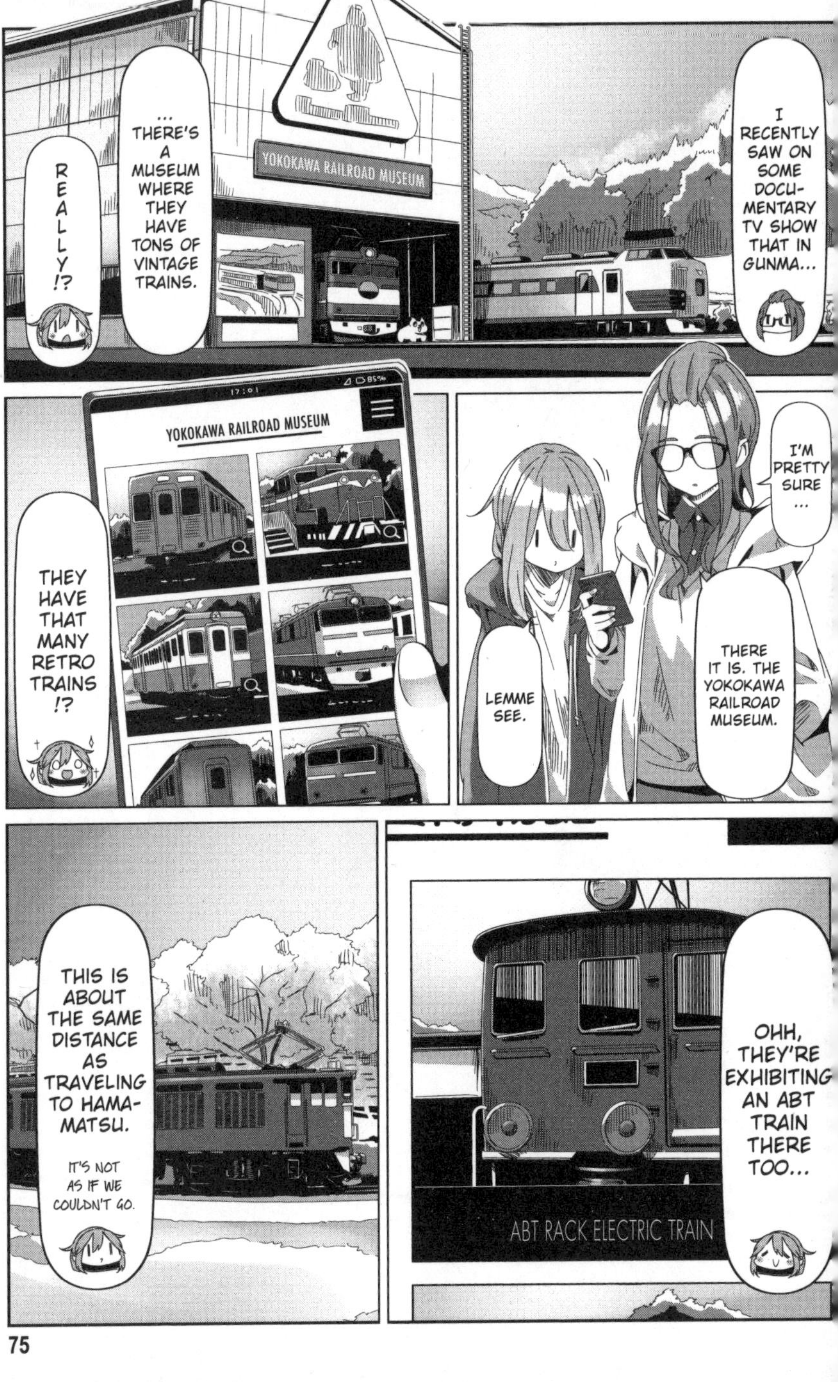
I RECENTLY SAW ON SOME DOCU-MENTARY TV SHOW THAT IN GUNMA...
... THERE'S A MUSEUM WHERE THEY HAVE TONS OF VINTAGE TRAINS.
YOKOKAWA RAILROAD MUSEUM
REALLY!?
I'M PRETTY SURE ...
THERE IT IS. THE YOKOKAWA RAILROAD MUSEUM.
LEMME SEE.
17:01
85%
YOKOKAWA RAILROAD MUSEUM
THEY HAVE THAT MANY RETRO TRAINS!?
OHH, THEY'RE EXHIBITING AN ABT TRAIN THERE TOO...
ABT RACK ELECTRIC TRAIN
THIS IS ABOUT THE SAME DISTANCE AS TRAVELING TO HAMA-MATSU.
IT'S NOT AS IF WE COULDN'T GO.

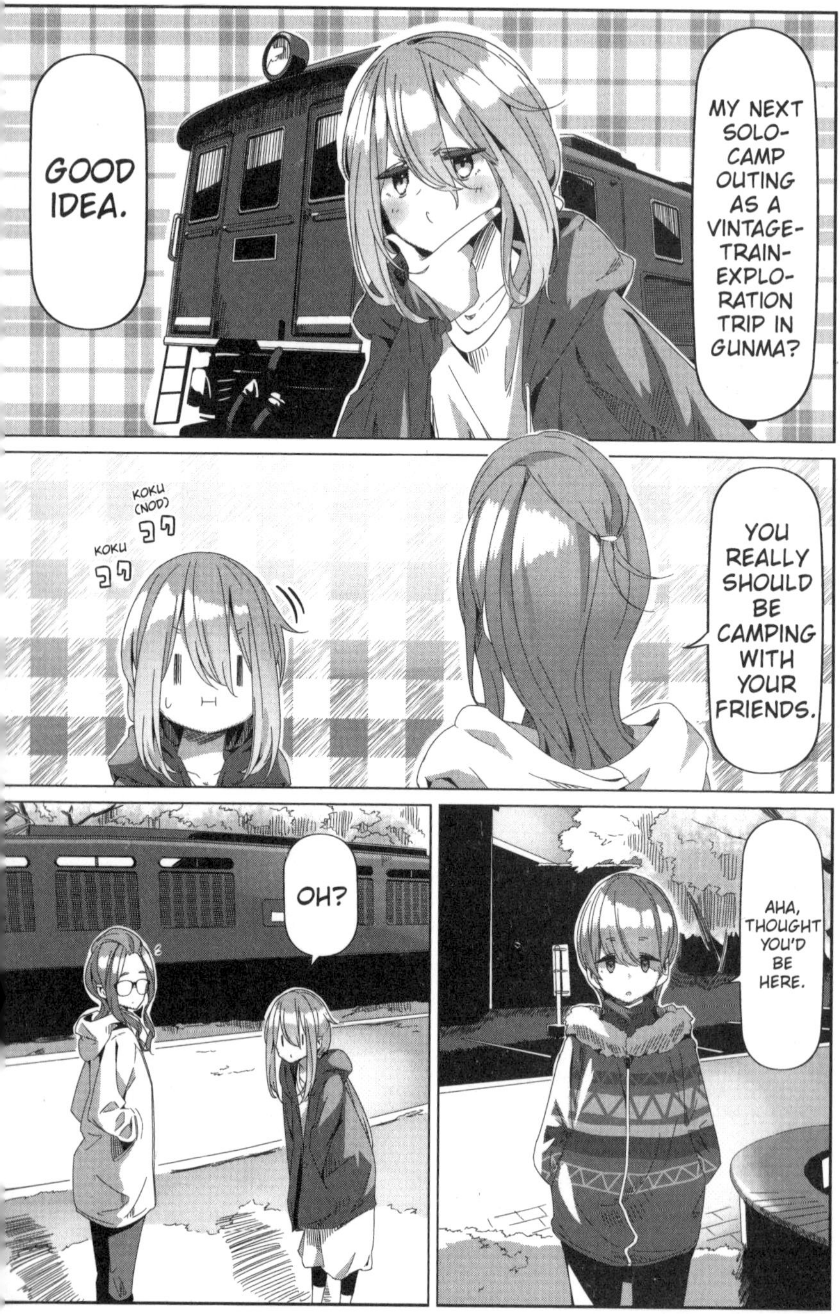
MY NEXT SOLO-CAMP OUTING AS A VINTAGE-TRAIN-EXPLORATION TRIP IN GUNMA?
GOOD IDEA.
YOU REALLY SHOULD BE CAMPING WITH YOUR FRIENDS.
KOKU (NOD)
KOKU
AHA, THOUGHT YOU'D BE HERE.
OH?

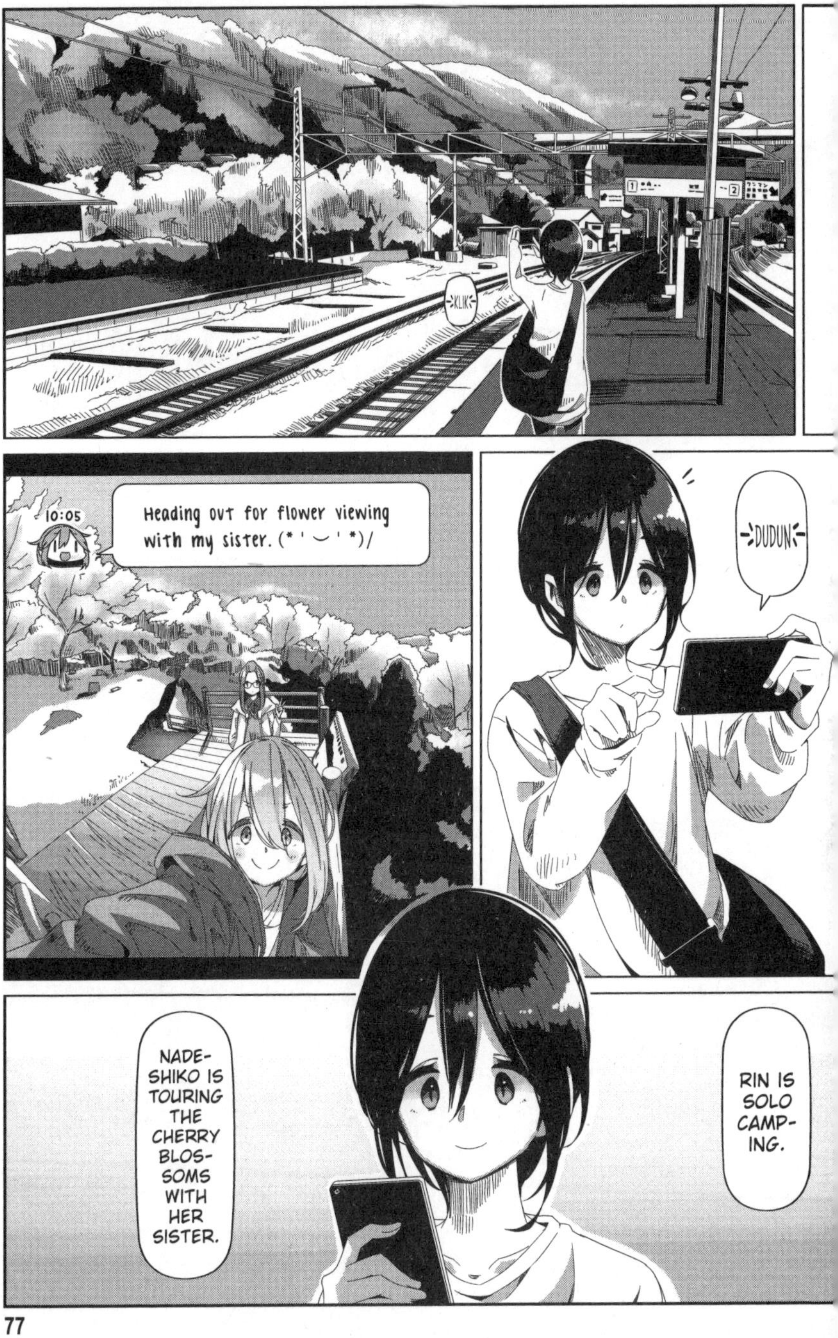
KLIK
DUDUN
10:05
Heading out for flower viewing with my sister. (*'︶'*)/
RIN IS SOLO CAMPING.
NADESHIKO IS TOURING THE CHERRY BLOSSOMS WITH HER SISTER.

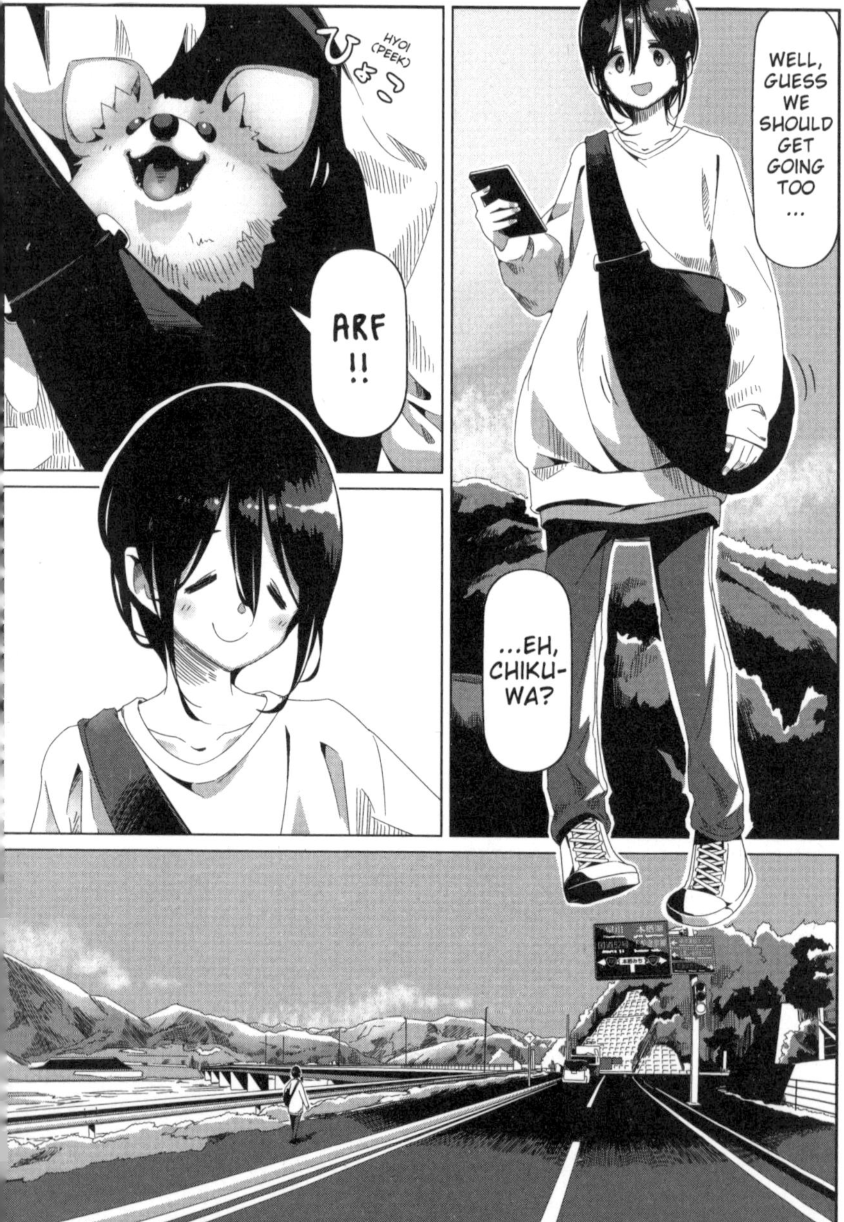
WELL, GUESS WE SHOULD GET GOING TOO ...
...EH, CHIKU-WA?
HYOI (PEEK)
ARF !!

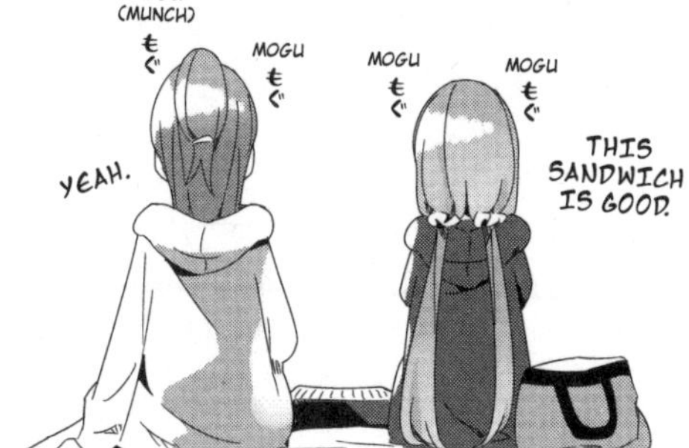
MOGU
もぐ
THIS SANDWICH IS GOOD.
MOGU
もぐ
MOGU
もぐ
MOGU (MUNCH)
もぐ
YEAH.

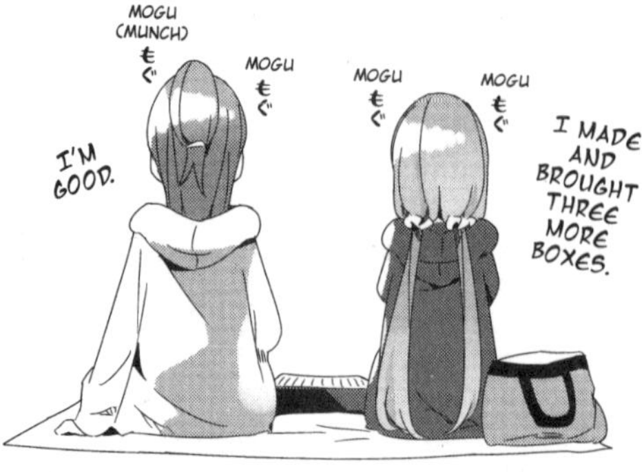
I MADE AND BROUGHT THREE MORE BOXES.
MOGU もぐ
MOGU もぐ
MOGU もぐ
MOGU (MUNCH) もぐ
I'M GOOD.

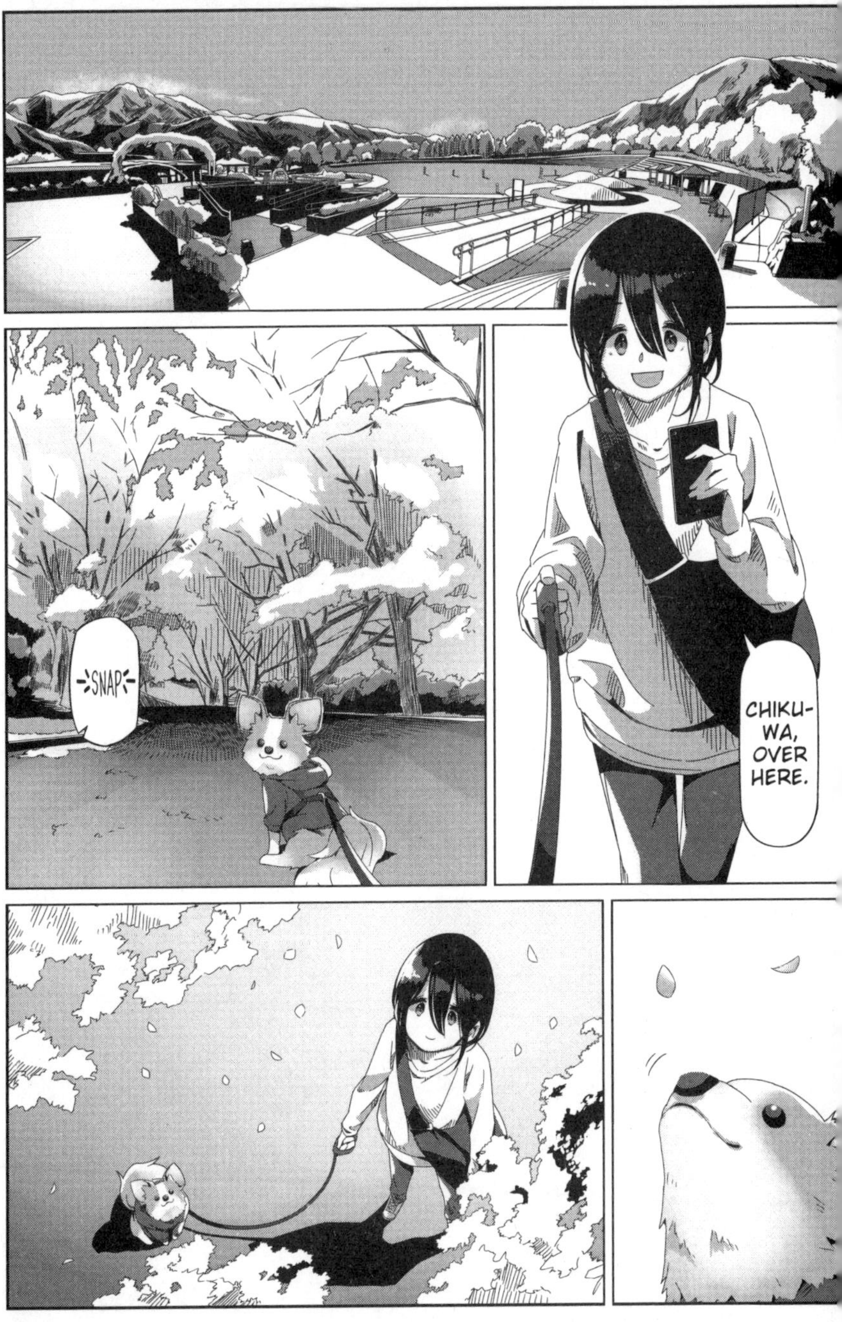
CHIKU-WA, OVER HERE.
SNAP

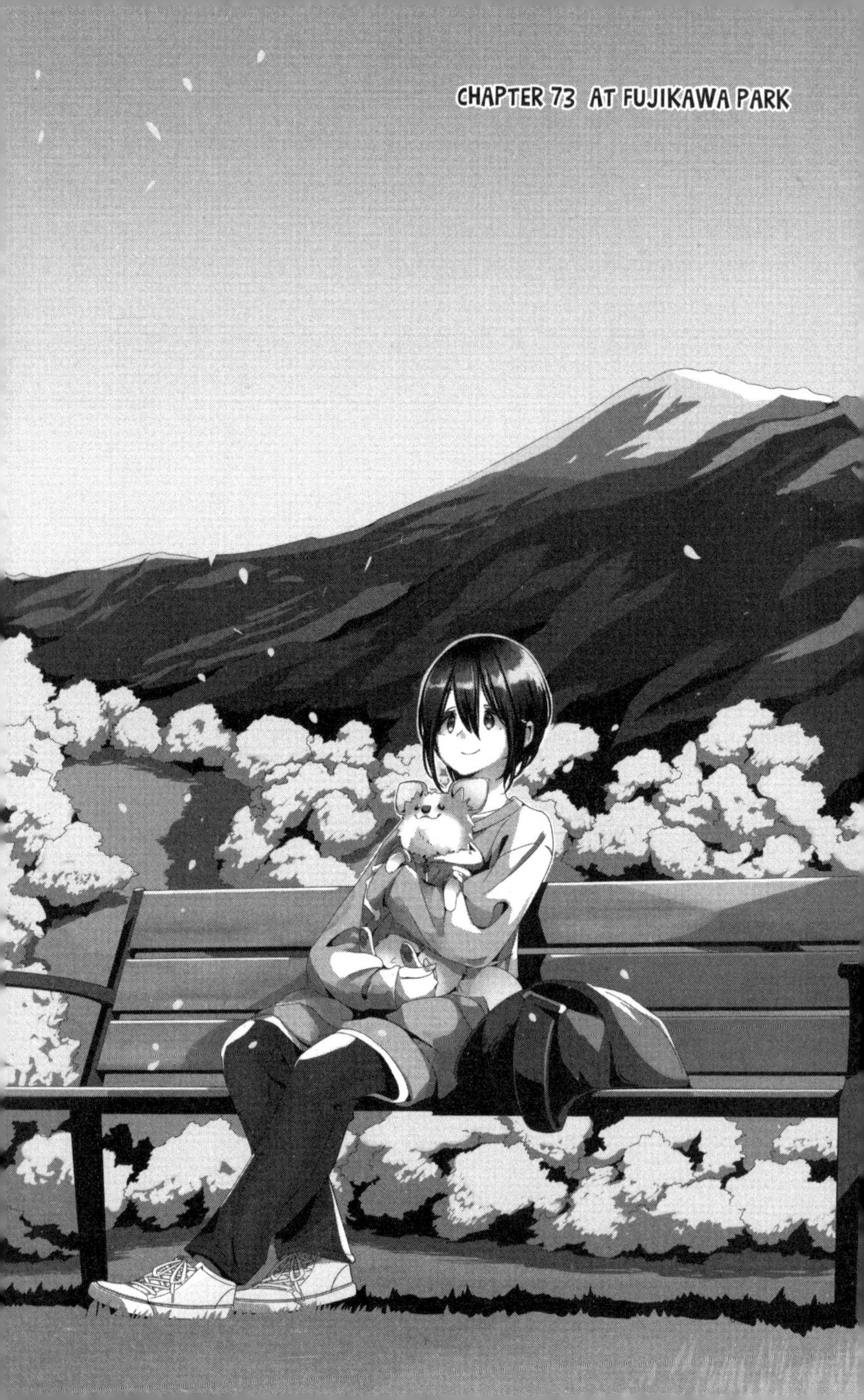
CHAPTER 73 AT FUJIKAWA PARK

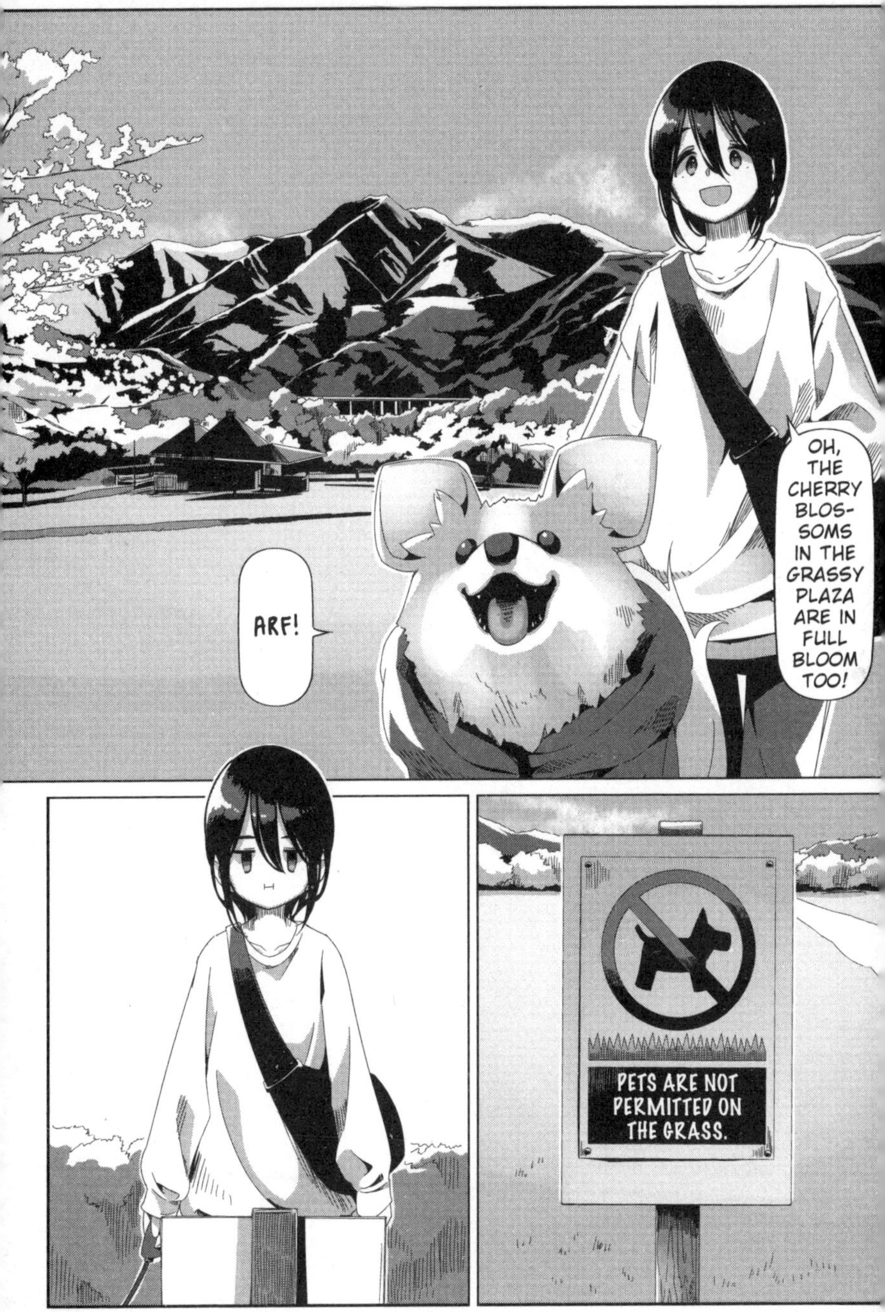
OH, THE CHERRY BLOSSOMS IN THE GRASSY PLAZA ARE IN FULL BLOOM TOO!
ARF!
PETS ARE NOT PERMITTED ON THE GRASS.

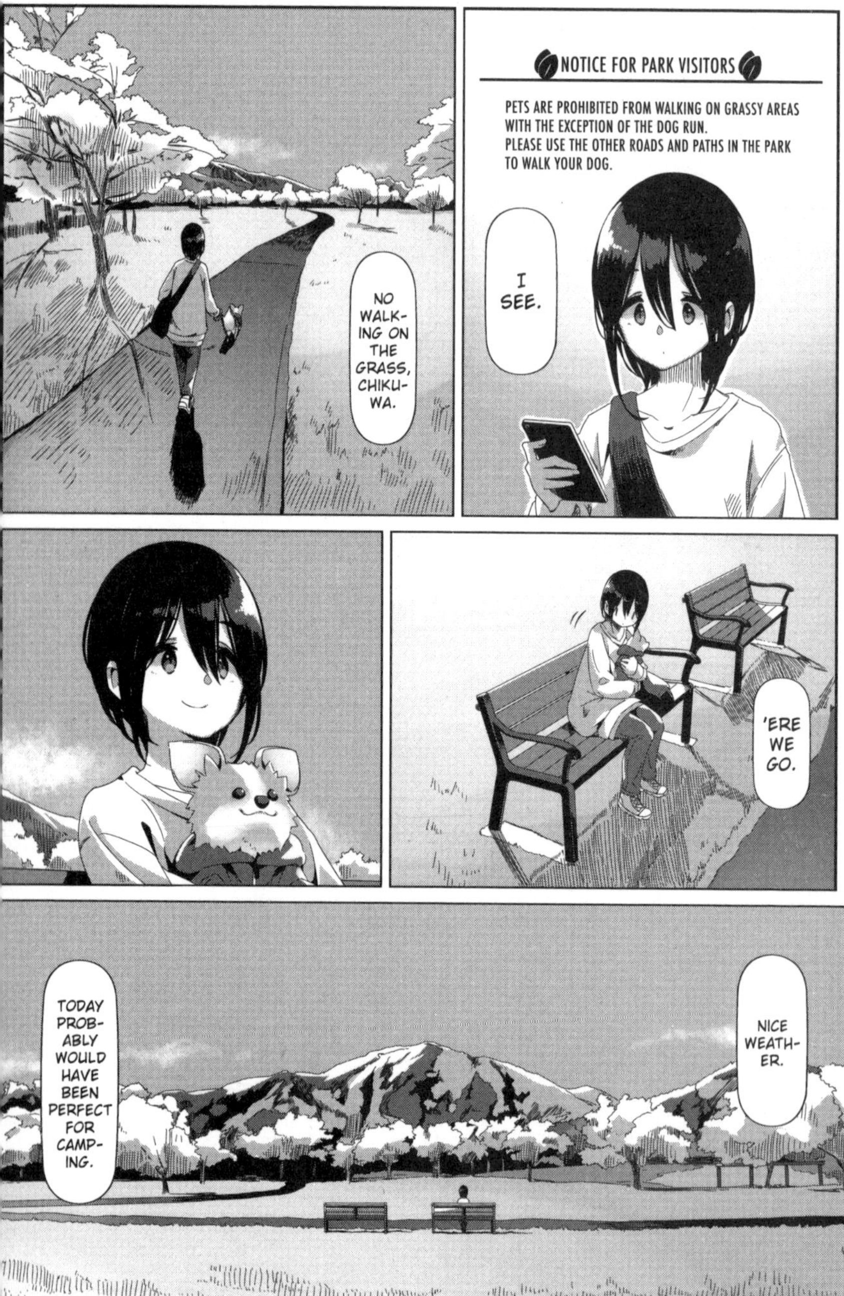
NOTICE FOR PARK VISITORS
PETS ARE PROHIBITED FROM WALKING ON GRASSY AREAS WITH THE EXCEPTION OF THE DOG RUN.
PLEASE USE THE OTHER ROADS AND PATHS IN THE PARK TO WALK YOUR DOG.
I SEE.
NO WALKING ON THE GRASS, CHIKUWA.
'ERE WE GO.
NICE WEATHER.
TODAY PROBABLY WOULD HAVE BEEN PERFECT FOR CAMPING.

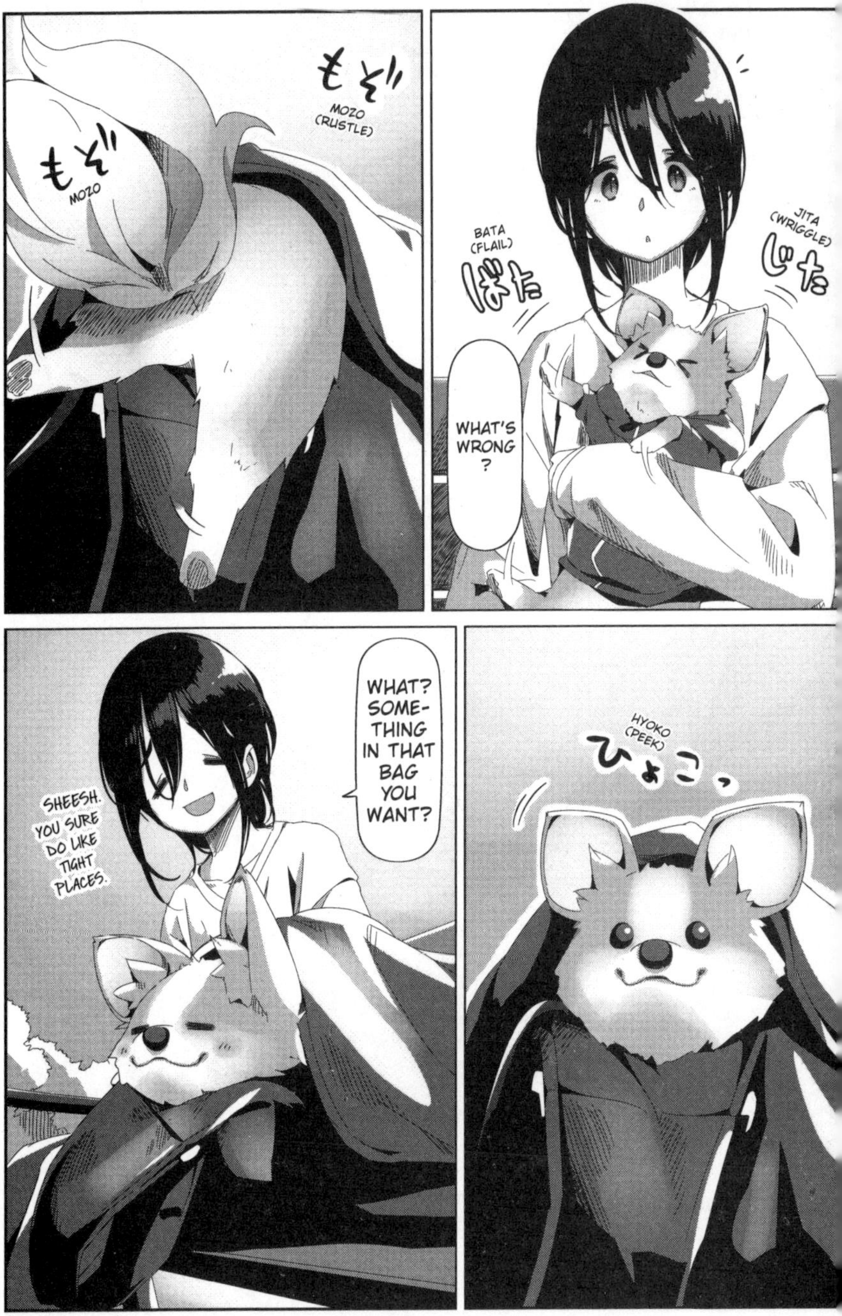
JITA (WRIGGLE)
じた
BATA (FLAIL)
ばた
WHAT'S WRONG?
もぞ
MOZO (RUSTLE)
もぞ
MOZO
HYOKO (PEEK)
ひょこっ
WHAT? SOME-THING IN THAT BAG YOU WANT?
SHEESH. YOU SURE DO LIKE TIGHT PLACES.

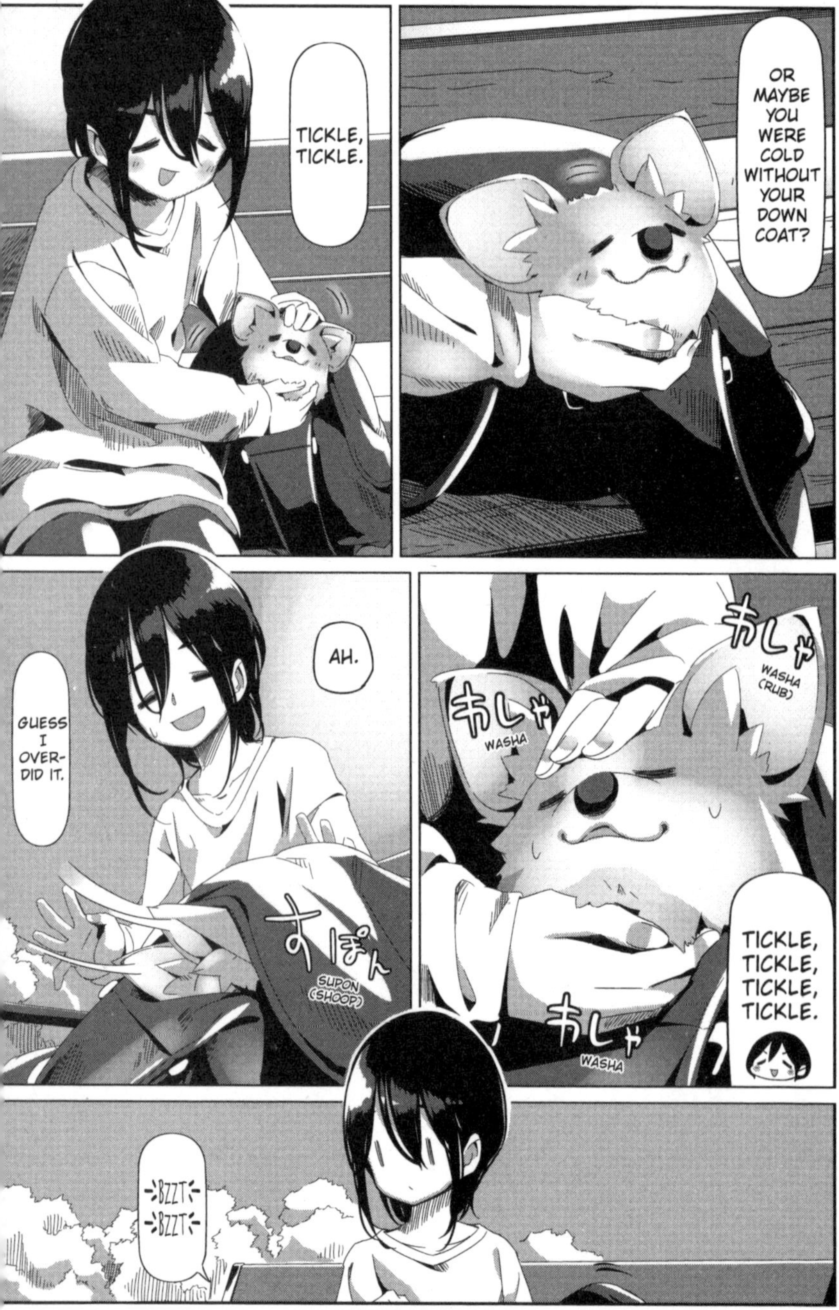
OR MAYBE YOU WERE COLD WITHOUT YOUR DOWN COAT?
TICKLE, TICKLE.
わしゃ
WASHA (RUB)
わしゃ
WASHA
TICKLE, TICKLE, TICKLE, TICKLE.
わしゃ
WASHA
AH.
GUESS I OVER-DID IT.
すぽん
SUPON (SHOOP)
BZZT BZZT

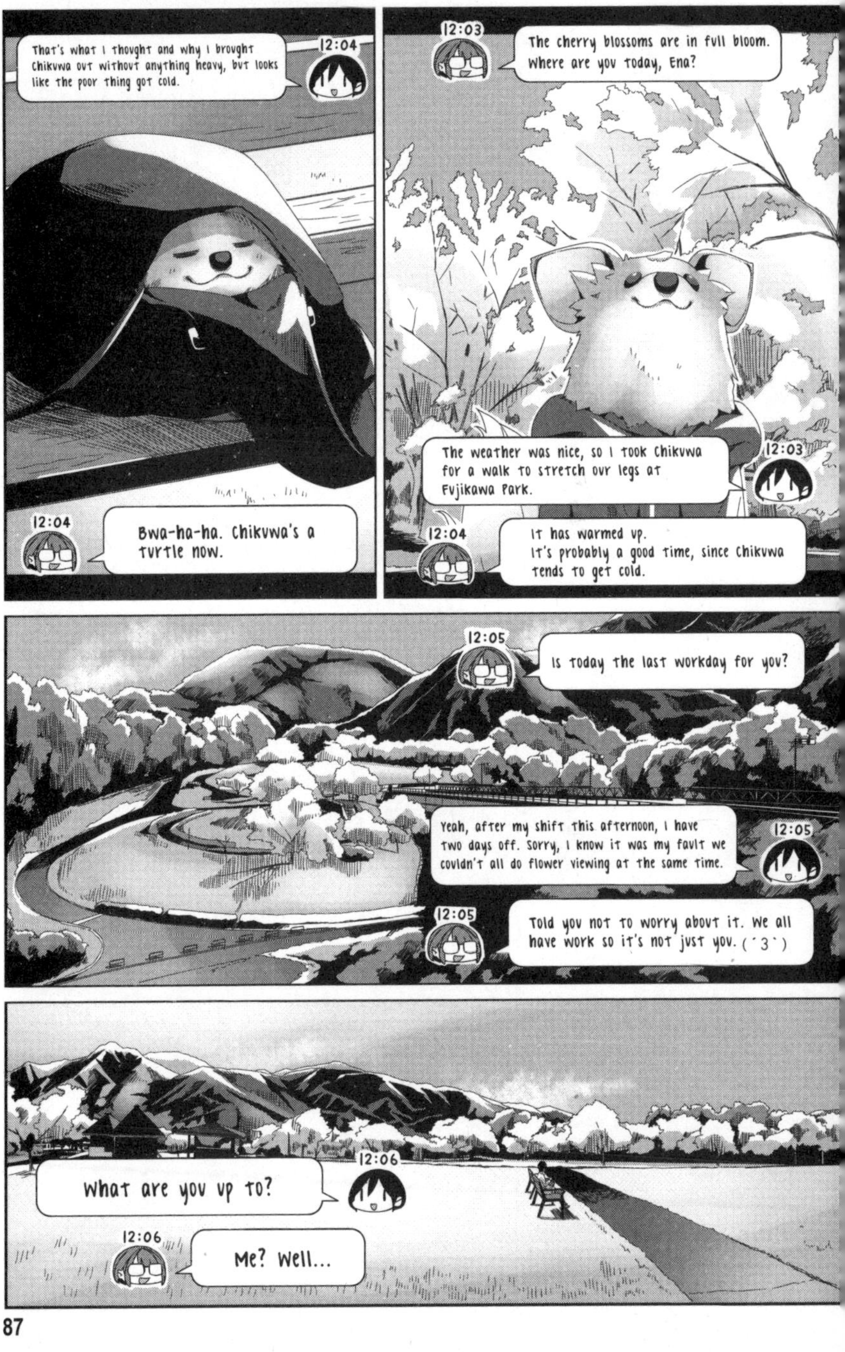
12:03
The cherry blossoms are in full bloom. Where are you today, Ena?
The weather was nice, so I took Chikuwa for a walk to stretch our legs at Fujikawa Park.
12:03
12:04
It has warmed up. It's probably a good time, since Chikuwa tends to get cold.
That's what I thought and why I brought Chikuwa out without anything heavy, but looks like the poor thing got cold.
12:04
12:04
Bwa-ha-ha. Chikuwa's a turtle now.
12:05
Is today the last workday for you?
Yeah, after my shift this afternoon, I have two days off. Sorry, I know it was my fault we couldn't all do flower viewing at the same time.
12:05
12:05
Told you not to worry about it. We all have work so it's not just you. (´3`)
What are you up to?
12:06
12:06
Me? Well...

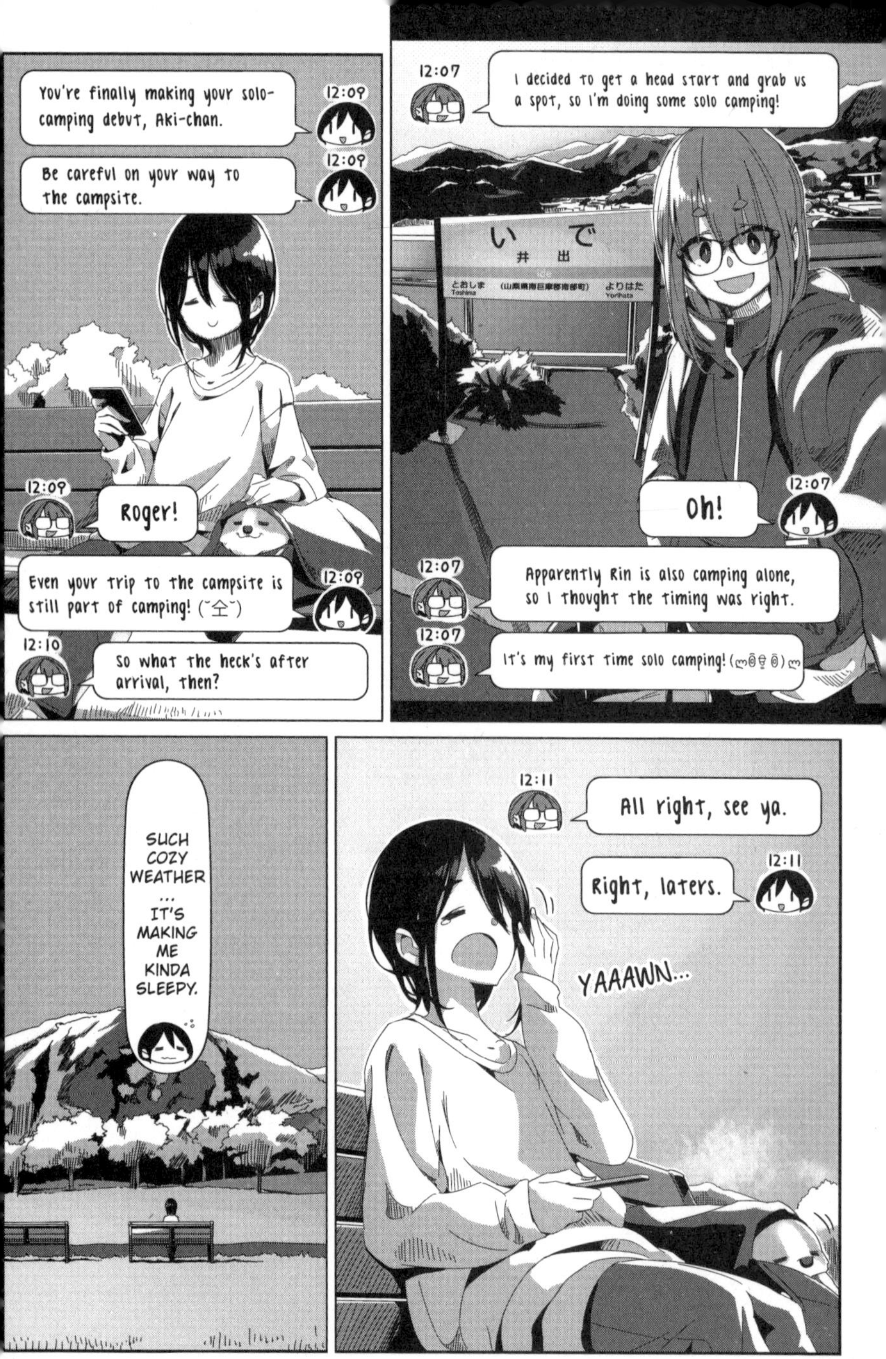
12:07
I decided to get a head start and grab us a spot, so I'm doing some solo camping!
12:07
Oh!
12:07
Apparently Rin is also camping alone, so I thought the timing was right.
12:07
It's my first time solo camping!
12:09
You're finally making your solo-camping debut, Aki-chan.
12:09
Be careful on your way to the campsite.
12:09
Roger!
12:09
Even your trip to the campsite is still part of camping!
12:10
So what the heck's after arrival, then?
12:11
All right, see ya.
12:11
Right, laters.
YAAAWN...
SUCH COZY WEATHER... IT'S MAKING ME KINDA SLEEPY.

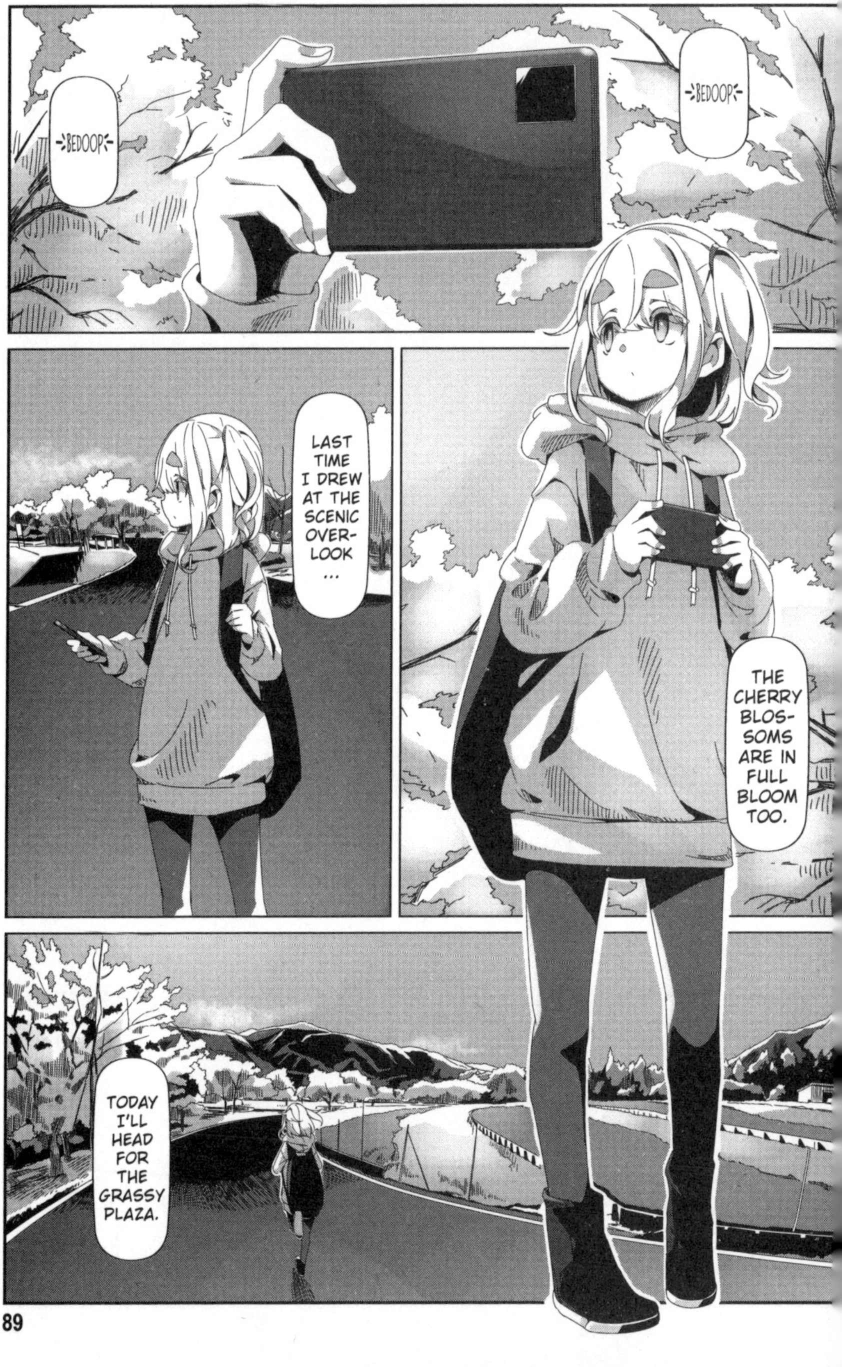
BEDOOP
BEDOOP
THE CHERRY BLOSSOMS ARE IN FULL BLOOM TOO.
LAST TIME I DREW AT THE SCENIC OVERLOOK ...
TODAY I'LL HEAD FOR THE GRASSY PLAZA.

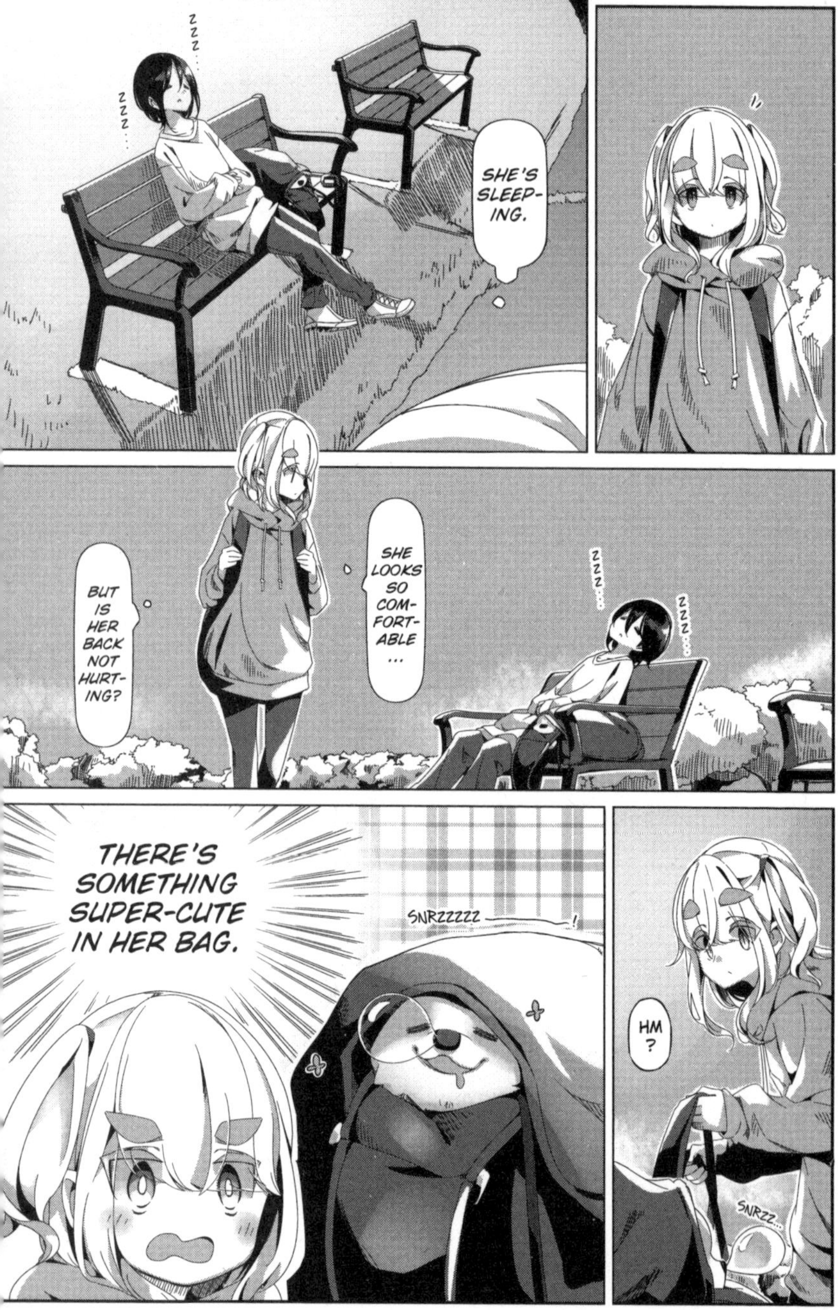
ZZZ...
ZZZ...
SHE'S SLEEP-ING.
ZZZ...
ZZZ...
SHE LOOKS SO COM-FORT-ABLE...
BUT IS HER BACK NOT HURT-ING?
HM?
SNRZZ...
SNRZZZZZ—!
THERE'S SOMETHING SUPER-CUTE IN HER BAG.

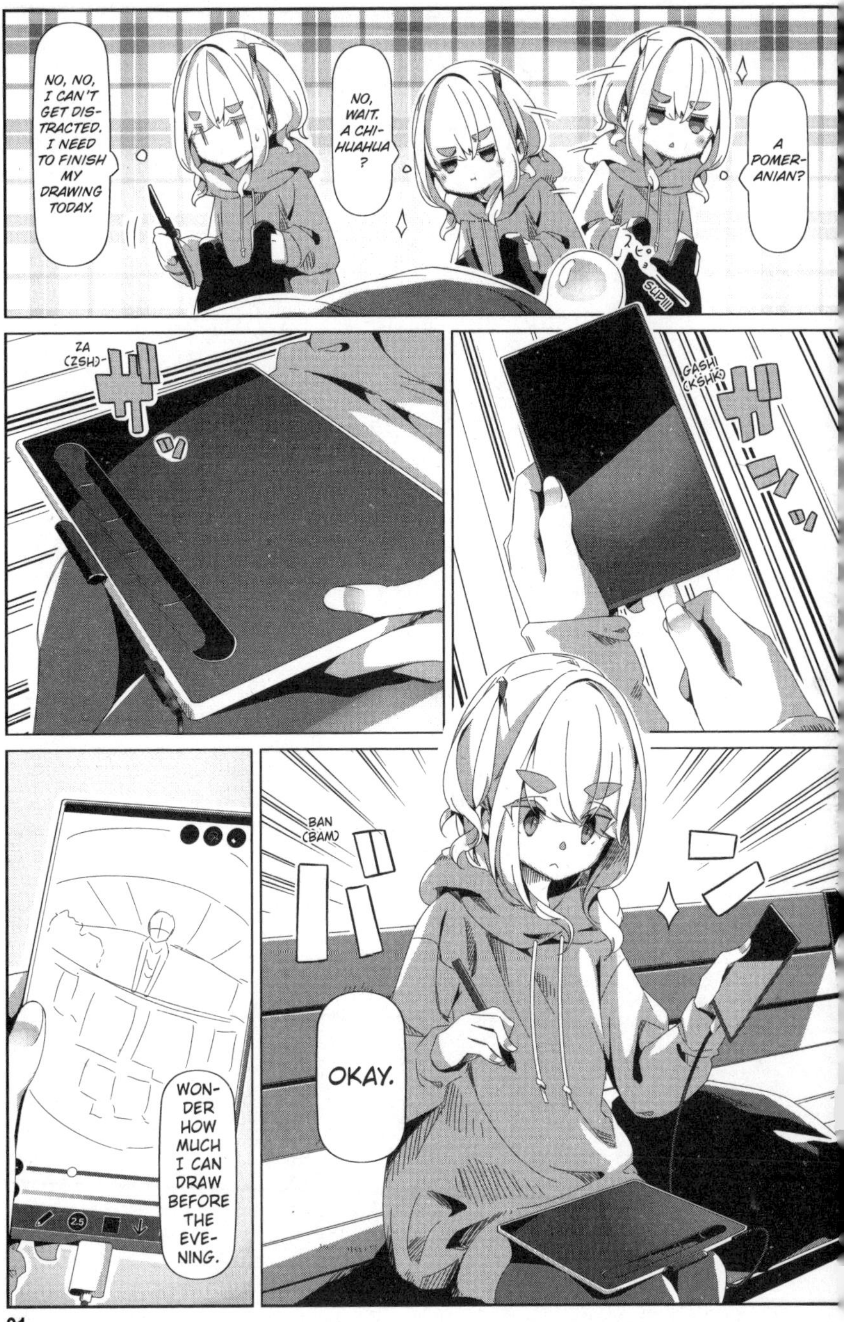
A POMERANIAN?
NO, WAIT. A CHIHUAHUA?
NO, NO, I CAN'T GET DISTRACTED. I NEED TO FINISH MY DRAWING TODAY.
SUPIII
GASHI (KSHK)
ZA (ZSH)
BAN (BAM)
OKAY.
WONDER HOW MUCH I CAN DRAW BEFORE THE EVENING.

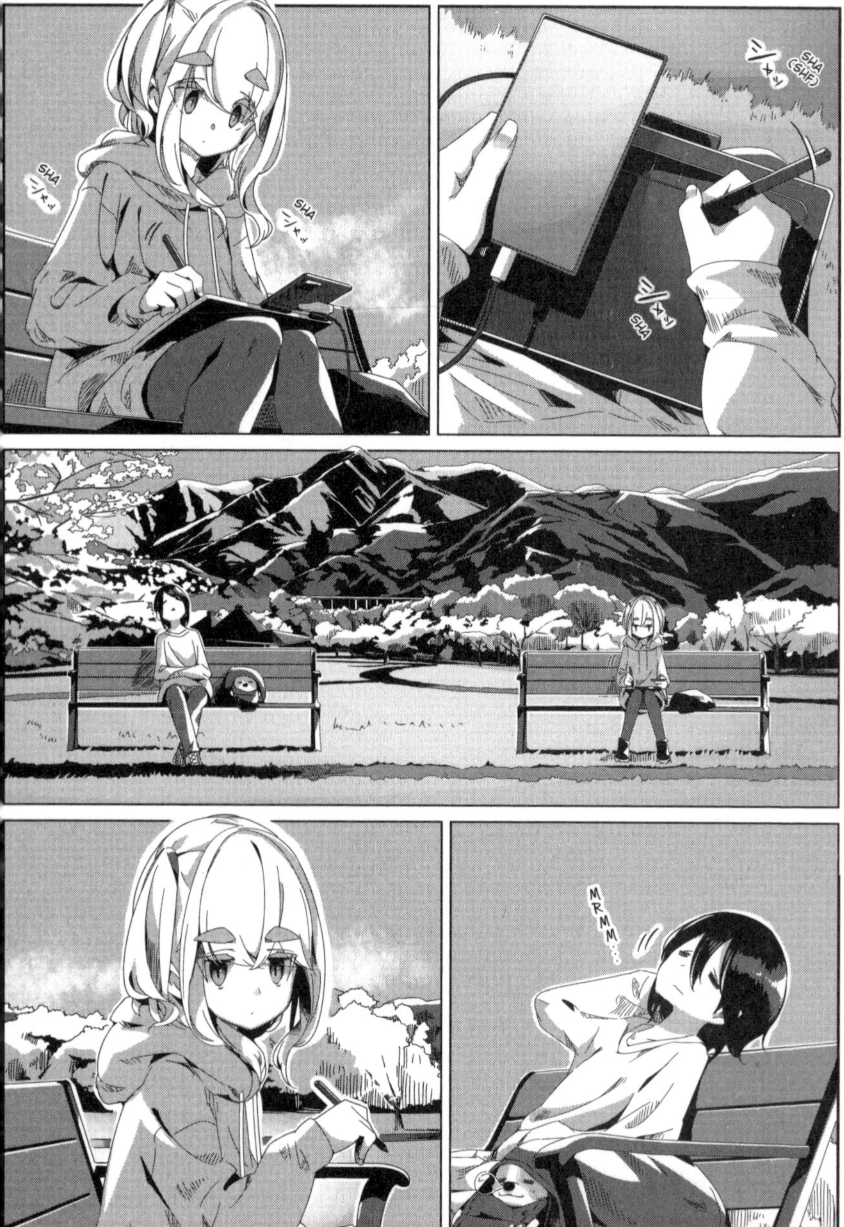
シャッ
SHA (SHF)
シャッ
SHA
SHA
シャッ
SHA
シャッ
MRMM...

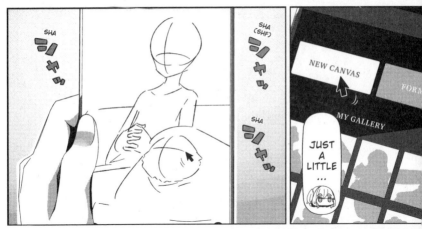

SHA

SHA
(SHF)

SHA

NEW CANVAS

FORM

MY GALLERY

JUST
A
LITTLE
...

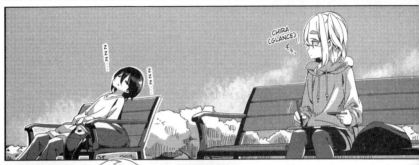

ZZZ...

ZZZ

CHIRA
(GLANCE)

PFFFF...

ZZZ

2.5

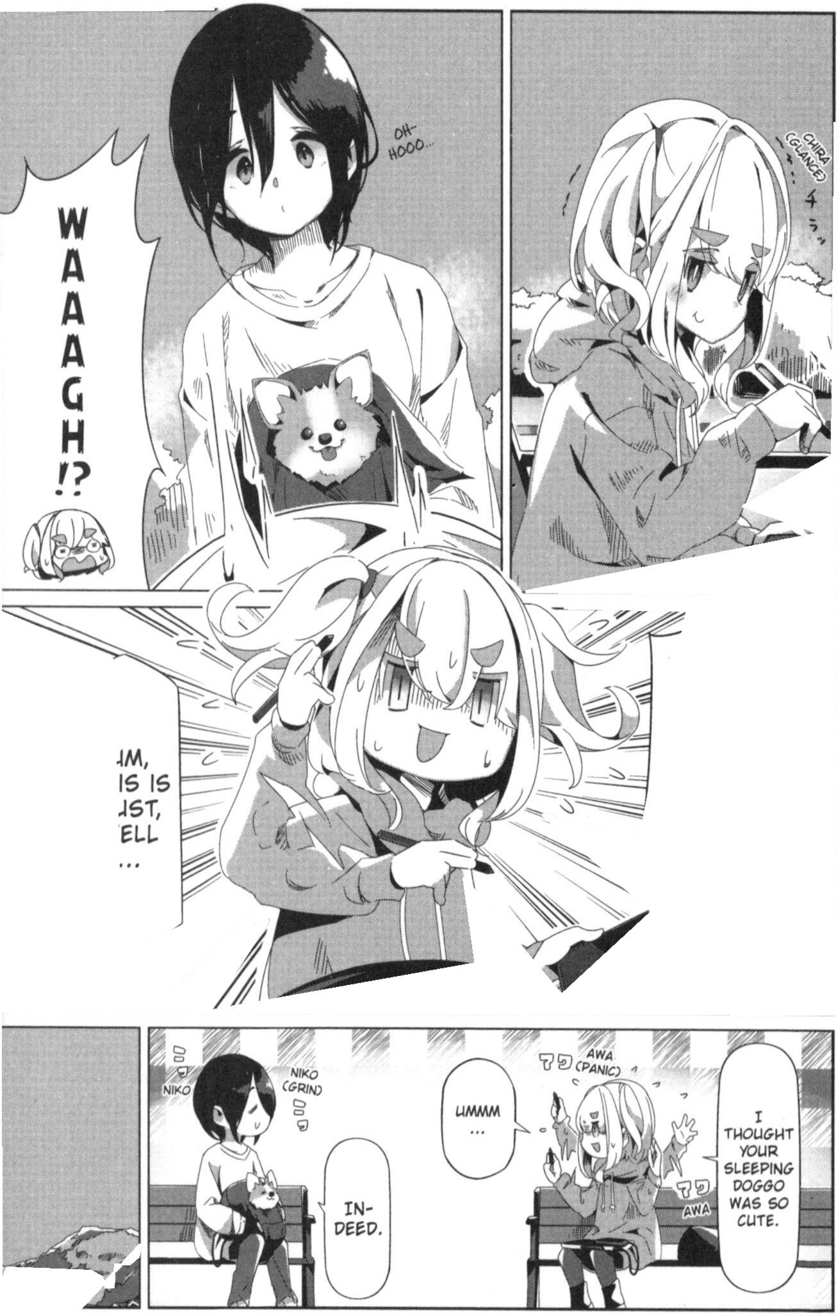
CHIRA (GLANCE)
チラッ
OH-HOOO...
WAAAAGH!?
M, IS IS ST, ELL ...
アワ AWA (PANIC)
I THOUGHT YOUR SLEEPING DOGGO WAS SO CUTE.
アワ AWA
UMMM ...
ニコ NIKO (GRIN)
ニコ NIKO
IN-DEED.

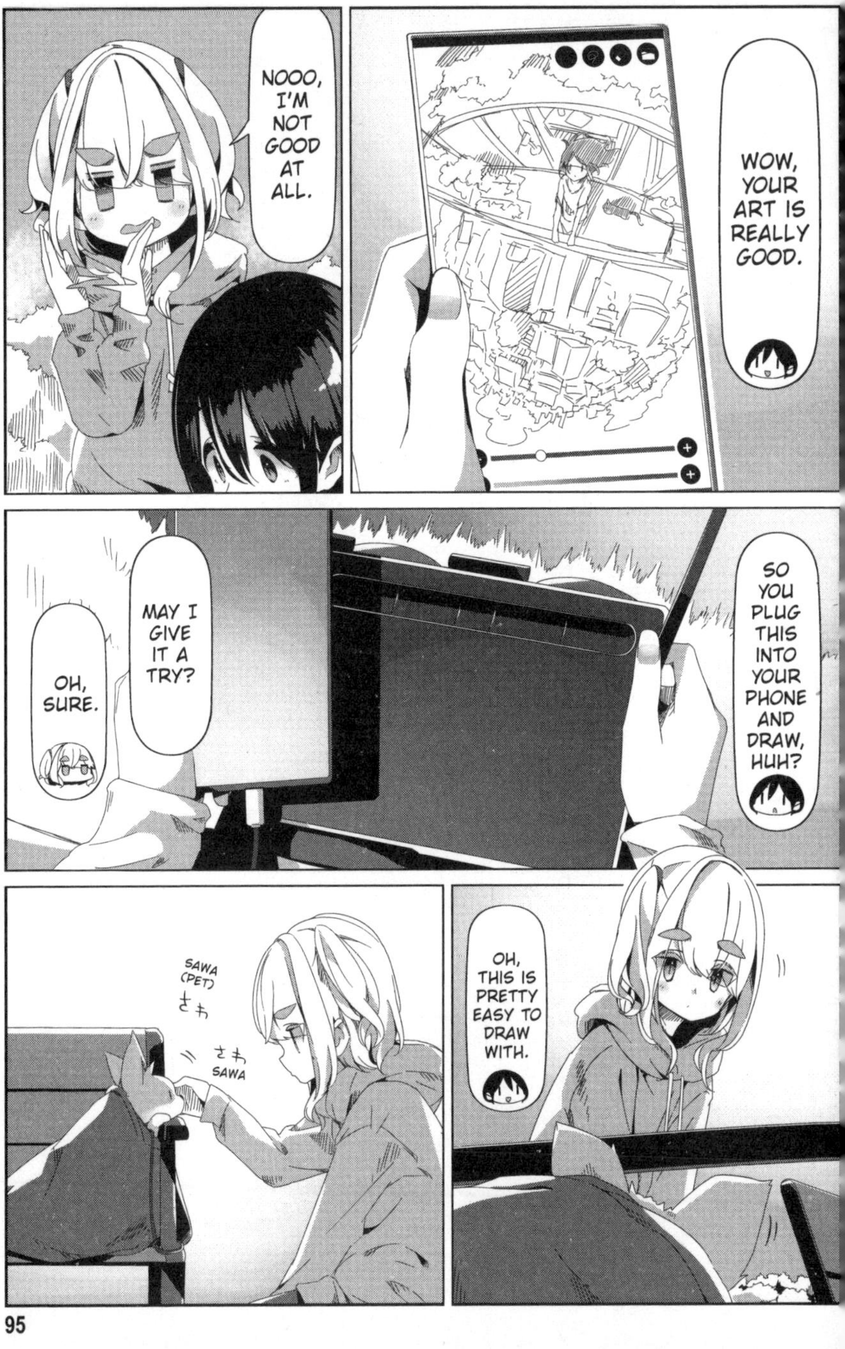
WOW, YOUR ART IS REALLY GOOD.
NOOO, I'M NOT GOOD AT ALL.
SO YOU PLUG THIS INTO YOUR PHONE AND DRAW, HUH?
MAY I GIVE IT A TRY?
OH, SURE.
OH, THIS IS PRETTY EASY TO DRAW WITH.
SAWA (PET)
さわ
さわ
SAWA

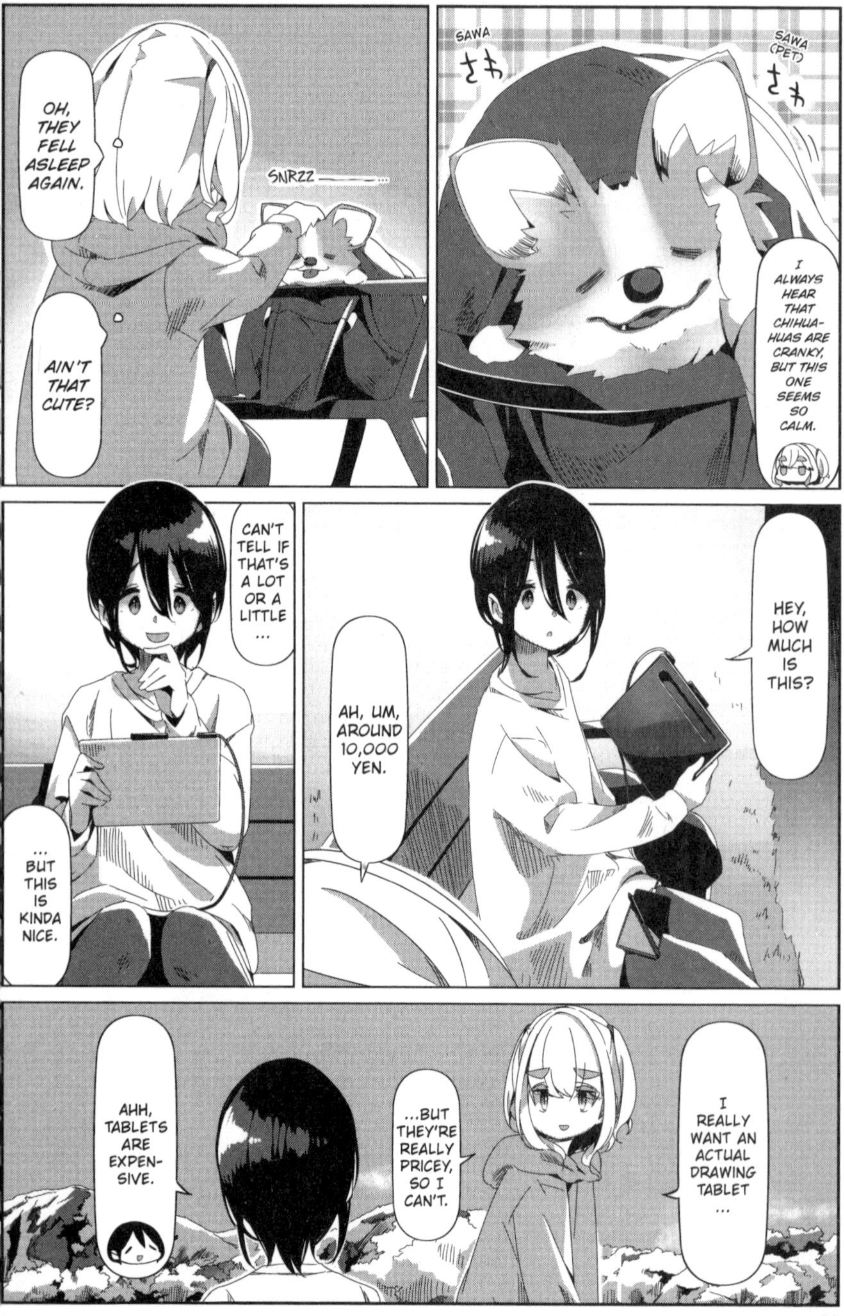
SAWA (PET)
さわ
SAWA
さわ
I ALWAYS HEAR THAT CHIHUAHUAS ARE CRANKY, BUT THIS ONE SEEMS SO CALM.
OH, THEY FELL ASLEEP AGAIN.
SNRZZ......
AIN'T THAT CUTE?
HEY, HOW MUCH IS THIS?
AH, UM, AROUND 10,000 YEN.
CAN'T TELL IF THAT'S A LOT OR A LITTLE...
...BUT THIS IS KINDA NICE.
I REALLY WANT AN ACTUAL DRAWING TABLET...
...BUT THEY'RE REALLY PRICEY, SO I CAN'T.
AHH, TABLETS ARE EXPEN-SIVE.

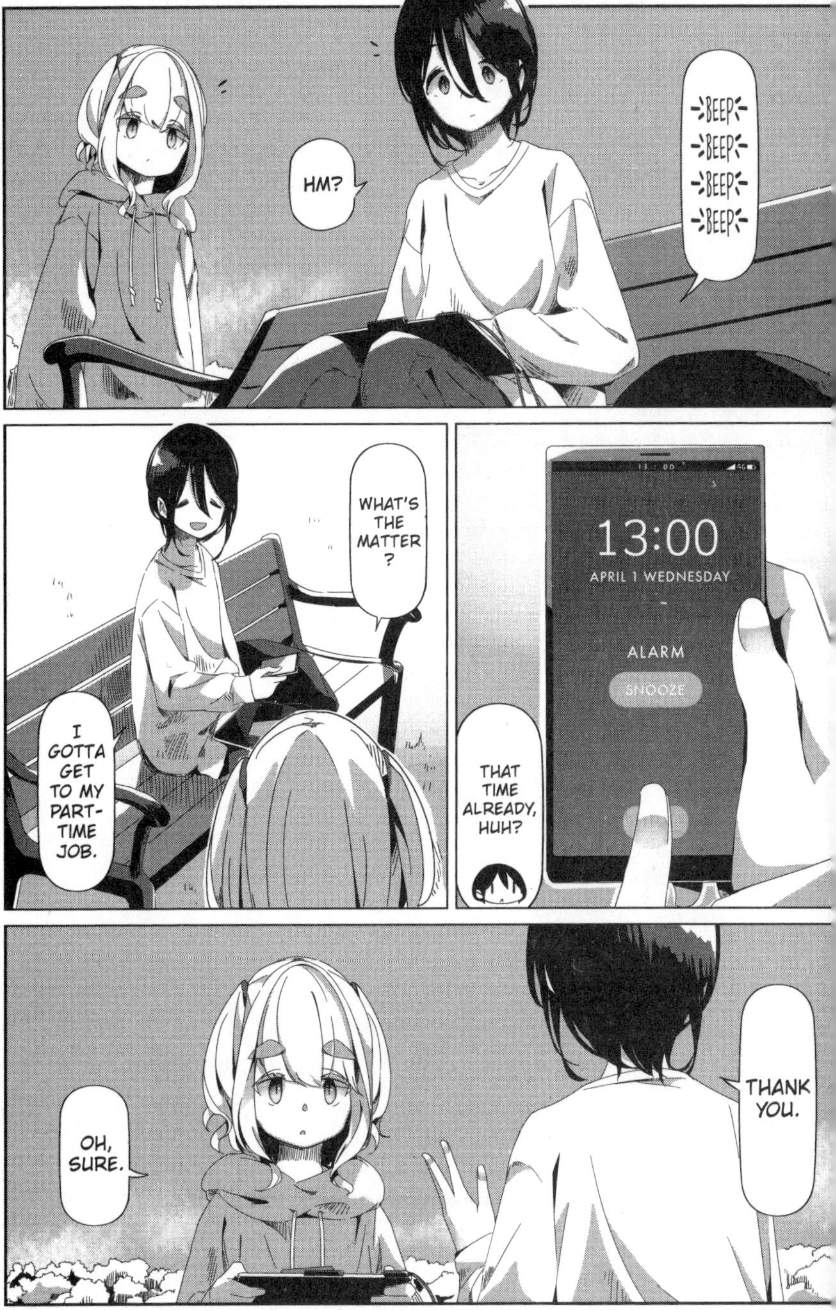
BEEP BEEP BEEP BEEP
HM?
13:00
APRIL 1 WEDNESDAY
ALARM
SNOOZE
THAT TIME ALREADY, HUH?
WHAT'S THE MATTER?
I GOTTA GET TO MY PART-TIME JOB.
THANK YOU.
OH, SURE.

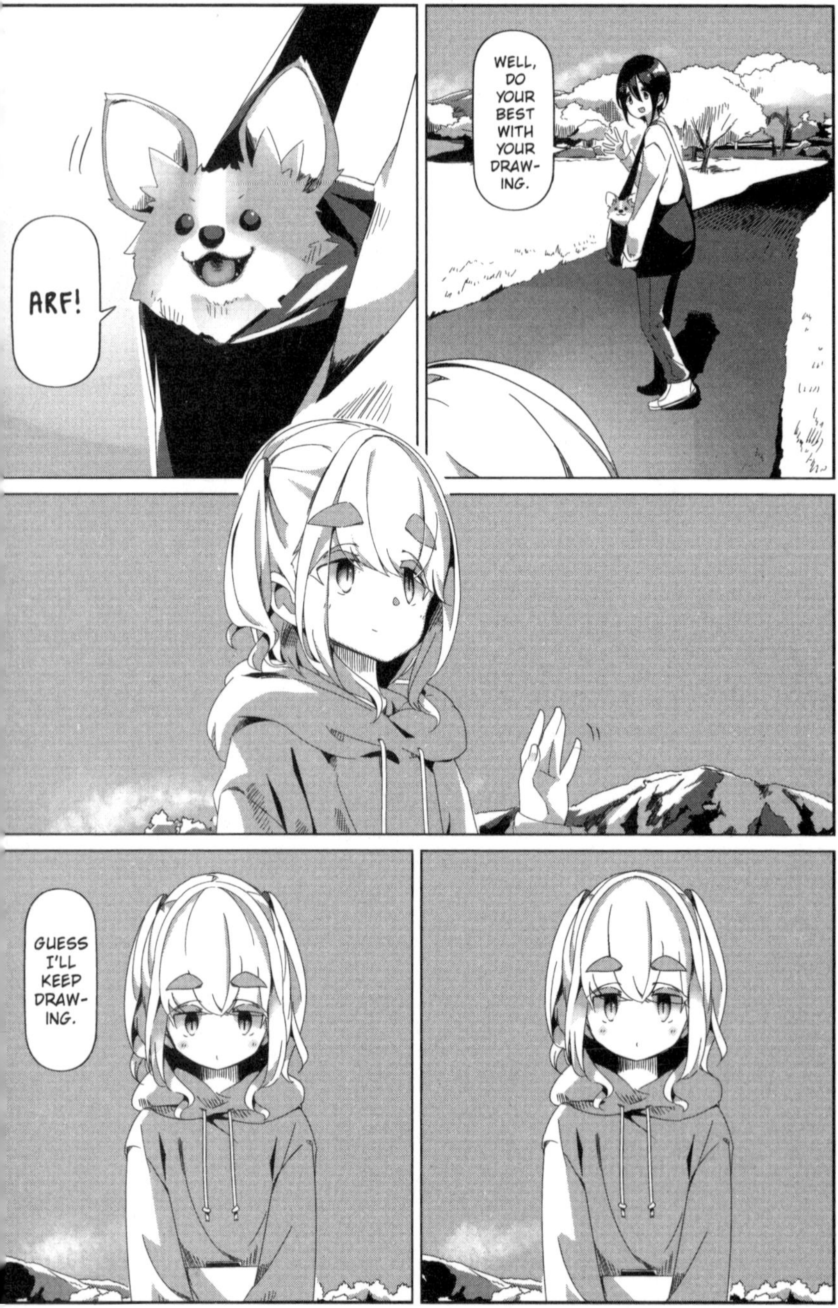
WELL, DO YOUR BEST WITH YOUR DRAW-ING.
ARF!
GUESS I'LL KEEP DRAW-ING.

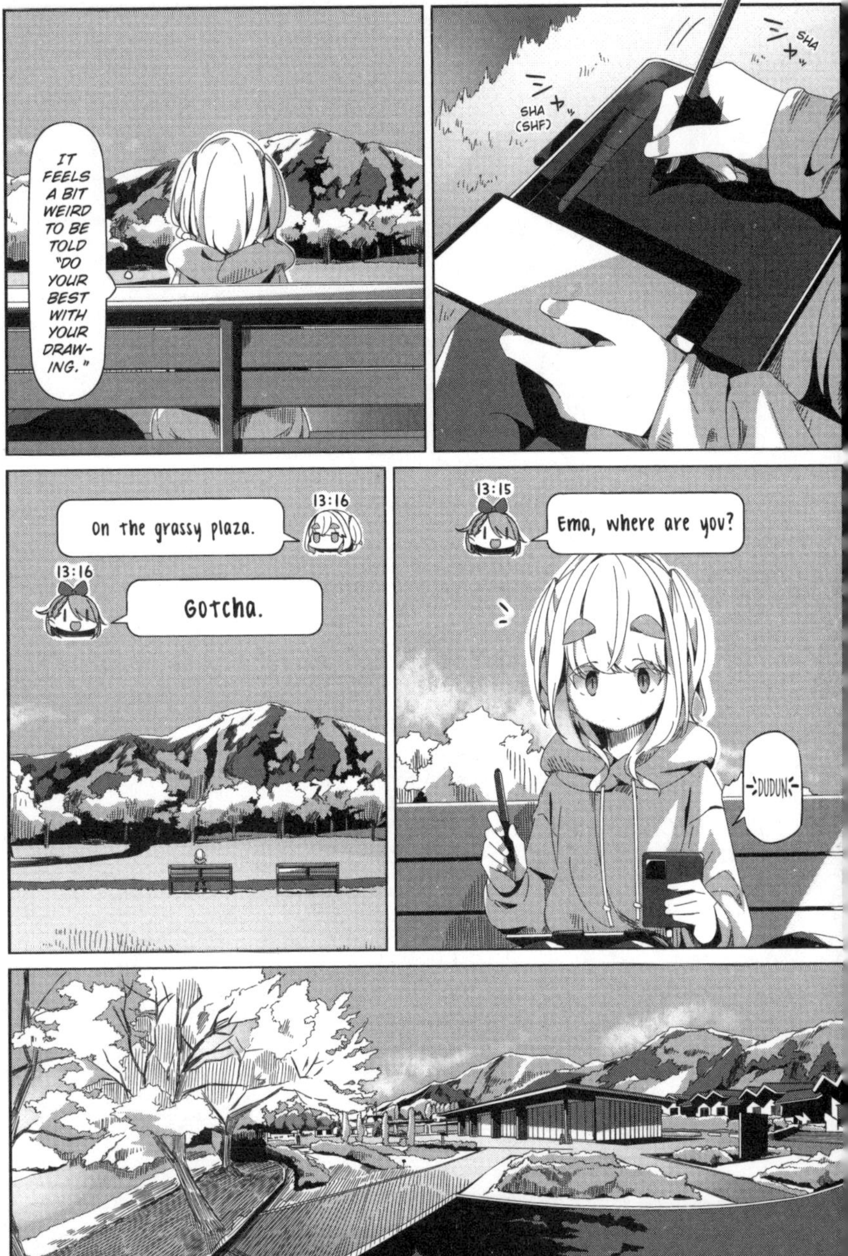

シャッ
SHA
シャッ
SHA (SHF)
IT FEELS A BIT WEIRD TO BE TOLD "DO YOUR BEST WITH YOUR DRAWING."
13:15
Ema, where are you?
DUDUN
13:16
On the grassy plaza.
13:16
Gotcha.

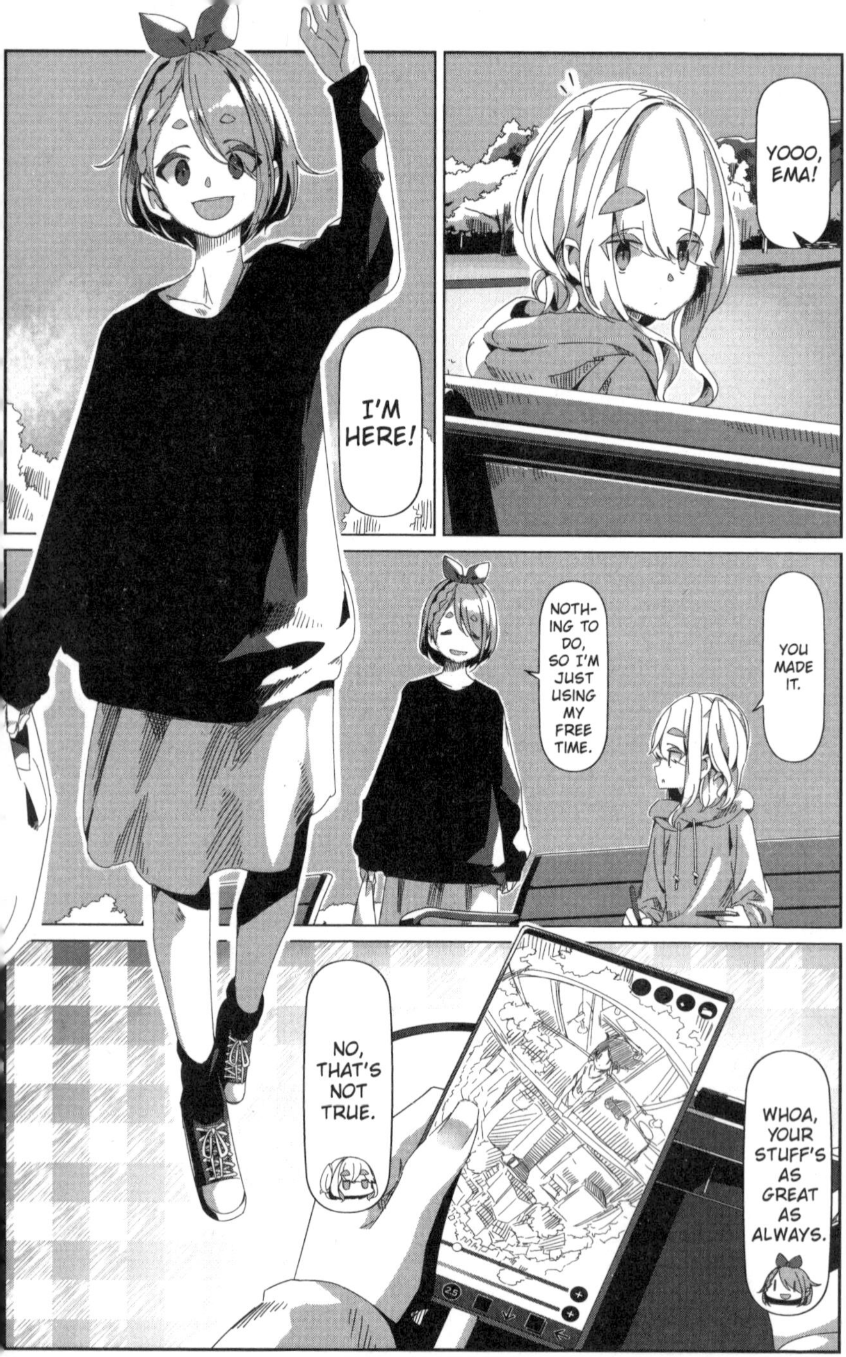
YOOO, EMA!
I'M HERE!
YOU MADE IT.
NOTHING TO DO, SO I'M JUST USING MY FREE TIME.
WHOA, YOUR STUFF'S AS GREAT AS ALWAYS.
NO, THAT'S NOT TRUE.

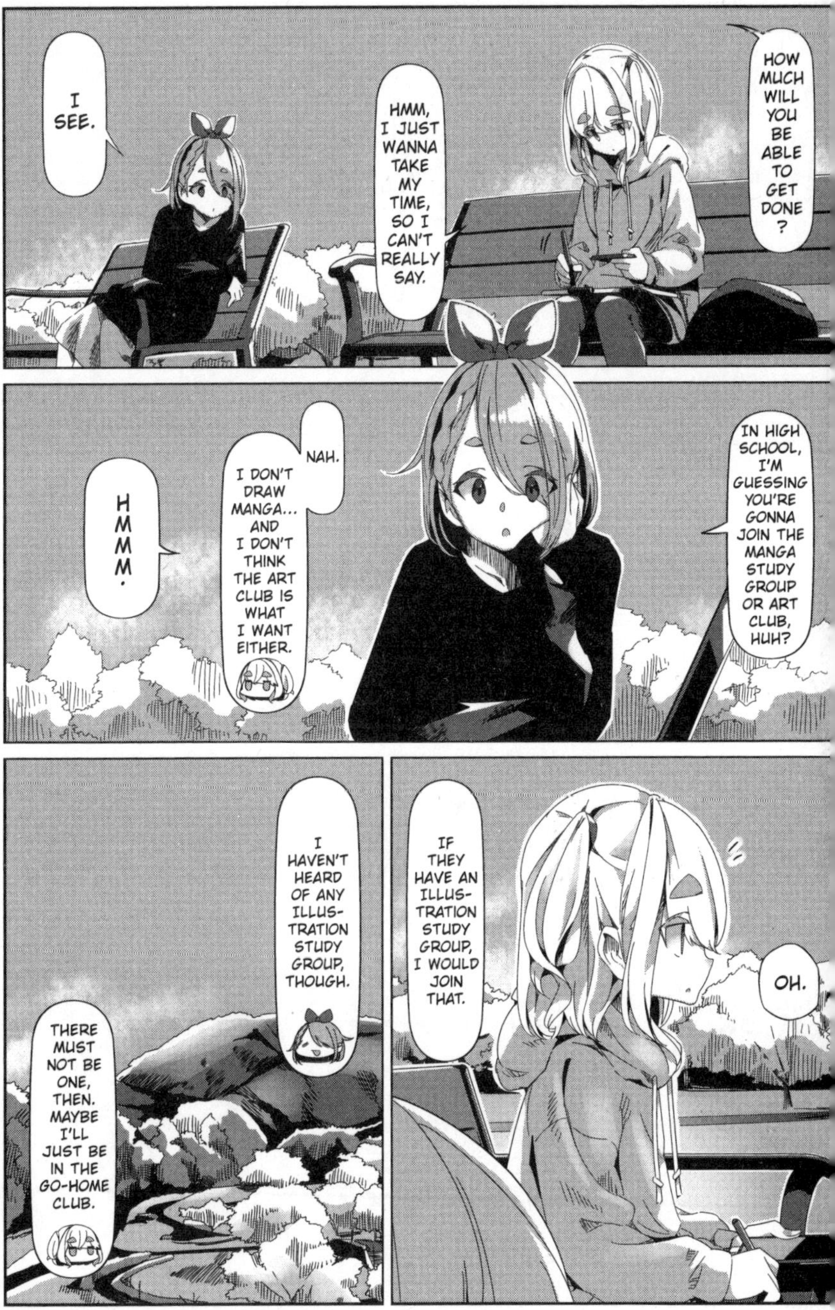
HOW MUCH WILL YOU BE ABLE TO GET DONE?
HMM, I JUST WANNA TAKE MY TIME, SO I CAN'T REALLY SAY.
I SEE.
IN HIGH SCHOOL, I'M GUESSING YOU'RE GONNA JOIN THE MANGA STUDY GROUP OR ART CLUB, HUH?
NAH.
I DON'T DRAW MANGA... AND I DON'T THINK THE ART CLUB IS WHAT I WANT EITHER.
HMMM.
OH.
IF THEY HAVE AN ILLUS-TRATION STUDY GROUP, I WOULD JOIN THAT.
I HAVEN'T HEARD OF ANY ILLUS-TRATION STUDY GROUP, THOUGH.
THERE MUST NOT BE ONE, THEN. MAYBE I'LL JUST BE IN THE GO-HOME CLUB.

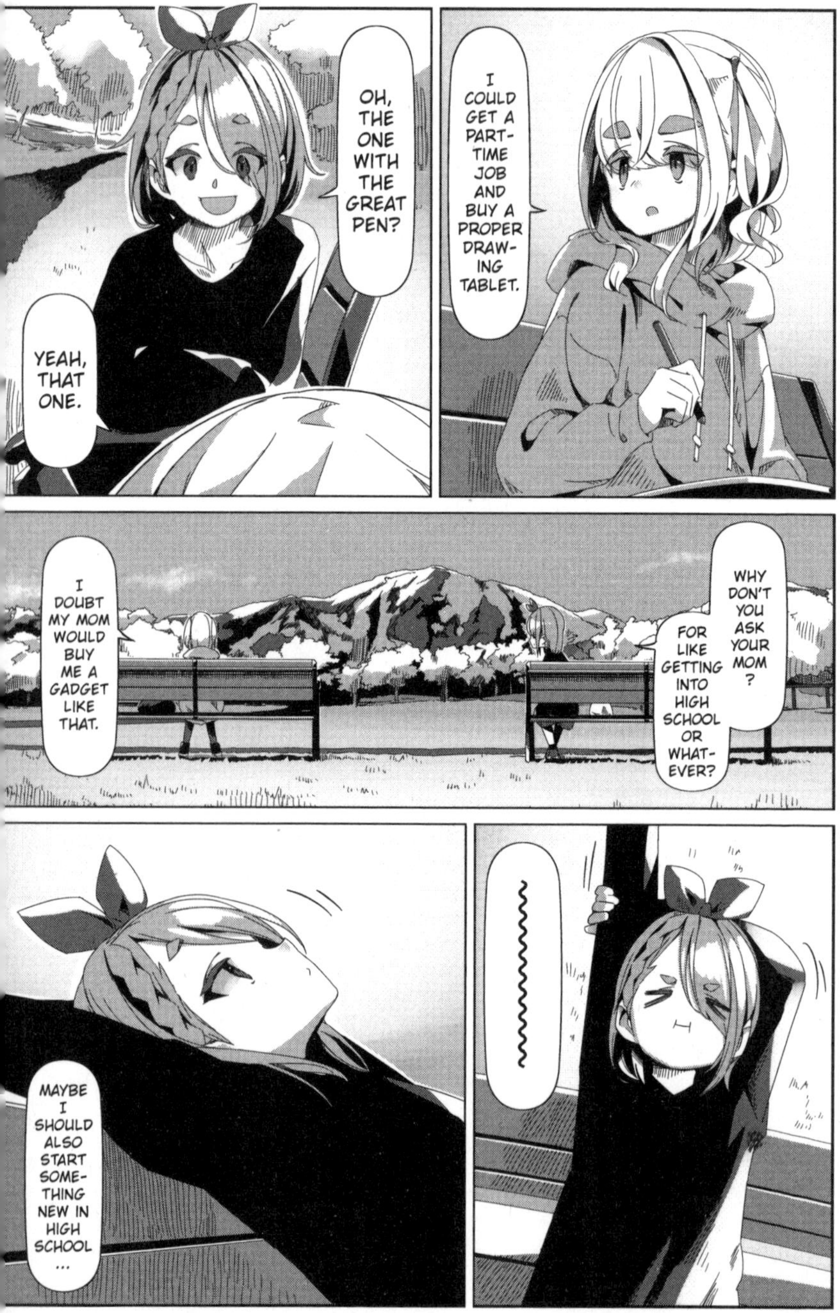
I COULD GET A PART-TIME JOB AND BUY A PROPER DRAWING TABLET.
OH, THE ONE WITH THE GREAT PEN?
YEAH, THAT ONE.
WHY DON'T YOU ASK YOUR MOM?
FOR LIKE GETTING INTO HIGH SCHOOL OR WHATEVER?
I DOUBT MY MOM WOULD BUY ME A GADGET LIKE THAT.
MAYBE I SHOULD ALSO START SOMETHING NEW IN HIGH SCHOOL ...

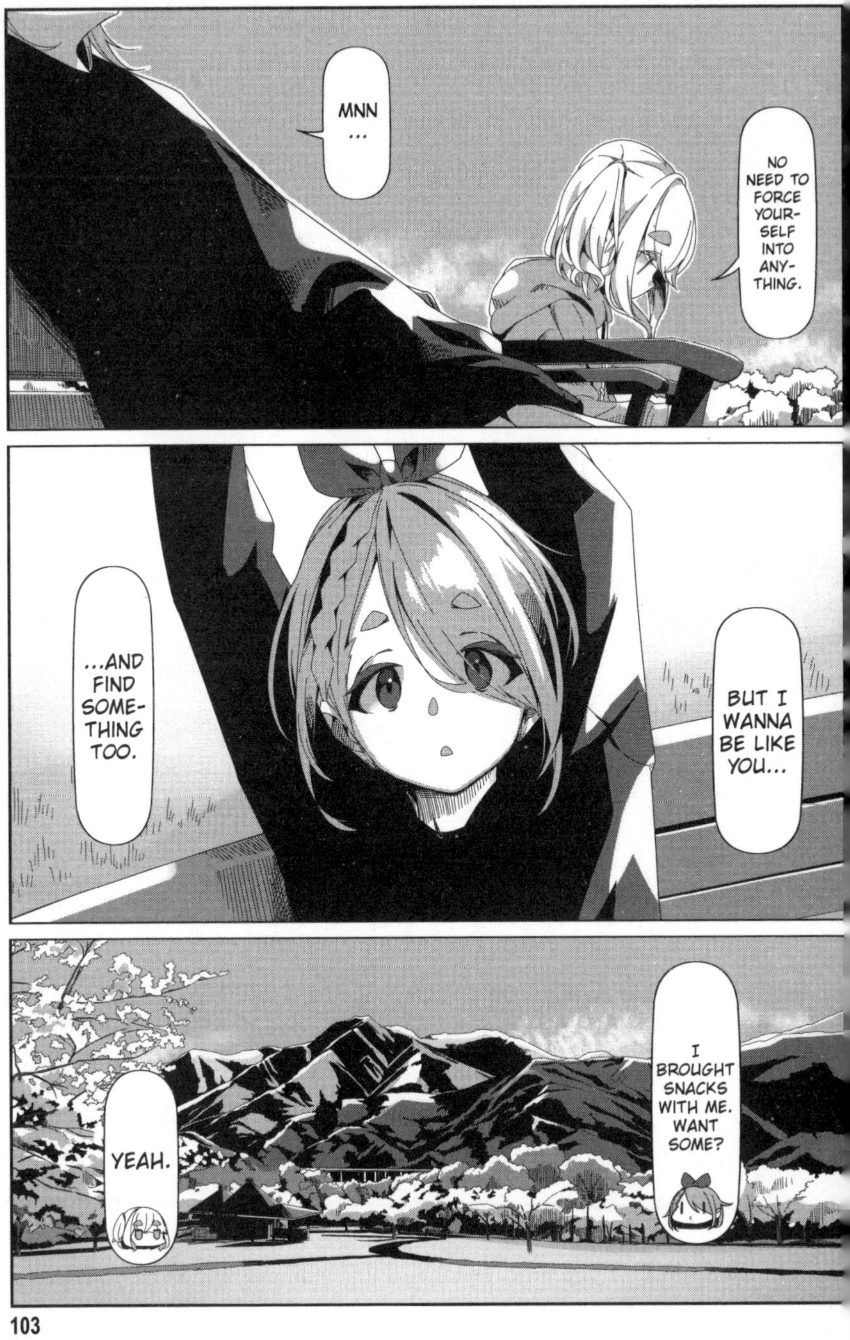
NO NEED TO FORCE YOURSELF INTO ANYTHING.
MNN ...
BUT I WANNA BE LIKE YOU...
...AND FIND SOMETHING TOO.
I BROUGHT SNACKS WITH ME. WANT SOME?
YEAH.

SIGN: IDE

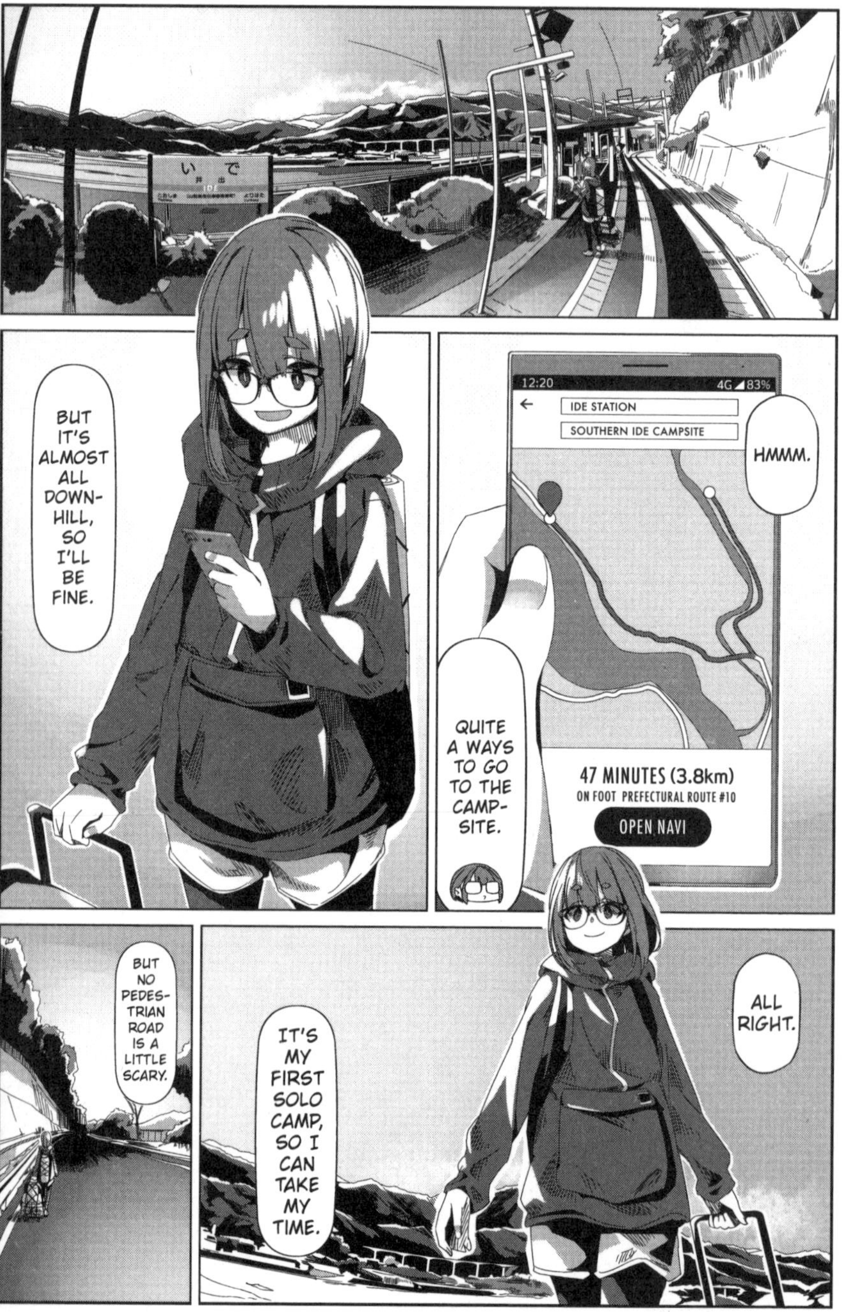

いで
井出
IDE
HMMM.
12:20
4G 83%
IDE STATION
SOUTHERN IDE CAMPSITE
47 MINUTES (3.8km)
ON FOOT PREFECTURAL ROUTE #10
OPEN NAVI
QUITE A WAYS TO GO TO THE CAMPSITE.
BUT IT'S ALMOST ALL DOWNHILL, SO I'LL BE FINE.
ALL RIGHT.
IT'S MY FIRST SOLO CAMP, SO I CAN TAKE MY TIME.
BUT NO PEDESTRIAN ROAD IS A LITTLE SCARY.

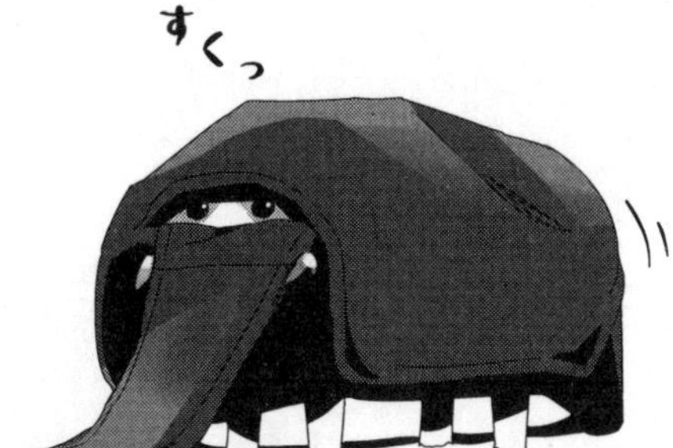
SUKU
(POP)
すくっ

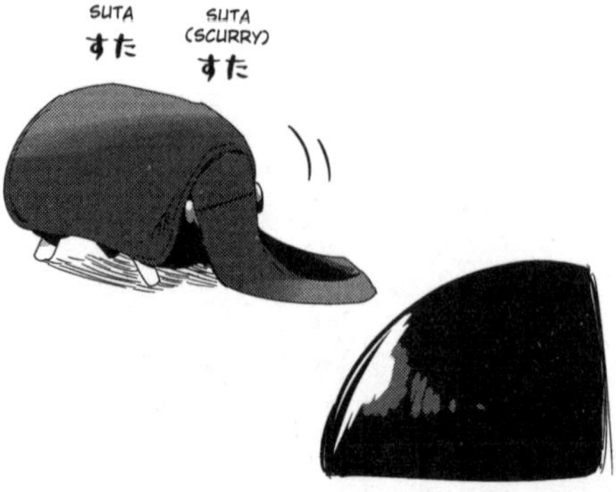
SUTA
すた
SUTA
(SCURRY)
すた

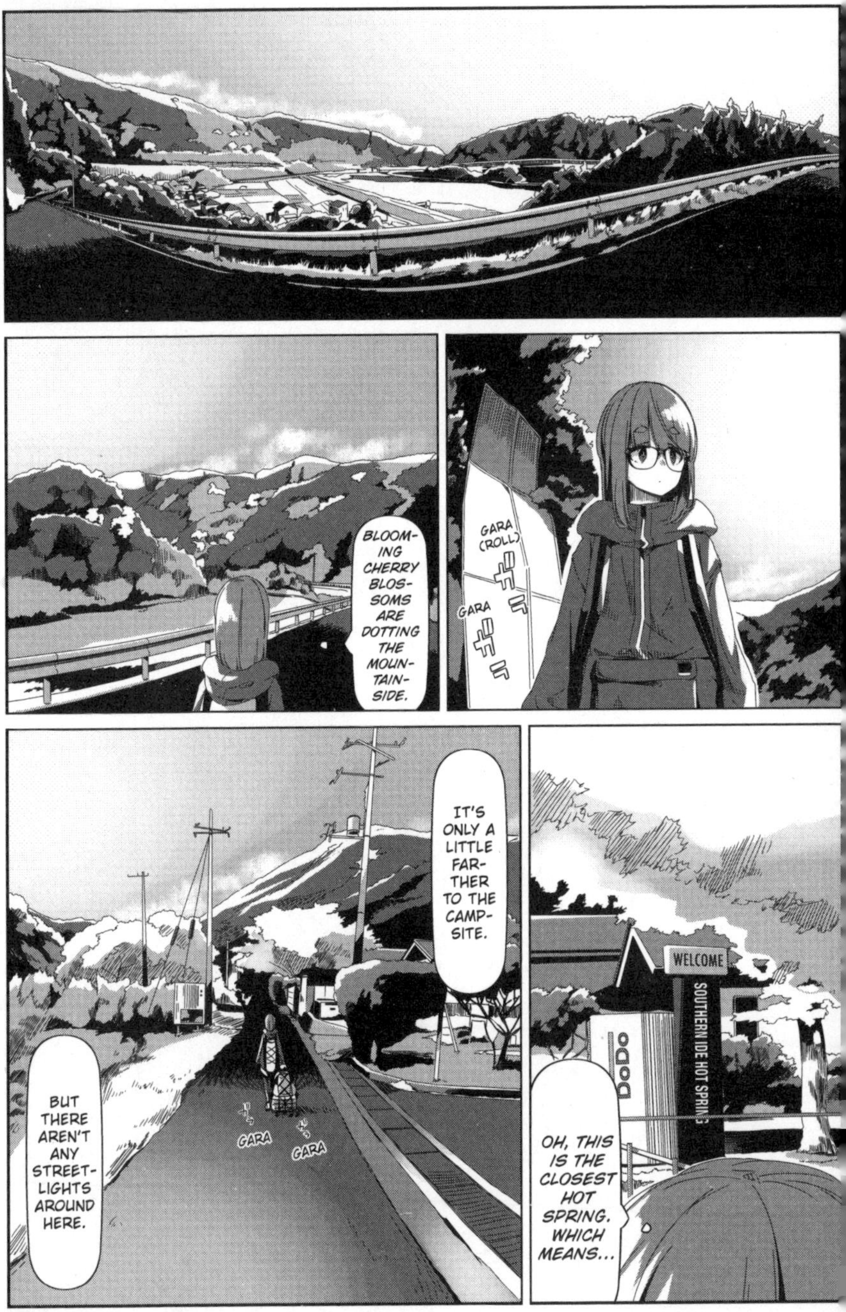
GARA (ROLL)
GARA
BLOOMING CHERRY BLOSSOMS ARE DOTTING THE MOUNTAINSIDE.
WELCOME
SOUTHERN IDE HOT SPRING
DoDo
OH, THIS IS THE CLOSEST HOT SPRING. WHICH MEANS...
IT'S ONLY A LITTLE FARTHER TO THE CAMPSITE.
BUT THERE AREN'T ANY STREETLIGHTS AROUND HERE.
GARA
GARA

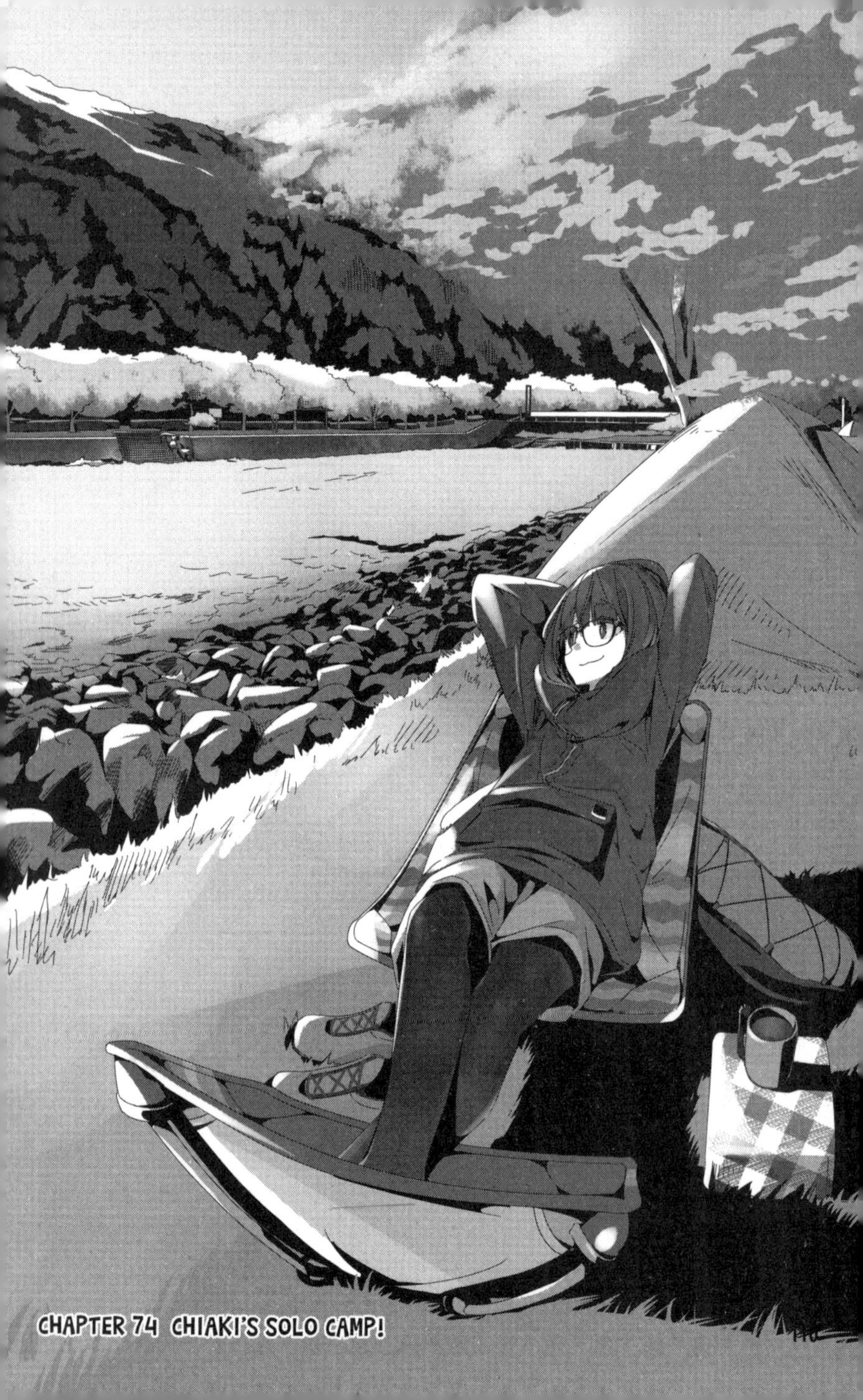

CHAPTER 74 CHIAKI'S SOLO CAMP!

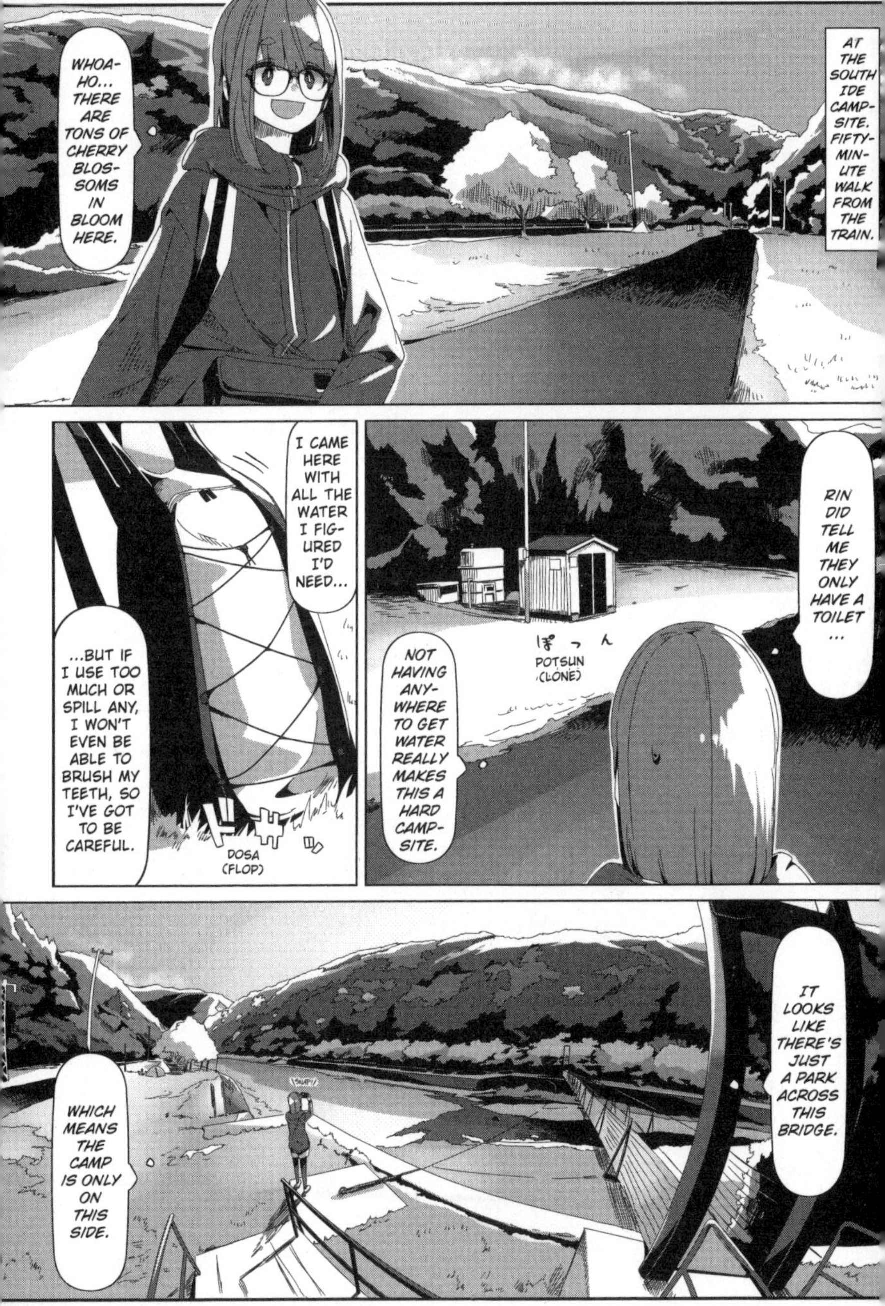
AT THE SOUTH IDE CAMPSITE. FIFTY-MINUTE WALK FROM THE TRAIN.
WHOA-HO... THERE ARE TONS OF CHERRY BLOSSOMS IN BLOOM HERE.
RIN DID TELL ME THEY ONLY HAVE A TOILET...
NOT HAVING ANYWHERE TO GET WATER REALLY MAKES THIS A HARD CAMPSITE.
ぽつん
POTSUN (LONE)
I CAME HERE WITH ALL THE WATER I FIGURED I'D NEED...
...BUT IF I USE TOO MUCH OR SPILL ANY, I WON'T EVEN BE ABLE TO BRUSH MY TEETH, SO I'VE GOT TO BE CAREFUL.
DOSA (FLOP)
IT LOOKS LIKE THERE'S JUST A PARK ACROSS THIS BRIDGE.
WHICH MEANS THE CAMP IS ONLY ON THIS SIDE.

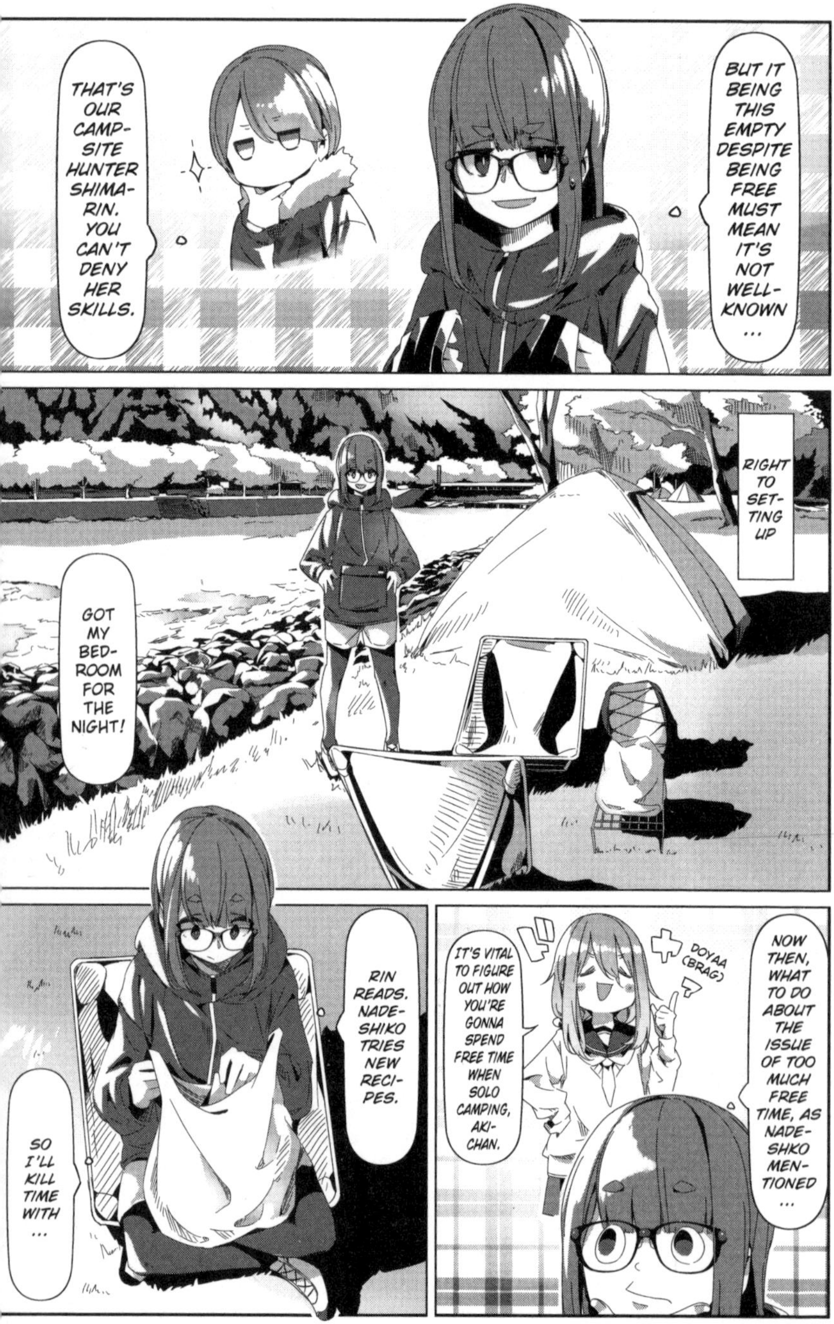

BUT IT BEING THIS EMPTY DESPITE BEING FREE MUST MEAN IT'S NOT WELL-KNOWN...
THAT'S OUR CAMPSITE HUNTER SHIMARIN. YOU CAN'T DENY HER SKILLS.
RIGHT TO SETTING UP
GOT MY BEDROOM FOR THE NIGHT!
NOW THEN, WHAT TO DO ABOUT THE ISSUE OF TOO MUCH FREE TIME, AS NADESHIKO MENTIONED...
DOYAA (BRAG)
IT'S VITAL TO FIGURE OUT HOW YOU'RE GONNA SPEND FREE TIME WHEN SOLO CAMPING, AKI-CHAN.
RIN READS. NADESHIKO TRIES NEW RECIPES.
SO I'LL KILL TIME WITH...

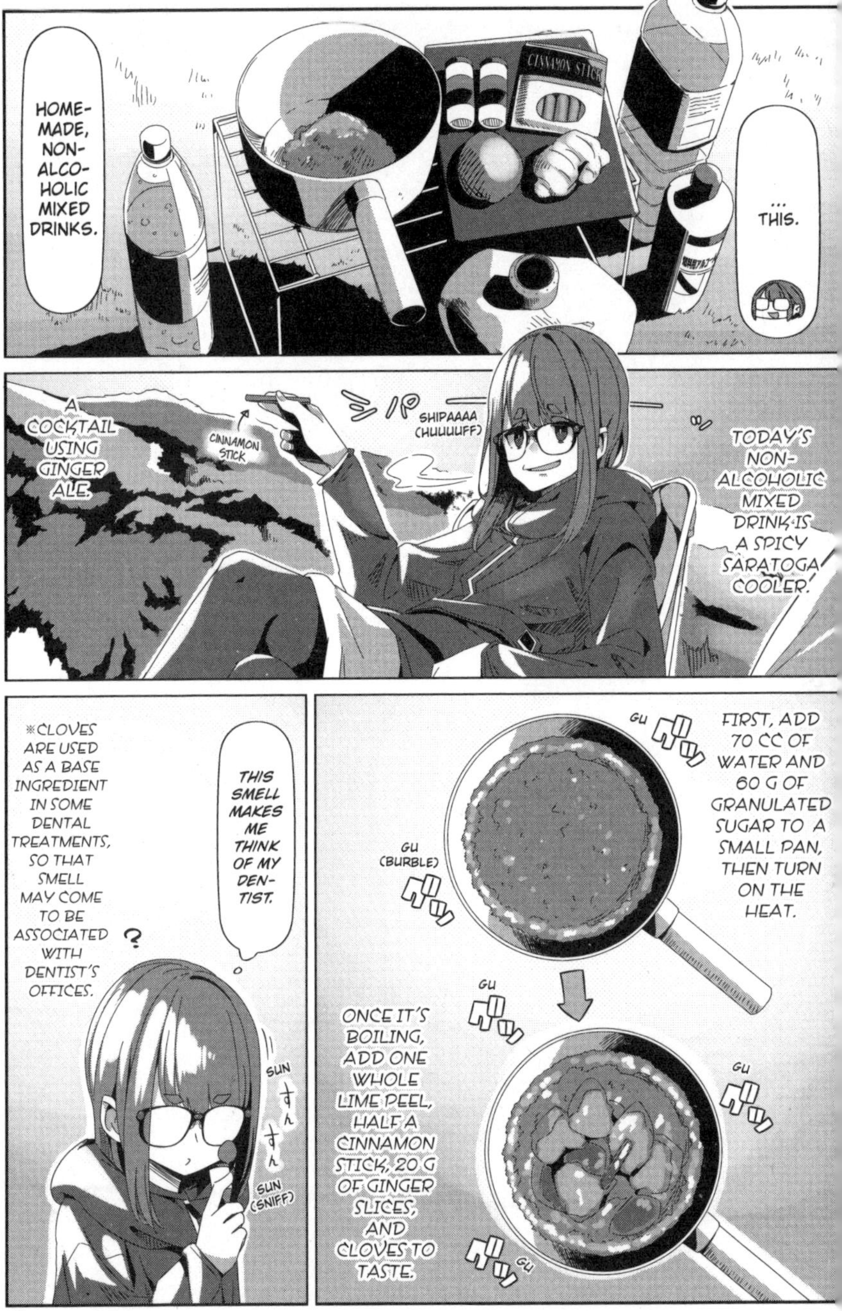
... THIS.
HOME-MADE, NON-ALCOHOLIC MIXED DRINKS.
TODAY'S NON-ALCOHOLIC MIXED DRINK IS A SPICY SARATOGA COOLER.
SHIPAAAA (HUUUUFF)
CINNAMON STICK
A COCKTAIL USING GINGER ALE.
FIRST, ADD 70 CC OF WATER AND 60 G OF GRANULATED SUGAR TO A SMALL PAN, THEN TURN ON THE HEAT.
GU
GU (BURBLE)
GU
ONCE IT'S BOILING, ADD ONE WHOLE LIME PEEL, HALF A CINNAMON STICK, 20 G OF GINGER SLICES, AND CLOVES TO TASTE.
GU
GU
THIS SMELL MAKES ME THINK OF MY DENTIST.
?
SUN
SUN (SNIFF)
※CLOVES ARE USED AS A BASE INGREDIENT IN SOME DENTAL TREATMENTS, SO THAT SMELL MAY COME TO BE ASSOCIATED WITH DENTIST'S OFFICES.

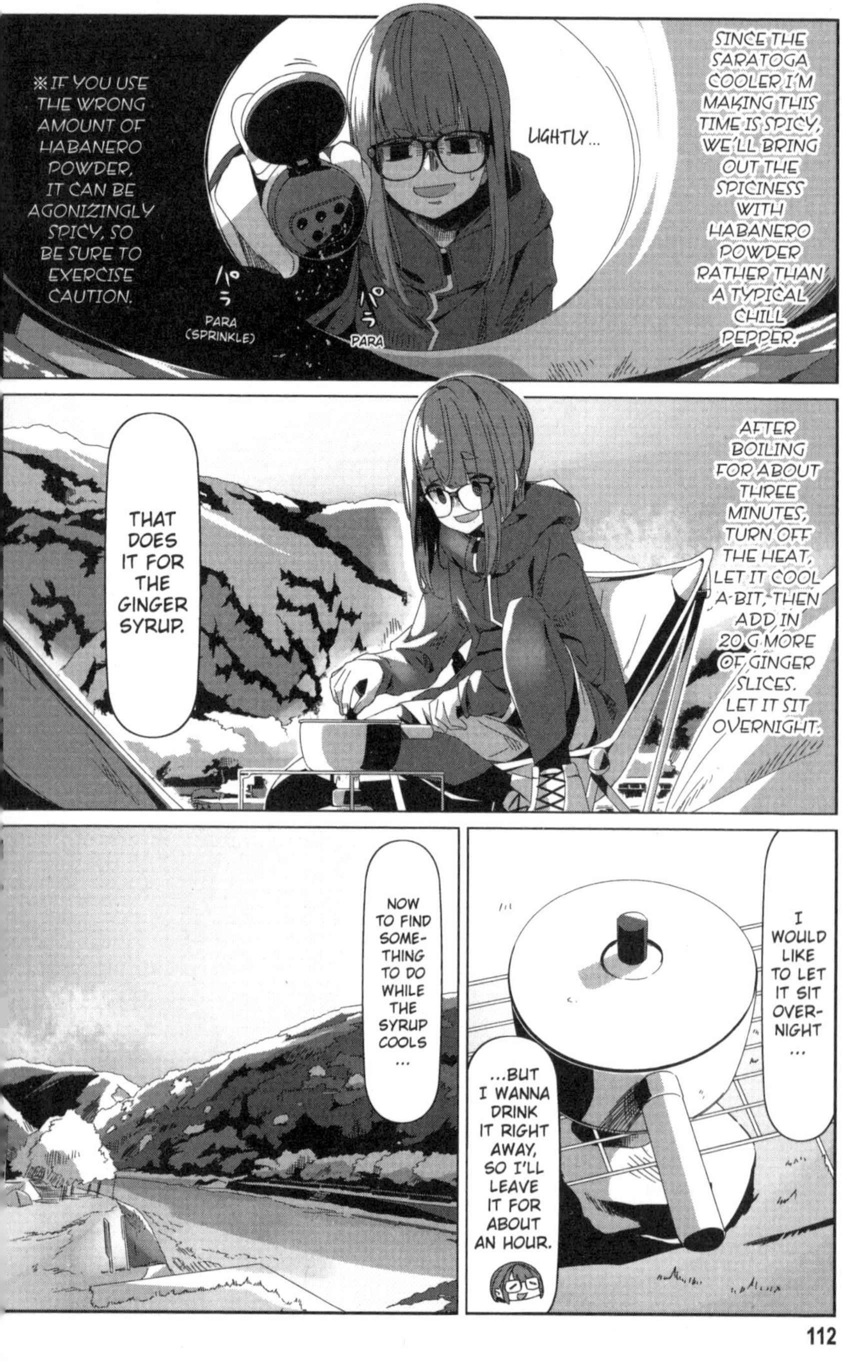
SINCE THE SARATOGA COOLER I'M MAKING THIS TIME IS SPICY, WE'LL BRING OUT THE SPICINESS WITH HABANERO POWDER RATHER THAN A TYPICAL CHILL PEPPER.
LIGHTLY...
※IF YOU USE THE WRONG AMOUNT OF HABANERO POWDER, IT CAN BE AGONIZINGLY SPICY, SO BE SURE TO EXERCISE CAUTION.
パラ
PARA
パラ
PARA (SPRINKLE)
AFTER BOILING FOR ABOUT THREE MINUTES, TURN OFF THE HEAT, LET IT COOL A BIT, THEN ADD IN 20 G MORE OF GINGER SLICES. LET IT SIT OVERNIGHT.
THAT DOES IT FOR THE GINGER SYRUP.
I WOULD LIKE TO LET IT SIT OVERNIGHT...
...BUT I WANNA DRINK IT RIGHT AWAY, SO I'LL LEAVE IT FOR ABOUT AN HOUR.
NOW TO FIND SOMETHING TO DO WHILE THE SYRUP COOLS...

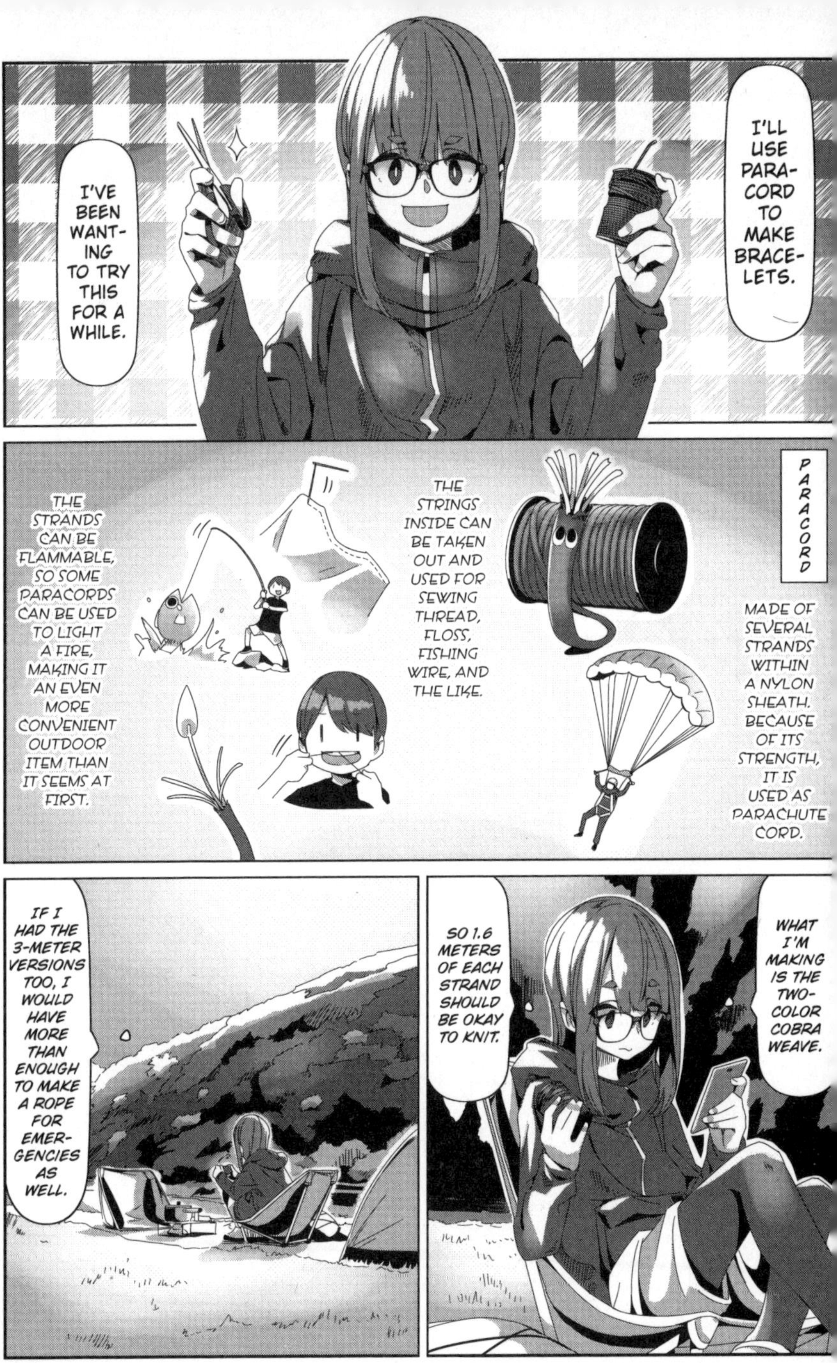
I'LL USE PARACORD TO MAKE BRACELETS.
I'VE BEEN WANTING TO TRY THIS FOR A WHILE.
PARACORD
MADE OF SEVERAL STRANDS WITHIN A NYLON SHEATH. BECAUSE OF ITS STRENGTH, IT IS USED AS PARACHUTE CORD.
THE STRINGS INSIDE CAN BE TAKEN OUT AND USED FOR SEWING THREAD, FLOSS, FISHING WIRE, AND THE LIKE.
THE STRANDS CAN BE FLAMMABLE, SO SOME PARACORDS CAN BE USED TO LIGHT A FIRE, MAKING IT AN EVEN MORE CONVENIENT OUTDOOR ITEM THAN IT SEEMS AT FIRST.
WHAT I'M MAKING IS THE TWO-COLOR COBRA WEAVE.
SO 1.6 METERS OF EACH STRAND SHOULD BE OKAY TO KNIT.
IF I HAD THE 3-METER VERSIONS TOO, I WOULD HAVE MORE THAN ENOUGH TO MAKE A ROPE FOR EMERGENCIES AS WELL.

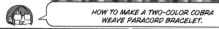

HOW TO MAKE A TWO-COLOR COBRA WEAVE PARACORD BRACELET.
① FIRST, USE A LIGHTER TO HEAT THE ENDS OF THE TWO STRANDS UNTIL THEY MELT A LITTLE...
JIJI (CH-CHK)
ONCE THEY'VE BEGUN TO MELT, YOU CAN PRESS THEM TOGETHER.
※BE CAREFUL NOT TO BURN YOURSELF.
GYU (SQUISH)
④ NEXT, WEAVE THE TWO STRANDS IN ALTERNATING KNOTS TOWARD THE CENTRAL FOLD.
② NEXT, FOLD IN HALF A SHORT BIT AWAY FROM THE CENTRAL FUSED POINT TO MAKE TWO STRANDS.
⑤ TAKE THE LOWER OF THE TWO STRANDS AND BRING IT OVER BOTH.
THE LOWER OF THE TWO STRANDS SHOULD BE COVERED ALREADY BY THE ONE STRAND, SO FEEDING THIS STRAND THROUGH THE LOOP AND KNOTTING IS THE IMPORTANT POINT HERE.
③ MAKE A LOOP AS SHOWN IN THE PICTURE, SLIGHTLY SMALLER THAN THE CIRCUMFERENCE OF YOUR WRIST, THEN KNOT.
SLIGHTLY SHORTER THAN THE OUTER CIRCUMFERENCE OF THE WRIST.
GYU
⑥ WHEN YOU REACH THE END, PASS THE STRANDS THROUGH THE LOOPS AS SHOWN.

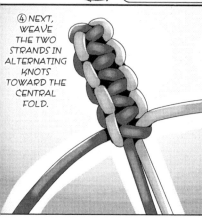

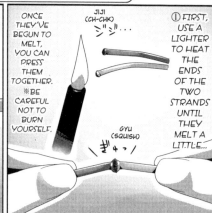

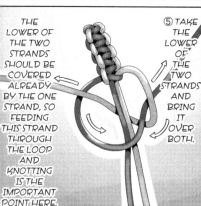

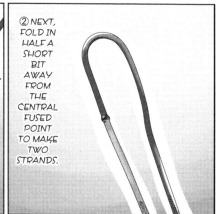

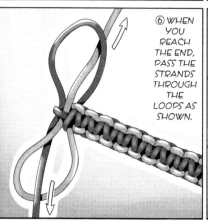

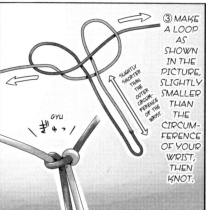

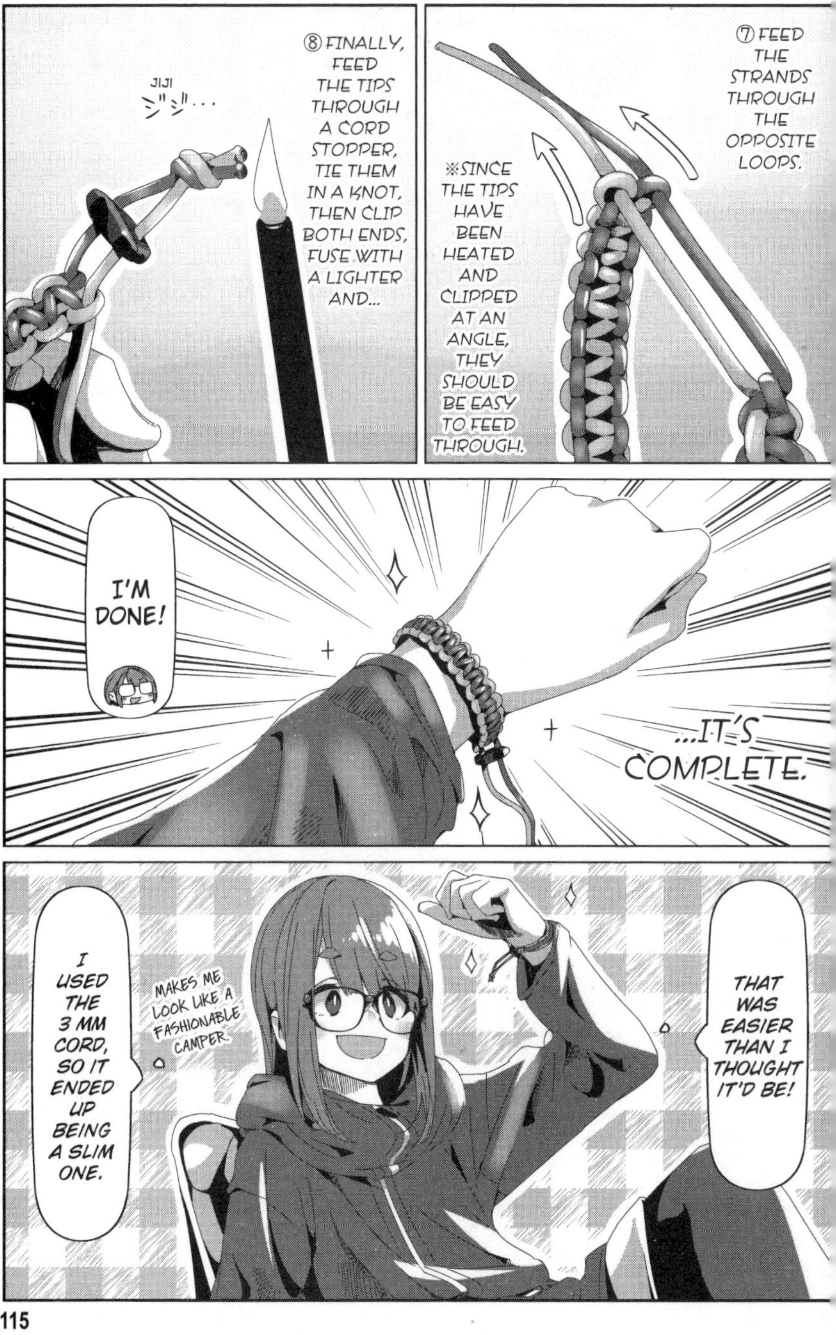
⑦ FEED THE STRANDS THROUGH THE OPPOSITE LOOPS.
※SINCE THE TIPS HAVE BEEN HEATED AND CLIPPED AT AN ANGLE, THEY SHOULD BE EASY TO FEED THROUGH.
⑧ FINALLY, FEED THE TIPS THROUGH A CORD STOPPER, TIE THEM IN A KNOT, THEN CLIP BOTH ENDS, FUSE WITH A LIGHTER AND...
JIJI
ジジ・・・
...IT'S COMPLETE.
I'M DONE!
THAT WAS EASIER THAN I THOUGHT IT'D BE!
MAKES ME LOOK LIKE A FASHIONABLE CAMPER.
I USED THE 3 MM CORD, SO IT ENDED UP BEING A SLIM ONE.

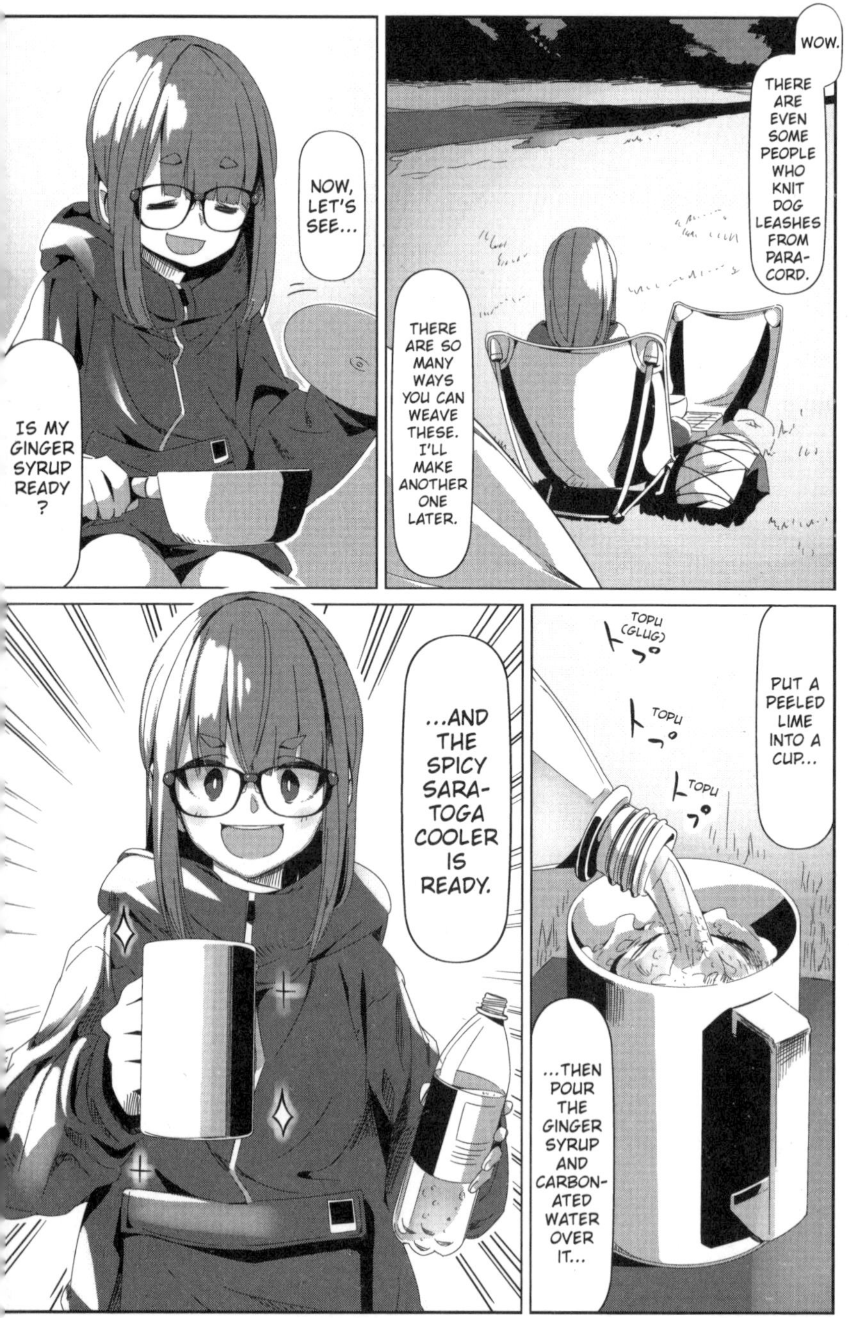

WOW.
THERE ARE EVEN SOME PEOPLE WHO KNIT DOG LEASHES FROM PARA-CORD.
THERE ARE SO MANY WAYS YOU CAN WEAVE THESE. I'LL MAKE ANOTHER ONE LATER.
NOW, LET'S SEE...
IS MY GINGER SYRUP READY?
TOPU (GLUG)
TOPU
TOPU
PUT A PEELED LIME INTO A CUP...
...THEN POUR THE GINGER SYRUP AND CARBON-ATED WATER OVER IT...
...AND THE SPICY SARA-TOGA COOLER IS READY.

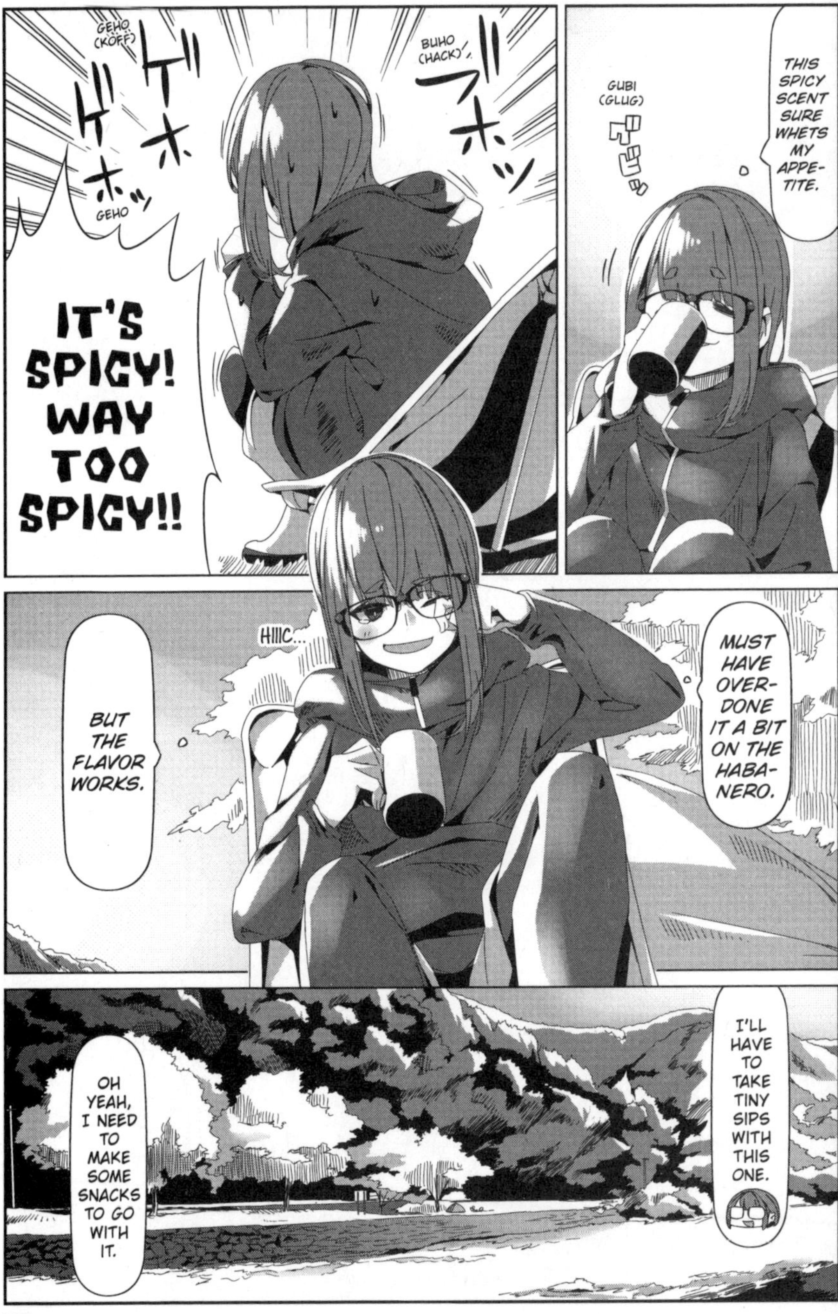
THIS SPICY SCENT SURE WHETS MY APPE-TITE.
GUBI (GLUG)
BUHO (HACK)
GEHO (KOFF)
GEHO
IT'S SPICY! WAY TOO SPICY!!
MUST HAVE OVER-DONE IT A BIT ON THE HABA-NERO.
HIIIC...
BUT THE FLAVOR WORKS.
I'LL HAVE TO TAKE TINY SIPS WITH THIS ONE.
OH YEAH, I NEED TO MAKE SOME SNACKS TO GO WITH IT.

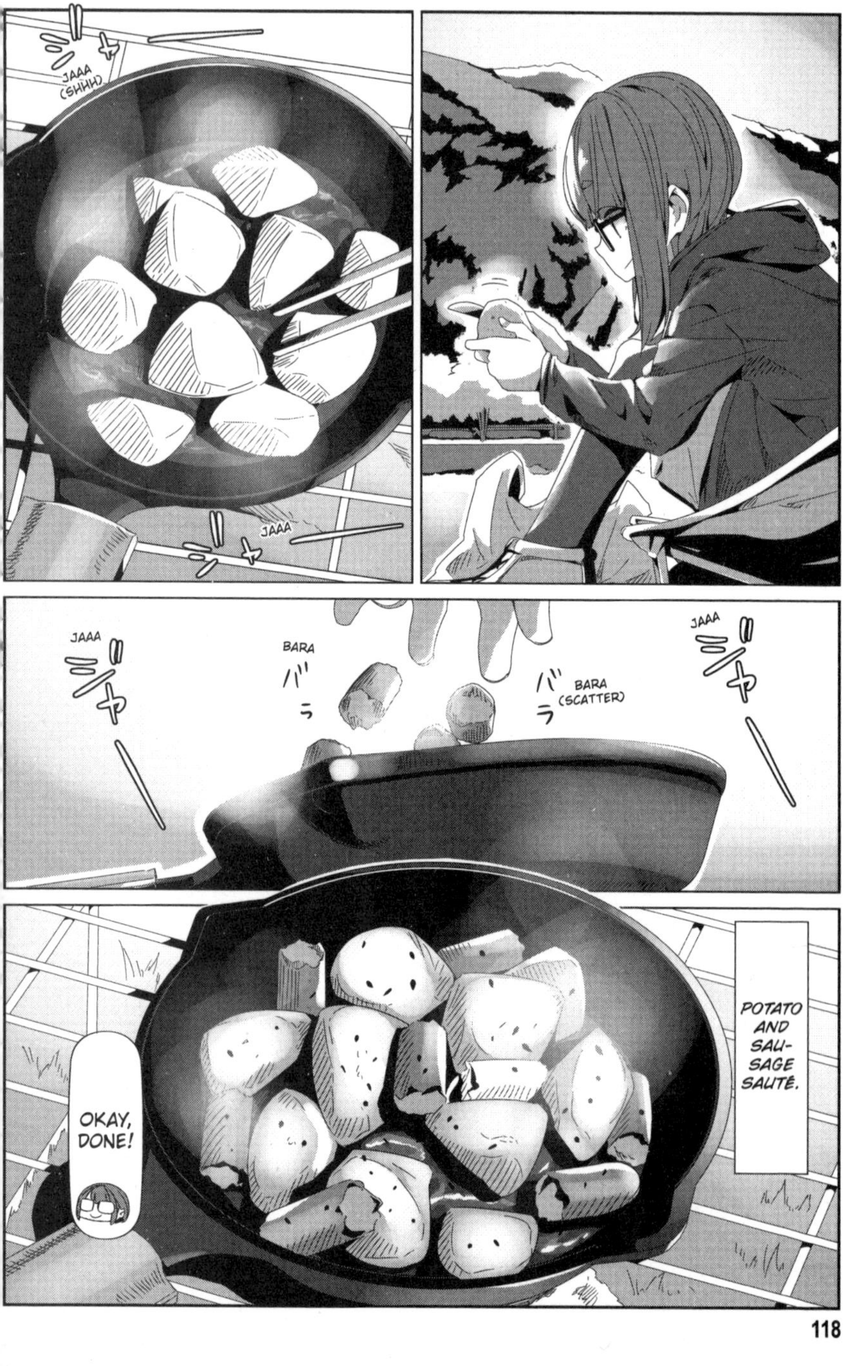

JAAA (SHHH)
ジャー
JAAA
ジャー
JAAA
ジャー
BARA (SCATTER)
バラ
BARA
バラ
JAAA
ジャー
POTATO AND SAU-SAGE SAUTÉ.
OKAY, DONE!

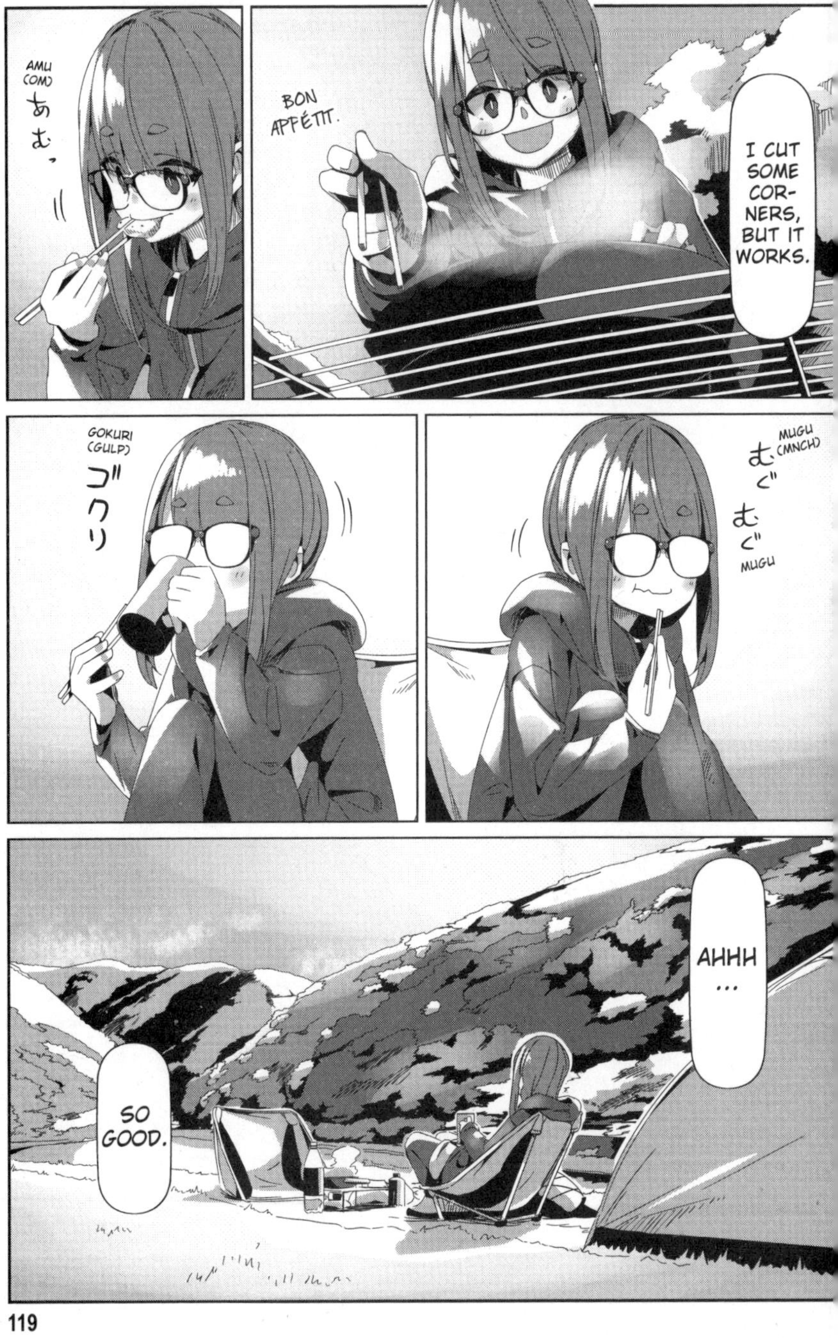
I CUT SOME CORNERS, BUT IT WORKS.
BON APPÉTIT.
AMU (OM)
あむっ
MUGU (MNCH)
むぐむぐ
MUGU
GOKURI (GULP)
ゴクリ
AHHH ...
SO GOOD.

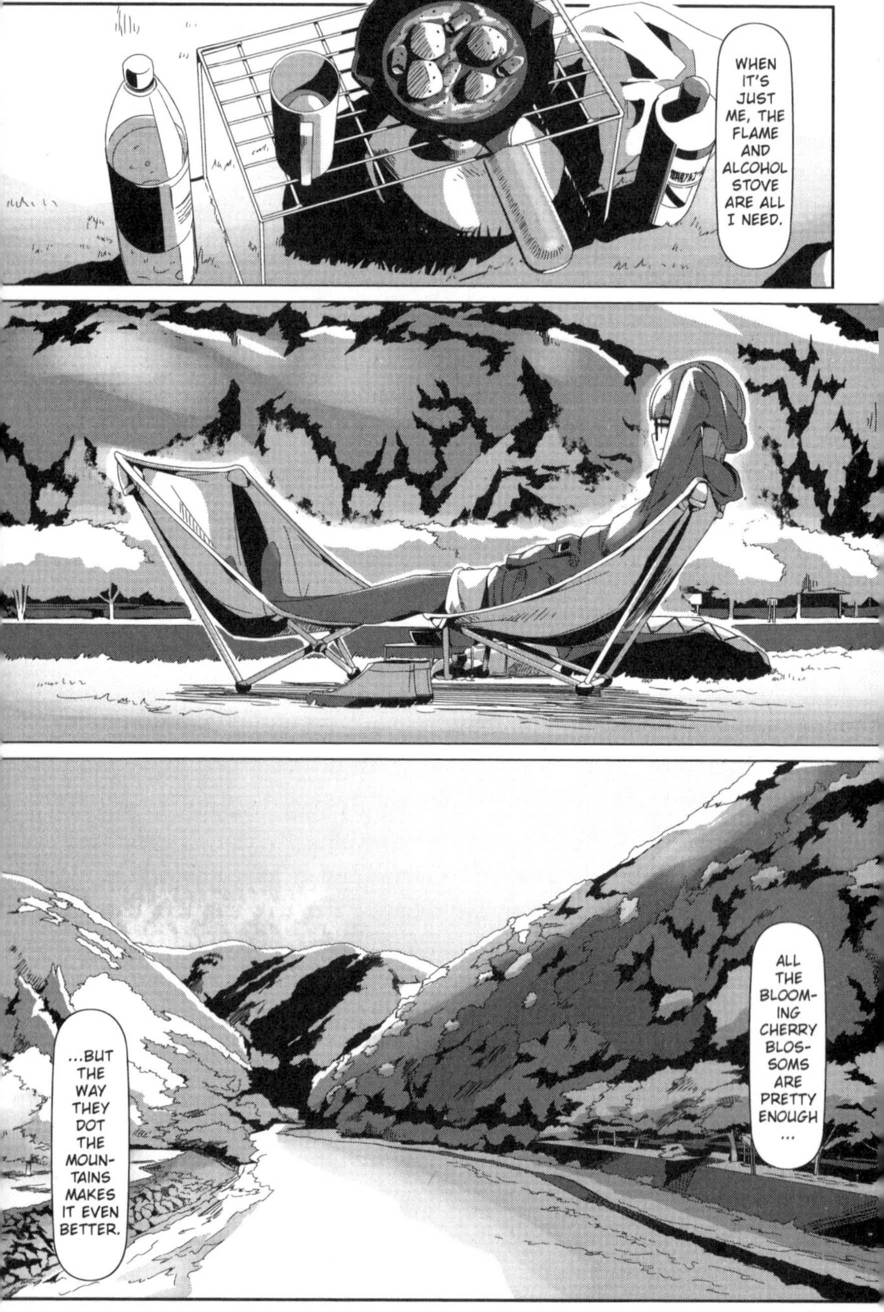
WHEN IT'S JUST ME, THE FLAME AND ALCOHOL STOVE ARE ALL I NEED.
ALL THE BLOOMING CHERRY BLOSSOMS ARE PRETTY ENOUGH...
...BUT THE WAY THEY DOT THE MOUNTAINS MAKES IT EVEN BETTER.

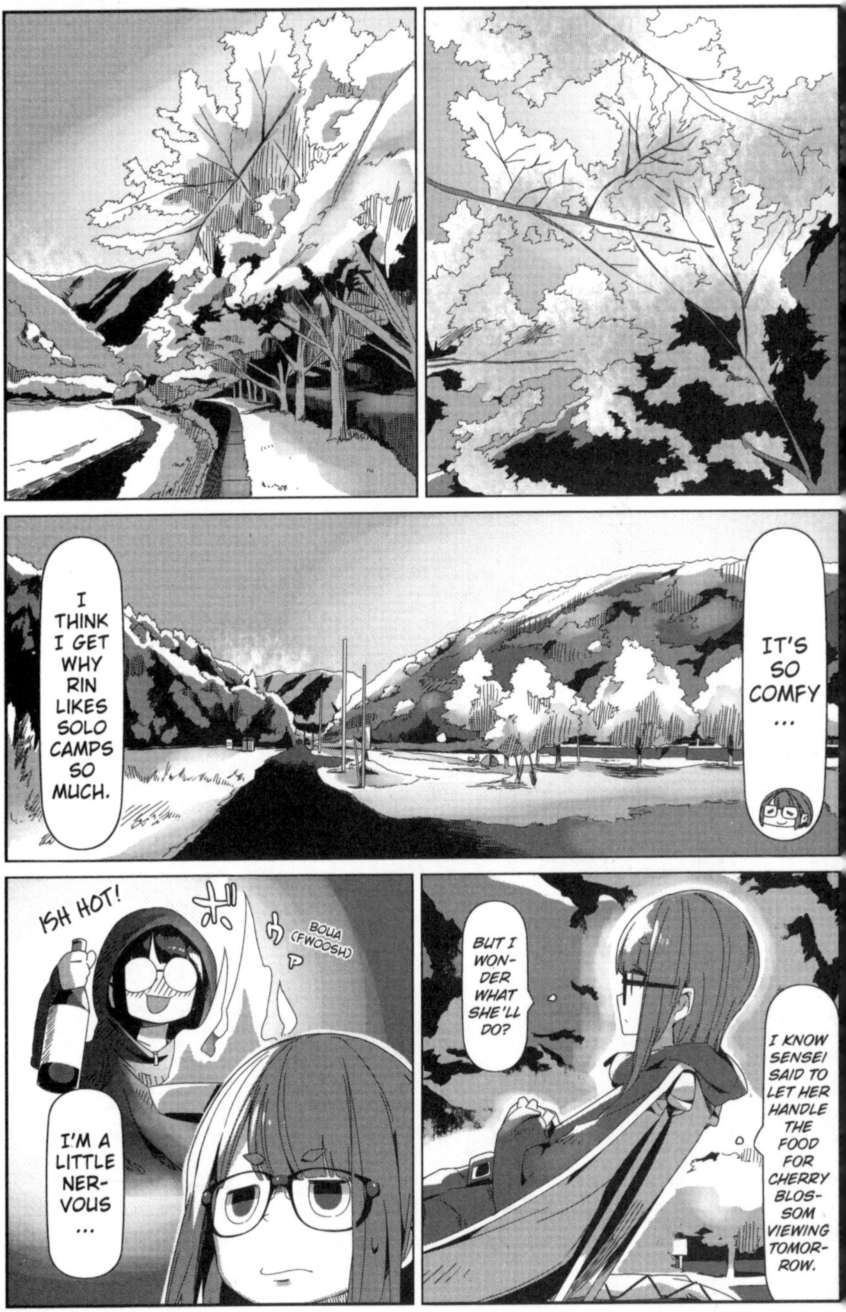
IT'S SO COMFY ...
I THINK I GET WHY RIN LIKES SOLO CAMPS SO MUCH.
I KNOW SENSEI SAID TO LET HER HANDLE THE FOOD FOR CHERRY BLOSSOM VIEWING TOMORROW.
BUT I WONDER WHAT SHE'LL DO?
ISH HOT!
ボウァ
BOUA (FWOOSH)
I'M A LITTLE NERVOUS ...

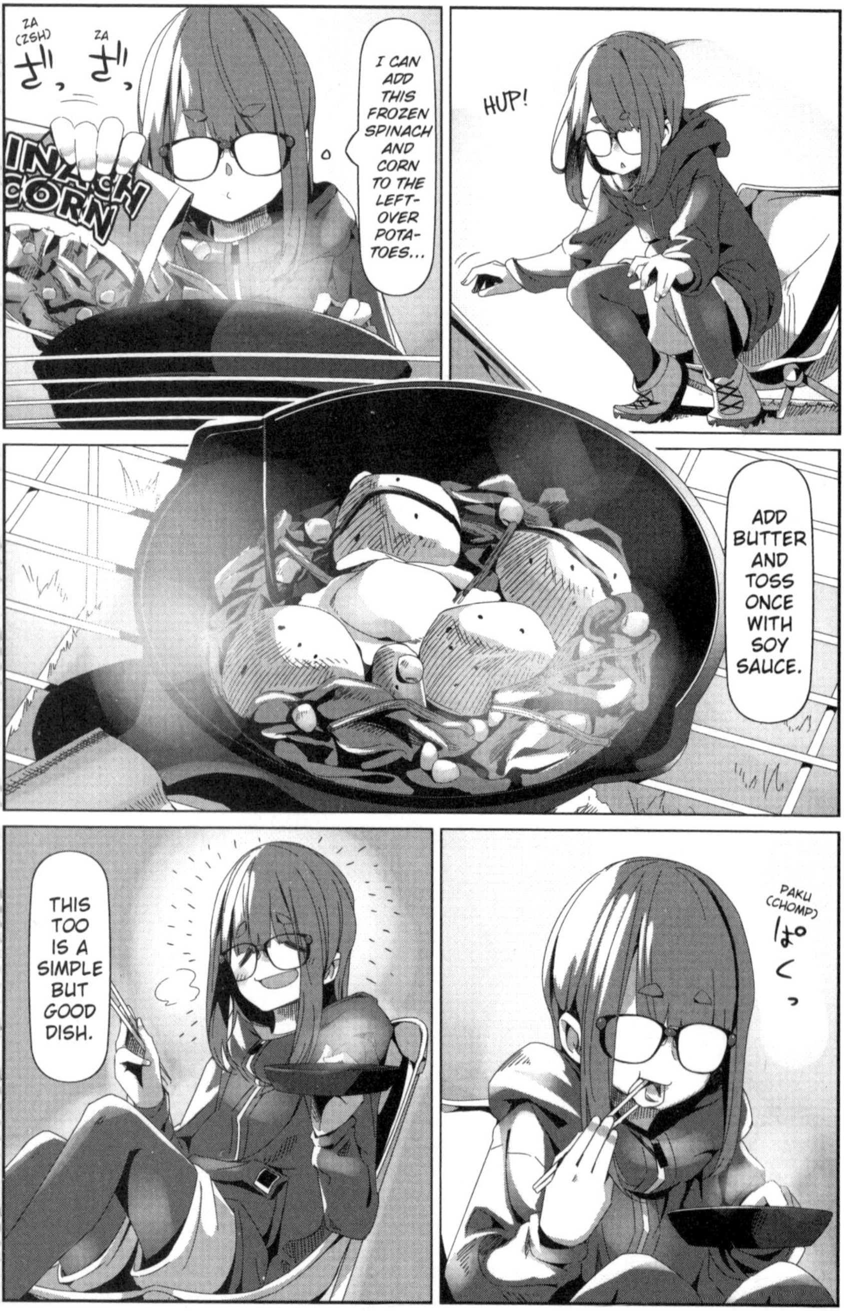
HUP!
ZA (ZSH) ZA
ざっざっ
INACH CORN
I CAN ADD THIS FROZEN SPINACH AND CORN TO THE LEFT-OVER POTATOES...
ADD BUTTER AND TOSS ONCE WITH SOY SAUCE.
PAKU (CHOMP)
ぱくっ
THIS TOO IS A SIMPLE BUT GOOD DISH.

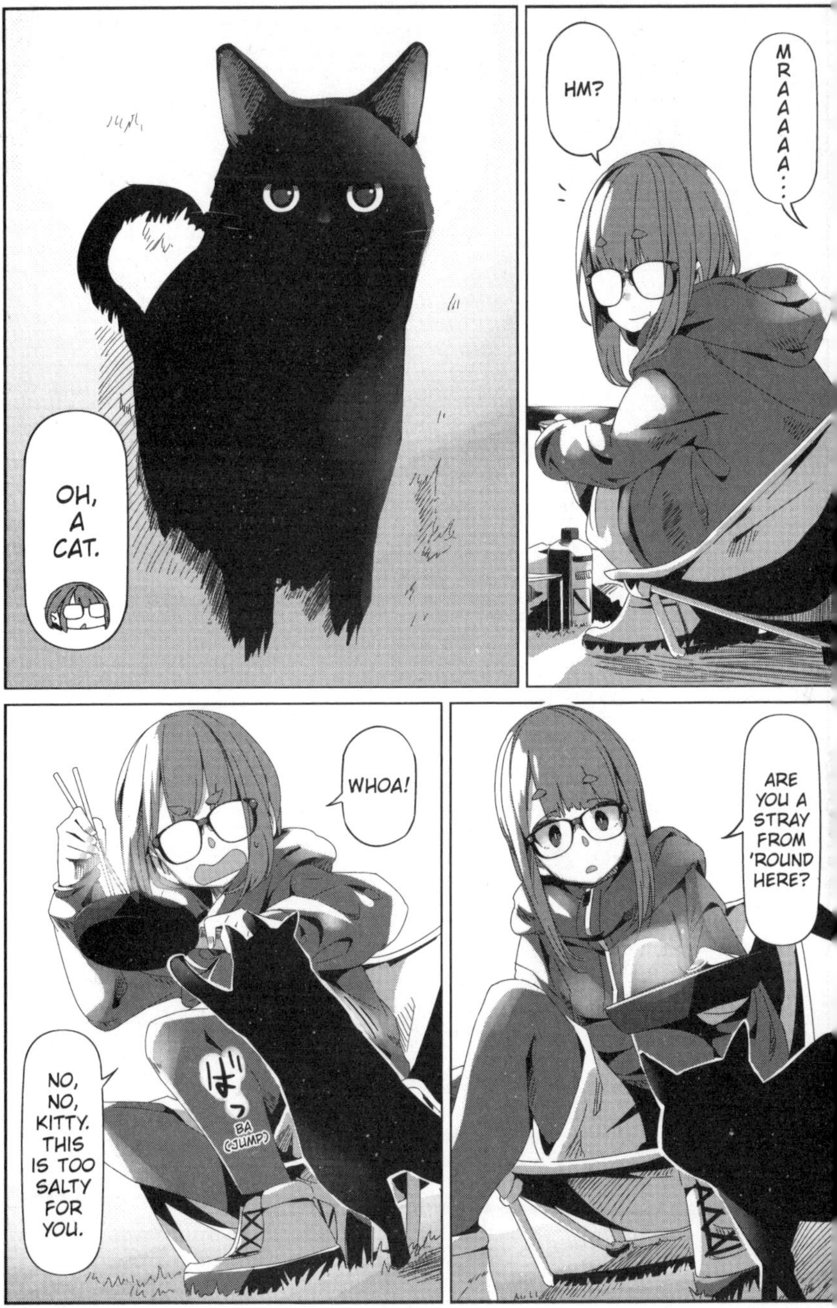
MRAAAAAA...
HM?
OH, A CAT.
ARE YOU A STRAY FROM 'ROUND HERE?
WHOA!
ばっ
BA (JUMP)
NO, NO, KITTY. THIS IS TOO SALTY FOR YOU.

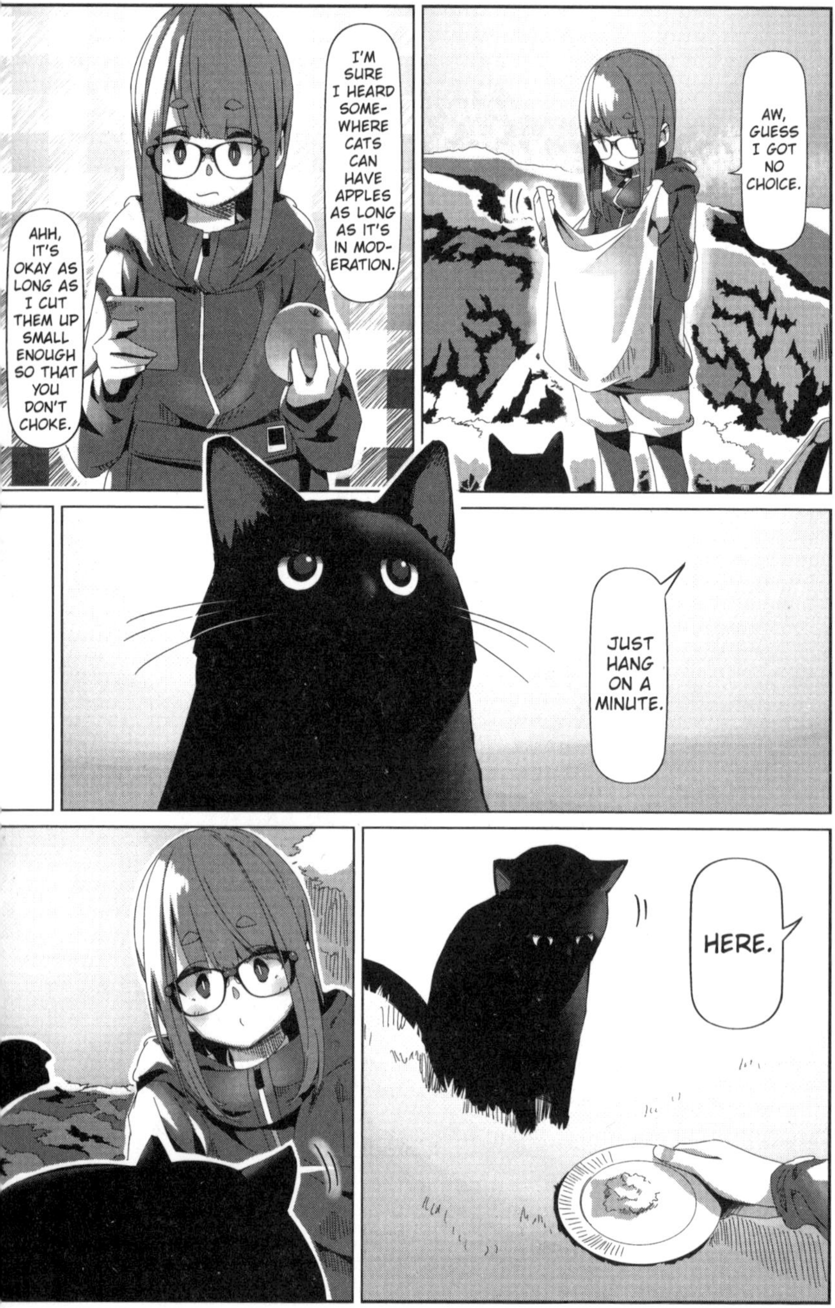
AW, GUESS I GOT NO CHOICE.
I'M SURE I HEARD SOME-WHERE CATS CAN HAVE APPLES AS LONG AS IT'S IN MOD-ERATION.
AHH, IT'S OKAY AS LONG AS I CUT THEM UP SMALL ENOUGH SO THAT YOU DON'T CHOKE.
JUST HANG ON A MINUTE.
HERE.

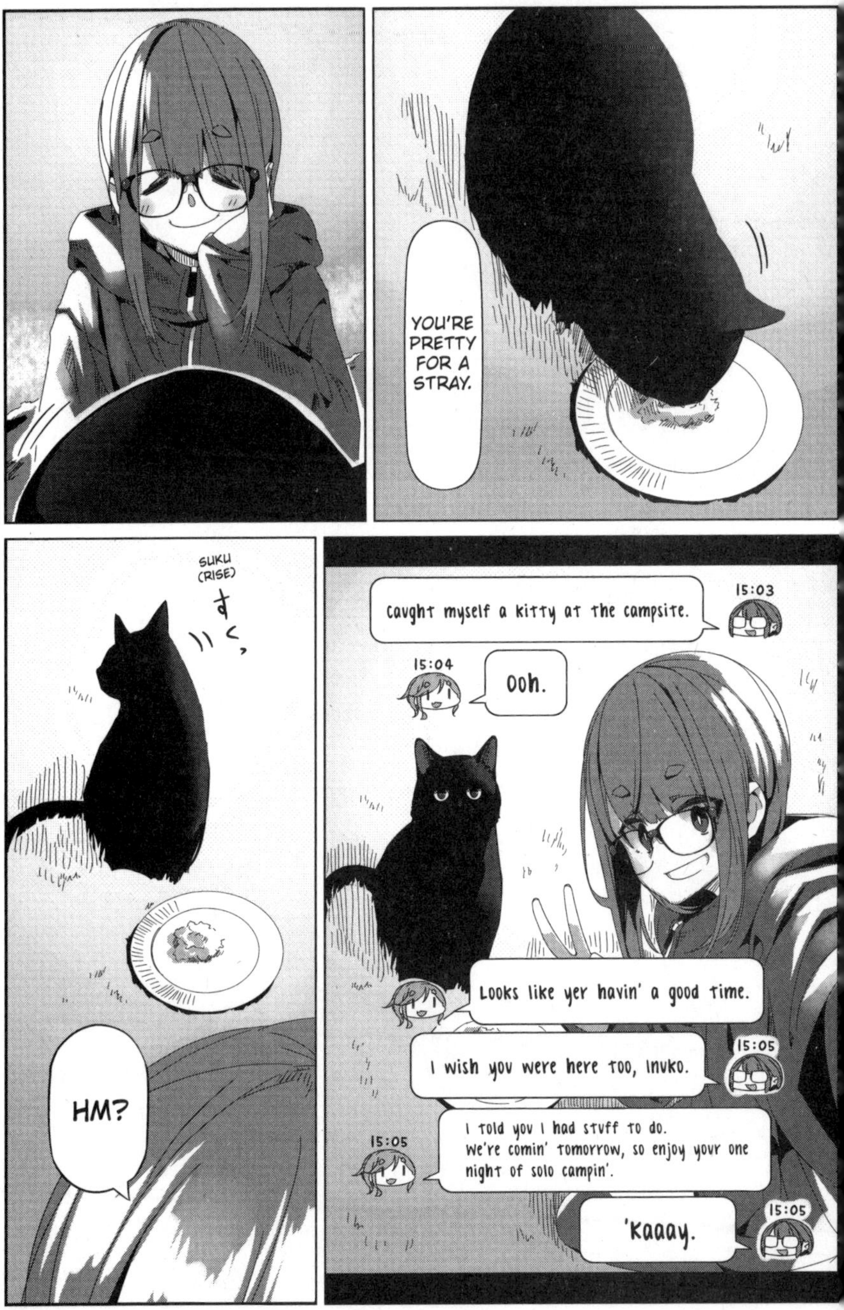
YOU'RE PRETTY FOR A STRAY.
15:03
Caught myself a kitty at the campsite.
15:04
Ooh.
Looks like yer havin' a good time.
15:05
I wish you were here too, Inuko.
15:05
I told you I had stuff to do. We're comin' tomorrow, so enjoy your one night of solo campin'.
15:05
'Kaaay.
SUKU (RISE)
すく
HM?

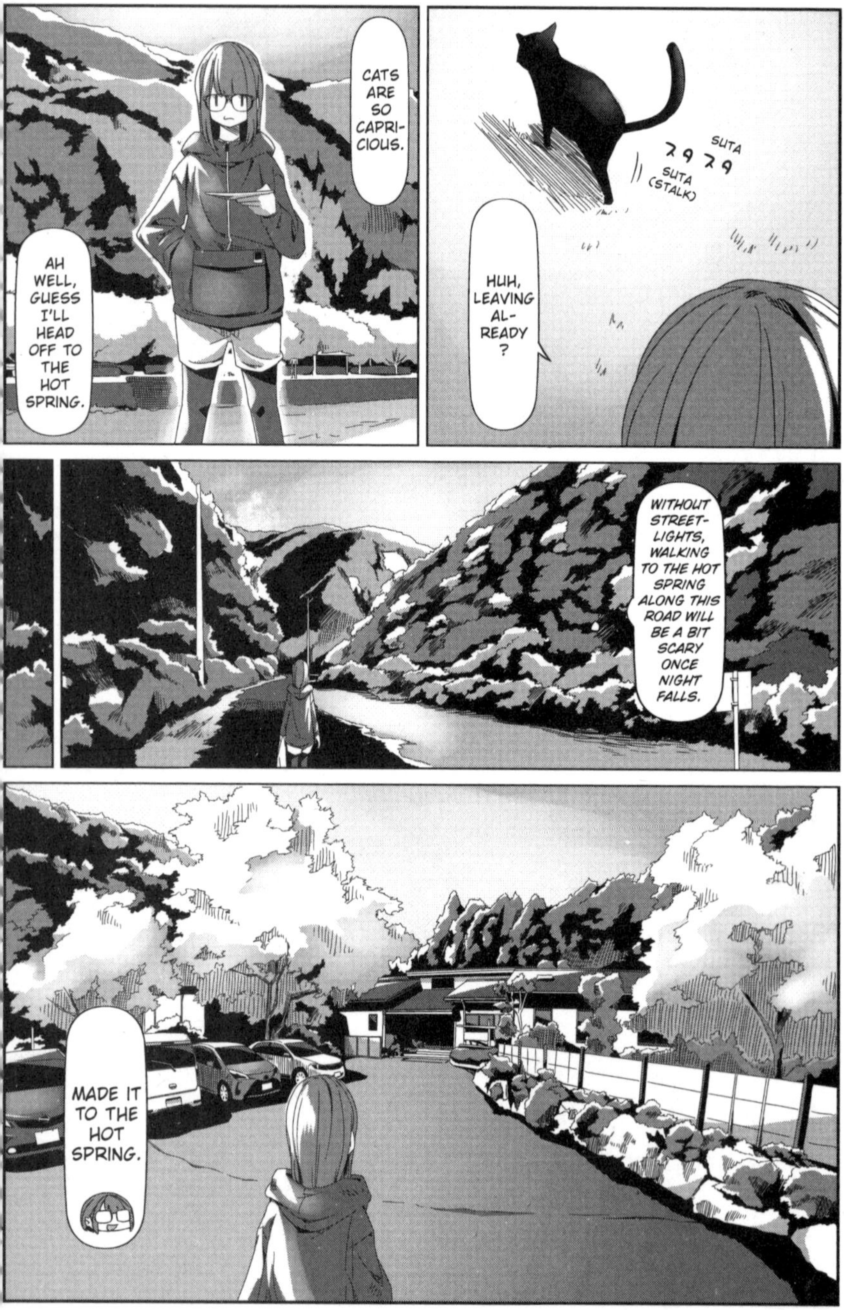
SUTA
スタスタ
SUTA (STALK)
HUH, LEAVING AL-READY?
CATS ARE SO CAPRI-CIOUS.
AH WELL, GUESS I'LL HEAD OFF TO THE HOT SPRING.
WITHOUT STREET-LIGHTS, WALKING TO THE HOT SPRING ALONG THIS ROAD WILL BE A BIT SCARY ONCE NIGHT FALLS.
MADE IT TO THE HOT SPRING.

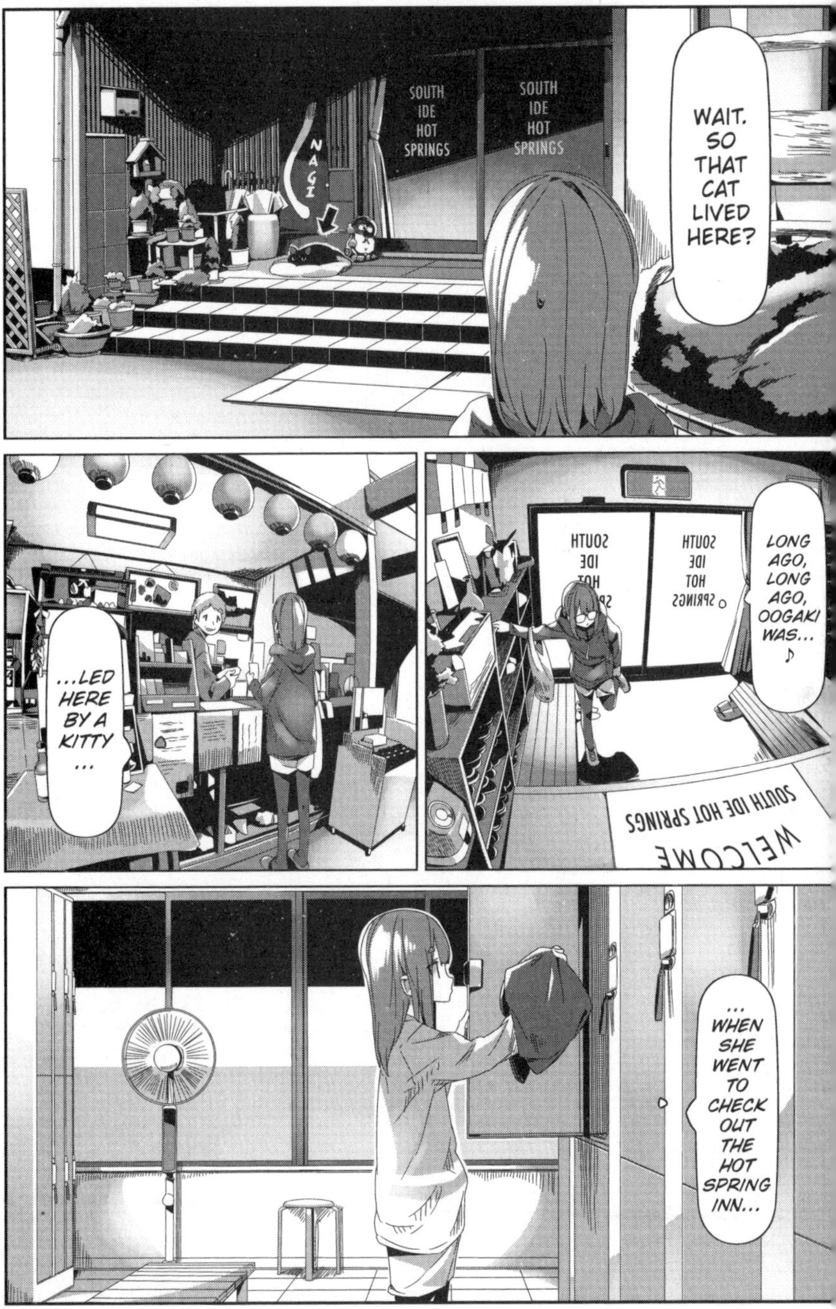
SOUTH IDE HOT SPRINGS
SOUTH IDE HOT SPRINGS
NAGI
WAIT. SO THAT CAT LIVED HERE?
LONG AGO, LONG AGO, OOGAKI WAS... ♪
WELCOME SOUTH IDE HOT SPRINGS
...LED HERE BY A KITTY ...
...WHEN SHE WENT TO CHECK OUT THE HOT SPRING INN...

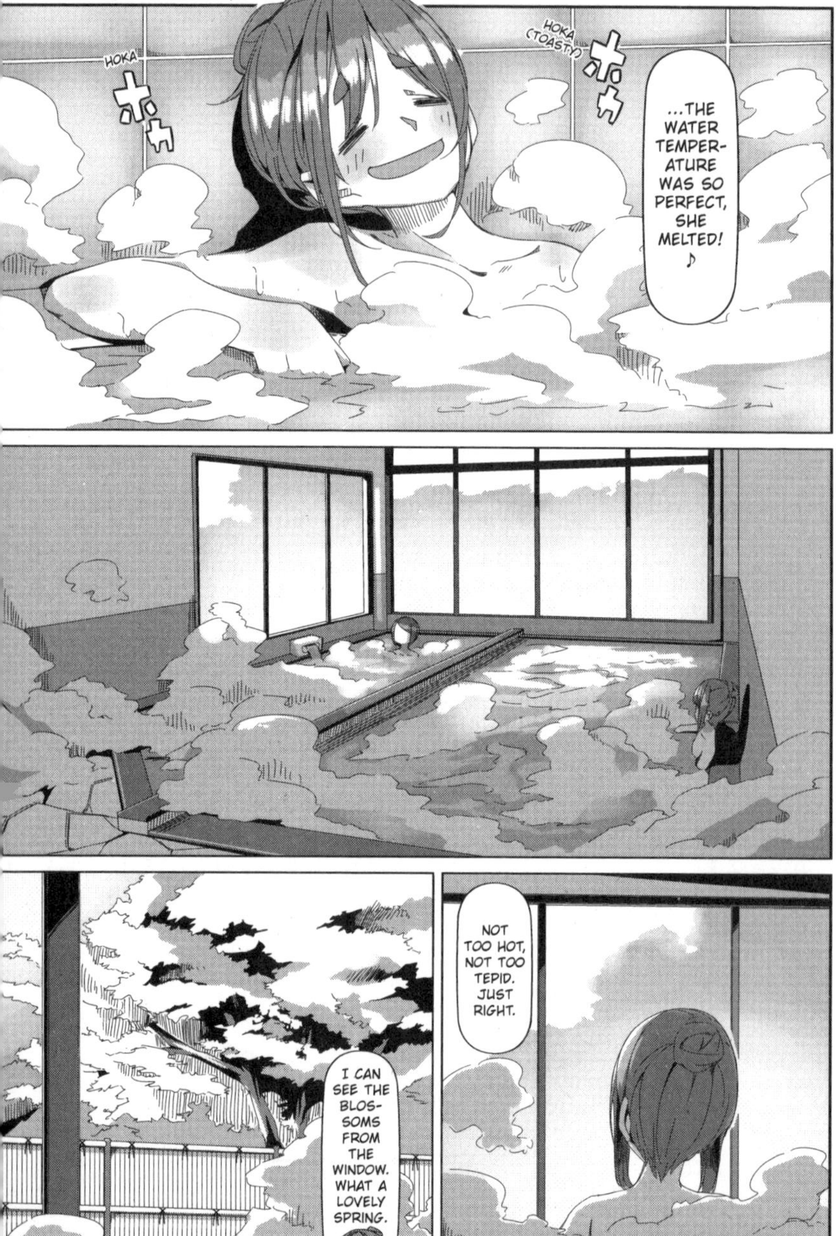
...THE WATER TEMPERATURE WAS SO PERFECT, SHE MELTED! ♪
HOKA (TOASTY)
HOKA
NOT TOO HOT, NOT TOO TEPID. JUST RIGHT.
I CAN SEE THE BLOSSOMS FROM THE WINDOW. WHAT A LOVELY SPRING.

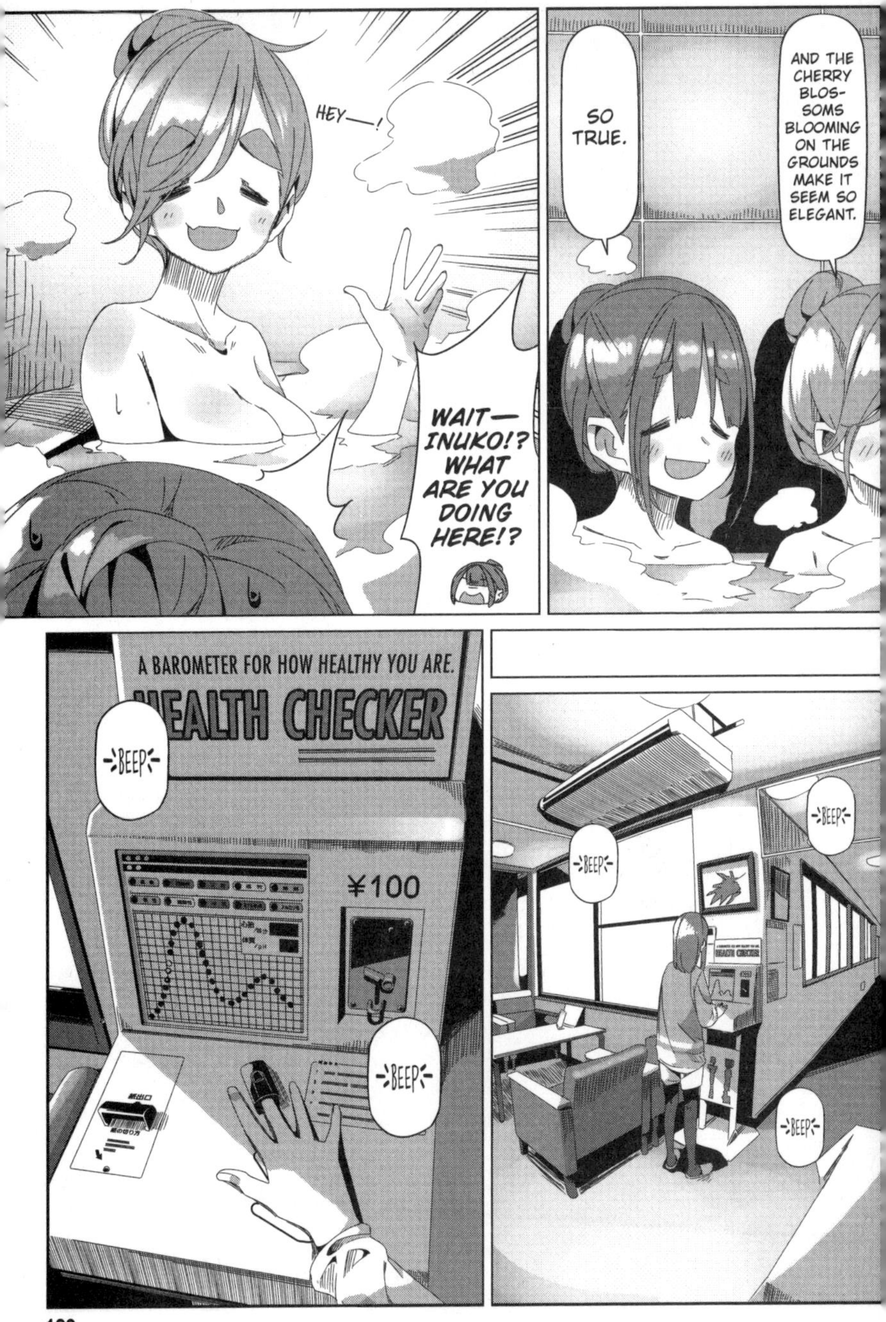

AND THE CHERRY BLOSSOMS BLOOMING ON THE GROUNDS MAKE IT SEEM SO ELEGANT.
SO TRUE.
HEY—!
WAIT— INUKO!? WHAT ARE YOU DOING HERE!?
BEEP
BEEP
BEEP
BEEP
A BAROMETER FOR HOW HEALTHY YOU ARE.
EALTH CHECKER
BEEP
¥100
BEEP

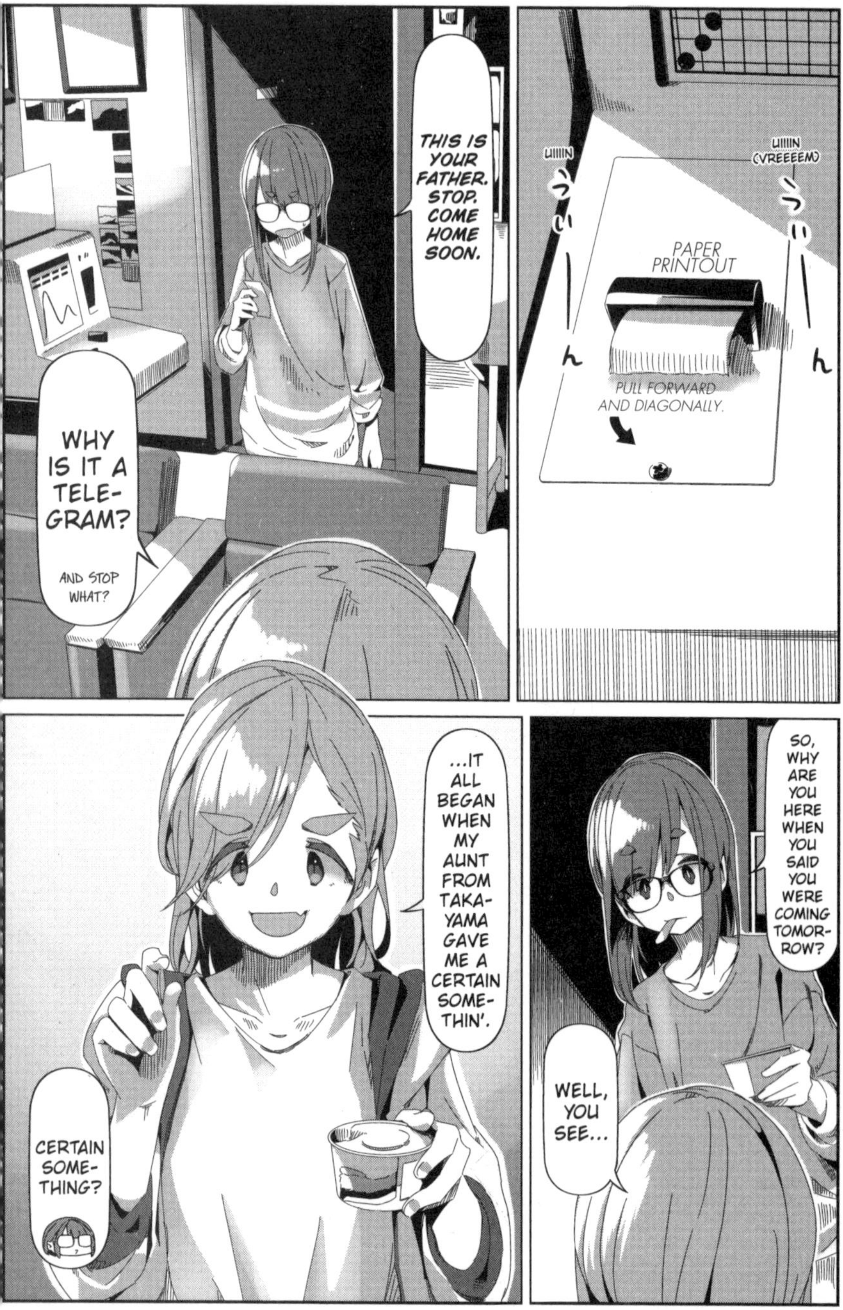
UIIIN (VREEEEM)
UIIIN
PAPER PRINTOUT
PULL FORWARD AND DIAGONALLY.
THIS IS YOUR FATHER. STOP. COME HOME SOON.
WHY IS IT A TELE-GRAM?
AND STOP WHAT?
SO, WHY ARE YOU HERE WHEN YOU SAID YOU WERE COMING TOMOR-ROW?
WELL, YOU SEE...
...IT ALL BEGAN WHEN MY AUNT FROM TAKA-YAMA GAVE ME A CERTAIN SOME-THIN'.
CERTAIN SOME-THING?

I MADE A SKILLET HANDLE COVER...
...WITH A PARACORD!!

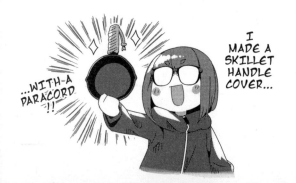

AAAAAAAAGH!
AAAAAAAAGH!
デロォ・・・
DEROO (DROOP)

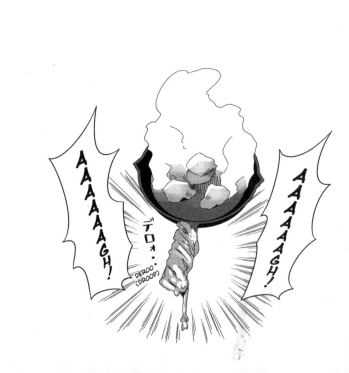

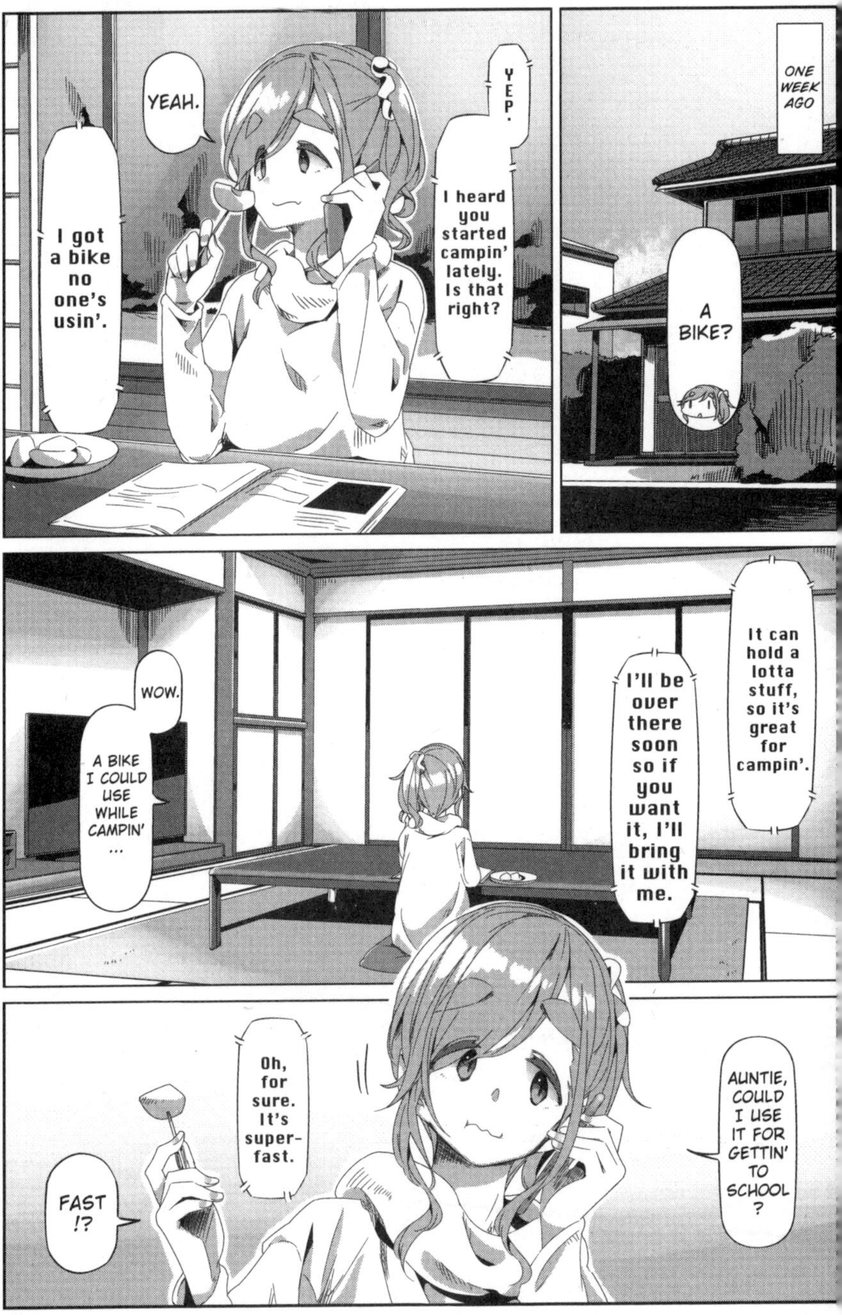
ONE WEEK AGO
A BIKE?
YEP.
I heard you started campin' lately. Is that right?
YEAH.
I got a bike no one's usin'.
It can hold a lotta stuff, so it's great for campin'.
I'll be over there soon so if you want it, I'll bring it with me.
WOW.
A BIKE I COULD USE WHILE CAMPIN'...
AUNTIE, COULD I USE IT FOR GETTIN' TO SCHOOL?
Oh, for sure. It's super-fast.
FAST!?

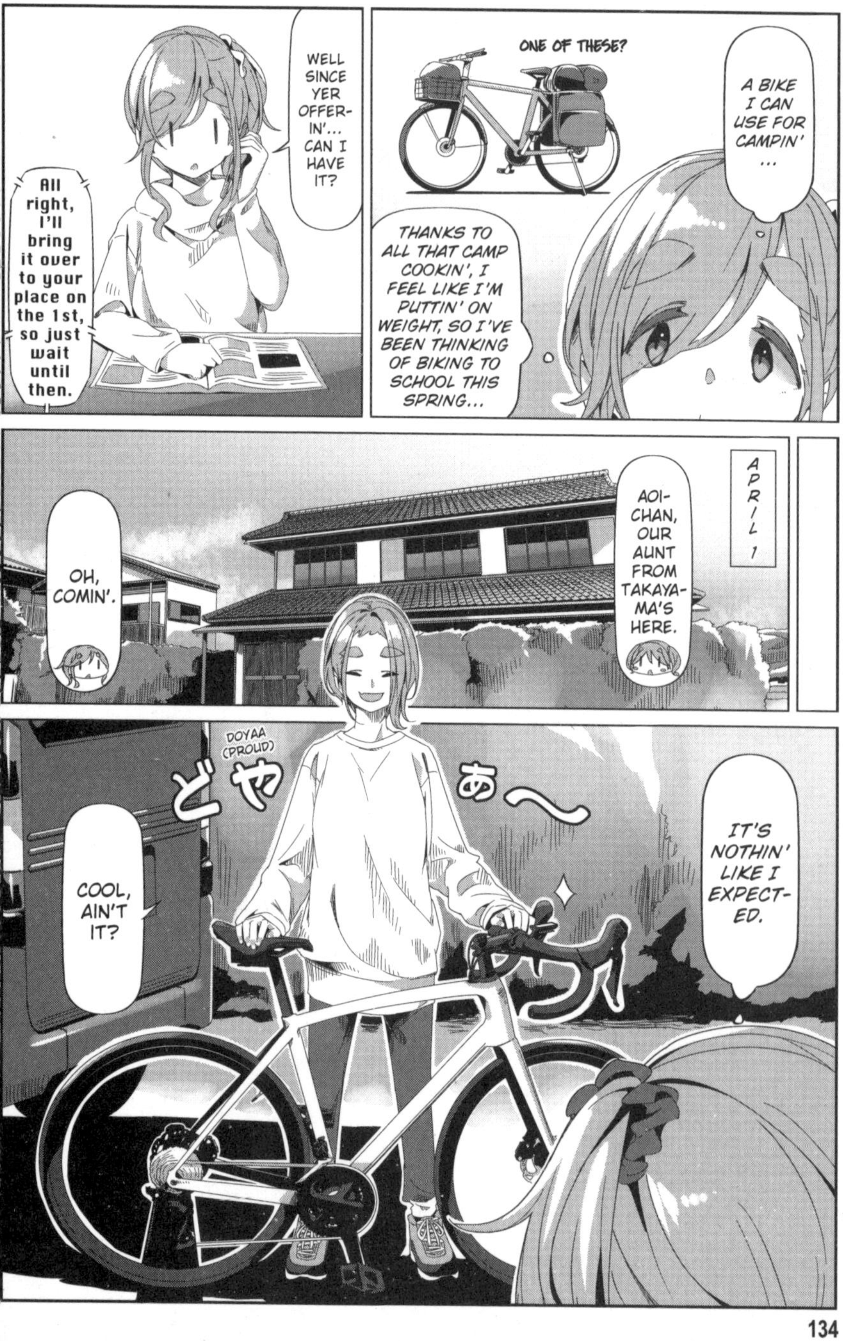
A BIKE I CAN USE FOR CAMPIN'...
ONE OF THESE?
THANKS TO ALL THAT CAMP COOKIN', I FEEL LIKE I'M PUTTIN' ON WEIGHT, SO I'VE BEEN THINKING OF BIKING TO SCHOOL THIS SPRING...
WELL SINCE YER OFFER-IN'... CAN I HAVE IT?
All right, I'll bring it over to your place on the 1st, so just wait until then.
APRIL 1
AOI-CHAN, OUR AUNT FROM TAKAYAMA'S HERE.
OH, COMIN'.
IT'S NOTHIN' LIKE I EXPECT-ED.
どやあ～
DOYAA (PROUD)
COOL, AIN'T IT?

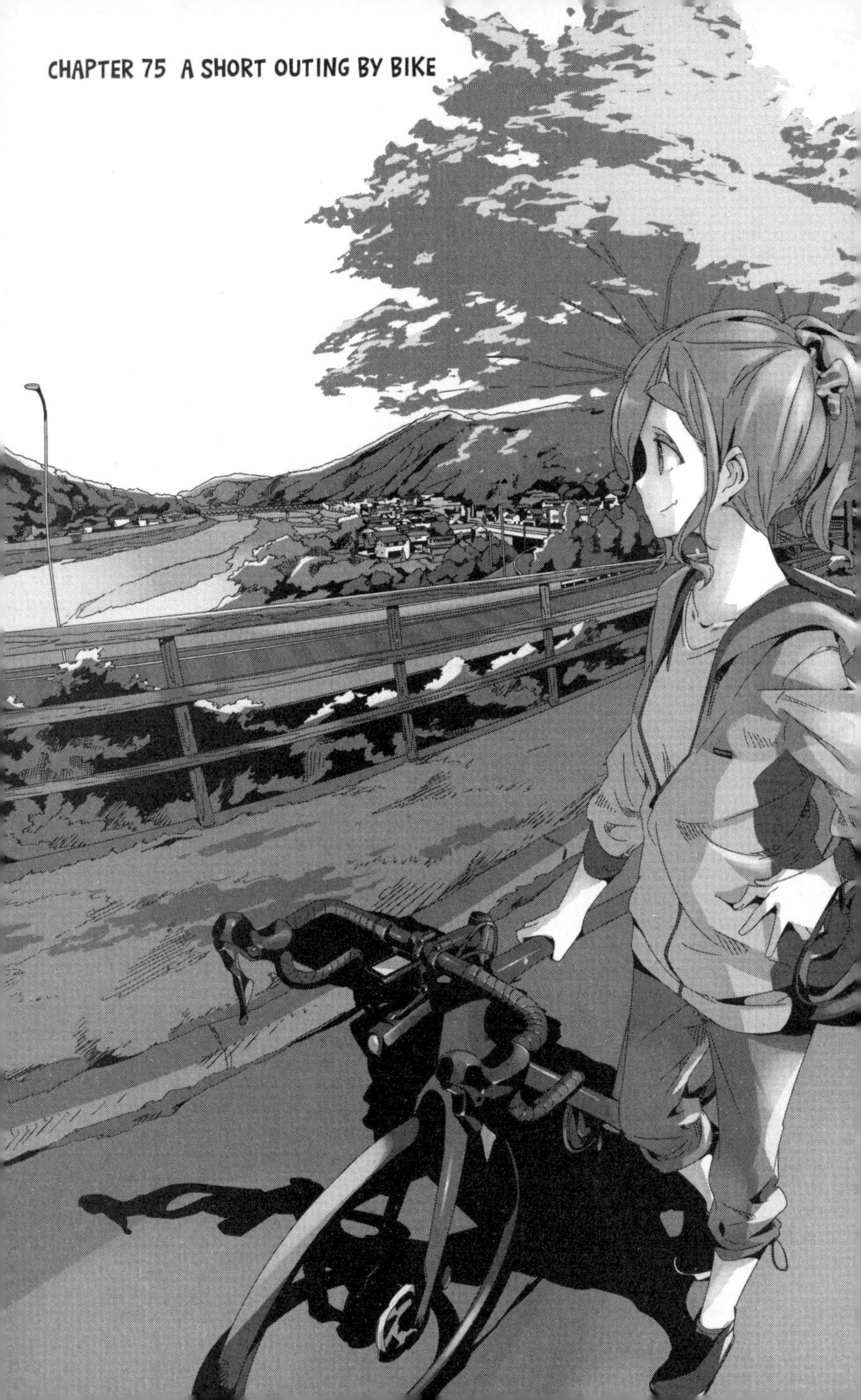
CHAPTER 75 A SHORT OUTING BY BIKE

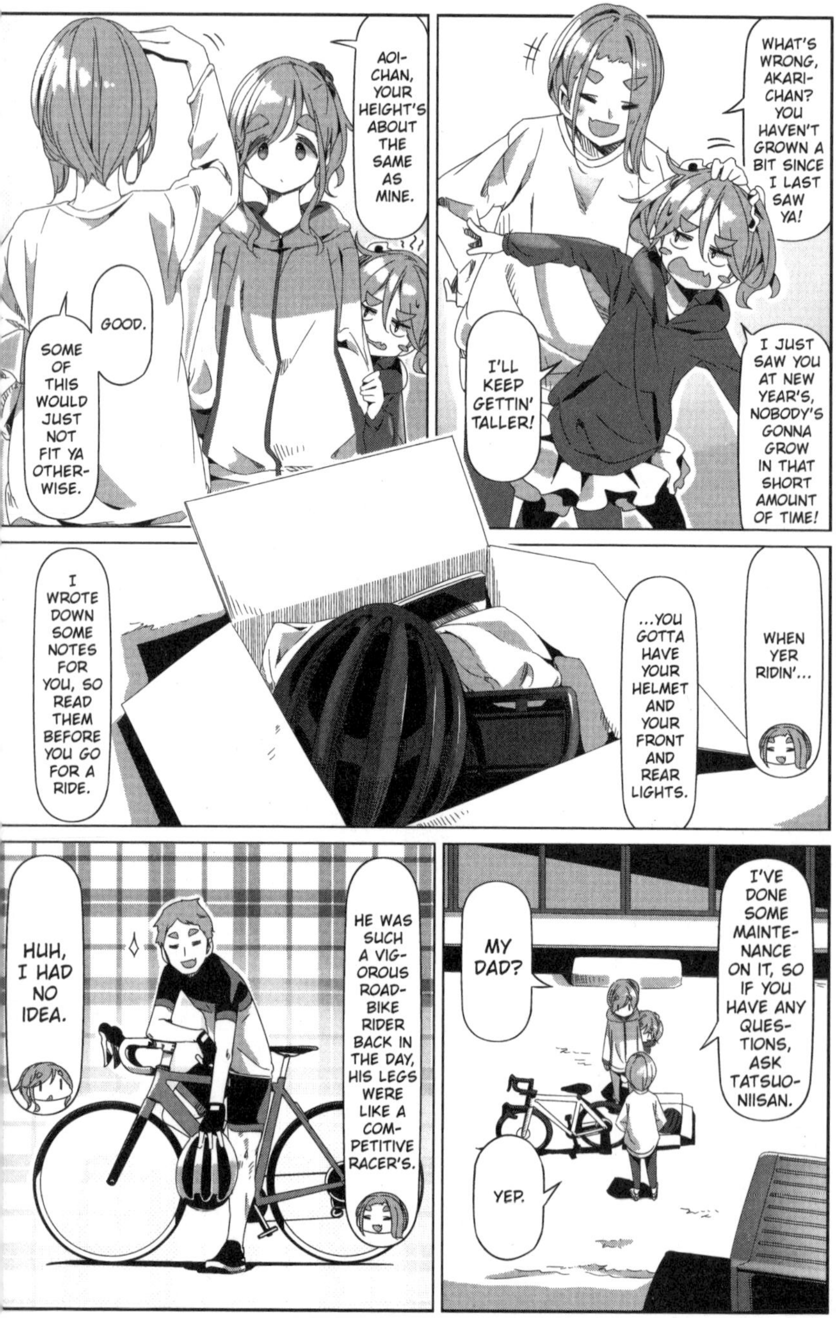
WHAT'S WRONG, AKARI-CHAN? YOU HAVEN'T GROWN A BIT SINCE I LAST SAW YA!
I JUST SAW YOU AT NEW YEAR'S, NOBODY'S GONNA GROW IN THAT SHORT AMOUNT OF TIME!
I'LL KEEP GETTIN' TALLER!
AOI-CHAN, YOUR HEIGHT'S ABOUT THE SAME AS MINE.
GOOD.
SOME OF THIS WOULD JUST NOT FIT YA OTHERWISE.
WHEN YER RIDIN'...
...YOU GOTTA HAVE YOUR HELMET AND YOUR FRONT AND REAR LIGHTS.
I WROTE DOWN SOME NOTES FOR YOU, SO READ THEM BEFORE YOU GO FOR A RIDE.
I'VE DONE SOME MAINTENANCE ON IT, SO IF YOU HAVE ANY QUESTIONS, ASK TATSUO-NIISAN.
MY DAD?
YEP.
HE WAS SUCH A VIGOROUS ROAD-BIKE RIDER BACK IN THE DAY, HIS LEGS WERE LIKE A COMPETITIVE RACER'S.
HUH, I HAD NO IDEA.

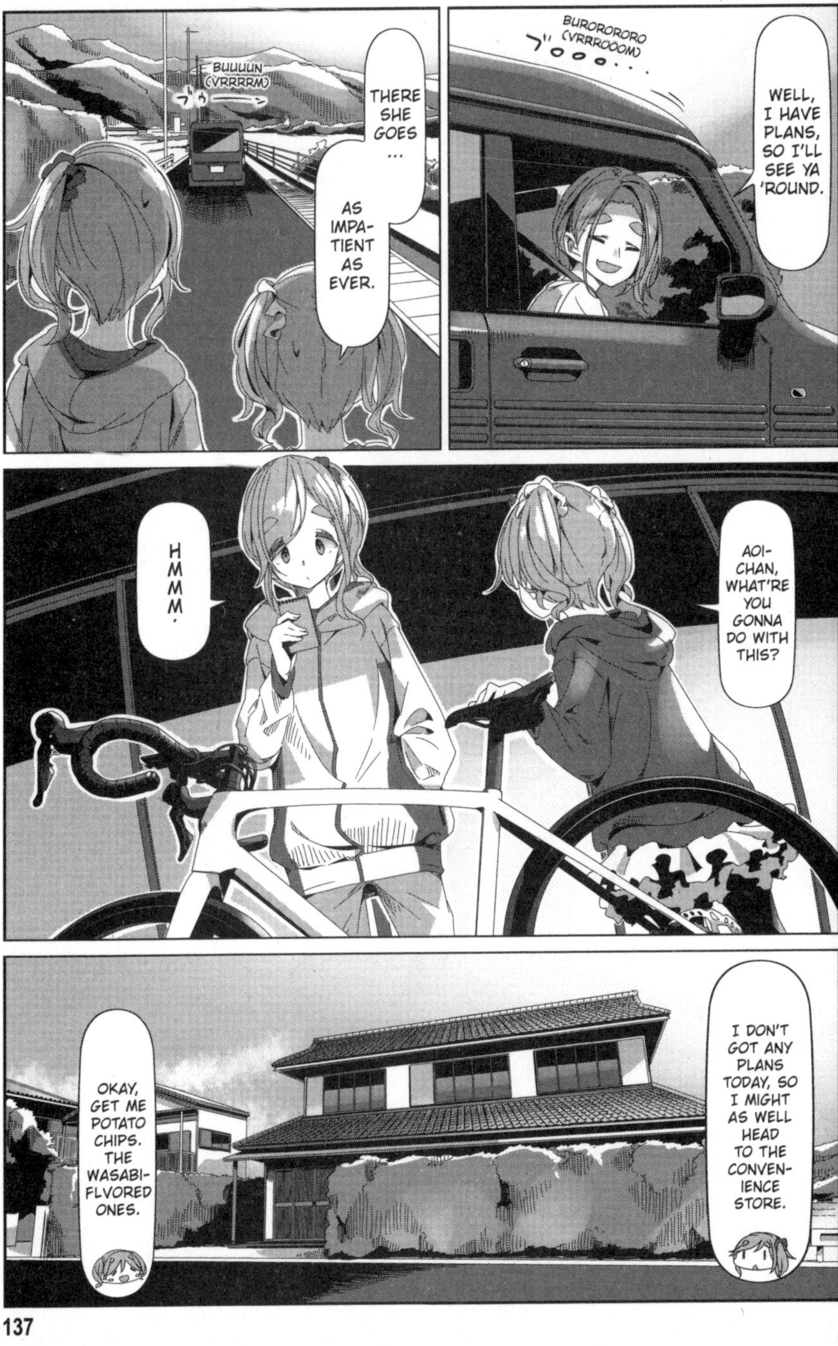
BURORORORO (VRRROOOM)
WELL, I HAVE PLANS, SO I'LL SEE YA 'ROUND.
BUUUUN (VRRRRM)
THERE SHE GOES...
AS IMPATIENT AS EVER.
AOI-CHAN, WHAT'RE YOU GONNA DO WITH THIS?
HMMM.
I DON'T GOT ANY PLANS TODAY, SO I MIGHT AS WELL HEAD TO THE CONVENIENCE STORE.
OKAY, GET ME POTATO CHIPS. THE WASABI-FLVORED ONES.

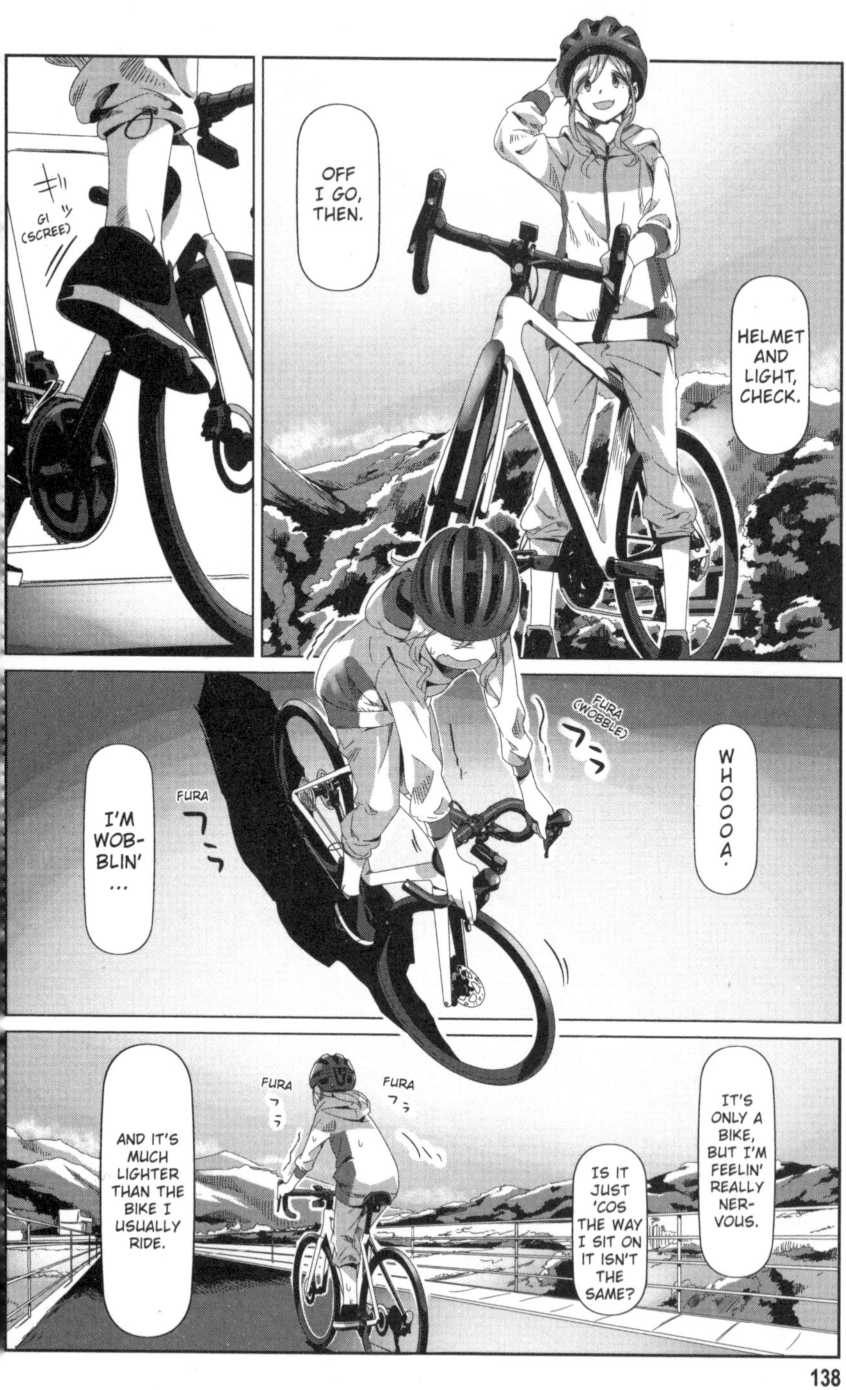
HELMET AND LIGHT, CHECK.
OFF I GO, THEN.
ギリ
GI ッ (SCREE)
WHOOOA.
フラ FURA (WOBBLE)
フラ FURA
I'M WOB-BLIN'...
IT'S ONLY A BIKE, BUT I'M FEELIN' REALLY NER-VOUS.
IS IT JUST 'COS THE WAY I SIT ON IT ISN'T THE SAME?
フラ FURA
フラ FURA
AND IT'S MUCH LIGHTER THAN THE BIKE I USUALLY RIDE.

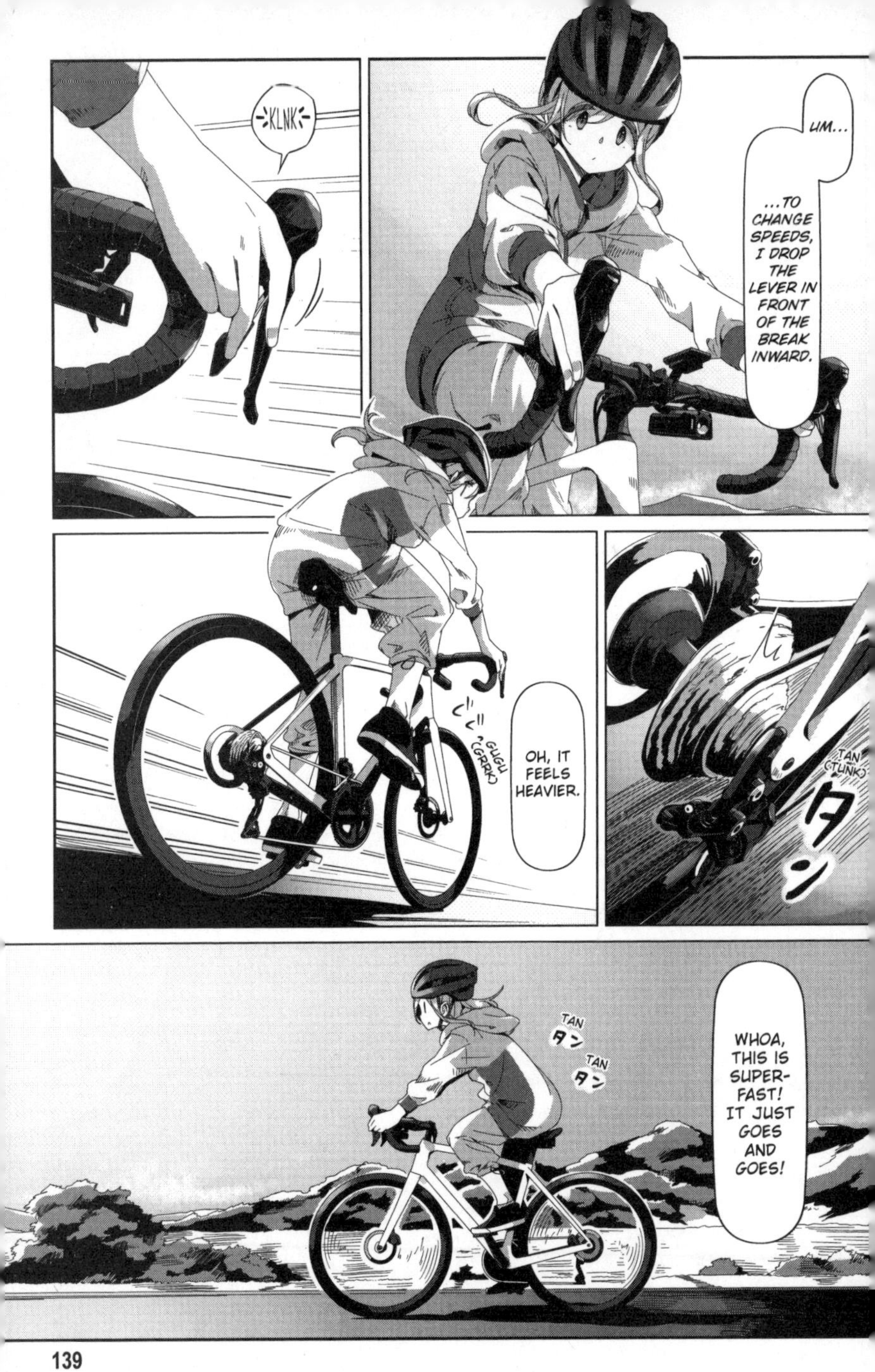
UM...
...TO CHANGE SPEEDS, I DROP THE LEVER IN FRONT OF THE BREAK INWARD.
KLNK
TAN (TUNK)
タン
OH, IT FEELS HEAVIER.
GUGU (GRRK)
ぐぐ
WHOA, THIS IS SUPER-FAST! IT JUST GOES AND GOES!
TAN
タン
TAN
タン

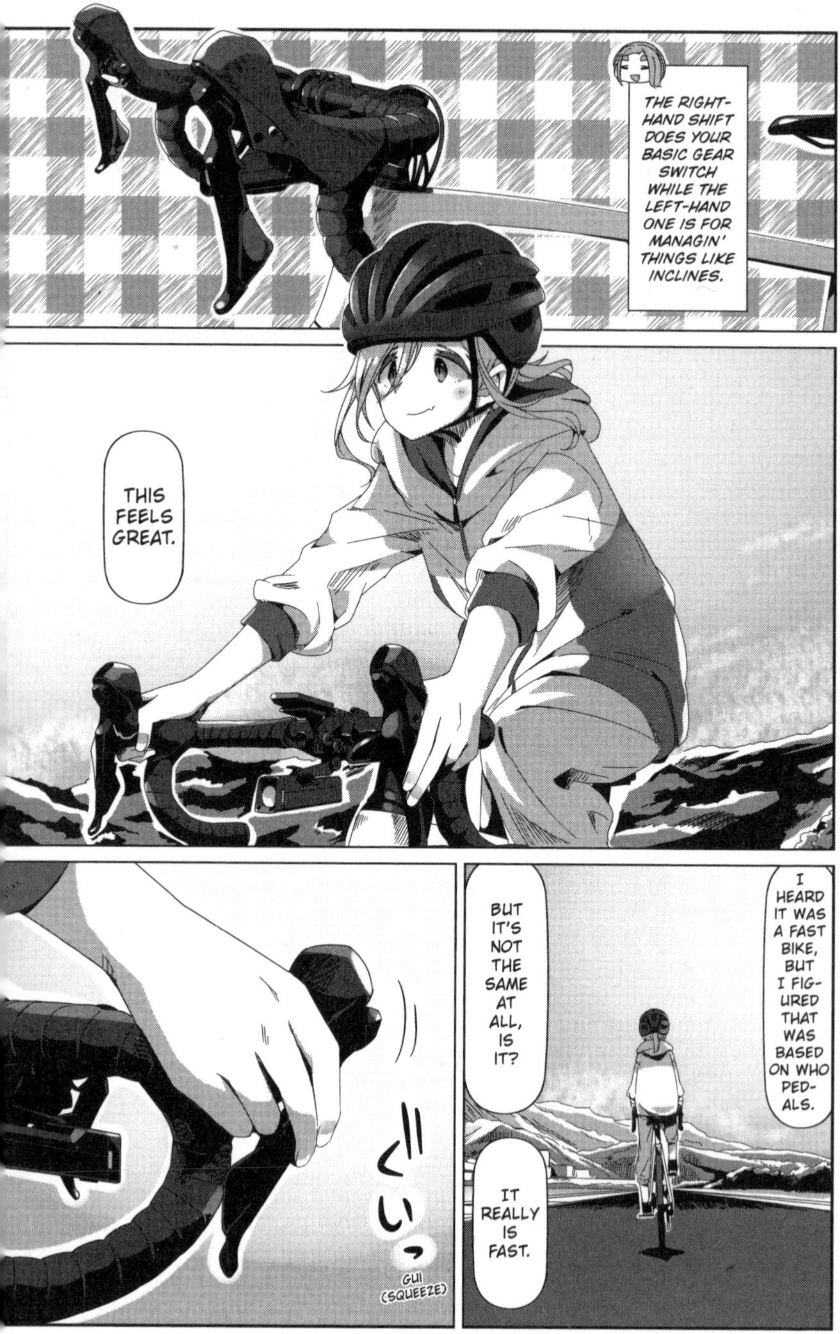
THE RIGHT-HAND SHIFT DOES YOUR BASIC GEAR SWITCH WHILE THE LEFT-HAND ONE IS FOR MANAGIN' THINGS LIKE INCLINES.
THIS FEELS GREAT.
I HEARD IT WAS A FAST BIKE, BUT I FIG-URED THAT WAS BASED ON WHO PED-ALS.
BUT IT'S NOT THE SAME AT ALL, IS IT?
IT REALLY IS FAST.
ぐいっ
GUI (SQUEEZE)

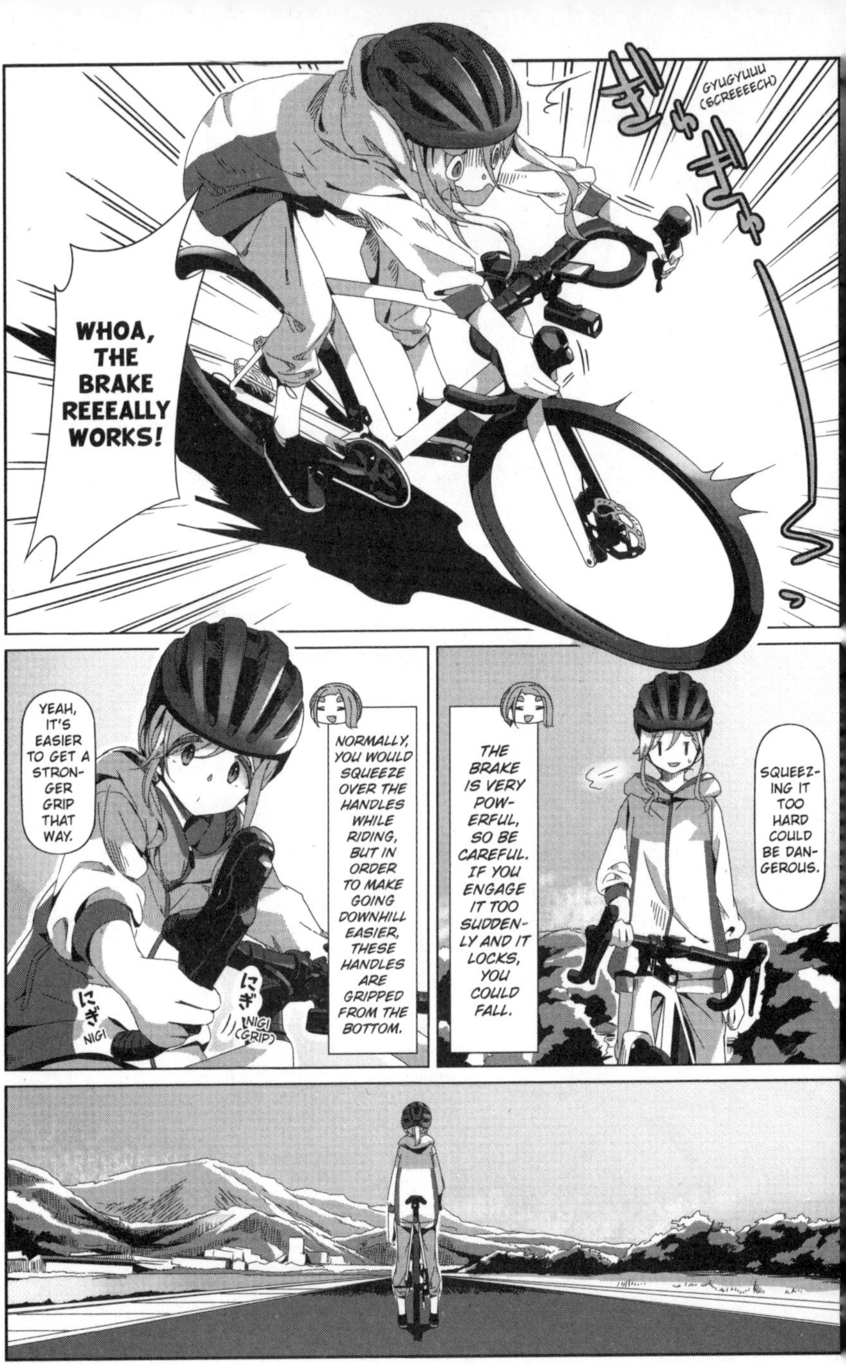
ぎゅぎゅ
GYUGYUUU (SCREEEECH)
WHOA, THE BRAKE REEEALLY WORKS!
SQUEEZING IT TOO HARD COULD BE DANGEROUS.
THE BRAKE IS VERY POWERFUL, SO BE CAREFUL. IF YOU ENGAGE IT TOO SUDDENLY AND IT LOCKS, YOU COULD FALL.
NORMALLY, YOU WOULD SQUEEZE OVER THE HANDLES WHILE RIDING, BUT IN ORDER TO MAKE GOING DOWNHILL EASIER, THESE HANDLES ARE GRIPPED FROM THE BOTTOM.
YEAH, IT'S EASIER TO GET A STRONGER GRIP THAT WAY.
にぎ
NIGI (GRIP)
にぎ
NIGI

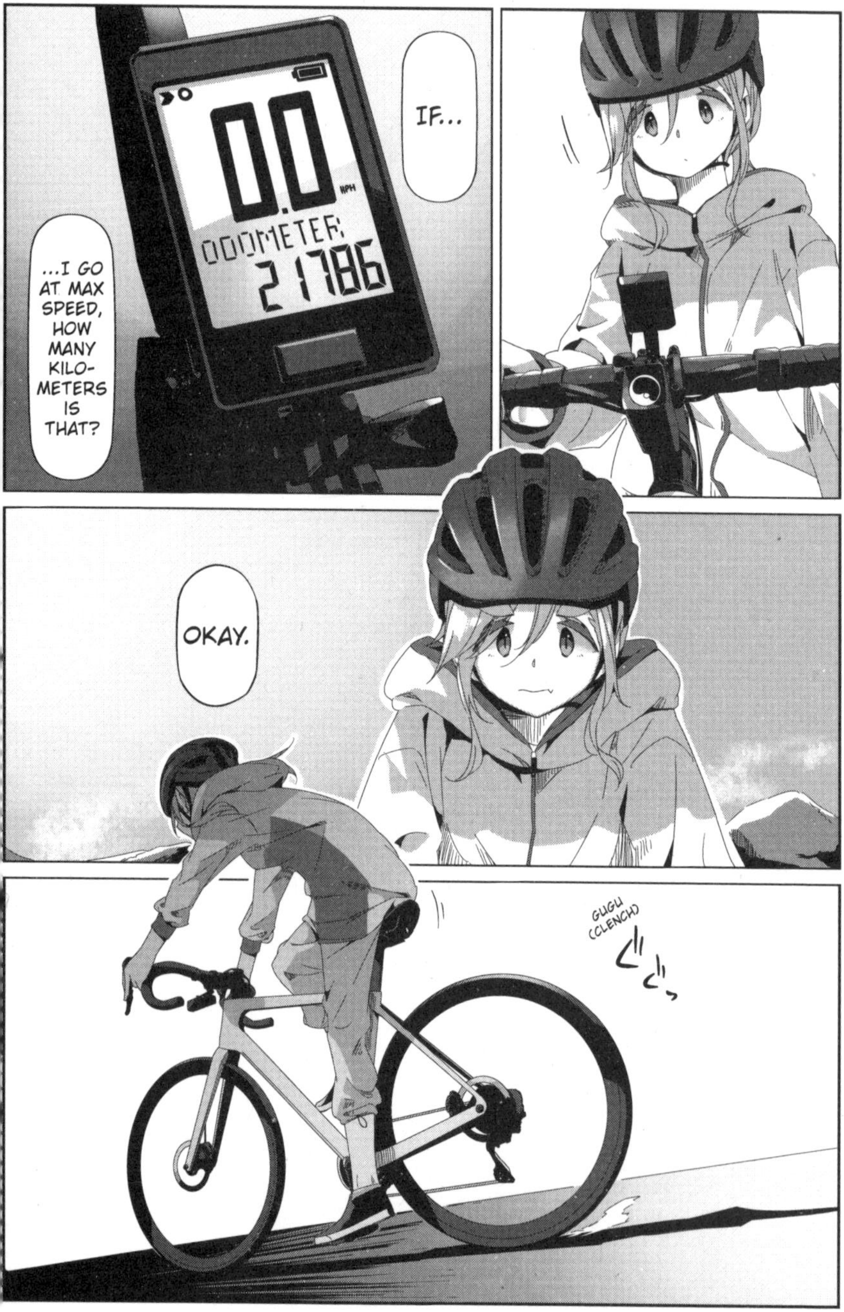
IF...
0.0
ODOMETER:
21786
...I GO AT MAX SPEED, HOW MANY KILO-METERS IS THAT?
OKAY.
GUGU (CLENCH)

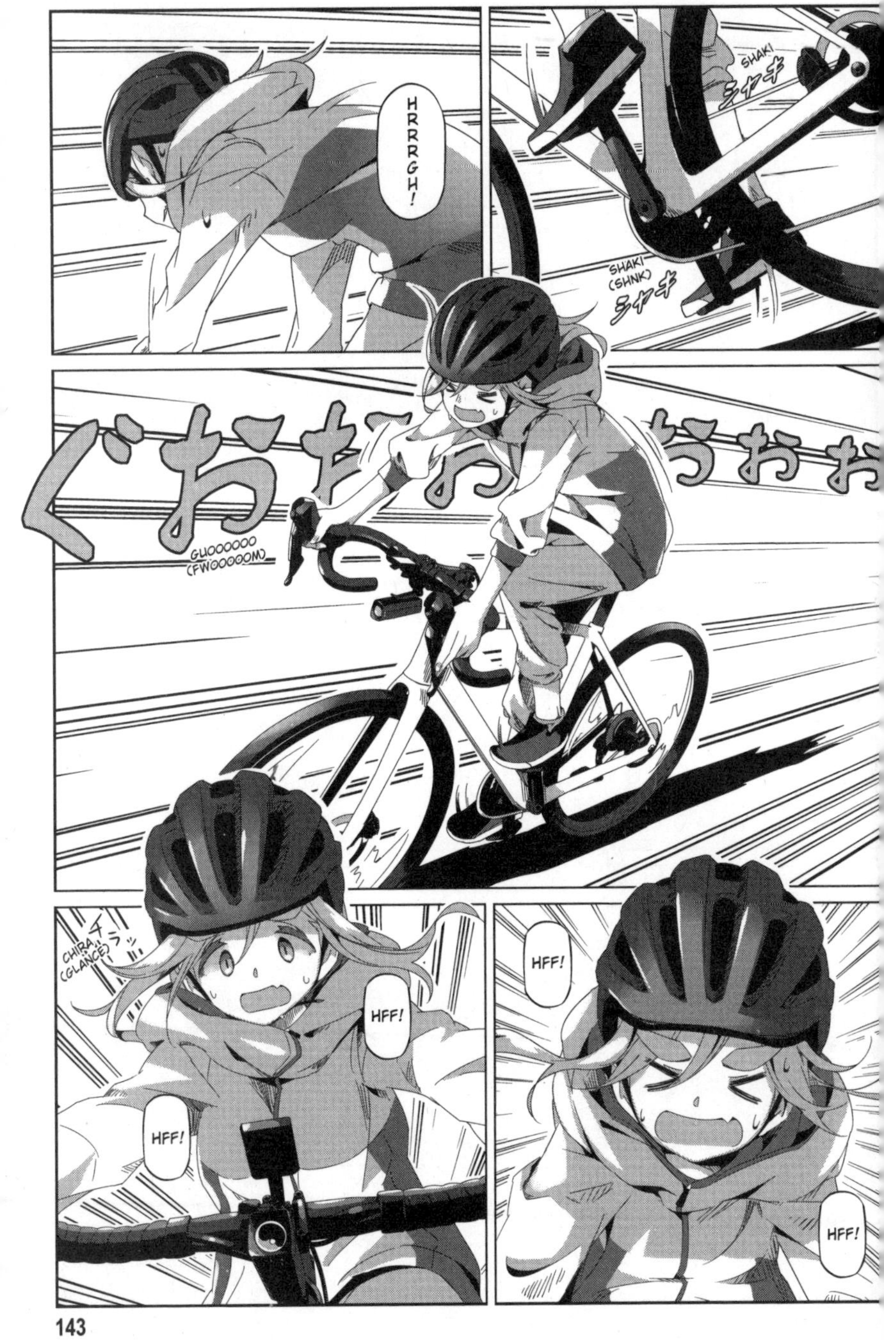

SHAKI
シャキ
SHAKI (SHNK)
シャキ
HRRRGH!
GUOOOOOO (FWOOOOOM)
HFF!
HFF!
CHIRA (GLANCE)
チラッ
HFF!
HFF!

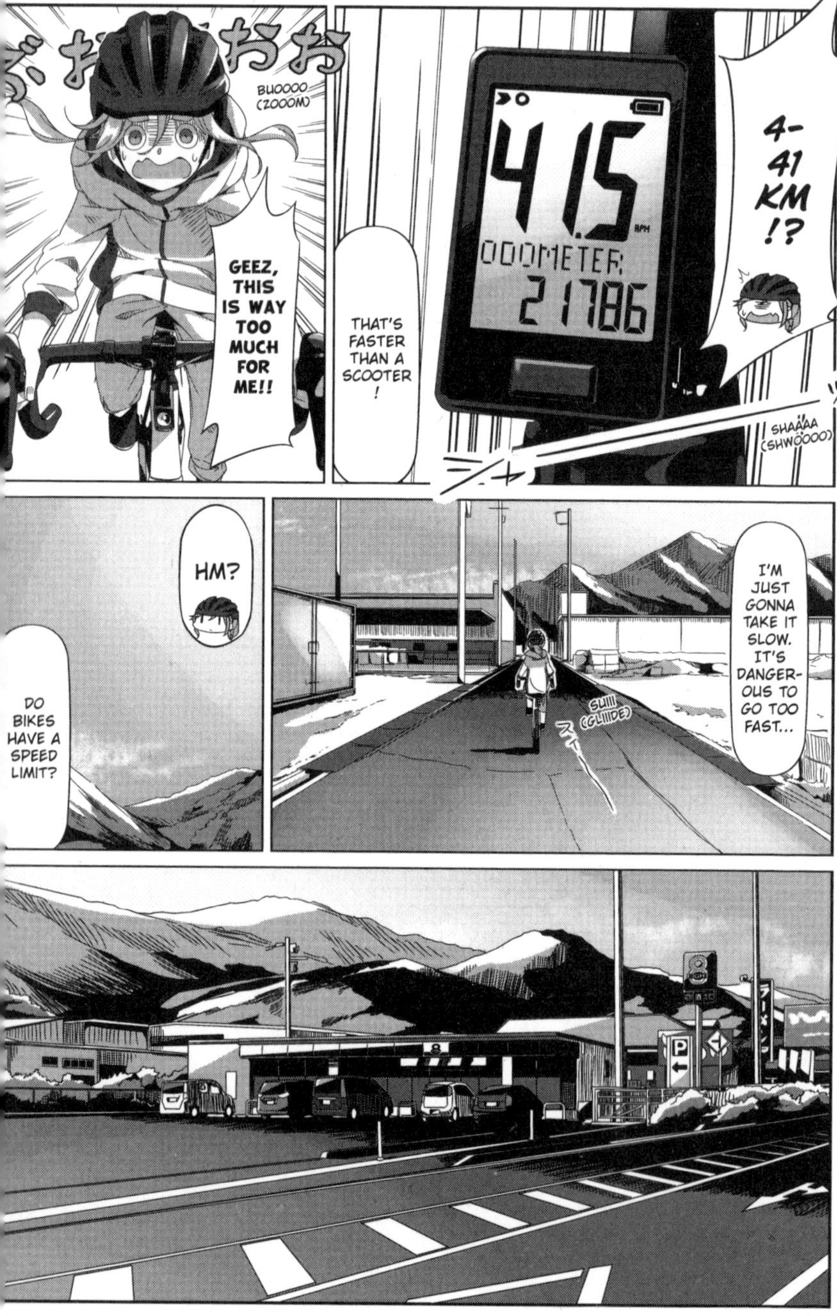
4-41 KM!?
41.5
ODOMETER: 21786
THAT'S FASTER THAN A SCOOTER!
SHAAAA (SHWOOOO)
BUOOOO (ZOOOM)
GEEZ, THIS IS WAY TOO MUCH FOR ME!!
I'M JUST GONNA TAKE IT SLOW. IT'S DANGEROUS TO GO TOO FAST...
SUIII (GLIIIDE)
HM?
DO BIKES HAVE A SPEED LIMIT?

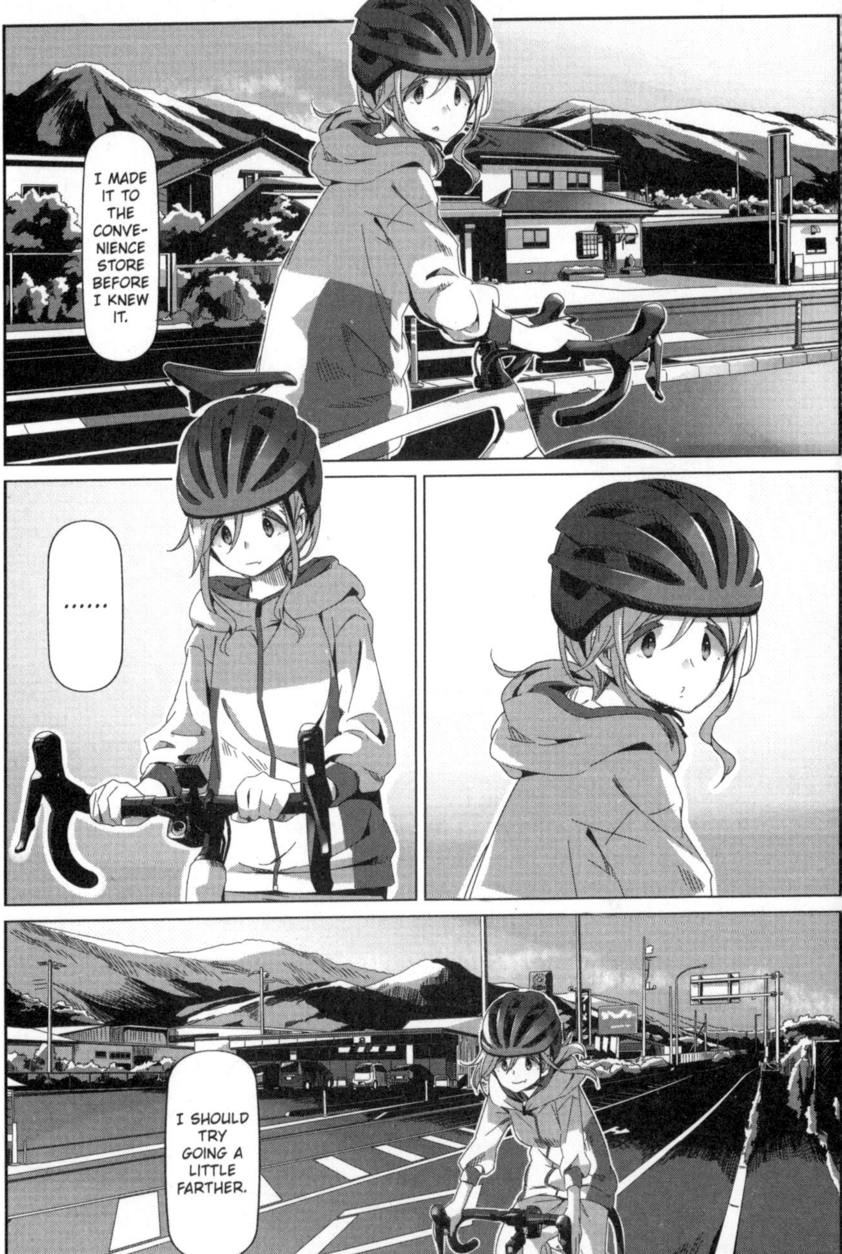
I MADE IT TO THE CONVE-NIENCE STORE BEFORE I KNEW IT.
......
I SHOULD TRY GOING A LITTLE FARTHER.

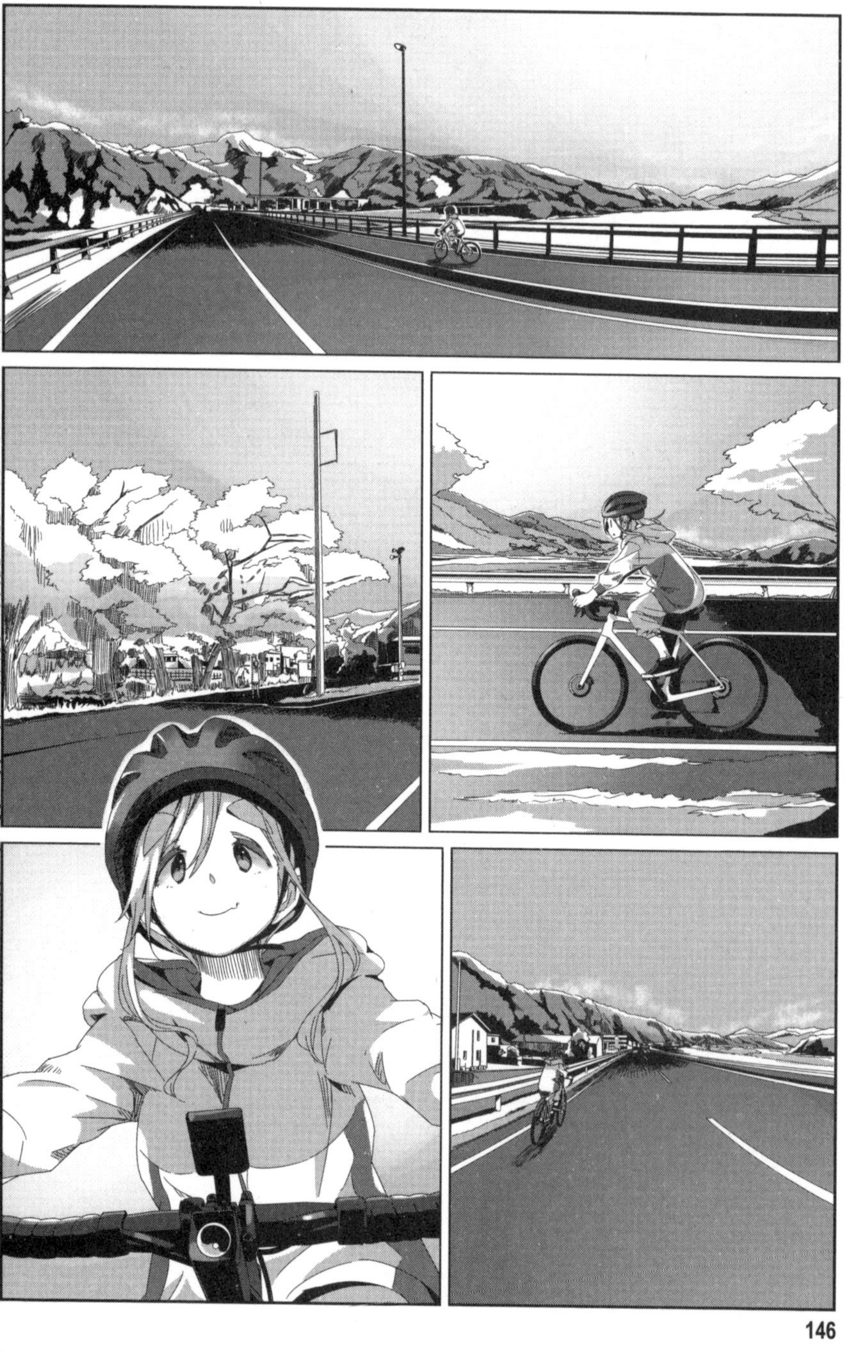

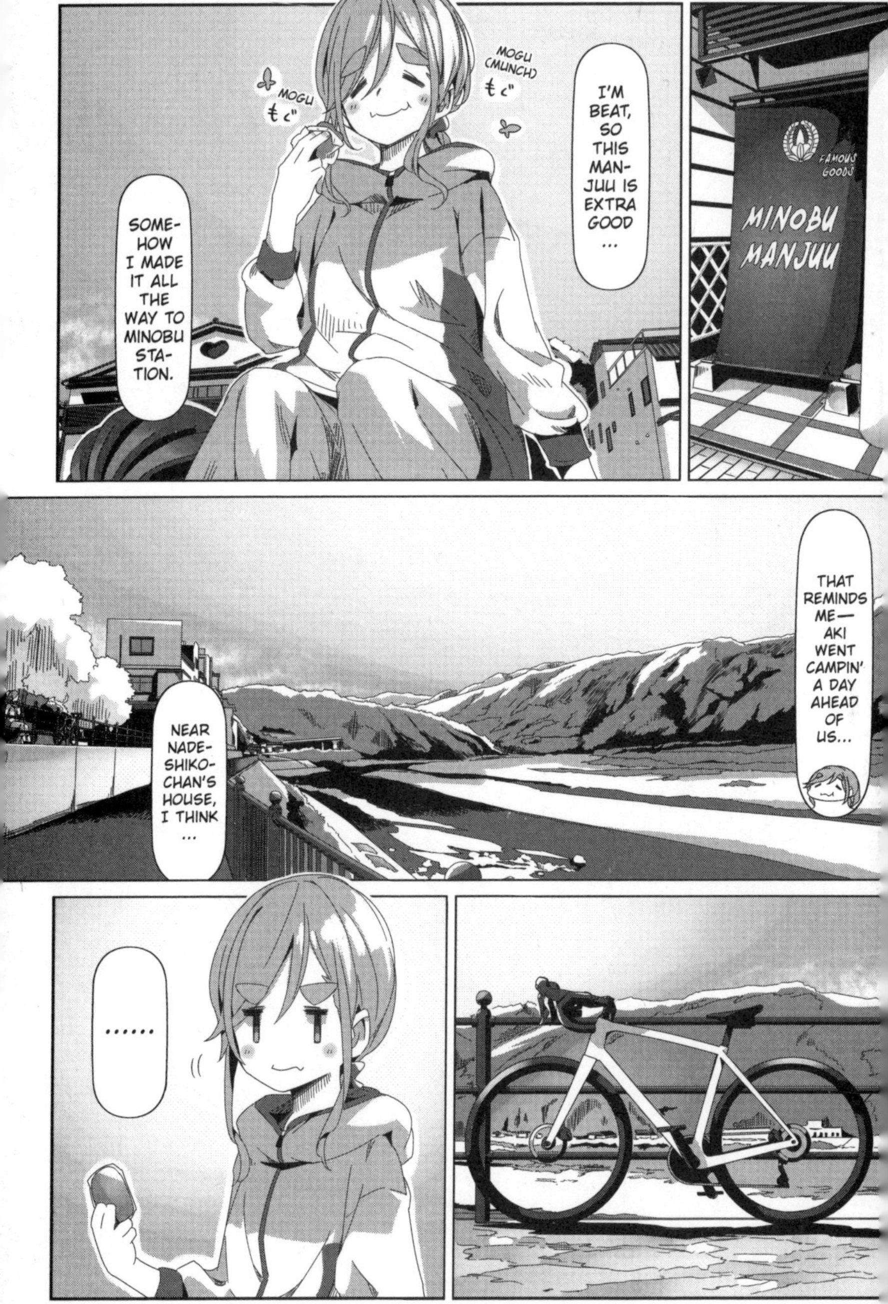
FAMOUS GOODS
MINOBU MANJUU
I'M BEAT, SO THIS MANJUU IS EXTRA GOOD...
MOGU (MUNCH)
もぐ
MOGU
もぐ
SOMEHOW I MADE IT ALL THE WAY TO MINOBU STATION.
THAT REMINDS ME—AKI WENT CAMPIN' A DAY AHEAD OF US...
NEAR NADESHIKO-CHAN'S HOUSE, I THINK...
......

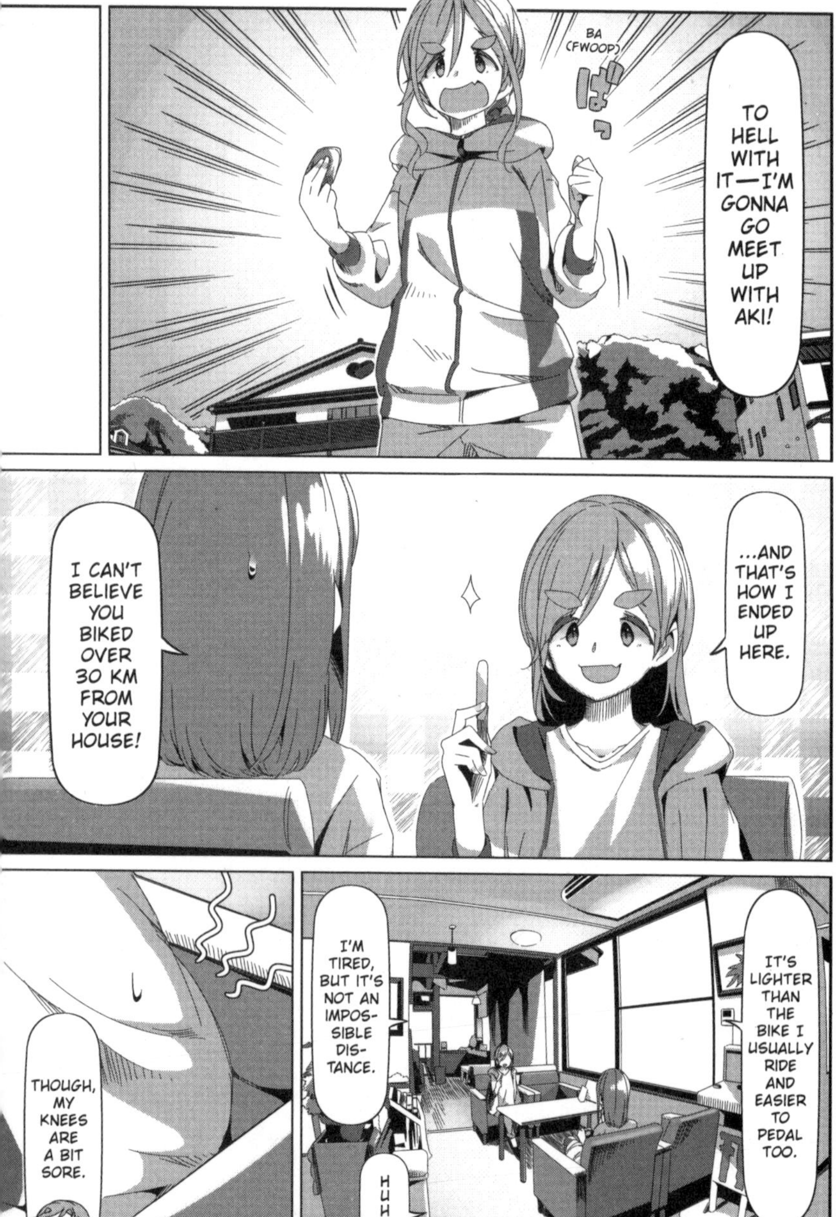
TO HELL WITH IT—I'M GONNA GO MEET UP WITH AKI!
BA (FWOOP)
...AND THAT'S HOW I ENDED UP HERE.
I CAN'T BELIEVE YOU BIKED OVER 30 KM FROM YOUR HOUSE!
IT'S LIGHTER THAN THE BIKE I USUALLY RIDE AND EASIER TO PEDAL TOO.
I'M TIRED, BUT IT'S NOT AN IMPOSSIBLE DISTANCE.
HUH...
THOUGH, MY KNEES ARE A BIT SORE.

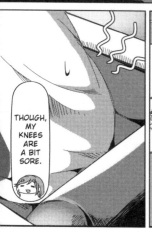

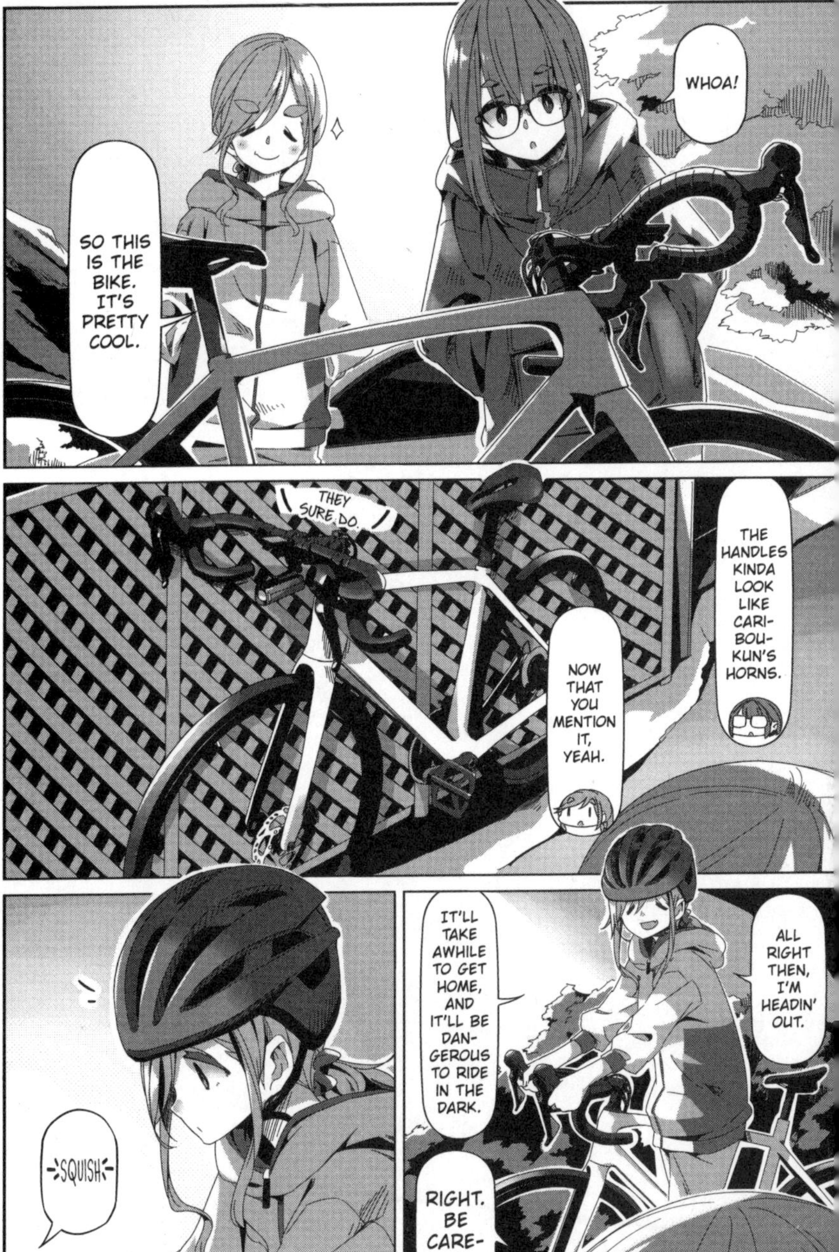
WHOA!
SO THIS IS THE BIKE. IT'S PRETTY COOL.
THE HANDLES KINDA LOOK LIKE CARI-BOU-KUN'S HORNS.
NOW THAT YOU MENTION IT, YEAH.
THEY SURE DO.
ALL RIGHT THEN, I'M HEADIN' OUT.
IT'LL TAKE AWHILE TO GET HOME, AND IT'LL BE DAN-GEROUS TO RIDE IN THE DARK.
RIGHT. BE CARE-FUL.
SQUISH

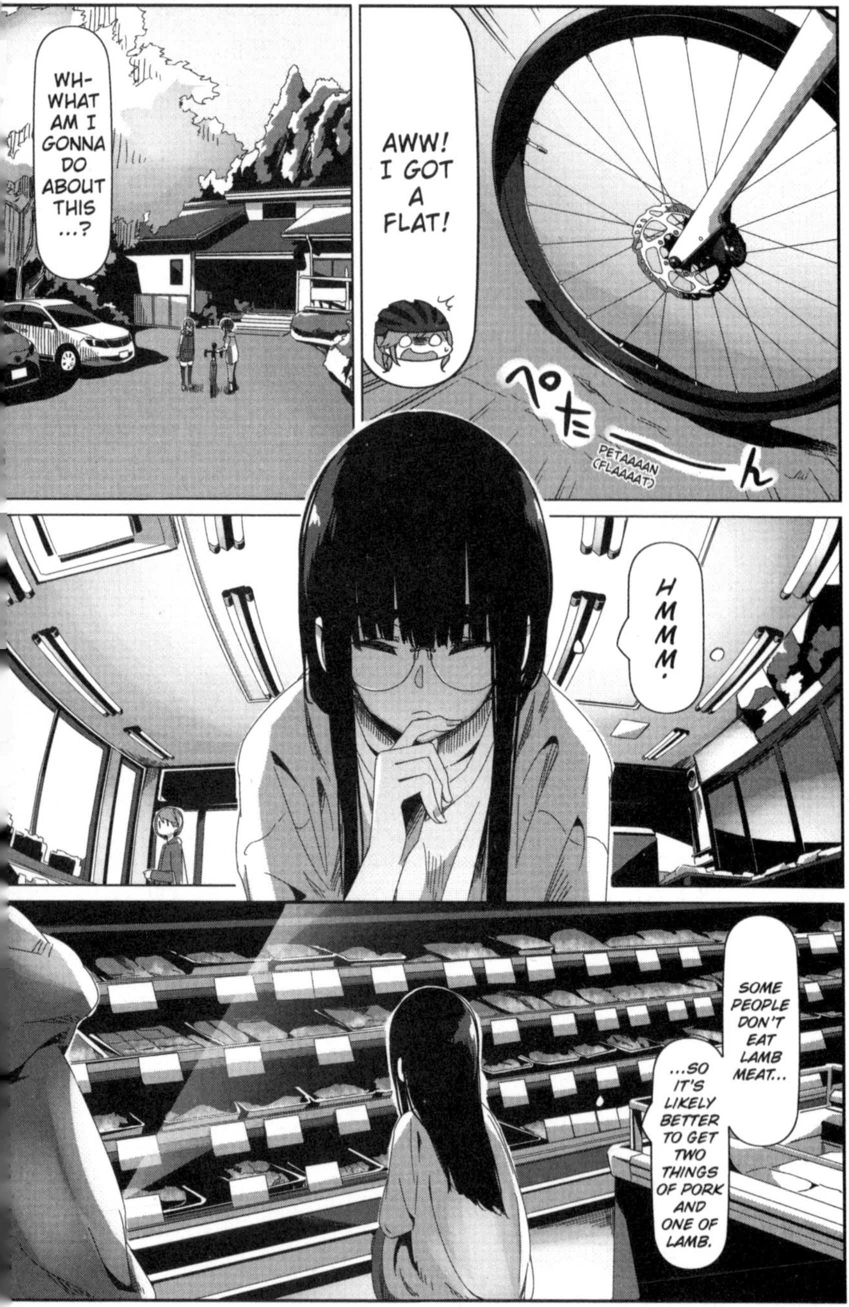
AWW! I GOT A FLAT!
ぺた ーん
PETAAAAN (FLAAAAT)
WH- WHAT AM I GONNA DO ABOUT THIS ...?
HMMM.
SOME PEOPLE DON'T EAT LAMB MEAT...
...SO IT'S LIKELY BETTER TO GET TWO THINGS OF PORK AND ONE OF LAMB.

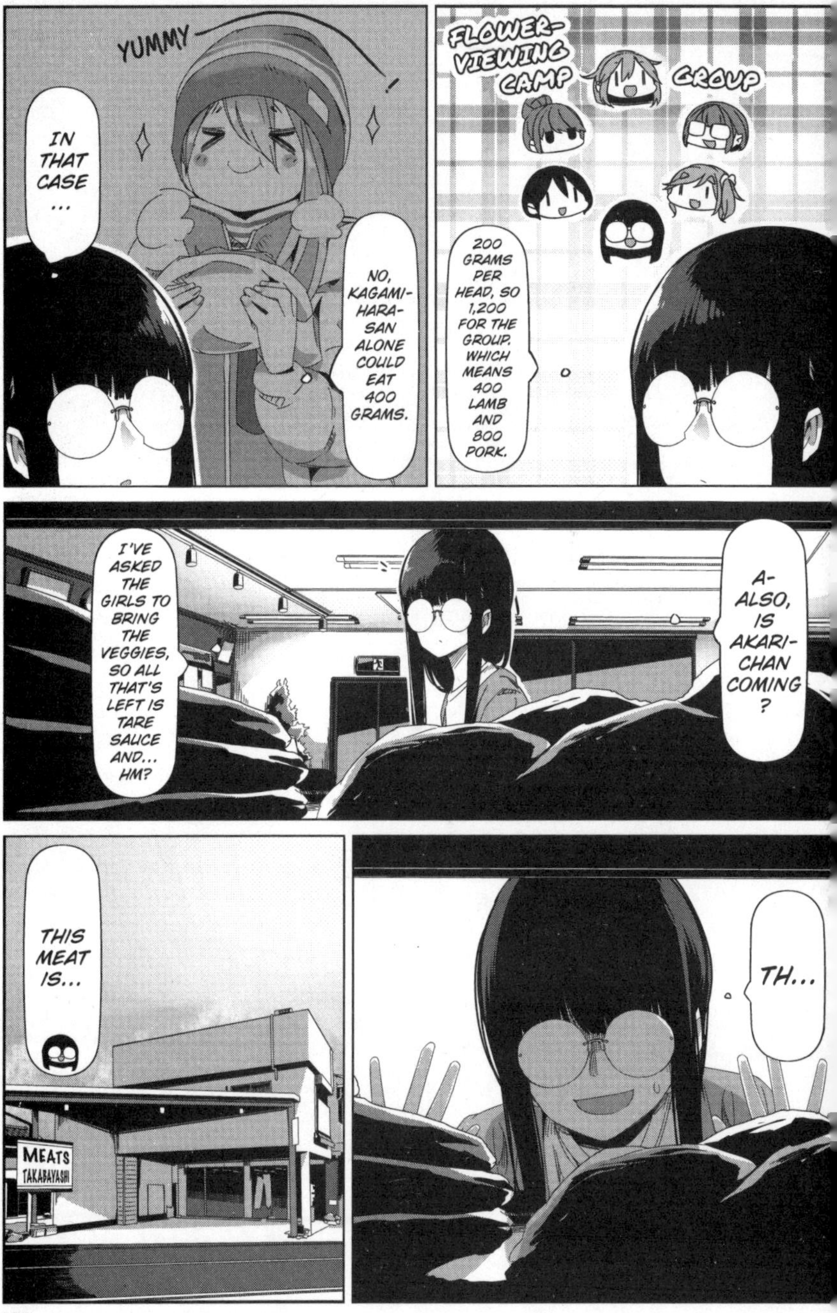
FLOWER-VIEWING CAMP GROUP
200 GRAMS PER HEAD, SO 1,200 FOR THE GROUP. WHICH MEANS 400 LAMB AND 800 PORK.
YUMMY
NO, KAGAMIHARA-SAN ALONE COULD EAT 400 GRAMS.
IN THAT CASE ...
A- ALSO, IS AKARI-CHAN COMING?
I'VE ASKED THE GIRLS TO BRING THE VEGGIES, SO ALL THAT'S LEFT IS TARE SAUCE AND... HM?
TH...
THIS MEAT IS...
MEATS
TAKABAYASHI

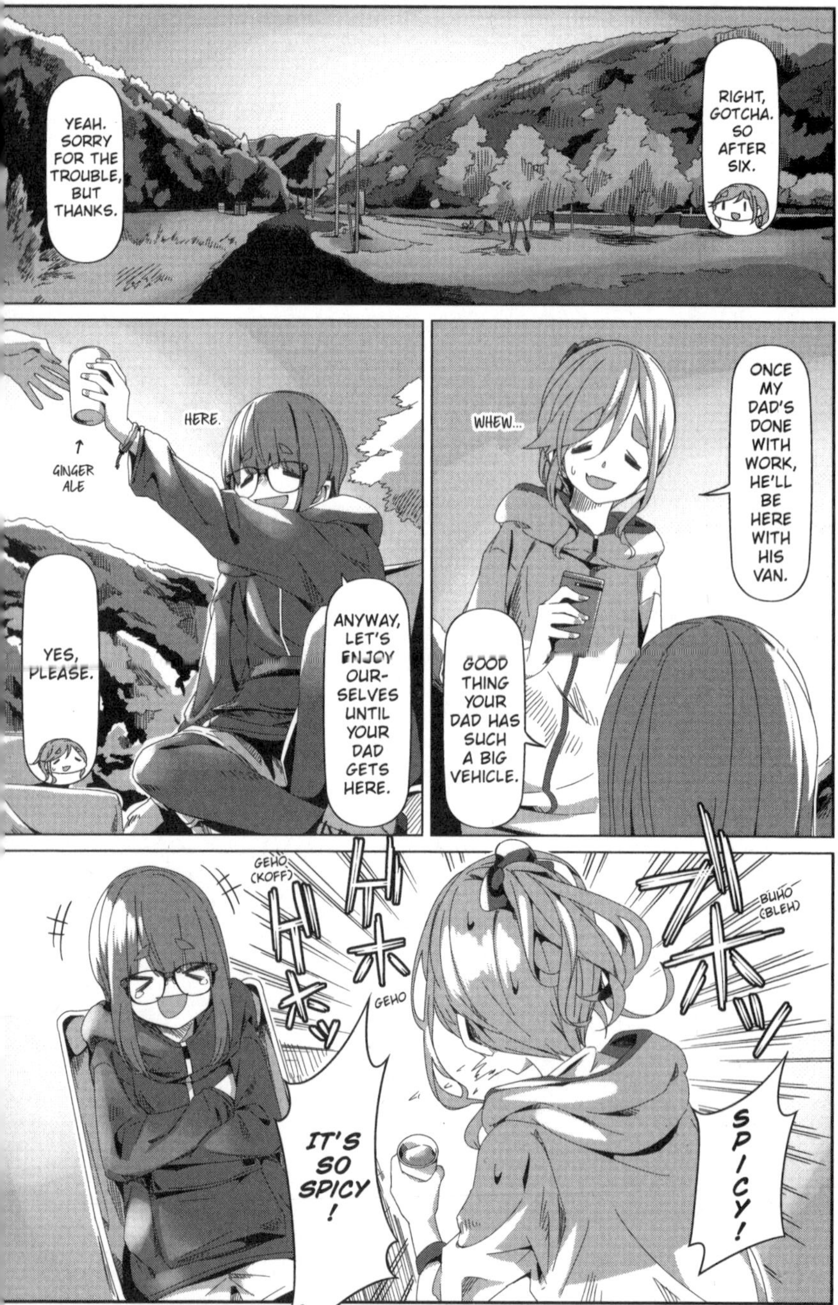
RIGHT, GOTCHA. SO AFTER SIX.
YEAH. SORRY FOR THE TROUBLE, BUT THANKS.
ONCE MY DAD'S DONE WITH WORK, HE'LL BE HERE WITH HIS VAN.
WHEW...
GOOD THING YOUR DAD HAS SUCH A BIG VEHICLE.
ANYWAY, LET'S ENJOY OUR-SELVES UNTIL YOUR DAD GETS HERE.
HERE.
↑ GINGER ALE
YES, PLEASE.
BUHO (BLEH)
SPICY!
GEHO (KOFF)
GEHO
IT'S SO SPICY!

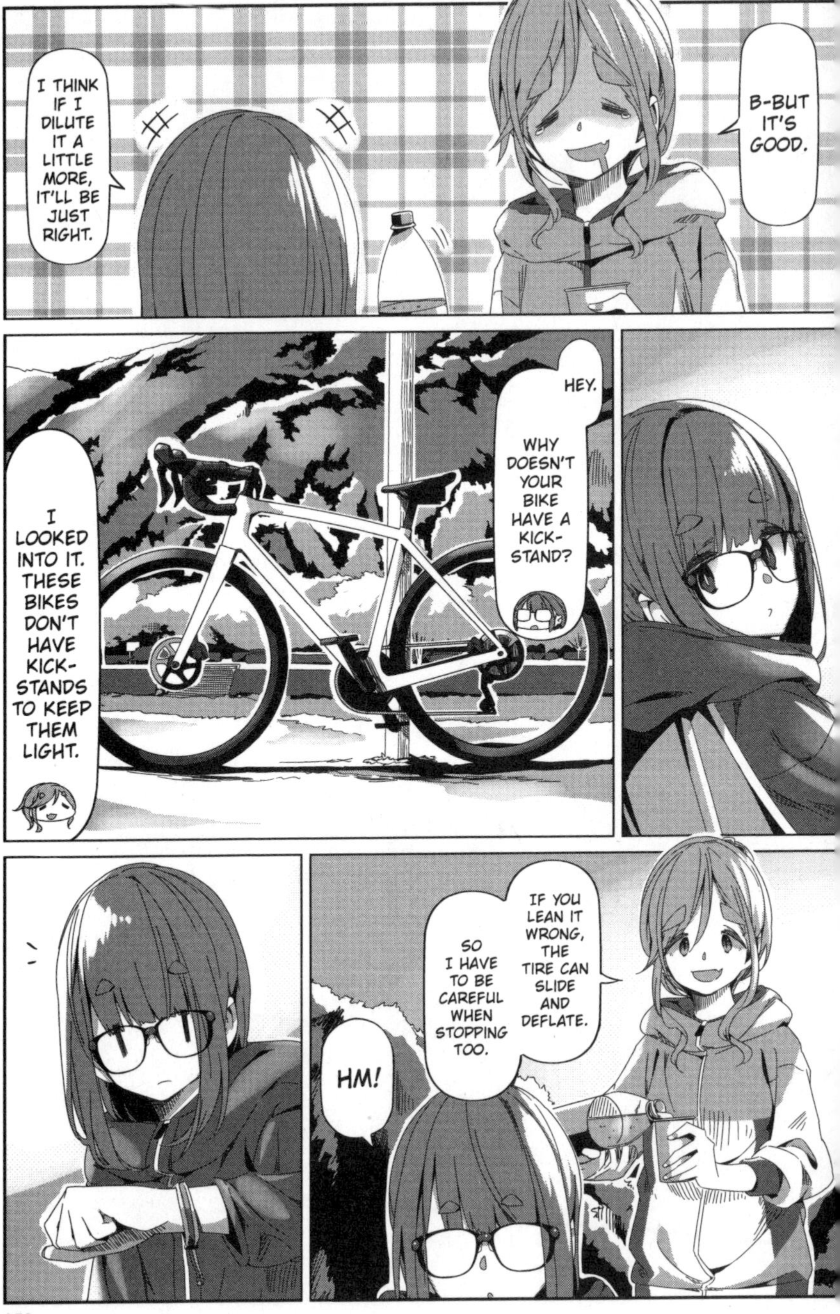
B-BUT IT'S GOOD.
I THINK IF I DILUTE IT A LITTLE MORE, IT'LL BE JUST RIGHT.
HEY.
WHY DOESN'T YOUR BIKE HAVE A KICK-STAND?
I LOOKED INTO IT. THESE BIKES DON'T HAVE KICK-STANDS TO KEEP THEM LIGHT.
IF YOU LEAN IT WRONG, THE TIRE CAN SLIDE AND DEFLATE.
SO I HAVE TO BE CAREFUL WHEN STOPPING TOO.
HM!

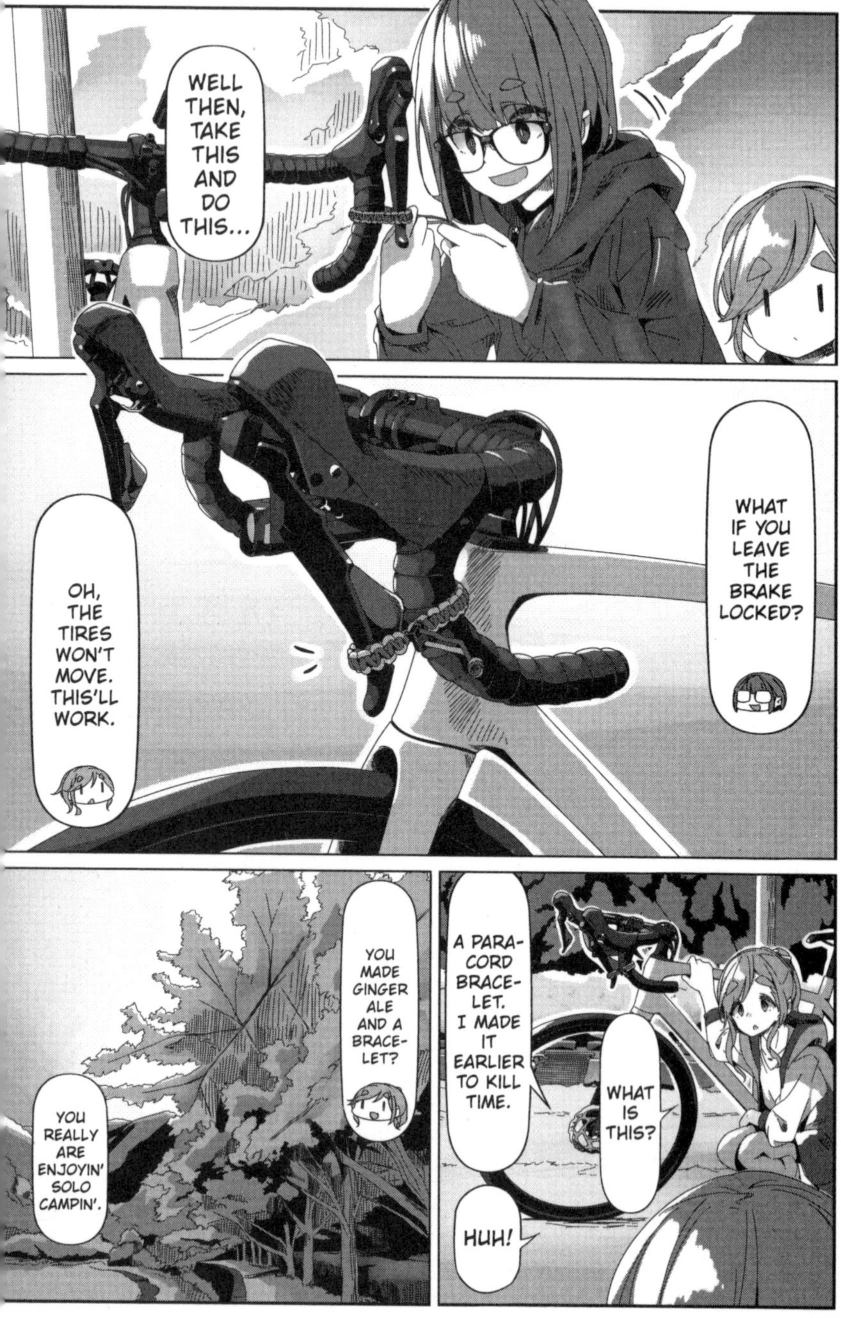
WELL THEN, TAKE THIS AND DO THIS...
WHAT IF YOU LEAVE THE BRAKE LOCKED?
OH, THE TIRES WON'T MOVE. THIS'LL WORK.
WHAT IS THIS?
A PARA-CORD BRACE-LET. I MADE IT EARLIER TO KILL TIME.
HUH!
YOU MADE GINGER ALE AND A BRACE-LET?
YOU REALLY ARE ENJOYIN' SOLO CAMPIN'.

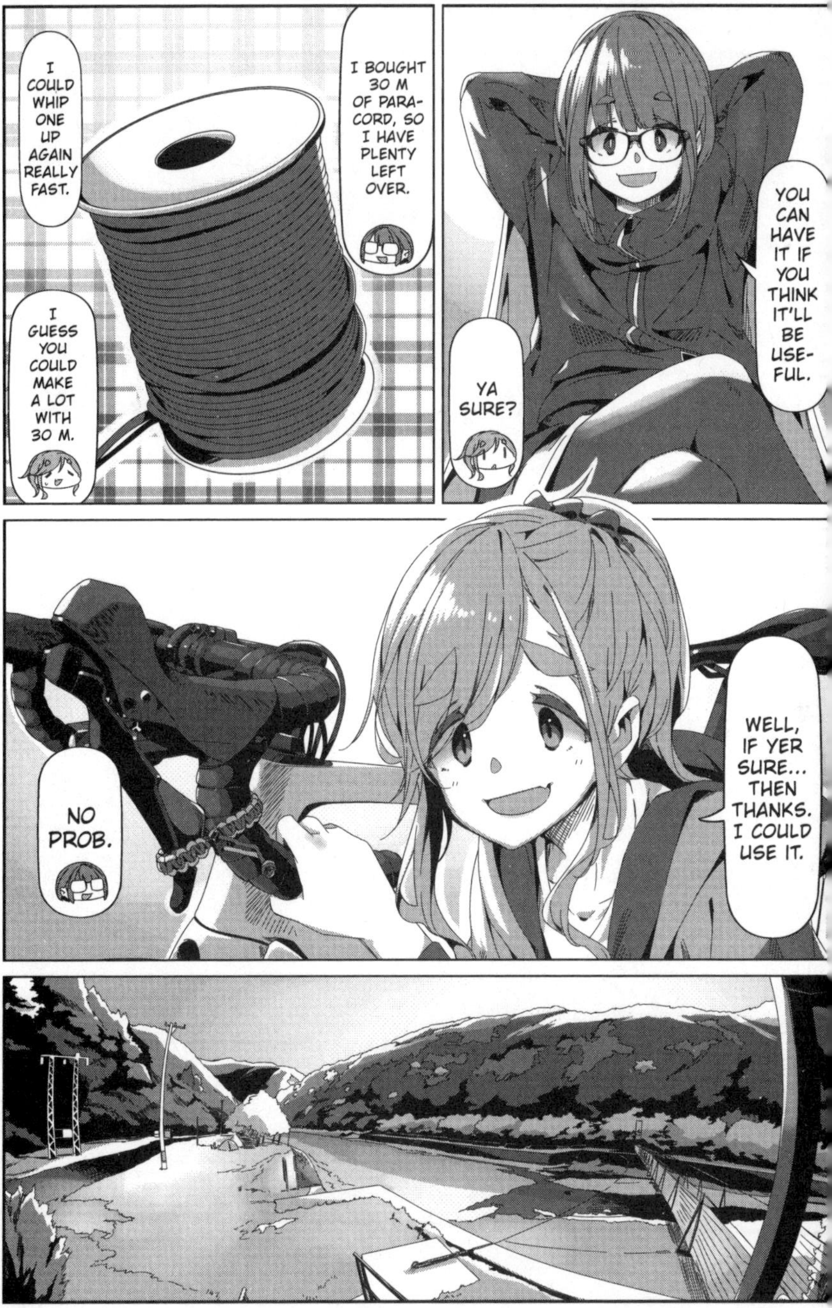
YOU CAN HAVE IT IF YOU THINK IT'LL BE USE-FUL.
YA SURE?
I BOUGHT 30 M OF PARA-CORD, SO I HAVE PLENTY LEFT OVER.
I COULD WHIP ONE UP AGAIN REALLY FAST.
I GUESS YOU COULD MAKE A LOT WITH 30 M.
WELL, IF YER SURE... THEN THANKS. I COULD USE IT.
NO PROB.

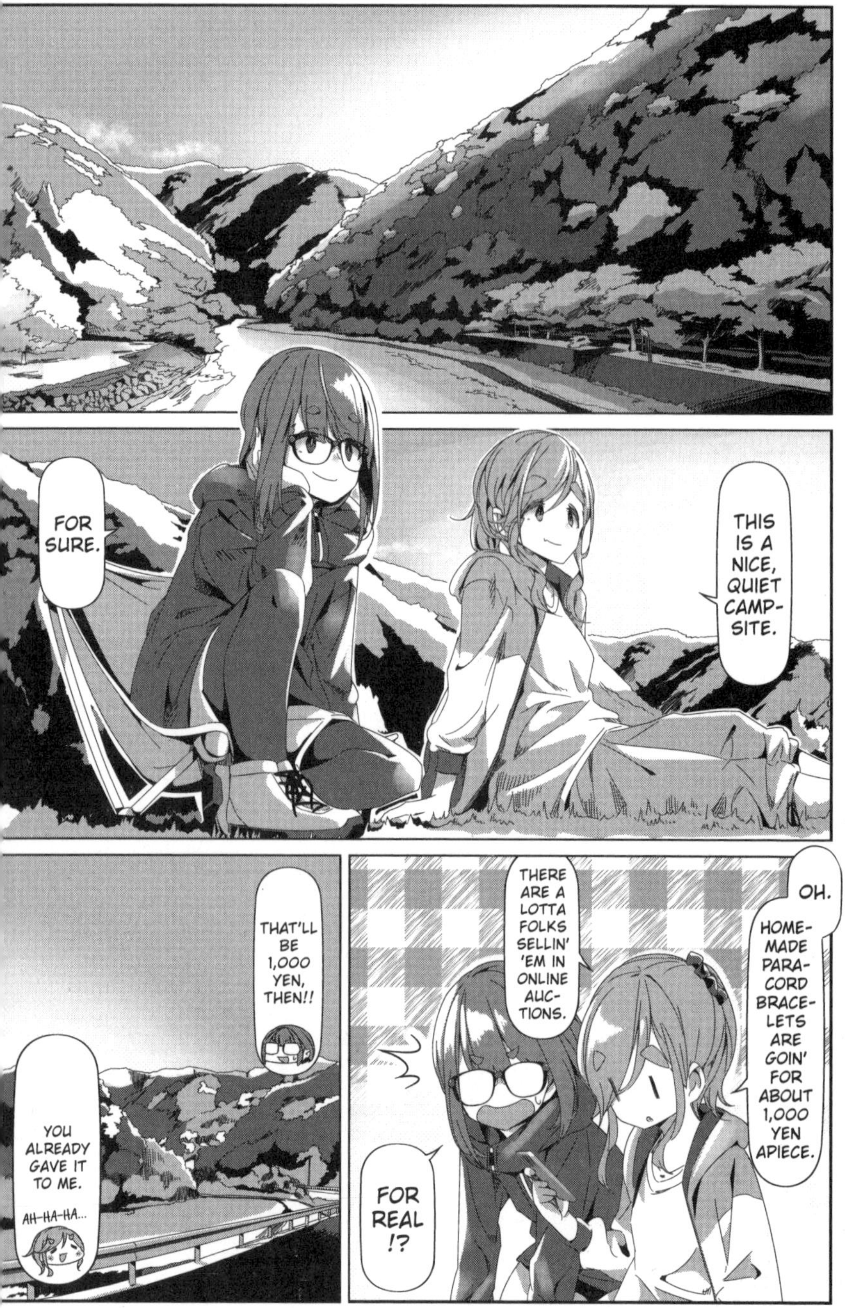
THIS IS A NICE, QUIET CAMP-SITE.
FOR SURE.
OH.
HOME-MADE PARA-CORD BRACE-LETS ARE GOIN' FOR ABOUT 1,000 YEN APIECE.
THERE ARE A LOTTA FOLKS SELLIN' 'EM IN ONLINE AUC-TIONS.
FOR REAL !?
THAT'LL BE 1,000 YEN, THEN!!
YOU ALREADY GAVE IT TO ME.
AH-HA-HA...

# TRANSLATION NOTES

COMMON HONORIFICS

no honorific: Indicates familiarity or closeness; if used without permission or reason, addressing someone in this manner would constitute an insult.
*-san*: The Japanese equivalent of Mr./Mrs./Miss. If a situation calls for politeness, this is the fail-safe honorific.
*-kun*: Used most often when referring to boys, this indicates affection or familiarity. Occasionally used by older men among their peers, but it may also be used by anyone referring to a person of lower standing.
*-chan*: An affectionate honorific indicating familiarity used mostly in reference to girls; also used in reference to cute persons or animals regardless of gender.
*-sensei*: A respectful term for teachers, artists, or high-level professionals.

*(o)nee*: Japanese equivalent to "older sis."
*(o)nii*: Japanese equivalent to "older bro."

100 yen is approximately 1 USD.
1 centimeter is approximately 0.39 inches. 1 kilometer is approximately 0.621 miles.

*PAGE 44*
***Touge***: Japanese for "mountain pass."

*PAGE 55*
**Western Line**: This is a cycling route in Yamanashi that circles the Koufu Basin at points and is meant to guide riders on the best routes to take in the lovely sights of blossoms in spring.

*PAGE 64*
**Fruit Line**: Like the Western Line, this is another cycling route around the Koufu Basin meant for viewing blossoms in the spring.

*PAGE 70*
**Standees**: The standees Nadeshiko is using here are Shingen Takeda and three of the women in his life: his mother (Goryounin Suwa, also called Koihime), his wife (Lady Sanjou), and one of his daughters (Matsuhime).

*PAGE 75*
**Gunma**: A prefecture in Japan located a bit north of Yamanashi and to the northwest of Tokyo.

*PAGE 130*
**"And stop what?"**: In the original Japanese, Inuko mixes up *kireji* ("stop" in the sense of telegram communications to indicate an ending punctuation) and its homophone, *kireji* ("bleeding hemorrhoids").

*PAGE 151*
***Tare* sauce**: A soy sauce–based sauce typically used for grilled meat.

**Meats Takabayashi**: This is a reference to an actual meat shop called Meat Takahashi.

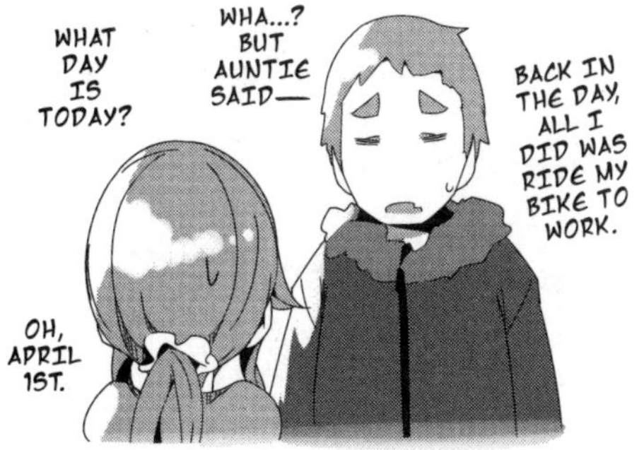
BACK IN THE DAY, ALL I DID WAS RIDE MY BIKE TO WORK.
WHA...? BUT AUNTIE SAID—
WHAT DAY IS TODAY?
OH, APRIL 1ST.

# TRANSLATION NOTES (continued)

*PAGE 159*
**Katsudon**: In its most commonly known form form, *katsudon* is a pork or chicken cutlet served over a **donburi** rice bowl. In *donburi*, the other ingredients are simmered together before being poured over the rice.

*PAGE 160*
**Fukui, Okinawa**: Different areas of Japan. Fukui is a prefecture west of Yamanashi along the Sea of Japan, and Okinawa is an island located far to the south of the Japan mainland.

**Police dramas**: The serving of *katsudon* to someone under interrogation is a trope of Japanese police dramas, and acts as a sort of "good cop" situation to tempt the suspect into confessing.

*PAGE 162*
**Ehoumaki**: A type of thick sushi roll made with seven fillings to symbolize good fortune. It's eaten on the holiday Setsubun—the day before the start of spring on the old Japanese lunar calendar.

*PAGE 165*
**Sukiyaki**: A hot-pot dish with fatty beef as the main ingredient.
**Nikujaga**: Stewed meat and potatoes.
**Acqua pazza**: An italian dish of white fish poached in an herb broth; sometimes, this refers to just the cooking method.
**Ajillo**: A Spanish dish made with garlic and guajillo chilis.

*PAGE 169*
**Carved a mountain into the shape of a dog**: Inuyama in Japanese is written with the characters for "dog" and "mountain."

*PAGE 171*
**Newly created kanji**: *Kanji*, one of the three writing systems used in Japanese, consists of ideograms in which meaning is contained within the character rather than treating it purely as an alphabet-esque letter. In Japan, there is an actual contest each year to think up new *kanji* to convey new ideas succinctly (though it's really only for fun, and they don't typically get adopted).

*PAGE 172*
**Yakiniku**: Grilled meat dishes, derived from Korean barbecue.

*PAGE 174–175*
**Mt. Fuji seen from...**: Unlike the previous part's *kanji* jokes, which utilize *kanji* to make shapes resembling what they're supposed to mean, this one is based on the meaning of existing *kanji* and how they can be broken into component parts, known as "radicals." While impossible to detail in full in a limited amount of space, here are some of the *kanji* used: 山 ("mountain"), 秩父多摩甲斐国立公園 ("Chichibu-Tama-kai National Park"—note that many of the *kanji* here have been squished into the single made-up character), 静岡 ("Shizuoka"), 山梨 ("Yamanashi"), 青 ("blue"), 争 ("conflict").

*INSIDE COVER (BACK)*
**Tatsuo, Kenjirou, Mitsuaki, Kyoushirou**: The younger brothers of Inuko's dad all have names that indicate their birth order, with Kenjirou being the second oldest and Kyoushirou being the fourth and youngest.

**Muromachi period**: An era in Japan from around 1336 to 1573 AD. It ended with the rise of Nobunaga Oda.

**Parallel world**: This is referring to the popular Japanese fictional trope of people being transported or reborn in other worlds, often with a fantasy setting. Also known as *isekai*.

◁ SIDE STORIES BEGIN ON THE NEXT PAGE ◁

# AFTER-SCHOOL 108 KATSUDON

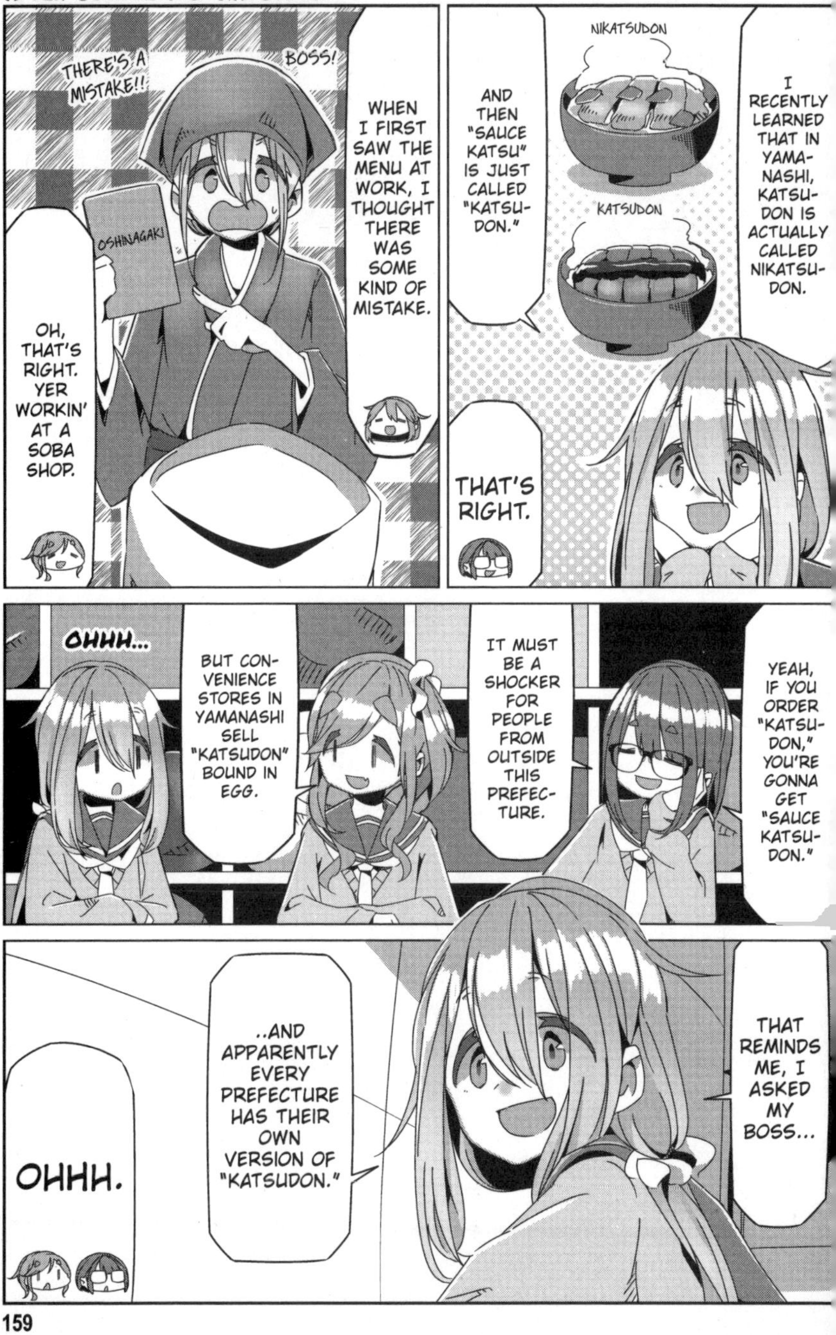
I RECENTLY LEARNED THAT IN YAMANASHI, KATSUDON IS ACTUALLY CALLED NIKATSUDON.
NIKATSUDON
KATSUDON
AND THEN "SAUCE KATSU" IS JUST CALLED "KATSUDON."
THAT'S RIGHT.
WHEN I FIRST SAW THE MENU AT WORK, I THOUGHT THERE WAS SOME KIND OF MISTAKE.
BOSS!
THERE'S A MISTAKE!!
OSHINAGAKI
OH, THAT'S RIGHT. YER WORKIN' AT A SOBA SHOP.
YEAH, IF YOU ORDER "KATSUDON," YOU'RE GONNA GET "SAUCE KATSUDON."
IT MUST BE A SHOCKER FOR PEOPLE FROM OUTSIDE THIS PREFECTURE.
BUT CONVENIENCE STORES IN YAMANASHI SELL "KATSUDON" BOUND IN EGG.
OHHH...
THAT REMINDS ME, I ASKED MY BOSS...
..AND APPARENTLY EVERY PREFECTURE HAS THEIR OWN VERSION OF "KATSUDON."
OHHH.

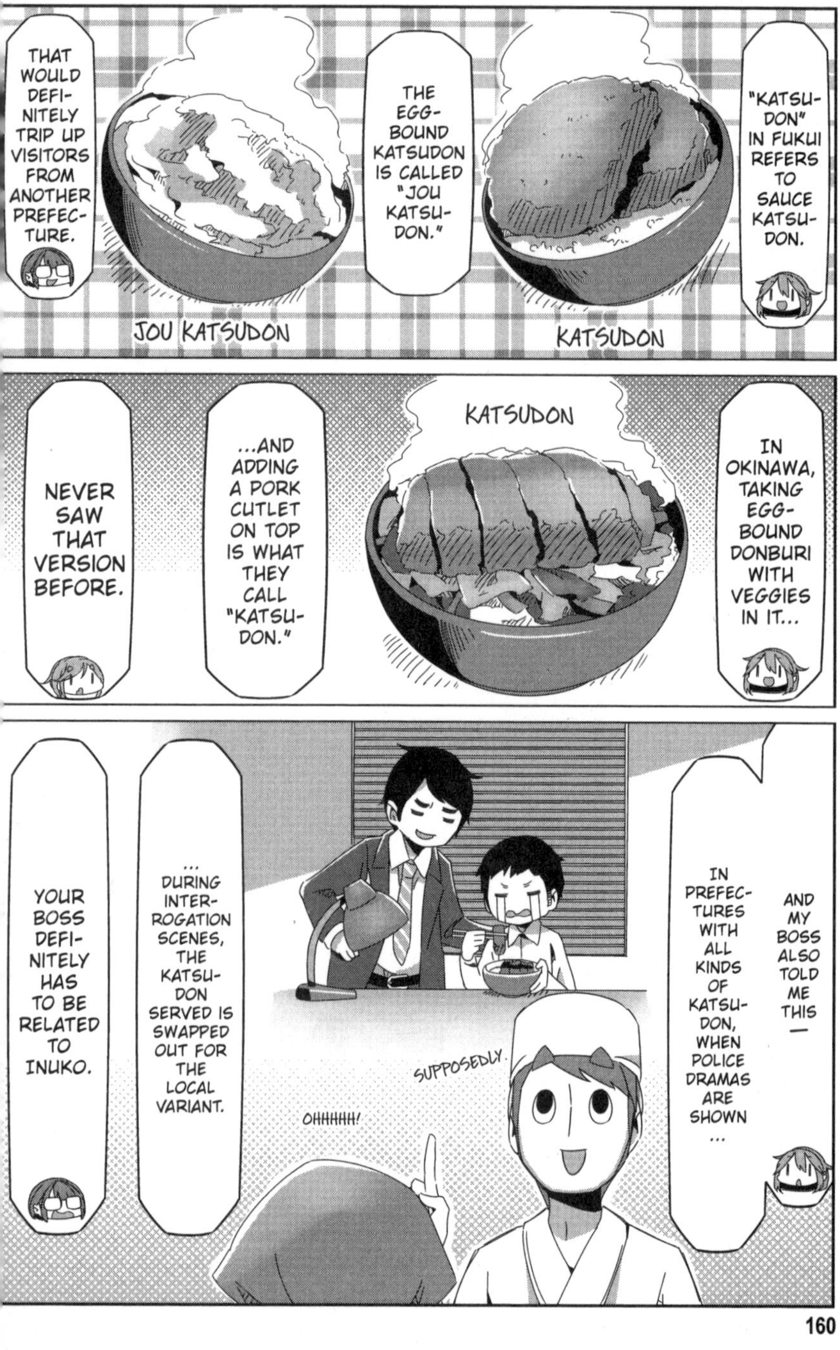
"KATSUDON" IN FUKUI REFERS TO SAUCE KATSUDON.
KATSUDON
THE EGG-BOUND KATSUDON IS CALLED "JOU KATSUDON."
THAT WOULD DEFINITELY TRIP UP VISITORS FROM ANOTHER PREFECTURE.
JOU KATSUDON
IN OKINAWA, TAKING EGG-BOUND DONBURI WITH VEGGIES IN IT...
KATSUDON
...AND ADDING A PORK CUTLET ON TOP IS WHAT THEY CALL "KATSUDON."
NEVER SAW THAT VERSION BEFORE.
AND MY BOSS ALSO TOLD ME THIS—
IN PREFECTURES WITH ALL KINDS OF KATSUDON, WHEN POLICE DRAMAS ARE SHOWN...
SUPPOSEDLY.
...DURING INTERROGATION SCENES, THE KATSUDON SERVED IS SWAPPED OUT FOR THE LOCAL VARIANT.
OHHHHHH!
YOUR BOSS DEFINITELY HAS TO BE RELATED TO INUKO.

## AFTER-SCHOOL 109 LEGEND OF NOUTORI

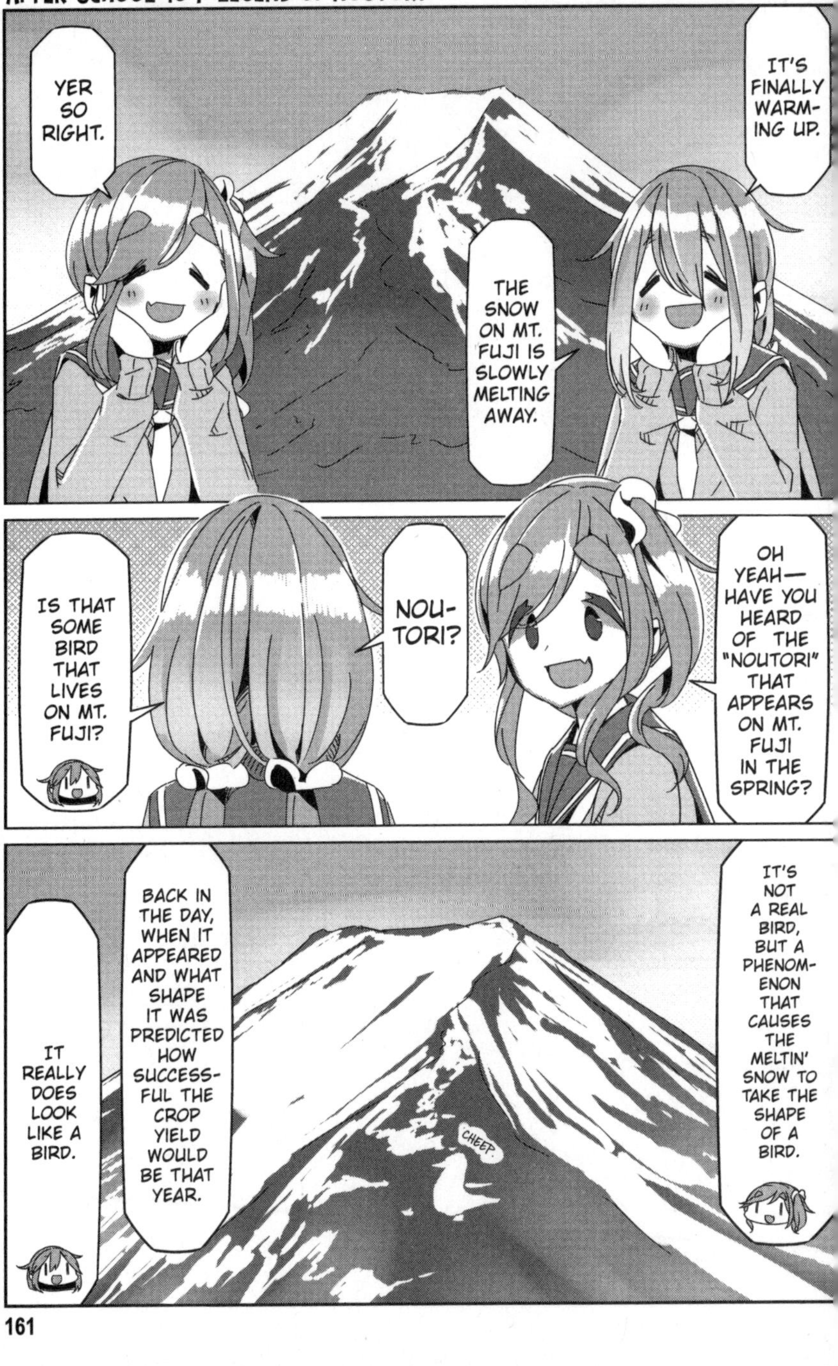
IT'S FINALLY WARMING UP.
THE SNOW ON MT. FUJI IS SLOWLY MELTING AWAY.
YER SO RIGHT.
OH YEAH—HAVE YOU HEARD OF THE "NOUTORI" THAT APPEARS ON MT. FUJI IN THE SPRING?
NOU-TORI?
IS THAT SOME BIRD THAT LIVES ON MT. FUJI?
IT'S NOT A REAL BIRD, BUT A PHENOMENON THAT CAUSES THE MELTIN' SNOW TO TAKE THE SHAPE OF A BIRD.
BACK IN THE DAY, WHEN IT APPEARED AND WHAT SHAPE IT WAS PREDICTED HOW SUCCESSFUL THE CROP YIELD WOULD BE THAT YEAR.
CHEEP
IT REALLY DOES LOOK LIKE A BIRD.

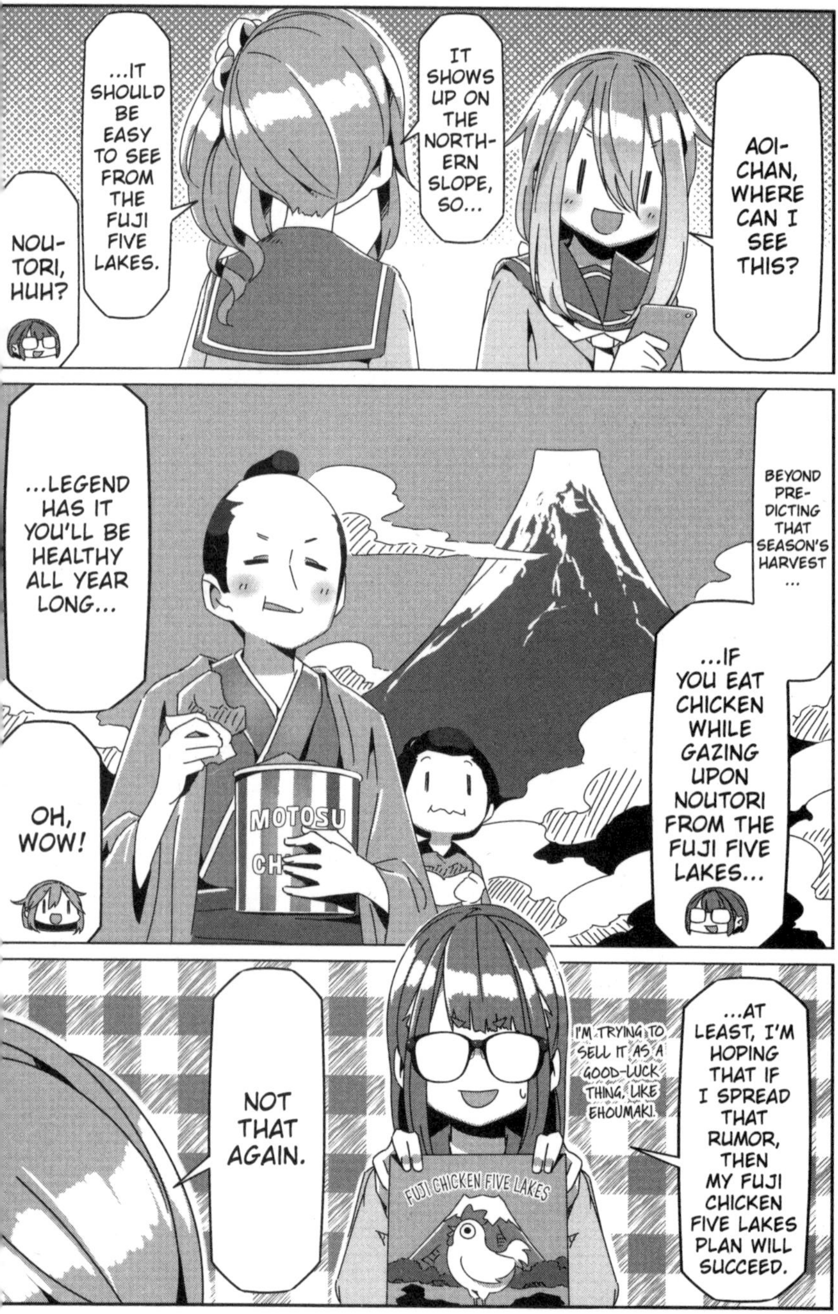
AOI-CHAN, WHERE CAN I SEE THIS?
IT SHOWS UP ON THE NORTHERN SLOPE, SO...
...IT SHOULD BE EASY TO SEE FROM THE FUJI FIVE LAKES.
NOU-TORI, HUH?
BEYOND PREDICTING THAT SEASON'S HARVEST...
...IF YOU EAT CHICKEN WHILE GAZING UPON NOUTORI FROM THE FUJI FIVE LAKES...
...LEGEND HAS IT YOU'LL BE HEALTHY ALL YEAR LONG...
MOTOSU
CH
OH, WOW!
...AT LEAST, I'M HOPING THAT IF I SPREAD THAT RUMOR, THEN MY FUJI CHICKEN FIVE LAKES PLAN WILL SUCCEED.
I'M TRYING TO SELL IT AS A GOOD-LUCK THING, LIKE EHOUMAKI.
FUJI CHICKEN FIVE LAKES
NOT THAT AGAIN.

## AFTER-SCHOOL 110 BROWS SHOWING THROUGH

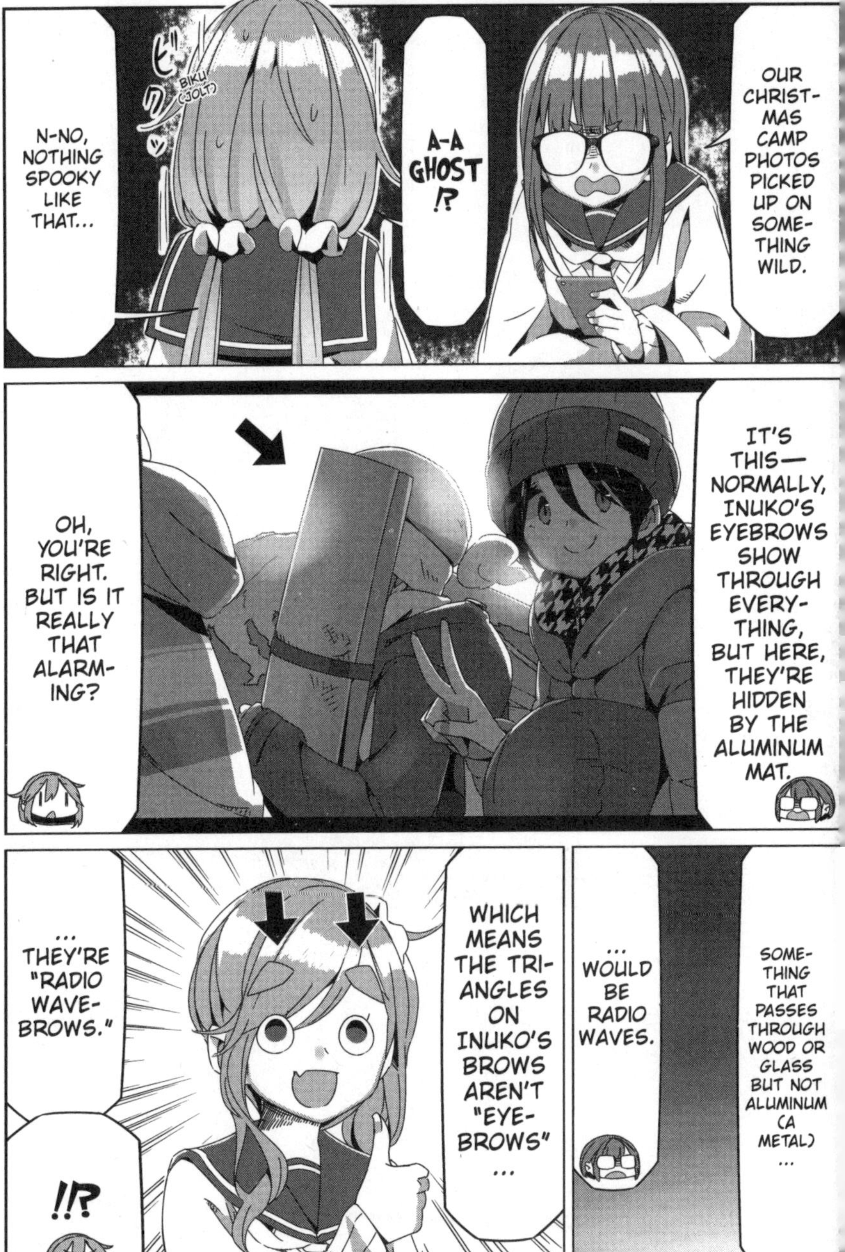

OUR CHRIST-MAS CAMP PHOTOS PICKED UP ON SOME-THING WILD.
A-A GHOST !?
BIKU (JOLT)
N-NO, NOTHING SPOOKY LIKE THAT...
IT'S THIS—NORMALLY, INUKO'S EYEBROWS SHOW THROUGH EVERY-THING, BUT HERE, THEY'RE HIDDEN BY THE ALUMINUM MAT.
OH, YOU'RE RIGHT. BUT IS IT REALLY THAT ALARM-ING?
SOME-THING THAT PASSES THROUGH WOOD OR GLASS BUT NOT ALUMINUM (A METAL) ...
... WOULD BE RADIO WAVES.
WHICH MEANS THE TRI-ANGLES ON INUKO'S BROWS AREN'T "EYE-BROWS" ...
... THEY'RE "RADIO WAVE-BROWS."
!!?

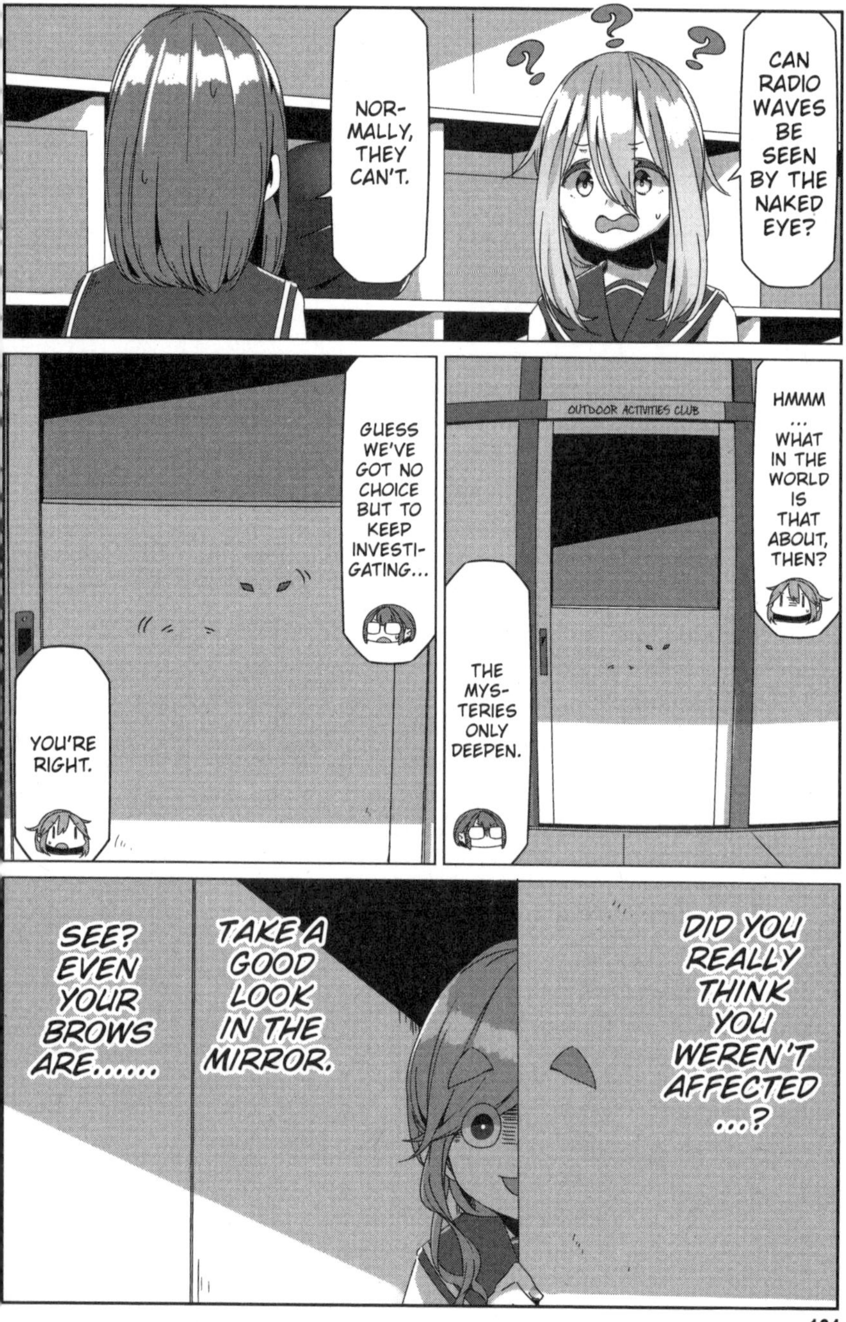
CAN RADIO WAVES BE SEEN BY THE NAKED EYE?
NOR-MALLY, THEY CAN'T.
HMMM... WHAT IN THE WORLD IS THAT ABOUT, THEN?
OUTDOOR ACTIVITIES CLUB
THE MYS-TERIES ONLY DEEPEN.
GUESS WE'VE GOT NO CHOICE BUT TO KEEP INVESTI-GATING...
YOU'RE RIGHT.
DID YOU REALLY THINK YOU WEREN'T AFFECTED ...?
TAKE A GOOD LOOK IN THE MIRROR.
SEE? EVEN YOUR BROWS ARE......

# AFTER-SCHOOL 111 THE PROBLEM OF OVER-REMIXING

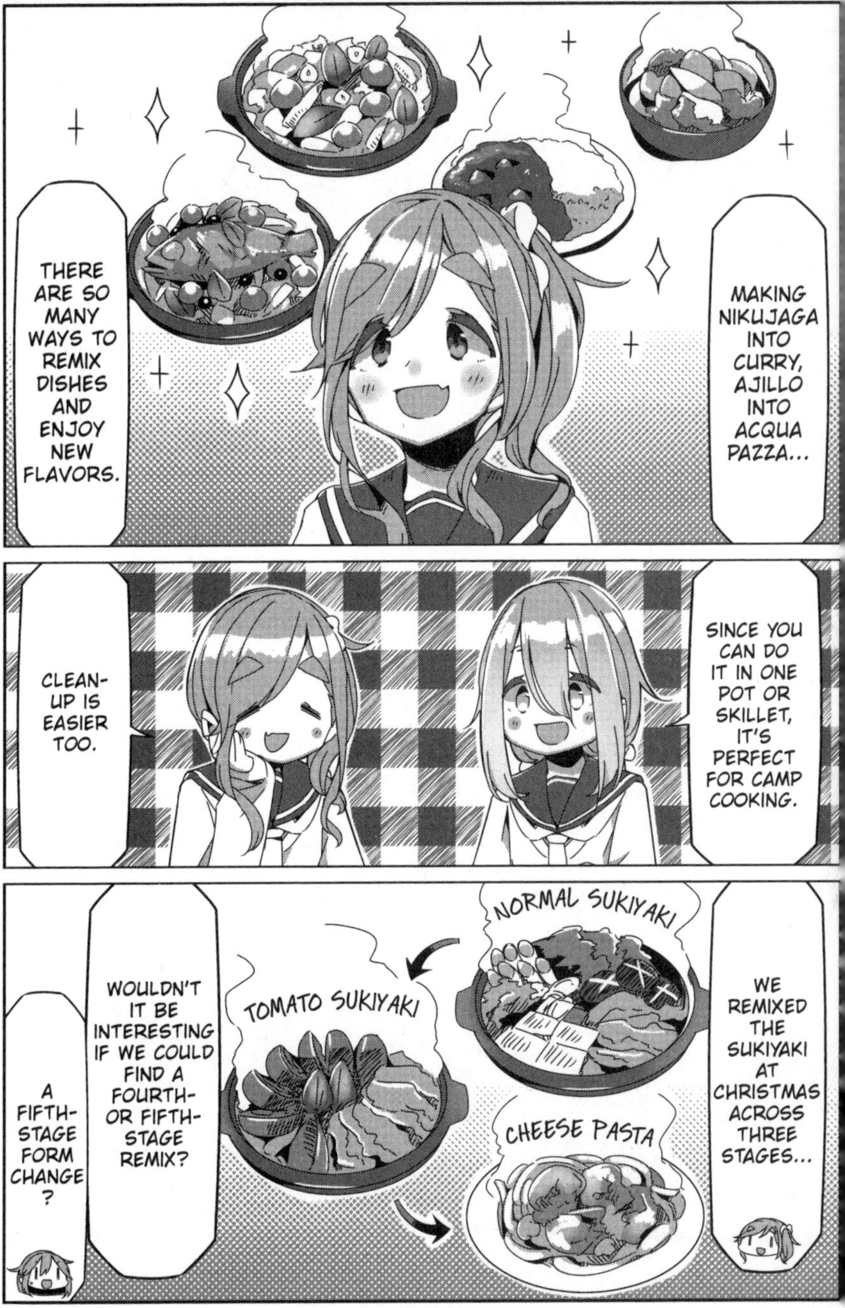
MAKING NIKUJAGA INTO CURRY, AJILLO INTO ACQUA PAZZA...
THERE ARE SO MANY WAYS TO REMIX DISHES AND ENJOY NEW FLAVORS.
SINCE YOU CAN DO IT IN ONE POT OR SKILLET, IT'S PERFECT FOR CAMP COOKING.
CLEAN-UP IS EASIER TOO.
WE REMIXED THE SUKIYAKI AT CHRISTMAS ACROSS THREE STAGES...
NORMAL SUKIYAKI
TOMATO SUKIYAKI
CHEESE PASTA
WOULDN'T IT BE INTERESTING IF WE COULD FIND A FOURTH- OR FIFTH-STAGE REMIX?
A FIFTH-STAGE FORM CHANGE?

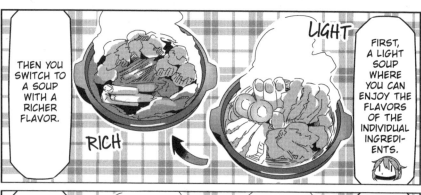

THEN YOU SWITCH TO A SOUP WITH A RICHER FLAVOR.

RICH

LIGHT

FIRST, A LIGHT SOUP WHERE YOU CAN ENJOY THE FLAVORS OF THE INDIVIDUAL INGREDIENTS.

BUT ADDING SPICY SEASONING TO KICK IT UP A NOTCH SOUNDS GOOD TOO.

SPICY

MILKY

NEXT WOULD BE SOMETHING CREAMY, LIKE WITH EGGS OR CHEESE...

| NADESHIKO | RIN | CHIAKI | INUKO |
|---|---|---|---|
| TUMMY: 3/10 | TUMMY: FULL | TUMMY: FULL | TUMMY: FULL |

IT'S LIKE THE FINAL BOSS IN AN RPG.

WITH HOW MANY TIMES IT CAN TRANSFORM, IT CANNOT BE BEATEN.

THAT RECIPE IS A FOURTH-STAGE FORM CHANGE.

PULL IT TOGETHER WITH SOME RICE OR SOBA IN A HOT POT, AND YOU GET SOMETHING LIKE THIS.

DANDAN NOODLES BECAME DANDAN GYOUZA HOT POT!!

# AFTER-SCHOOL 112 THE ROUGH MAP OF YAMANASHI

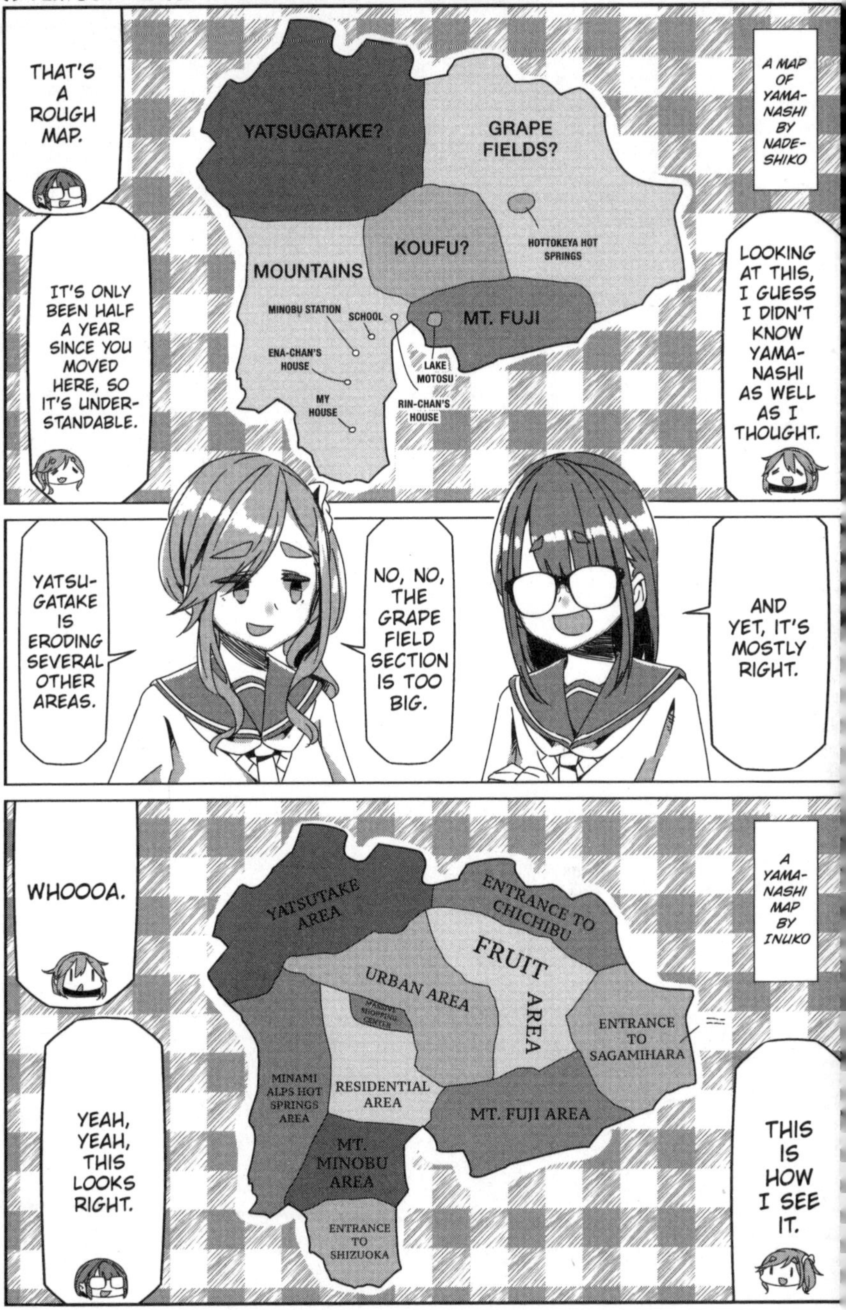
A MAP OF YAMANASHI BY NADESHIKO
LOOKING AT THIS, I GUESS I DIDN'T KNOW YAMANASHI AS WELL AS I THOUGHT.
YATSUGATAKE?
GRAPE FIELDS?
HOTTOKEYA HOT SPRINGS
KOUFU?
MOUNTAINS
MT. FUJI
MINOBU STATION
SCHOOL
ENA-CHAN'S HOUSE
LAKE MOTOSU
MY HOUSE
RIN-CHAN'S HOUSE
THAT'S A ROUGH MAP.
IT'S ONLY BEEN HALF A YEAR SINCE YOU MOVED HERE, SO IT'S UNDERSTANDABLE.
AND YET, IT'S MOSTLY RIGHT.
NO, NO, THE GRAPE FIELD SECTION IS TOO BIG.
YATSUGATAKE IS ERODING SEVERAL OTHER AREAS.
A YAMANASHI MAP BY INUKO
THIS IS HOW I SEE IT.
ENTRANCE TO CHICHIBU
YATSUTAKE AREA
FRUIT AREA
URBAN AREA
MASSIVE SHOPPING CENTER
ENTRANCE TO SAGAMIHARA
MINAMI ALPS HOT SPRINGS AREA
RESIDENTIAL AREA
MT. FUJI AREA
MT. MINOBU AREA
ENTRANCE TO SHIZUOKA
WHOOOA.
YEAH, YEAH, THIS LOOKS RIGHT.

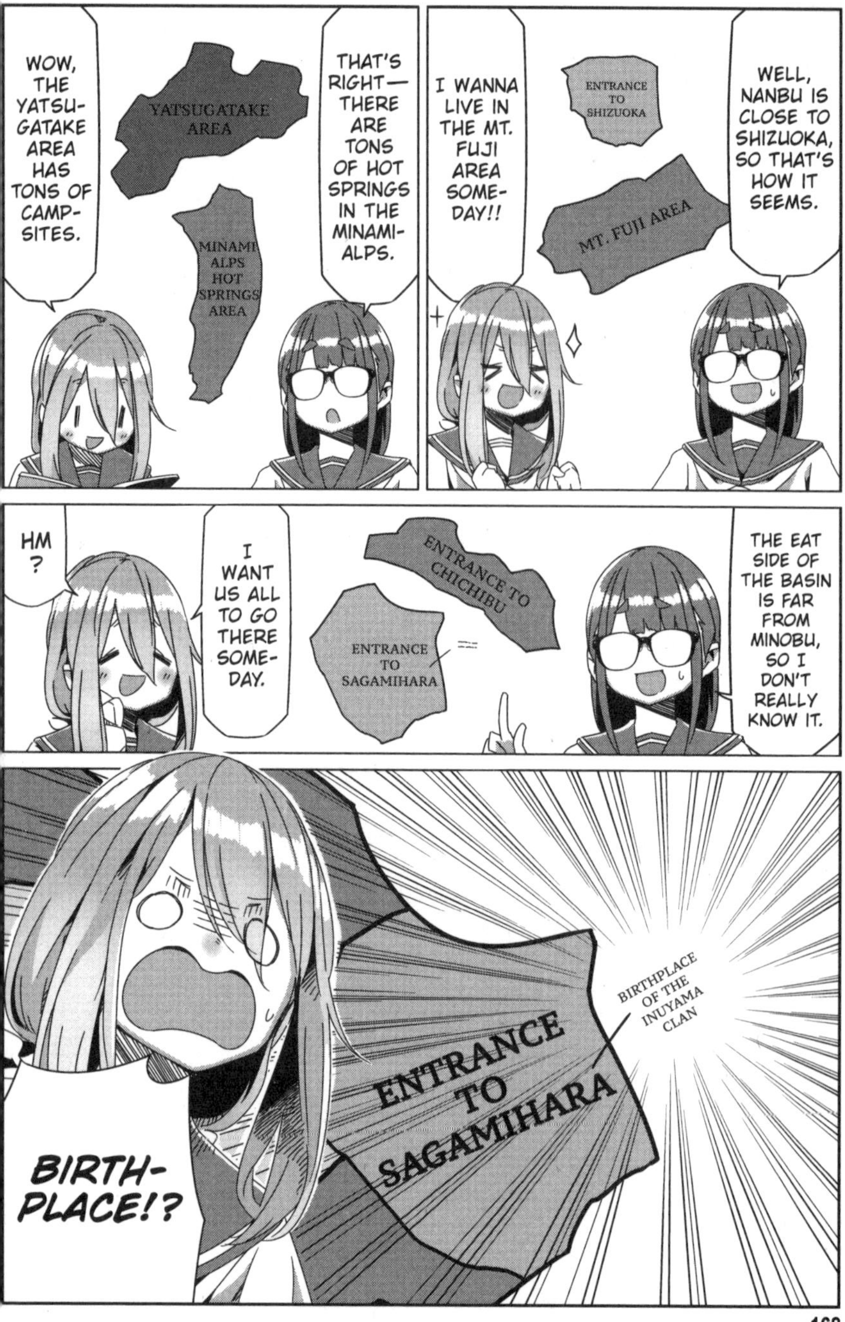
WELL, NANBU IS CLOSE TO SHIZUOKA, SO THAT'S HOW IT SEEMS.
ENTRANCE TO SHIZUOKA
MT. FUJI AREA
I WANNA LIVE IN THE MT. FUJI AREA SOMEDAY!!
WOW, THE YATSUGATAKE AREA HAS TONS OF CAMPSITES.
THAT'S RIGHT—THERE ARE TONS OF HOT SPRINGS IN THE MINAMI-ALPS.
YATSUGATAKE AREA
MINAMI ALPS HOT SPRINGS AREA
THE EAT SIDE OF THE BASIN IS FAR FROM MINOBU, SO I DON'T REALLY KNOW IT.
ENTRANCE TO CHICHIBU
ENTRANCE TO SAGAMIHARA
I WANT US ALL TO GO THERE SOMEDAY.
HM?
BIRTHPLACE OF THE INUYAMA CLAN
ENTRANCE TO SAGAMIHARA
BIRTH-PLACE!?

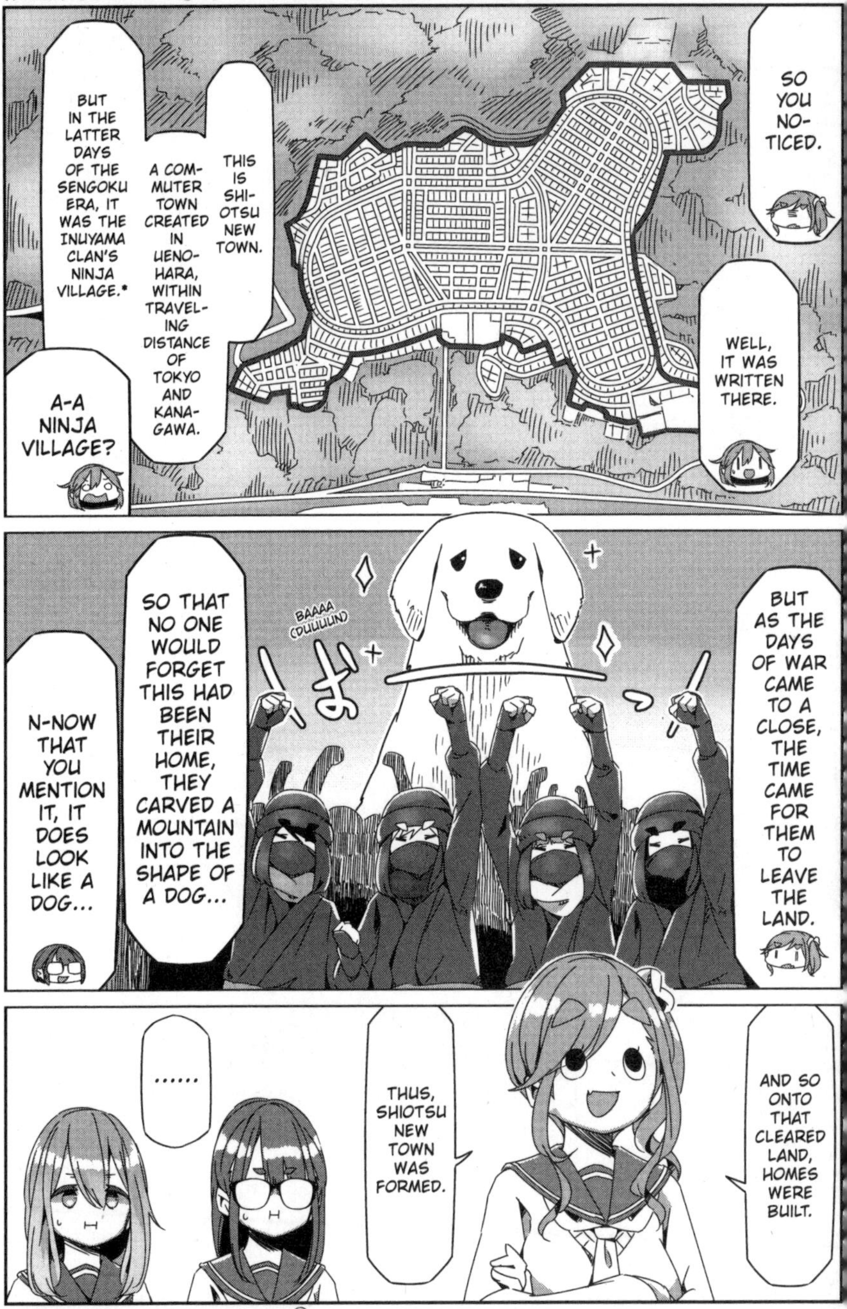
SO YOU NOTICED.
WELL, IT WAS WRITTEN THERE.
THIS IS SHIOTSU NEW TOWN.
A COMMUTER TOWN CREATED IN UENOHARA, WITHIN TRAVELING DISTANCE OF TOKYO AND KANAGAWA.
BUT IN THE LATTER DAYS OF THE SENGOKU ERA, IT WAS THE INUYAMA CLAN'S NINJA VILLAGE.*
A-A NINJA VILLAGE?
BUT AS THE DAYS OF WAR CAME TO A CLOSE, THE TIME CAME FOR THEM TO LEAVE THE LAND.
SO THAT NO ONE WOULD FORGET THIS HAD BEEN THEIR HOME, THEY CARVED A MOUNTAIN INTO THE SHAPE OF A DOG...
BAAAA (DUUUUN)
N-NOW THAT YOU MENTION IT, IT DOES LOOK LIKE A DOG...
AND SO ONTO THAT CLEARED LAND, HOMES WERE BUILT.
THUS, SHIOTSU NEW TOWN WAS FORMED.
......

※ *SEE THE INSIDE COVER OF LAID-BACK CAMP ⑩*

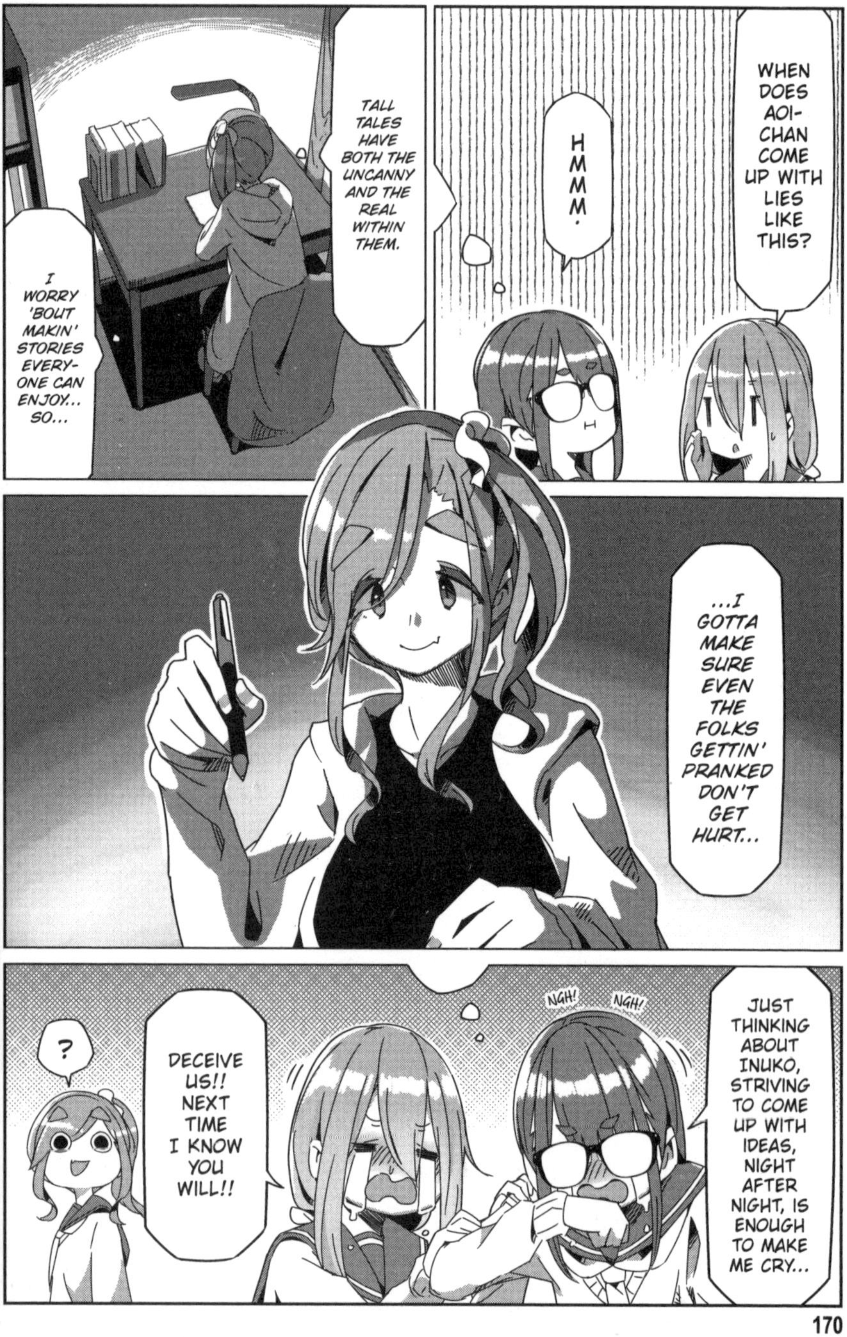
WHEN DOES AOI-CHAN COME UP WITH LIES LIKE THIS?
HMMM.
TALL TALES HAVE BOTH THE UNCANNY AND THE REAL WITHIN THEM.
I WORRY 'BOUT MAKIN' STORIES EVERY-ONE CAN ENJOY... SO...
...I GOTTA MAKE SURE EVEN THE FOLKS GETTIN' PRANKED DON'T GET HURT...
JUST THINKING ABOUT INUKO, STRIVING TO COME UP WITH IDEAS, NIGHT AFTER NIGHT, IS ENOUGH TO MAKE ME CRY...
NGH! NGH!
DECEIVE US!! NEXT TIME I KNOW YOU WILL!!
?

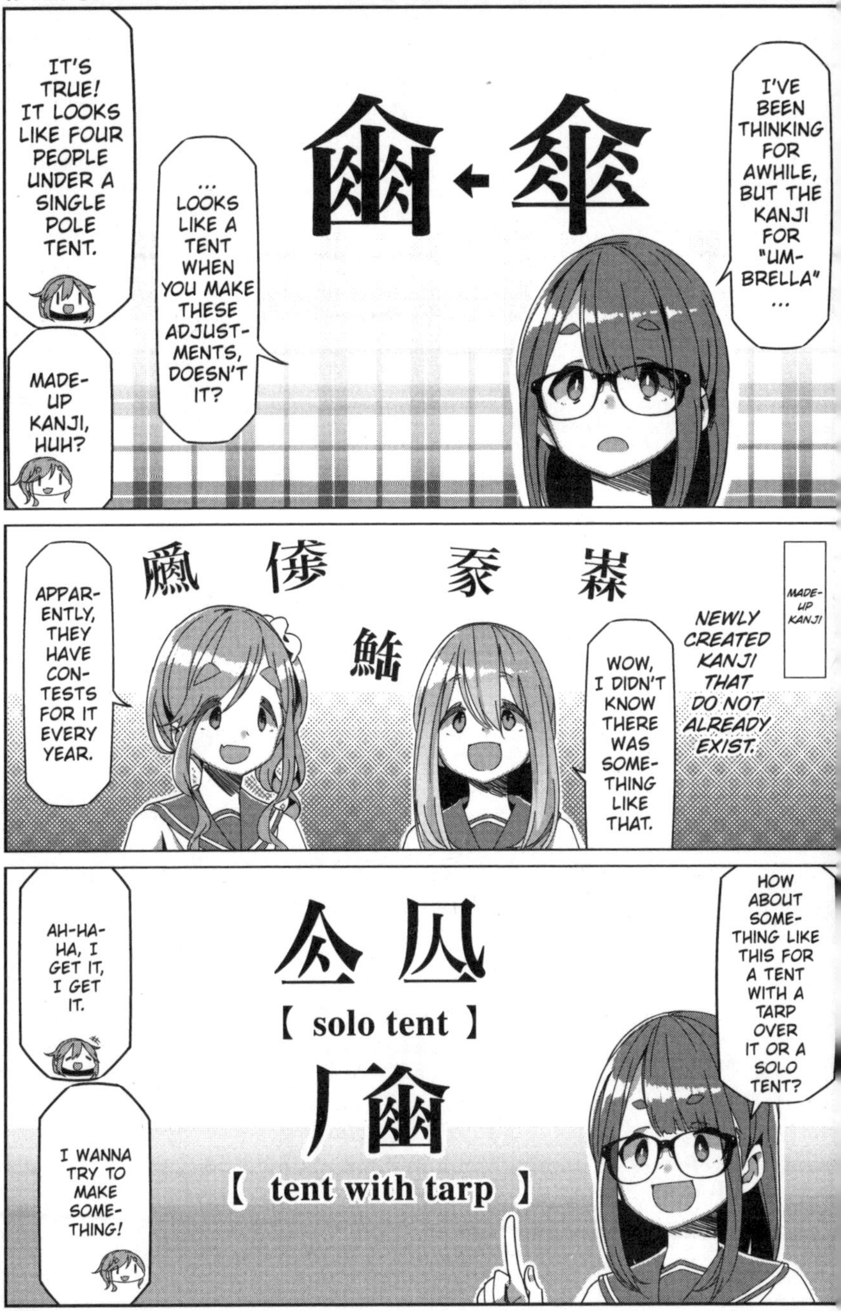
I'VE BEEN THINKING FOR AWHILE, BUT THE KANJI FOR "UM-BRELLA" ...
傘
... LOOKS LIKE A TENT WHEN YOU MAKE THESE ADJUST-MENTS, DOESN'T IT?
IT'S TRUE! IT LOOKS LIKE FOUR PEOPLE UNDER A SINGLE POLE TENT.
MADE-UP KANJI, HUH?
MADE-UP KANJI
NEWLY CREATED KANJI THAT DO NOT ALREADY EXIST.
WOW, I DIDN'T KNOW THERE WAS SOME-THING LIKE THAT.
APPAR-ENTLY, THEY HAVE CON-TESTS FOR IT EVERY YEAR.
HOW ABOUT SOME-THING LIKE THIS FOR A TENT WITH A TARP OVER IT OR A SOLO TENT?
【 solo tent 】
【 tent with tarp 】
AH-HA-HA, I GET IT, I GET IT.
I WANNA TRY TO MAKE SOME-THING!

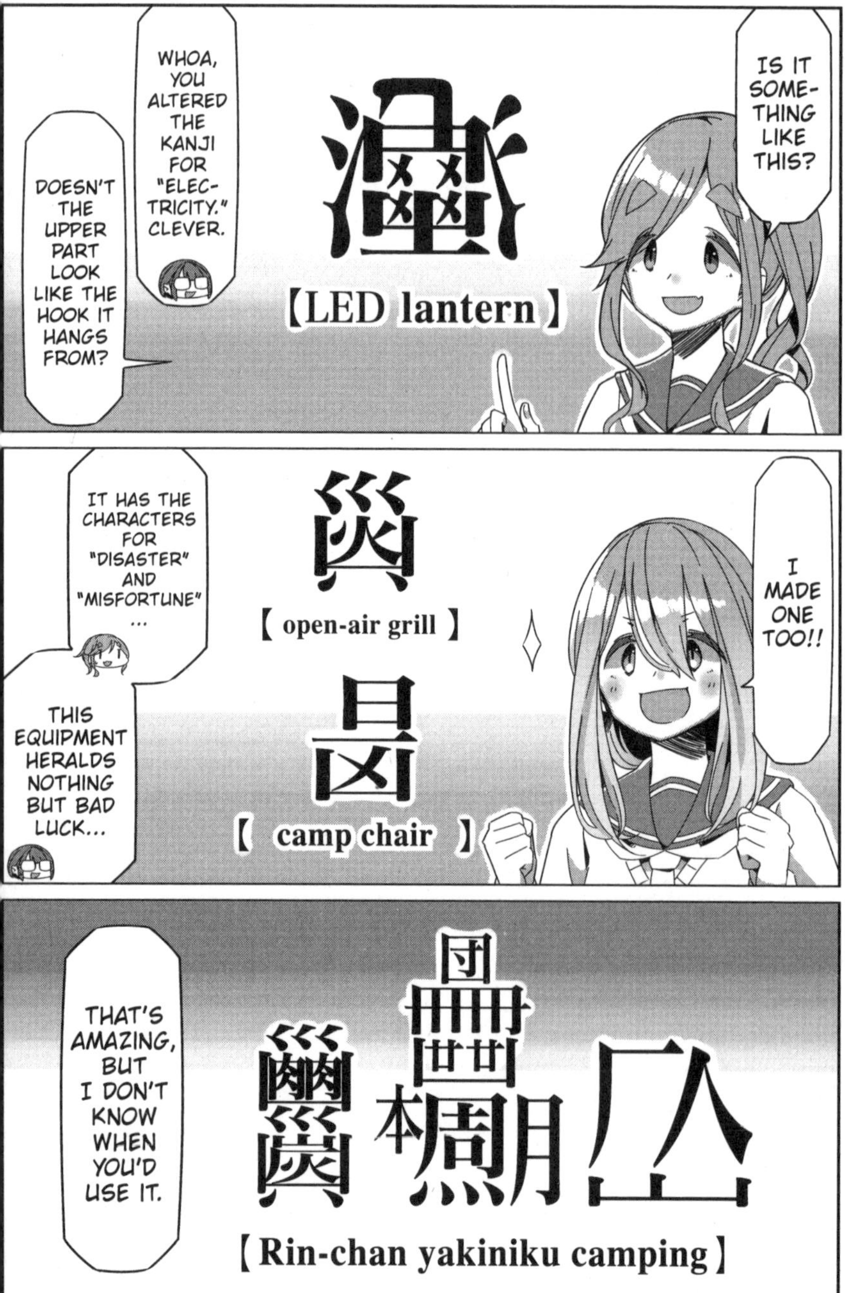

IS IT SOMETHING LIKE THIS?
【LED lantern】
WHOA, YOU ALTERED THE KANJI FOR "ELECTRICITY." CLEVER.
DOESN'T THE UPPER PART LOOK LIKE THE HOOK IT HANGS FROM?
I MADE ONE TOO!!
【open-air grill】
【camp chair】
IT HAS THE CHARACTERS FOR "DISASTER" AND "MISFORTUNE"...
THIS EQUIPMENT HERALDS NOTHING BUT BAD LUCK...
【Rin-chan yakiniku camping】
THAT'S AMAZING, BUT I DON'T KNOW WHEN YOU'D USE IT.

# AFTER-SCHOOL 115 KANJI CREATION, MOUNTAIN ARC

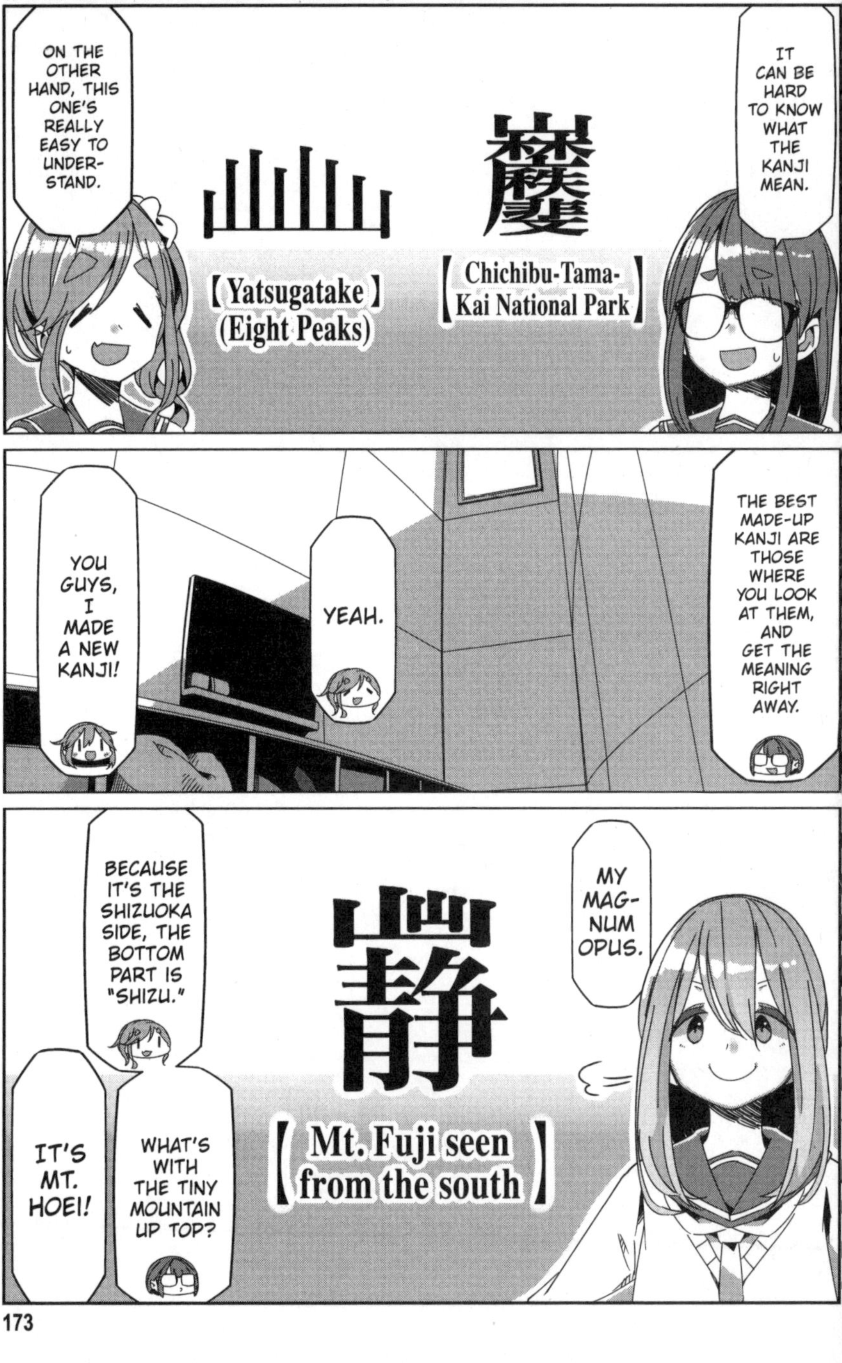
IT CAN BE HARD TO KNOW WHAT THE KANJI MEAN.
【Chichibu-Tama-Kai National Park】
【Yatsugatake】 (Eight Peaks)
ON THE OTHER HAND, THIS ONE'S REALLY EASY TO UNDER-STAND.
THE BEST MADE-UP KANJI ARE THOSE WHERE YOU LOOK AT THEM, AND GET THE MEANING RIGHT AWAY.
YEAH.
YOU GUYS, I MADE A NEW KANJI!
MY MAG-NUM OPUS.
【Mt. Fuji seen from the south】
BECAUSE IT'S THE SHIZUOKA SIDE, THE BOTTOM PART IS "SHIZU."
WHAT'S WITH THE TINY MOUNTAIN UP TOP?
IT'S MT. HOEI!

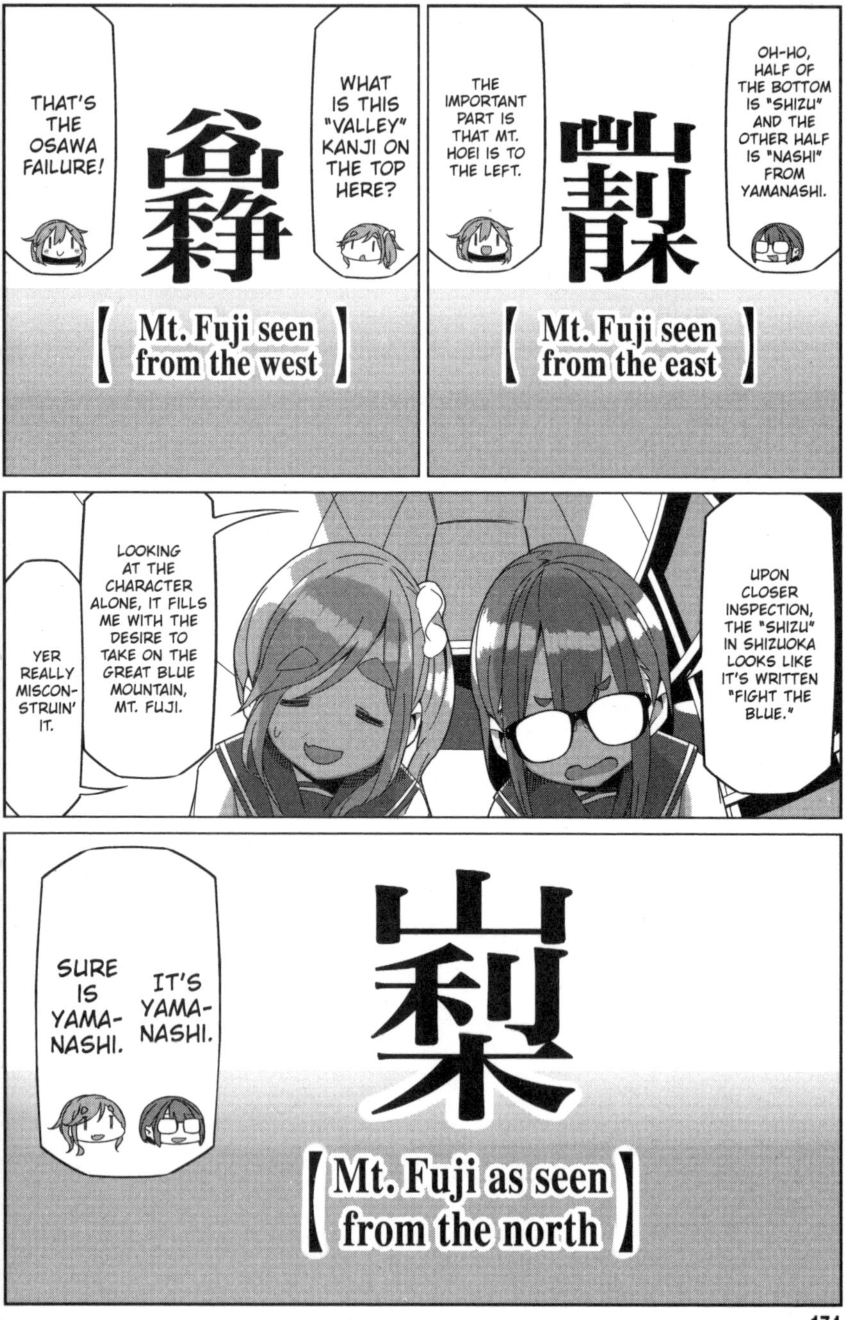
OH-HO, HALF OF THE BOTTOM IS "SHIZU" AND THE OTHER HALF IS "NASHI" FROM YAMANASHI.
THE IMPORTANT PART IS THAT MT. HOEI IS TO THE LEFT.
【Mt. Fuji seen from the east】
WHAT IS THIS "VALLEY" KANJI ON THE TOP HERE?
THAT'S THE OSAWA FAILURE!
【Mt. Fuji seen from the west】
UPON CLOSER INSPECTION, THE "SHIZU" IN SHIZUOKA LOOKS LIKE IT'S WRITTEN "FIGHT THE BLUE."
LOOKING AT THE CHARACTER ALONE, IT FILLS ME WITH THE DESIRE TO TAKE ON THE GREAT BLUE MOUNTAIN, MT. FUJI.
YER REALLY MISCON-STRUIN' IT.
IT'S YAMA-NASHI.
SURE IS YAMA-NASHI.
【Mt. Fuji as seen from the north】

## AFTER-SCHOOL 116 RAINY DAY OFF

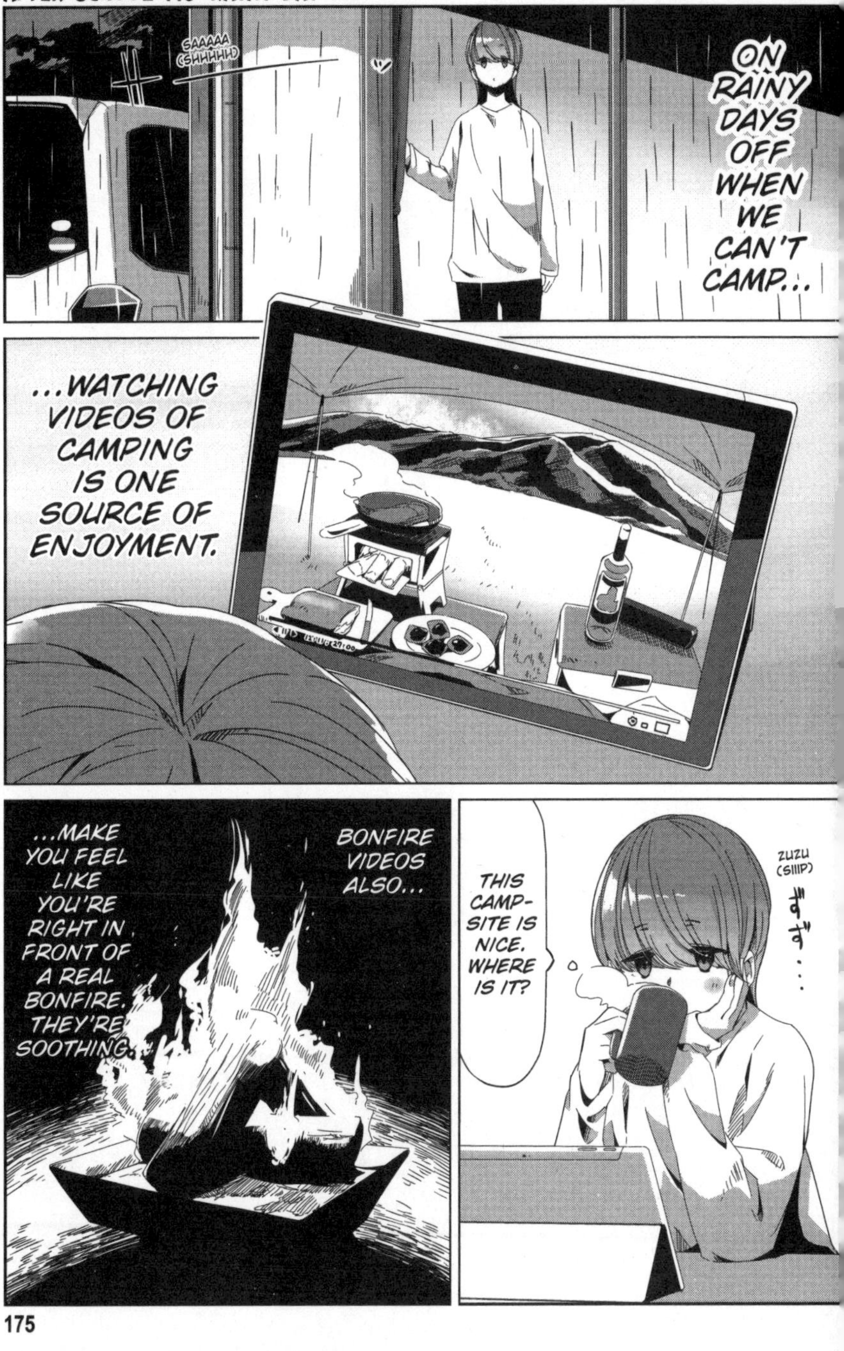
ON RAINY DAYS OFF WHEN WE CAN'T CAMP...
SAAAAA (SHHHHH)
...WATCHING VIDEOS OF CAMPING IS ONE SOURCE OF ENJOYMENT.
ZUZU (SIIIP)
ずず…
THIS CAMP-SITE IS NICE. WHERE IS IT?
BONFIRE VIDEOS ALSO...
...MAKE YOU FEEL LIKE YOU'RE RIGHT IN FRONT OF A REAL BONFIRE. THEY'RE SOOTHING.

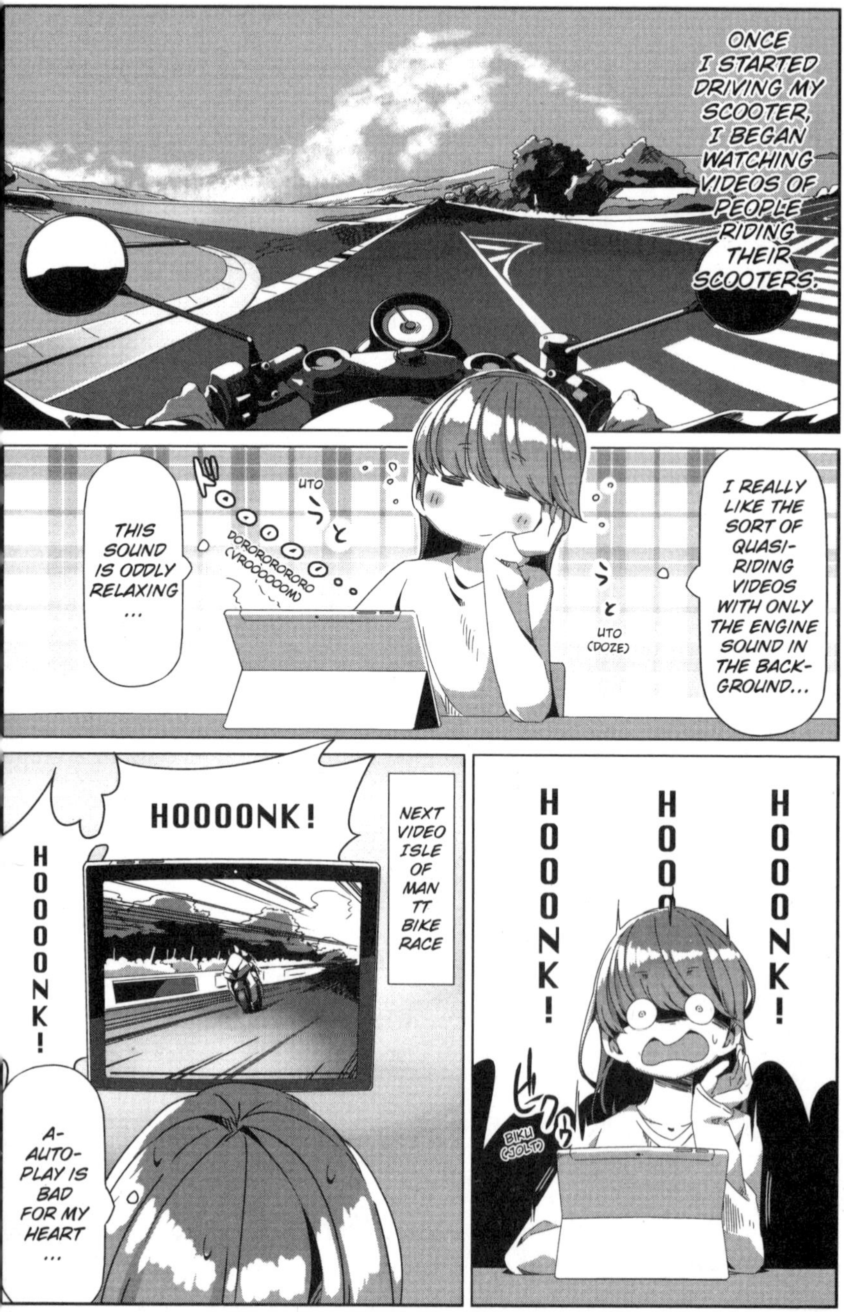
ONCE I STARTED DRIVING MY SCOOTER, I BEGAN WATCHING VIDEOS OF PEOPLE RIDING THEIR SCOOTERS.
I REALLY LIKE THE SORT OF QUASI-RIDING VIDEOS WITH ONLY THE ENGINE SOUND IN THE BACK-GROUND...
UTO (DOZE)
UTO
DOROROROROROROROR (VROOOOOOOM)
THIS SOUND IS ODDLY RELAXING ...
HOOOONK!
HOOO
HOOOONK!
BIKU (JOLT)
HOOOONK!
NEXT VIDEO ISLE OF MAN TT BIKE RACE
HOOOOONK!
A-AUTO-PLAY IS BAD FOR MY HEART ...

THIS WAS *LAID-BACK CAMP*, VOLUME 13.
THIS VOLUME CONTINUES THE FIRST PART OF THE CHERRY-BLOSSOM-VIEWING ARC.

IT DIDN'T COME UP IN THE STORY, BUT YAMANASHI HAS FAMOUS SPOTS FOR VIEWING PEACH BLOSSOMS AND PLUM BLOSSOMS, SO PLEASE TRY INCLUDING THOSE WHEN YOU GO CHERRY-BLOSSOM VIEWING IN THE AREA.
EVEN NOW, IT'S STILL HARD FOR ME TO TELL WHICH IS WHICH.

THIS HAS BEEN AFRO.

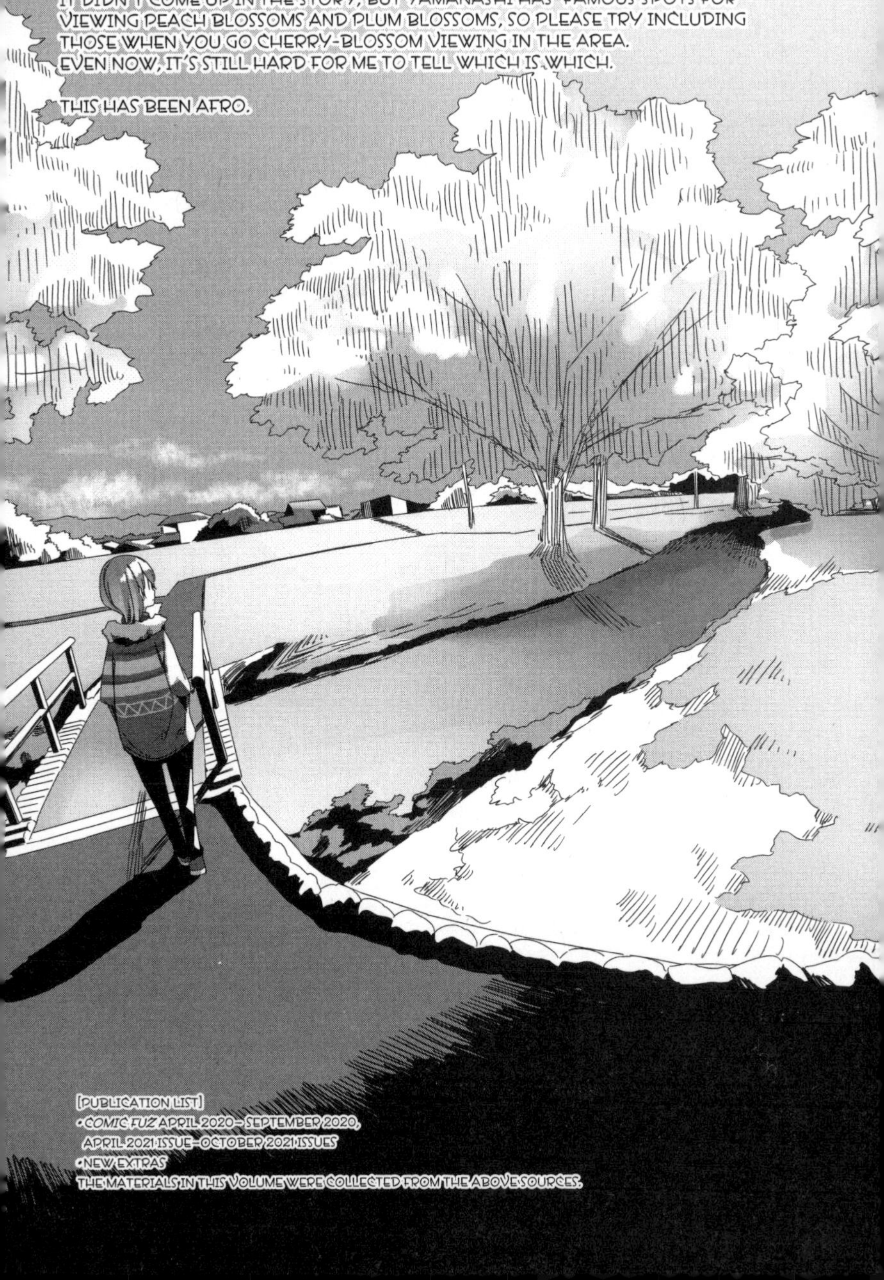

[PUBLICATION LIST]
• *COMIC FUZ* APRIL 2020– SEPTEMBER 2020,
APRIL 2021 ISSUE–OCTOBER 2021 ISSUES
• NEW EXTRAS
THE MATERIALS IN THIS VOLUME WERE COLLECTED FROM THE ABOVE SOURCES.

# LAID & BACK CAMP ⑬

## Afro

Translation: **Amber Tamosaitis** ✳ Lettering: **DK**

YURUCAMP Vol. 13
© 2022 afro. All rights reserved. First published in Japan in 2021 by HOUBUNSHA CO., LTD., Tokyo. English translation rights in United States, Canada, and United Kingdom arranged with HOUBUNSHA CO., LTD. through Tuttle-Mori Agency, Inc., Tokyo.

English translation © 2023 by Yen Press, LLC

Yen Press
150 West 30th Street, 19th Floor
New York, NY 10001

Visit us at yenpress.com
facebook.com/yenpress
twitter.com/yenpress
yenpress.tumblr.com
instagram.com/yenpress

First Yen Press Edition: April 2023
Edited by Yen Press Editorial: Carl Li
Designed by Yen Press Design: Eddy Mingki, Wendy Chan

Yen Press is an imprint of Yen Press, LLC.
The Yen Press name and logo are trademarks of Yen Press, LLC.

Library of Congress Control Number: 2017959206

ISBNs: 978-1-9753-5174-8 (paperback)
       978-1-9753-5175-5 (ebook)

10 9 8 7 6 5 4 3 2 1

WOR

Printed in the United States of America